AMERICAN CUT AND ENGRAVED GLASS

GLASS

THE BRILLIANT PERIOD
IN HISTORICAL PERSPECTIVE

MARTHA LOUISE SWAN

Published in Radnor, Pennsylvania 19089, by Wallace-Homestead,
a division of Chilton Book Company

Library of Congress Catalog Card No. 84-052053
ISBN 0-87069-713-7

Cover and text design by Anthony Jacobson

Pictured on the facing page: Fig. C.3. Pitcher, 8½″ x 5″,
green-cut-to-clear, is cut in floral and rococo forms above a
band of nailhead diamonds near base, which is cut in sixty-four
rays. Handle has a full-length tear. Identified as Dorflinger's
work, it came from Louis Iorio collection. (Gerritse, with
photograph by Tom Gordon.)

2 3 4 5 6 7 8 9 0   3 2 1 0 9 8 7 6 5

To Earle,
lover of beauty in all of its manifestations

Contents

Preface

This book was written to satisfy a "felt need," as the educational psychologists would say. Thoughtful reading, with careful attention to details, will benefit several categories of readers.

The antique dealer, perhaps a specialist in clocks or art glass, can hardly know every type of glass. He may buy a general collection containing some items of cut glass, about which he knows little.

The new collector should be armed with knowledge that will help him choose wisely from the beginning, thus avoiding costly mistakes.

The advanced collector not only shares our joy in acquiring fine glassware, but may heighten appreciation of his own glass by learning more of its history. Learning about glass in relation to its period in time, as a part of the environment of once-living people, brings the past to life.

The investor in antiques (including cut and engraved glassware) should gain from this book the necessary information to recognize a "good buy" when he sees one, and to discern the difference between old and new, foreign and American.

Finally, for the lover of beautiful objects, the photographs will delight the eye. Since it is not always possible to have access to a large number of prime examples of fine glassware, and since verbal descriptions are inadequate, good photographs are essential to educate the taste.

Most of the black-and-white photographs were taken by Tom Gordon; the remainder by Conkling, Inc. (Both firms are in Portland, Oregon.) Black-and-white pictures by Conkling are so marked; all others are by Gordon. Each color plate is labeled individually.

The beauty achieved and skills developed by artists and artisans during the Brilliant Period in America, extending roughly from 1876 to 1916, will be shown and described. The original setting of the glassware in the home and the high place it held in the social life of the period will be explained. To comprehend the importance of this lavish glassware, one must know a good deal about the era in which it was made, including the economy, politics, the status of women in society, and life-styles.

For years, some contributors to expensive publications on antique furnishings have "looked down their noses" at American Brilliant cut glass, considering it to be garish and too ornate. For too long, this precious part of our heritage was overlooked. But the finest pieces have doubled, tripled, and even quadrupled in price since our first item was bought in 1967.

Viewers of our collection have asked questions that have given direction in the writing of this volume. Those questions include:

What do you mean by "cut" glass?

How can you tell whether a piece is cut or pressed?

How do you know how much to pay?

How can you tell a good piece from a poor one?

Do you consider it an investment? (One viewer remarked wryly that it couldn't be much worse than the stock market.)

Don't you worry about burglars and vandals?

Can you get insurance for breakage as well as for theft?

What if we have an earthquake?

You must have been collecting for years! Do you mind telling me how you got started?

How do you clean the glass? How often do you wash it?

Do you actually use any of these while entertaining?

How do you know it isn't old European or even modern? I've seen cut glass for sale in jewelry and department stores.

When was it made? Is it antique?

Where have you found your pieces? Do you buy at auctions, in shops, or from individuals?

How much lead is in this glass? Could you tell me how it was made?

What pattern is this?

What do you mean, "signed"? Should I buy only signed glass?

All of these questions and more will be answered. Hopefully, the facts are arranged in an articulate and pleasant manner, so that reading the text may be as joyful as perusing the illustrations. Dates are used often to clarify the reader's orientation in time. Whenever possible, the works are assembled by maker to aid in recognition of a manufacturer's products, as well as to exemplify change in basic design chronologically.

Advice on where to buy, how to care for, insure, and display your glass is based on our experience. Collecting cut glass can be an expensive hobby, but not necessarily for those only in the upper brackets.

The scope of this book must have limitations. Some companies will be described in detail, as prototypes to illustrate production of cut glass at its zenith of popularity and quantity in our country, but no attempt will be made to duplicate authoritative volumes already in print. Historical background will be given in order to put this period in perspective. The author has tried to distill essential facts concerning the origin and evolution of cut glass dating back to ancient Egypt. A complete history could not be contained here, yet salient points should greatly increase appreciation of our relics of a romantic age. A few illustrations from life in the Golden Age will provide "atmosphere."

Since patterns or designs (here the words are used interchangeably) are composed of elements that, like musical notes, can be combined in an infinite variety of ways, not every design will be identified by name or company. Although hundreds of hours were spent searching through books, catalogs, periodicals, and patent documents, some well-known patterns may have been overlooked through sheer mental fatigue. It would be impossible to find all of the designs anyway, since, of the thousands cut, only a few were patented; of the many catalogs of the period, relatively few survived to be consulted or reprinted.

An annotated bibliography is provided for sources of further study. Rest assured that facts stated are derived from these references.

Acknowledgments

We are grateful to the following friends who lent us their glassware. (Surnames only will appear at the end of legends for the sake of brevity.) Most are from Portland, Oregon, and environs.

Bob & Fran's Antiques (Vancouver, Washington), Mr. and Mrs. Charles Cornwell, Mr. and Mrs. Richard E. Dolan, Fran Frané's Tickled Pink Gift Shop, Ida Frazer, Jo Frazier, Mr. and Mrs. Leonard Gerritse, Bernice Gilbert, Mr. and Mrs. John F. Hamstreet, Hilby's Antiques, Bert Hilby, David Hoglund, Karl Jernes (antique car), Betty Kriska, Sybil and Carol Matye, Eleanor McCoy, Roberta McKaig (Idaho), Mr. and Mrs. Robert H. Meyer (South Dakota), David and Patty Miles, Theresa Nash, Mr. and Mrs. Richard L. Rice, Mr. and Mrs. John Rieder, Florence Swetland Roberts, Janet Rolland, Mr. and Mrs. Paul Serres, Mary Seymour, Bernice Snead, Taylor's Treasures (Aurora, Oregon), Jean Voorhees, Weir's House of Glass (Waitsburg, Washington), Christine Willits, and Earleen of Wilson Antiques.

Thanks to these well-known dealers for sharing knowledge: Mildred Jones, J. Michael Pearson, Alexander Tisnado, and Herbert Wiener. Pearson and Wiener are authors of books on cut glass as well.

Louise Boggess, co-author of *American Brilliant Cut Glass*, supplied information and encouragement.

Maudie Eastwood, author of *The Antique Doorknob*, sent notes on the manufacture of glass doorknobs and gave me photographs.

Albert Christian Revi, author of several books on glassware and editor of the *Spinning Wheel* periodical, gave permission to reproduce the photograph of a cut glass windowpane that appeared in his article in the November 1968 issue.

Nancy O. Merrill, director-curator of the Sandwich Historical Society (Cape Cod, Massachusetts), sent a color photograph taken of the ruby window in the Sandwich Museum.

Thanks to Bill Schroeder, publisher of the *Value Guide*, by Jo Evers (1975), for permission to copy two illustrations of celery trays, copied from catalogs.

Wallace Turner (Tuthill Cut Glass Company Museum in Middletown, New York) helped identify glassware.

Robert Bryden, Manager of Pairpoint Glass Company, Inc., (Sagamore, Massachusetts) identified patterns and verified facts concerning history of the firm.

Mrs. Penrose Hawkes kindly answered several queries concerning history of the T.G. Hawkes Company and the role played by her husband in the firm.

Louise Ream, in 1977 president of Heisey Collectors of America, Inc., supplied information not yet published.

To Cecelia H. Caneschi, Reference Department of the Meriden Public Library, who supplied information on the J.J. Niland Company to Dorothy Reynolds (who passed it on to me from Caldwell, Idaho), we are grateful.

Concerning the connection between Meriden (Connecticut) cut glass and similar Canadian designs, our thanks go to E.P. Hogan, historian of the International Silver Company. Virginia Wright, assistant librarian of the Corning Museum of Glass, pointed the way to publications on several Canadian firms. Hazen Wright, head office buyer at Henry Birks & Sons, Ltd., of Montreal, not only answered questions, but kindly bought a book and mailed it to me when it could not be found here. Mrs. C. White, head of Processing Division, from the office of the Commissioner of Patents in Ottawa, and Janet Holmes, curatorial assistant of the Royal Ontario Museum, provided valuable assistance.

Martha Ziegler, customer service manager of Interpace Corporation, maker of Franciscan Crystal (Tiffin, Ohio), clarified late manufacture of Hawkes glassware.

Alan Zell (Zell Brothers Jewelers in Portland, Oregon) put me in touch with Baccarat in New York. André Vulliet, executive vice president and general manager of Baccarat, sent my query to their Paris office.

S.R. Eveson, director of Dema Glass Ltd. (incorporating Edinburgh Crystal Glass Company)/Thomas Webb & Sons of Stourbridge, England, identified the English bowl and the decanter with central hole.

During research in the Multnomah County Library (Oregon), Ellen Byrnes, Barbara Bush, and Carmelita Smith were willing and cheerful assistants.

Many dealers, collectors, and friends have encouraged our efforts.

The hours spent by my daughter Noreen as she read the manuscript aloud to catch errors or to detect repetition were most helpful. Thanks, also, to my granddaughter Stephanie, for many trips down a narrow, winding stairway at the library, where she carried heavy Patent Gazette volumes to the duplicating machine to copy registered designs.

Introduction

"You collect what? How on earth did you become interested in cut glass?"

"I never dreamed such beautiful pieces existed! I preferred something with color until I saw these."

Visitors frequently remark, "I suppose you have been collecting for many years."

Actually, my parents had no cut glass in our home. Mother inherited from *her* mother (married in 1888) a lovely "imitation cut glass" jelly compote (fig. 13) and a footed cake stand, both of which were pressed glass. There were other mementos, such as a ruby flashed toothpick holder, brought back from the World's Fair of 1904 at St. Louis by her father, but no cut glass. Even though Grandfather Brower owned a restaurant and a grocery store, he and Grandmother worked hard for a living and could not afford luxuries. Grandmother baked the pastries served in the restaurant, but did not work outside the home. She died of "Childbed fever" and overwork at the age of thirty-five after the birth of her third child.

Father's parents had a farm in the Ozark Mountains in southern Missouri. Hard work resulted in "a living" with no money left over for decorative furnishings.

The Legacy

My husband, on the other hand, grew up with a closetful of cut glass, but was unaware of its charm and value until his adoptive mother passed away at age 98 in 1966. She was a genteel but sturdy lady from New England, descended from a line of sea captains traced back to 1636.

Mother Swan's marriage license is dated 1889, at least nine years into the Brilliant Period, which most experts agree lasted from 1880 to 1905 or 1910. As an 1899 Higgins & Seiter catalog suggested,

> Nothing was more appropriate for the expression of affection and esteem than something choice in Glass or China. For weddings and anniversaries their use has become traditional—they are as much a part of the bride's expectations as a wedding ring or trousseau.

Since my husband and I lived in the Pacific Northwest at the time of his mother's death, it seemed expedient to dispose of her Victorian furniture back East. Later, when he was no longer confused by grief Earle regretted selling the rosewood parlor set with lion heads on the arms and paws on the legs, the swivel-top card table of mahogany and the gilt mirror from the hall, the oval-back settee and chairs from the living room, the round oak dining table and six chairs to match, and even the tall chamber pot or commode that had rested in the guest room closet.

He did, of course, keep her personal and family mementos. Then, sadly, he packed her hand-painted china, which he had watched her decorate, to pass on to our four children. The Limoges china (purchased in white, then painted by hand) included a gilded chocolate set; a berry bowl and six matching saucers, each painted with a different fruit; dessert plates with the same design; a master nut dish in the shape of a leaf with six small individual leaf dishes; the miniature sugar and creamer that the maid brought upstairs on his tray when he was ill; a toothpick holder; a squatty milk jug; a dresser set consisting of tray, puff jar, hair receiver and cologne bottle; a covered box for hairpins; and a collar button jar. There was also a sterling silver camel's-hair brush, embosed with an Art Nouveau lady with flowing hair, a button hook, and two silver-backed clothes brushes.

He shipped West the old oak china closet (with curved glass front, glass shelves, and a mirrored back) and about a dozen pieces of cut glass, including a 10", two-piece punch bowl.

As we unpacked the shipment, Earle recalled memories of his youth, when his mother entertained in the twelve-room Connecticut house, where Mother Swan closed the shutters from inside on hot days and during the "line storm" that occurred each fall.

The house had three stories and a basement, in which Father Swan had installed a kiln for baking his wife's hand-painted porcelain. China painting was a popular pastime of upper-middle-class ladies early in this century.

When Earle and I were married in 1938, the year of the first hurricane in New England since 1823, the large carriage barn had long ago been converted to a four-car garage. Earle's adoptive father, who died in 1936 at the age of seventy-one, had owned the second automobile in town, a Stanley Steamer, which had to be crated and shipped to New York for restoration whenever a repair was beyond the capabilities of the local blacksmith. The car was purchased in 1902 for $600 directly from the factory in Toledo, Ohio.

Mother Swan was probably the first lady in town to have her own car. Several times during her later years, my husband brought up the subject of safety and showed concern for her competing with the fast drivers of this age. She would draw herself up imperiously and, with brown eyes flashing, state, "No one in Norwich has driven as long as I have!" That always closed the subject, for no one could argue with the fact.

When Father Swan brought friends home from the Arcanum Club (for men only, of course), or Mother Swan had a meeting of ladies from the church, out came the hand-painted china and the cut glass, establishing an aura of elegance for the occasion.

As Earle and I assembled the china closet and solemnly placed each item on a glass shelf, we looked at the pieces with a nostalgic awareness of their connection with a far-away age.

A New Hobby

Earle and I met through our mutual love of music. As singers in an oratorio society, we talked and discovered that my piano accompaniment was just what he needed when he played violin solos. This association led to marriage in less than a year. I gave up teaching school and he became an accountant. We moved West and raised a family.

After our four children were grown (and dancing lessons and orthodontia were no longer a strain on the budget), we had some money to spend as we pleased. Earle was well into gun collecting, and together we restored and decorated a fine old Georgian colonial house.

Then it happened! We attended an antiques dealers' show in August 1967 and saw cut glass more beautiful than any we had inherited. Relying only on careful observation and joint artistic judgment, we bought over a thousand dollars' worth from one dealer that day.

The experience was frightening. Had we acted impulsively and made a mistake? The only way to find out was to learn what we had, to try to get an accurate picture of the market for cut glass, and hopefully to gauge its future worth. We bought every book on cut glass we could find and eagerly studied all facets of the subject. We located other collectors and observed and discussed their glass.

We were astonished by a tale told of a businessman whose wife refused to have cut glass in the house. She insisted it was incompatible with her décor. He solved the dilemma by building shelves in his office, where he displays his treasures.

Two months after our first purchase of cut glass in the fall of 1967, my husband suffered a massive coronary occlusion. My only concern was for his recovery.

We gave up all thoughts of our new hobby. We decided to sell the largest pieces in preparation for moving to a smaller house with no stairs. A "blind ad" in the newspaper brought four letters from prospective buyers. We answered two and sold all we wished to sell at current dealer prices, not losing a cent.

After an apparently good recovery, Earle's interest in cut glass was renewed. He sold most of his guns, as well as the stocks we owned, and turned all of his energy toward locating beautiful glass. Every vacation was a treasure hunt. We traveled up and down the Coast, sometimes to private homes, but mainly to dealers.

A Plan for the Future

Earle and I planned to move out of the city at retirement time and establish a museum to display our glass. We would have a small shop on the side. We spent many happy hours planning model rooms with authentic furniture of the period as a setting for some of the glass. The rest of the pieces were to be placed on velvet-covered steps in another room.

Then, as we both realized that Earle's health was failing, we abandoned this ambitious project and decided to photograph the collection while it was still intact, and to share our experiences in a book for the enjoyment of fellow collectors.

Earle passed away in April 1970. I am certain that he would have wanted me to complete the book. It is dedicated to Earle, lover of beauty in all of its manifestations, whether in music, art objects, or nature.

1
Learning about Glassmaking

Collectors of glass need at least a cursory knowledge of the history of glassmaking. Just as a class in music appreciation opens up the mind to a more sensitive enjoyment of this sophisticated art, so does study of the role played by glassmaking in the development of civilization.

Imagine a world without glass — not just decorative glass, but glass in architecture or photography. Recreation uses binoculars, motion picture projectors, even thermos bottles. Laboratory research relies on the microscope invented in 1590. Reading glasses date from the fourteenth century. Where would we be in medicine without the hypodermic needle and Galileo's fever thermometer? Astronomy has employed the telescope since 1609 to explore outer space.

Glass has even been used for personal adornment. Fashionable English ladies in the seventeenth century wore blown glass ships with widespread sails and glass flowers on their heads.

Ignorance concerning cut glass and the time of its zenith in America is common. Recently a teacher in a high school overheard a colleague who had seen our collection exclaiming about the glass. She said, "Oh, I thought cut glass was worthless. Only crystal is valuable."

More books on American history should go beyond names of presidents, political parties, and the dates of battles and wars. They should also describe changes in mores, attitudes, life-styles, and accoutrements of daily living. They surely would be more interesting to read.

Dealers

In an ideal situation, the customer can rely upon the knowledge and integrity of the dealer for guidance. Unfortunately, there are a few unscrupulous antiques dealers and some ignorant people in the business.

On a recent tour of eight shops in small towns, I found two shops heavily laced with reproductions of art, carnival, and cut glass. An import catalog lists several of the exact pieces of low quality. On the counter was a mold-blown yacht decanter of poor glass.

When we questioned the merchant, he replied, "My wife knows more about the glass; she's not in today." Later we returned to the shop when the wife was on duty and received the same reply concerning her husband.

Most shops that carry authentic, high-class antique items do not handle reproductions. A few stores may have a mixture of fine old pieces, more recent "collectibles" (such as Depression glass), good furniture made as late as the 1930s, and perhaps reproductions of carnival glass clearly labeled "new." These dealers generally can be relied upon to be truthful.

A famous name, however, is no guarantee. Earle and I bought an expensive bowl signed Hawkes in San Francisco at a large, well-known establishment. A few modern imports were not labeled "new" in any way. And a huge two-part punch bowl of wavy, inferior glass carried a spurious signature.

Even honest dealers make errors in judgment. Unless they specialize in one area and study this field in depth, they cannot hope to know all antiques equally well, even after many years.

Early in our collecting experience, Earle and I found a large compote in a shop where we had bought several pieces. It was heavy and fairly brilliant, and was cut in typical American motifs. The price was $115. Something about the base and the "feel" of the cutting bothered me. I asked, "Are you sure it is American and old?"

The lady looked annoyed and replied, "Of course! It came from a local home with several other old pieces. I will give you a written statement of guarantee."

I looked at Earle. He said we would think it over. The dealer indignantly repeated her declaration.

I searched through the four books we owned and became more convinced than ever that the compote was not from the American Brilliant Period. It might, however, be from the Middle Period, for it seemed to resemble some pieces circa 1860. It certainly did not look Irish or English.

The next day, in a continuing effort to identify it, I went to jewelry stores that carry good modern European imports. Wandering through a shopping mall, I noticed cut glass in a store that handles fireplace equipment, items in wrought iron from Spain, statues from Italy, and elaborate lamps. On a display table was an exact duplicate of the compote. It was labeled "Made in West Germany" and was priced at $37.50!

I called the lady, told her as kindly as possible what I had found, and begged her to see it for her own protection. She did so and called me back to apologize. I did not blame her then and have dealt with her since the incident. She had obviously been fooled by one modern piece among several old ones. If we had bought the compote, then made the discovery, she would surely have refunded our money. But it might not have been so easy if we had made such a mistake while traveling. One can imagine all sorts of complications in undoing a sale made in a strange city.

What Is Glass

Glass has been described as a congealed solution of a number of substances, including silica and alkali. The American Society for Testing Materials gives this definition: "Glass is an inorganic product of fusion which has cooled to a rigid condition without crystallizing." The temperature at which fusion takes place is governed by the amount of alkali present. Alkali acts as a flux that causes fusion and promotes the melting of the remaining ingredients at a lower temperature.

The primary ingredient of glass is silica in the form of sand. The whitest sand obtainable, preferably free from iron that would discolor the finished product, is refined and purified. The aim is to make the glass "crystal clear," which simply means colorless and not cloudy. The word *crystal* comes from a Greek word meaning *clear-ice*. Transparent quartz was named *rock crystal* because an ancient myth contended that it was a sort of permanent ice formed by intense cold. When crushed, real rock crystal becomes silica or quartz, from which all glass is made.

The alkali can be either potash or soda. Long ago, the alkalis were derived from wood-ash (potash-glass) or by burning seaweed (soda-glass). Potash-glass is hard and brilliant, passing rapidly from liquid to solid.

Soda-glass remains longer in a plastic state and is more easily manipulated. Lime hardens the *metal*, as glass workers call glass, and makes it easy to work; borax also gives it hardness. If soda is used, lime carbonate is added as a hardener. If potash is chosen, red lead can be added to produce *lead glass*, sometimes called *flint glass*, which is more fusible and more easily cut and engraved.

Early Venetian glassmakers made glass from crystal pebbles found in the Po and Ticino rivers as well as in the ground. They added lime from crushed seashells or powdered marble and soda ash imported from Spain or Egypt. This made a light and thin-walled soda-lime glass. When the Venetians first went to England, they used native flints for glassmaking. This was closest in appearance to natural rock crystal.

After the change to silicious sand, the name *flint* remained. Yet it is an error to call lead glass "flint" and vice versa. There was no lead in the original flint glass. Lead glass is the type used for fine tableware. It is especially suitable for cutting. About 30 to 50 percent fluxed with lead, it refracts light, especially when cut into facets. The finest specimens in our collection have a "watery" and "silvery" appearance.

To satisfy the curiosity of technically minded readers, here is the formula for "crystal glass on the European standard" revealed by Deming Jarves, long associated with the famous Boston & Sandwich Glass Company. (The words in parentheses are mine.)

1,200 lbs. silex (sand, a form of silica)
  800 lbs. red lead (oxide of lead)
  400 lbs. pearl ash (which we call potash)
   50 lbs. nitre
   10 lbs. phosphate of lime
   10 ozs. white oxide of antimony
   24 ozs. manganese
   32 ozs. arsenic
   20 ozs. borax

Most companies in every land have used black oxide of manganese (called Glassmaker's Soap) and arsenic to decolorize the glass by neutralizing the iron particles. Too much lead caused striae in glass (some early Bakewell, for example); fires that were too hot produced air bubbles (as in some pieces by George Dummer); too much soda in English and some old Danish glass resulted in a yellowish or brownish cast. At any rate, American glass of the Brilliant Period finally surpassed any made in Europe in clarity and brilliance.

The chemistry of glassmaking is a fascinating subject. Metal oxides, obtained by grinding minerals or mineral earth to a powder, give beautiful colors to glass. These have been discovered by experimentation through the centuries. For example, ambers and olive-greens are "natural" colors caused by the presence of ferric iron (yellow) and ferrous iron (green) in the sand. "Artificial" colors include deep sapphire-blue, made by adding cobalt oxide, and a brilliant red, made by adding gold chloride. About one ounce of gold is used for every sixty pounds of batch. Copper in varied forms produces brilliant blue, green, and intense red. Silver nitrate makes an opaque yellow, while oxide of tin produces white opaque glass.

Vaseline glass, so-called because its yellow-green color resembles petroleum jelly, is known as *lemon-escent* in England. It was developed by Bohemian glassmakers in the second quarter of the nineteenth century. At first it was blown and cut, then later pressed into molds. (Colored glass was extremely popular in America from 1815 to 1848.) We find vaseline glass especially interesting in this atomic age because uranium, a source of atomic energy, is the ingredient responsible for the unique color of the glass. Exposed to "black light," the glass glows. It causes a violent Geiger counter reaction, yet is considered safe for serving food.

How the Glass Was Made

The proper mixtures of dull-looking ingredients were placed in preheated clay pots inside the furnace and brought to a white heat of 2,500 degrees Fahrenheit over a raging fire. The firepot had to be of the best grade of clay, carefully seasoned for months before it was used. Once it was placed in the furnace, it never cooled until it was replaced by a new one, perhaps three months later. By that time, its walls were thin and weak, in danger of breaking and spilling the molten glass.

Changing pots was a dangerous job. The pot first was fired in a kiln and brought to a great heat, then transferred to the furnace, while still red-hot. Some men were fined for shirking the job.

It was found that adding broken glass, called *cullet*, produced a much better quality. Cullet was constantly called for in advertisements in both English and American newspapers. Of course, all scraps and items rejected or accidentally broken went into the cullet bin.

Wood was the first fuel for heating the glass furnace. Natural gas was discovered in the United States in 1775 in Kanawha County, West Virginia, and soon became the most desired source of heat. (The first commercial gas well was drilled in 1821 in Fredonia, New York. Gas was being used for lighting by 1824.) Coal was used where gas was not available, but, after the first successful oil well began operating in Titusville, Pennsylvania, in 1859, petroleum was favored because it provided controlled temperatures and even better fusing of ingredients.

About forty hours were required for complete fusion, during which time some undissolved particles had dropped to the bottom. Others, in the form of a saline, whitish scum called *glass gall* or *sandever*, had risen to the top. These were skimmed off with shovels or sabers, then glass samples were taken. Then the temperature was lowered until the glass had a somewhat thicker, taffy-like consistency, and could be worked.

In order to learn the terms used by the profession, let us describe a hypothetical scene in a large glasshouse in America or Europe during that fabulous era.

When the *batch* reached the proper state, a *gang* or *shop* of workmen (called a *chair* in England) acted in harmony to produce a blown *blank*, an article ready to be decorated by cutting, engraving, or both.

The master blower was called a *gaffer*. His assistant, the *gatherer*, took up from the pot the needed amount of molten glass, or *gather*, on the end of an iron *blowpipe* about four to six feet long. He or a *servitor* formed it into the desired shape by rolling it on an iron table known as a *marver*. Then he passed it to the gaffer, who inflated it and created the correct form.

To blow a bubble in the glass, the gaffer moistened his mouth with water before blowing. The water, converted into steam inside the glass, aided in extension of the *bell* or hollow ball formed at the end of the pipe. After making a bubble in the gather by blowing through the blowpipe, the gaffer could elongate the blob of glass by swinging it in a circle. A trench may have been dug in the floor to give him room to swing. He could shorten the bell by holding the pipe with the bubble at its top for a short time.

When the glass became too cool to work, the *middle-boy* reheated it in the *glory hole*, then handed it back to the gaffer. The hole for reheating was sometimes a small aperture in the same furnace, called a *nose* or *bye hole*. In other cases, it was in a small, separate furnace. At the proper time, one of the assistants brought a small glob of molten glass on the end of a solid, flat-topped *pontil rod*. This was applied to the swell of glass opposite the blowpipe. The gaffer broke the entire shape away from the blowpipe by touching it near the point of contact with a piece of iron dipped in cold water, then he gave it a sharp tap. The other end of the article could then be finished, using the pontil rod as the axis of rotation.

The master blower or gaffer worked with the glass attached to the pontil rod and fashioned it with wooden and metal tools. The wooden tools were dipped into water periodically to prevent charring. The gaffer seated himself and rested the rod on the slanting arms of the *chair,* a crude structure of wood with metal bands along the edges of the arms. He kept rolling the iron with his left hand (to keep the form symmetrical) while shaping the object with the tools in his right hand. The end of the broad seat of the chair held the tools to be used for shaping the malleable glass. A *bit-boy* brought small bits of glass to add handles, feet, or other appurtenances to the piece (fig. 1). The base of the *parison,* as the partially formed blank was called, was flattened by means of a *paddle* or *battledore.*

The foot of stemware may have been shaped by inserting it between wooden *clappers.* Metal tools included *calipers* to measure the piece for symmetry, *pucellas* to widen or narrow the opening, *tongs* to handle the hot object, and *shears* to trim off excess material while red hot. As tumblers, bowls, globes, and similar objects are spherical in shape when blown, they had to be cut to form an opening. This was accomplished after the piece had cooled by marking the rim line with a diamond point and using a thin flame to crack off unwanted portions. The piece was held down on a rotating iron or sandstone disk and fed with abrasive and water to grind the edge evenly.

The rim was reheated, *fire-finished* and smoothed, rounded and perfected with grayness removed. This is one of the signs of hand-blown glass and should be remembered when you buy tumblers, cups, or goblets. If a chipped piece has been ground down to eliminate the chip, the edge has become flat. The buyer should be aware of the alteration and pay less.

When the piece was finally broken off from the pontil rod, a rough mark or scar called the *pontil mark,* was left on the base. This was usually ground off, leaving a smooth concave circle, or it may have been made flat and cut in a star or other design when the blank was decorated.

Most pieces were free-blown, but some were blown into a paste mold (plain or patterned) made of iron and lined with a resinous beeswax. *Blown-mold* seems to have been an American invention circa 1820, adapted by the English, Irish, and French. A metal mold in two to six or more pieces was fitted around a bubble of glass at the end of a blowpipe and locked. After blowing, the mold was unlocked to permit removal of the finished piece. Walls of the vessel were about the same thickness throughout. Therefore, where there were depressed sections on the outside, they appeared as protuberances on the inside, and vice versa.

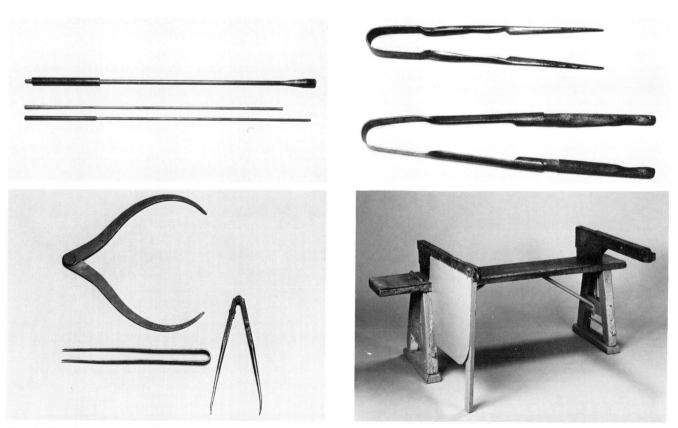

Fig. 1. Glassblower's tools. Top to bottom, left to right: Blowpipe; mouthpiece insulated with wood or twine; two pontil rods: wood and steel jacks or pucellas, used as spreaders; a spring tool, called pincers, used in pincer work and for applying handles; compasses for measuring to achieve uniform heights on goblets and other vessels; calipers or dividers for measuring diameters; bench or chair. (The Corning Museum of Glass, Corning, New York)

By using molds shaped to transfer the principal motifs of the "cut" design to the blank, labor costs were saved late in the Brilliant Period when quality was declining. Indeed, much of the European imported glass today is of this ersatz variety.

Resuming our visit to a glass factory, some articles, such as a square or rectangular box, had to be *press-molded.* The first man gathered glass on a rod, held it over the hollow of a one-piece mold, and cut off just enough. Instantly the second man brought down with lever power a *follower* of brass to shape the inside of the object. Melted glass was compressed to fill the cavity of the mold, which was then turned bottom up. With a little tap, the article (tumbler or box) dropped red-hot on the stone table. If the item was a tumbler, a boy with an iron rod with a bit of hot glass on its end pressed it against the bottom, to which it adhered. He held the tumbler in the glory hole, twirling it rapidly, then passed it to a third man who whirled it on the arms of a chair, removing roughness from the edge with an iron tool. This man passed the rod to a boy who separated it from the piece, which was immediately placed in the annealing oven. These five men produced a beautiful tumbler in forty-five seconds!

A complicated piece was reheated again and again in the glory hole. In its final form, it was received on a wooden paddle (held steady by asbestos-covered tongs) by a young apprentice called the *taker-in* or *carry-in* and was placed by him in an annealing oven for a day, or even a week, to decrease the heat gradually until it could withstand room temperature. The thicker and larger the glass item, the longer it took to cool.

The oven was called the *leer* or *lehr.* It was like a tunnel, thirty to 440 feet long, with a moving belt carrying the glass from 1,400 degrees Fahrenheit to room temperature. The oven was sealed against drafts that would crack the glass. Annealing reduced the porosity and made the glass more durable and less liable to break while being cut. If it cooled too quickly, the glass became brittle and cracked spontaneously on the shelf or burst if placed in sunshine.

Ornamental Cutting

Cutting is done by holding the blank against a revolving iron wheel and pressing down against it. Power for turning the wheel evolved from a treadle (pumped by the right foot of the cutter) to lathes (turned by boy apprentices) to water power (which may have been used in Egypt and Syria 200 years B.C., since miter, square, and panel scoops appear on very early glass). The Kensington Glasshouse in Philadelphia used waterpower in 1790. Bakewell may have used steam as early as 1817, although some firms used horsepower to turn the lathes. Electric motors finally made possible the deep miter (spelled *mitre* in England) cuttings of the Brilliant Period in America.

Although one artisan alone could complete all the phases of cutting, assembly-line work was more economical in a large house. A piece could be handed from one artisan to the next for different stages according to an artisan's expertise. This also obviated changing wheels for each phase of cutting. Some one-man home shops had four lathes so the cutter could move from one to the next without changing wheels. Let us describe a cutting shop circa 1900.

Visualize long rows of frames, each of which carries between two main supports removable spindles with abrasive wheels of iron. Wheels of many sizes and materials — stone, wood, walrus hide or leather, cork, felt — hang on a rack to one side. Each frame has an individual belt linked to a pulley of an overhead shaft driven by an electric motor (fig. 2).

A blank is brought from the storeroom. The design to be cut has been devised by a master cutter or designer. Either he has cut his creation freehand, thus making an actual sample to copy, or he has sketched a design to follow. Usually the outlines are drawn on the glass with a brush in hairlines. The artist may use a mixture of resin, red lead, and turpentine, or brunswick black diluted with turpentine.

Whoever puts the design on the glass hands the blank to the *rougher,* who makes the first deep incisions by holding it against a large iron or steel wheel called a *mill.* Onto the edge of the mill drips a stream of fine, wet sand from a hopper. The sand does the actual cutting; the water prevents overheating from friction.

In following the designer's marks, the rougher can hardly see the contact points because of the sand, and

Fig. 2. Glasscutter at work. This man worked in the exhibit of the Libbey Glass Company at the 1893 World's Columbian Exposition in Chicago. (From Bancroft's *Book of the Fair,* Vol. II, p.891.)

because he is looking down into the dish from inside to outside. While cutting a bottle, decanter, or vase, he looks through two layers of glass. If he cuts a miter groove too deeply, the piece will break. In more shallow cutting — flutes, relief diamonds, or bull's-eyes — there is less risk. Most cutters start as roughers. Boys in their apprenticeship are first allowed to cut edges, then panels, as danger of breakage is minimal.

The *smoother*, using a stone wheel called a *craigleith* imported from Scotland refines the first cuts and adds smaller cuts. All cuts are a whitish gray at this stage until polished to restore clarity by the *polisher*.

Before acid-polishing was introduced in the 1890s to eliminate the gray appearance and to polish away wheels marks, wooden wheels with rouge or putty powder (oxide of tin and lead) were used. Polish was often further improved by brushing with putty powder. Finally, a paste of pumice or rottenstone was used with cork, felt, or walrus-hide wheels. This was a slow process, but it left a soft luster never equaled by acid-polishing, used generally after 1900.

A Dorflinger advertisement in *Harper's Magazine*, October 1896, declared: "A lot of cut glass is now polished by chemicals. Our ware is all cut and finished *by hand*, and will keep its brilliancy."

Thatcher Brothers in New Bedford, Massachusetts, were supposed to have invented this faster method of polishing by dipping the glass into acid. They turned down an offer of $50,000 for their process. Soon other factories perfected their own acid treatment. The acid bath sometimes left a slick, oily-feeling surface to the touch. Overexposure often smoothed the edges to resemble pressed glass, or imparted a grainy appearance to the surface. Besides all this, it was a dangerous process for the workmen.

A mixture of sulphuric and hydrofluoric acids was held in tanks. The fumes had to be sucked up through overhanging hoods by powerful fans. Even then it was deemed necessary for the workmen to wear rubber masks with inserts of wet gauze, as well as heavy rubber aprons.

The early method of dipping consisted of filling the piece with wax, into which was inserted a wooden handle. Later, the inside surface and other surfaces requiring no polish were coated with wax, and several pieces were placed in a wire basket. In either case, the articles were immersed in the tank containing the secret formula of acids (sometimes in two or three of varying concentrations), while the immersion was timed on a stopwatch. Finally, they were rinsed by dipping into or spraying with water to stop the action of the acids.

Only certain shops had this equipment; some accomplished better results than others. If done well, the method was a great boon for those who cut intricate, fine patterns. Polishing, which may have taken six hours by means of the wooden wheel, could now be done in five minutes.

Fire-polishing was also used to some extent. An August 1904 patent assigned to Libbey, called "Art of Fire-Polishing Glass," by Cornelius J. Nolan, describes the process as rotating the piece and applying heat to one surface, while subjecting the opposite side to cooling influences so that the article retained its shape. A jet of flame was applied on one side; a cooling jet of air on the other.

In October 1904 Mr. Nolan published another patent for fire-polishing:

> Subjecting article to action of a flame containing unconsumed combustible (carbonizing flame) which lays down a coating, then to heated gases rich in oxygen which consumes or burns off the coating whereby the article is polished, at the same time cooling it.

When a dealer points out that a piece is wood-polished, you will know that it is worth more and may be older than a similar acid-polished item. You will never hear a dealer say proudly, "This is acid-polished." Examine enough pieces to learn the difference.

Women employees washed all traces of polishing powders and guide markings from the glass, then passed it to a sharp-eyed inspector for detection of flaws. Schoolgirls helped out during busy periods. In Corning, women could become chief inspectors or supervisors. Hunt's business manager was a woman. Revi found in his research that the Pitkin & Brooks factory in Valparaiso, Indiana, opened in 1911, was the first to employ women as glass artists. During the life of Laurel Cut Glass Company of Jermyn, Pennsylvania, women were hired as polishers and as cutters of simple designs. But in the main, men were dominant in the industry.

Bottles, cruets, and decanters frequently had identical numbers scratched on the stopper and inside the neck, in case the two parts were separated in shipping. Hand-blown articles differ slightly in size and shape and so require stoppers made to fit each one. We often can tell that a bottle has its original stopper by discovering these tiny numerals.

Finally, an employee would acid-stamp the signature (if one had been adopted) on each piece, or on one of a set, or paste on a paper label.

Types of Cutting Wheels

Cutting wheels can be grouped into three major contours with some fifty variants. The three major categories are the pointed or V-shaped rim edges for miter or bevel cuts, the flat rim edges producing panel cutting, and convex rims for hollow cuts. The mitered wheel might have had a single V-shaped edge, with the bottom of the V forming a sharp cutting edge, or it might have had several parallel sharp edges produced by cutting a flat-edged wheel by turning it toward a hard steel rod, sometimes tipped with a diamond. This type was essential for cutting silver diamond, fine-line cutting, or any motif with parallel lines. It was called a *gang* wheel

Fig. 3. Berry bowl, 9″ × 4″. Deep miter cuts divide design into major and minor motifs. Around a central sixteen-point hobstar are small areas of simple hobnail — a button with six sides. Four deeply cut sixteen-point hobstars alternate with kites of clear-button cane around sides. Small triangles of crosshatching (silver diamond) and small fans fill remaining spaces. Note depth of cutting, seen on lower curve. (Matye)

and was introduced in 1913. Sinclaire and Hawkes used fine-line bands with engraved motifs, especially in the 1920s (fig. 311).

Early in the period, stones imported from England and Scotland were used for smoothing. Later, Carborundum wheels were used. Carborundum is a man-made stone second only to the diamond in hardness. It's produced by heating sand and carbon together in an electric resistance furnace. The smoothing wheels were kept wet with dripping water, which was less messy than sand and water. They ranged from 18″ in diameter by ⅝″ to 1½″ thick, down to 4″ in diameter by ½″ thick.

By means of combining cuts in various directions and angles, elements of design or *motifs* were developed. These included diamonds of diverse depth and size (such as relief, strawberry, chequered, and cross-cut), fluting, notching or beading, bull's-eyes (called *printies* or *punties* in England and *kugeln* in Germany), fans, prismatic cutting, splits, stars of various types, hobstars, and vesicas. The bowl shown (fig. 3) has typical motifs used in geometrical cutting.

In 1904, Charles B. Bishop of New Britain, Connecticut, patented a machine for cutting glass mechanically. It provided a means of holding the blank, rolling and swinging it against the cutting tool, and indexing the design to be cut. Cheap ware, pressed in molds to standard dimensions, could be cut by this method. Such an inferior product is of no interest to the collector.

Engraving

On early Bohemian glass, noted for its fine engraving, shallow Baroque engraving was often spread over the object in a lacy pattern to conceal tiny bubbles and unmelted sand. Modern glass is more perfect, so the engraving is often concentrated in a single, dramatic motif or figure that stands out against the clear background. Later Bohemian and present-day Steuben are in this category. During the Brilliant Period, copper wheel engravers came to Corning, New York, from Central Europe (most were from Bohemia). Here they trained American engravers to use European methods.

They used copper wheels of many diameters, from around 2″ inches to pinhead size, and some so small that a magnifying glass is needed to study the details in the finished decoration. These exquisite designs were expensive and time-consuming. The wheels were fed with a mixture of oil or water and an abrasive — generally emery of different grits. A small felt pad hanging at the rear of the wheel held and spread the mixture on the wheel. The artisan let go of the article every thirty to fifty seconds, dipped his fingers into the emery, and rubbed it on the wheel. As it spread over the design, he wiped it away. He held the piece under the over-hanging wheel and brought the glass upward against it, resting his elbows on cushions to steady his hands.

Engraving may be shallow or deep. The most shallow, often called *surface engraving*, was done by means of a copper wheel on glass too thin for the cutter. In this category were monograms, coats of arms, even pictures. In deep engraving, we use the word *intaglio*, translated "engraved" or "sculptured" from the Italian. It should be pronounced een-tahl-yee-o. Some of the deepest intaglio sculpturing was abraded by means of sandstone wheels or by those of aloxite, an electrically fused aluminum.

Engraving requires more artistry, skill, and training than mere cutting. It compares favorably with cameo work. In fact, it is the reverse of cameo cutting, in which the background is cut away, leaving the "picture" in relief. While engraving in the intaglio manner, the artist carves freehand into the glass at varying depths. Most engraving was left gray, a *mat* or *matte* lusterless finish, for contrast with the clear, uncut areas of the surface, but some of the finest examples were partially polished. Others were entirely polished, in which case they are said to be *rock crystal*.

The luncheon plate (fig. 4) has a partially polished design. A 1911 R.T. & Company Jeweler's Wholesale Supply House (Chicago) catalog shows a comparable plate. It was called a sandwich plate and came in 6″ through 10″ sizes. The 9″ plate, described as of "finest quality, highly polished," sold for $10 to the retailer. Even a peanut butter sandwich would seem elegant served on this plate.

Fig. 4. Luncheon plate, 9¼", ⅜" base, is heavy for its size. Blazed or feathered leaf design is cut on finest blank, probably by Libbey. Central flower, miter leaves, and thumbprint buds are polished, but feathered edges and crosshatched flower center are left gray.

The small Libbey compote in Chapter 14 (fig. 279) is left gray in the matte finish, while the Hawkes compote in Chapter 15 (fig. 316) is entirely in rock crystal.

Some engraving in the Brilliant Period followed intricate, lacy designs that were repetitious and geometrically precise (Pairpoint and Sinclaire, for example). Others were like freehand drawings with only a plan to guide the engraver. Some engravings depicted coats of arms or monograms, while others showed views of buildings, such as Mt. Vernon on a goblet by the Dithridge Flint Company circa 1876 (pl.. 18 in *Cut and Engraved Glass* by Daniel). Fruits, flowers, butterflies, and various animals were favorite subjects from nature. Although cut on a pressed blank late in the period, a cream and sugar set (fig. 5) with engraved birds and flowers is charming and is made of good lead crystal.

Another type of engraving, by *needle-point*, was used from about 1910 into the 1920s. A design was programmed in a machine that produced a mechanically uniform pattern on the sides of thin metal tumblers and stemware as the revolving objects were pressed against the needle. We have three examples under Fry glass in Chapter 17 (fig. 395) to illustrate this technique.

Acid Etching

Most *acid etching* dates after 1875. Briefly explained, the making of gray or frosted pictures by acid etching upon the glass was done sometimes by using a stencil as a guide. The finest etching resulted when a skillful artist dipped a piece in a wax resist (such as asphaltum), drew the pattern on the wax, then cut through the wax freehand to provide a design before dipping the item into acid, exposing it to acid vapor, or painting over it with acid paste. After the etching had reached the proper depth, action of the acid was stopped by application of warm water. Joseph Locke of the New England Glass Company worked with his friend Edward Drummond Libbey to do outstanding etching. Locke used only hydrofluoric acid with alkali of ammonium fluorides for matte (satin) etchings.

Shades for lamps were in great demand throughout the century, and for gas chandeliers and electric lights beginning in the 1890s. A matte finish to diffuse the light was produced by acid etching or by sandblasting. Some globes or shades had an intricate pattern. Others employed literal designs, such as a Masonic emblem, or words, such as FIRE ESCAPE or STAIRS, for use in public buildings. These were produced by stencils or acid resist. In some cases, the matte finish was engraved in a polished design, as in the Grape and Leaf pattern. The shade shown (fig. 6) was taken from a house built in 1913.

Fig. 5. Cream and sugar set, 2½" h, 3" sq, has an unusual shape. Lip of creamer thins toward the edge, as it was drawn out of the side while still malleable. Engraved bird in flight, with a straw in its beak, and flowers in matte finish contrast with polished leaves. By Fry, similar to "Oriole." (Bert Hilby)

Fig. 6. Light shade, 8″ d × 5¼″ h, frosted, then cut to clear.

Etching of any kind is neither cut nor engraved, yet many people, including dealers, now say "etched" when they mean "engraved."

Cased, Overlay, and Flashed

Cased and *overlay* can be made the same way. When a gaffer has achieved the shape he wants in the gather of glass on the end of his blowpipe, he removes it from the pipe, spreads an opening in the end, places the cuplike shell into a metal shell, then gently blows a gather of clear or color inside the first. Reheating fuses the pieces into a single unit. In cased glass, the layers are of equal thickness; in overlay, the outer layer is thinner than the base shape. Another method of making overlay is to blow a clear blank, cool it, then spread molten colored glass over the clear blank. The covering must not be so hot that it melts the inner form, but warm enough to adhere to it.

Flashed glass has an outer coating no thicker than varnish on furniture. The object made of glass with a high melting point is dipped into a colored bath of glass with a low melting point. Its shape does not warp in the cooler bath. Less expensive Bohemian glass has been made this way. Sometimes part of the flashing has worn off, making this treatment less desirable than casing.

In all three types, the outer layer was cut or engraved to reveal the inner color (figs. C. 2 and 3). It is easy to see the difference by observing the edges of the cut design. This "Bohemian" type of cut glass was popular in America about 1862. Interest was aroused by displays of French and Austrian glass at New York's Crystal Palace in 1853.

Teardrops, Air-twist Stems, and Bubbles

Another form of decoration was the *tear*, an empty space that was globular at one end and tapered to a point at the other. It was implanted in the stems of goblets, wines, compotes, candlesticks, and occasionally in knife rests. These were made in several ways: by injecting a drop of alcohol into the stem while the glass was still ductile; by pushing a needlelike snout of a bellows into the stem, then blowing a tear of the desired size; or by pushing a sharp-pointed tool into the stem to the correct depth. Air was sealed in the cavity by crimping or adding a small gather of glass over the hole. Tears were early forms of stem adornment. They often were used in early English baluster stems, dating from 1680.

Air-twist stems on wines and candle- and tapersticks were popular in eighteenth-century England. The American colonies imported them, but did not make them at that time. The air-twist stem was made by punching a series of holes in the lower end of the gather of glass, which was to form the stem. Air was entrapped by nipping or adding glass to create bubbles. As the glass was rotated and stretched, the bubbles were elongated, forming a group of air-twists. This technique was seldom used during the Brilliant Period, but Carder did again employ this type of decoration in making a wide variety of cut, engraved, and colored ware, especially in the 1920s.

Accidental bubbles were the bane of early glass-makers, who strove for clear, flawless glass. Carder, however, loved bubbles. To produce *random bubbles*, he would send workmen out to cut fresh poles from willows growing on the banks of the Chemung River. Just before bubbled pieces were to be made, a willow pole four to five feet long would be pushed into the pot opening, through the molten glass all the way to the bottom. It then was withdrawn at once. This "sticking the pot" released gas, causing the glass to form bubbles of various sizes for the next half hour or longer. When necessary, the process was repeated.

Controlled bubbles were produced either by flat spike molds or two-piece, hinged iron molds. The flat mold was a wooden slab about 1″ thick. Spikes protruded about ½″ in the planned bubble pattern. With the slab placed on the marver, a gather of glass was rolled over it, punching holes into the surface of the glass. Another gather was applied to lock in the air and preserve the design.

The other method required a dip or hinged iron mold with spikes arranged in the desired pattern on the inside. The holes produced were likewise sealed shut with additional molten glass.

Pairpoint, from 1910 into the 1920s, used so many spherical or oval knops containing air traps that the "bubble ball" became almost a trademark of the company. A Pairpoint vase is shown in Chapter 9 (fig. 78). Dorflinger also used this form of decoration.

Appreciation of Glassmakers

Having seen how complex glassmaking was, we should truly appreciate the dedication of the artisans to their craft.

When I complained to my music professor in college about the difficulty of learning harmony and counterpoint in order to write music correctly, he replied, "Louise, you do well, considering that you waited so long to learn music theory. Remember that the great composers of the past were apprenticed as children to their master teachers, perhaps as early as seven years of age. They lived with the master and composed daily, just as you learned to read and write words."

Master glassmakers also started young, often as early as seven years of age in Europe. In the United States during the Brilliant Period, the usual starting age was fourteen. Long hours of working under supervision of highly skilled makers and cutters, year after year, naturally led to high achievement in the art of glassmaking.

2

Our Glass Heritage
in History

The earliest glass we know of is nature's shiny black obsidian. It is similar to English wine bottle glass and may be seen in Yellowstone National Park in the phenomenon aptly named Glass Mountain. Natural glass made excellent arrowheads and knives, such as the sacrificial knife held by a Mayan priest, found in bas-relief on a *stele* (stone slab). Victims laid out on a bloodstone block were dispatched with an obsidian knife or axe. Temple walls are still stained with their blood.

The most ancient man-made glass has been found in Egypt, a country protected from enemies by natural barriers. Egypt had the necessary ingredients (silica and alkali) and fuel (from papyrus, tamarisk trees, and acacia groves). A green glass bead, discovered in a tomb at Thebes, was analyzed and found to have been made of soda and lime by human hands. This proves that Egyptians possessed technical knowledge of glass-making 3500 years B.C. According to J.R. Vávra of Prague in his erudite study of Bohemian glass, *Five Thousand Years of Glass-Making,* Professor Dr. Springer and H.C. Beck place the art of glass-melting at 4000 years B.C. Beads dug from under the foundations of the temple tower in Assur date Mesopotamian glass at 2900 B.C.

Tutankhamen (circa 1371 to 1352 B.C.), pharoah of Egypt for nine years, married the third daughter of Ikhnaton, and succeeded his father-in-law in 1361 B.C. His otherwise undistinguished reign, which ended at the untimely age of nineteen, became famous following the discovery of his tomb at Thebes in the Valley of the Kings in 1922.

Relevant to our study is the exciting proof that glass colored by metal oxides was used on an equal basis with precious stones in the carefully executed gold jewelry of the boy-king. His death mask of solid gold, which was placed over the head and shoulders of the mummy outside the bandages, is as beautifully detailed in back as are the exquisite facial features. The stripes of the headdress are of blue glass, an imitation of lapis lazuli. Large earrings with a green glass center were found in the tomb and are presumed to be his. A wide, flamboyant collar of gold was composed of 166 plaques inlaid with colored opaque glass. Its design portrays the vulture goddess of el-Kab, Nekhbet, beside the cobra goddess of Buto.

False emeralds of good size have been found, but the most astounding discovery was an obelisk sixty feet high in the temple of Jupiter Ammon. This was of emerald-green glass, colored by copper oxide.

First the Egyptians, then the Syrians, learned to make a vitreous glaze, opaque and colored, to cover objects of stone or of molded sand mixed with clay. If thick enough, the glass needed nothing for support. It could be made into beads and small pieces for inlay work. Subsequently, someone found that it could be gathered on a core. When the core was removed, a small vessel or bottle was left behind. It is supposed that cosmetics, perfumes, and medicines were carried in these *unguentaria*. Other Mediterranian lands also left a few sand-core examples.

According to some authorities, enlightenment was a long time in coming, because the earliest glass vessels, shaped by molding, date circa 1500 B.C. They were in many colors. Vávra, however, states that he possesses "fragments of a vase from the year 3300 B.C. Its green glaze carried the name of the first Egyptian pharoah, MENNY." At this time they used glazes to cover entire walls! Vávra also confirms discoveries of small pieces of glass dating from 2000 to 1788 B.C. These were used to replace lost turquoise in a bracelet and a small mosaic calf, found among the jewels of a princess. They prove that the cloisonné and millefiori techniques passed from Egypt to Rome.

From 1375 B.C., there was a thousand-year decline in Egyptian glassmaking. Before dying out, many beautiful vases, goblets, and bowls were made exclusively for the upper classes. With the loss of Egyptian supremacy over Asia Minor, luxury glass declined practically to extinction.

Discovery of the Blowpipe

The Syrians or Egyptians may have invented the long blowpipe for shaping about three centuries before Christ. Drawings on a tomb at Beni Hassan depict naked figures at a fire with what seem to be blowpipes in the time of Pharaoh Usetesen I, 1900 B.C. F.L. Griffith, however, declares that the figures are smiths bellowing their fire on an open hearth. Perhaps he was wrong. Many discoveries continually change our "facts" about ancient times. Some credit an artisan of Sidon (now in Lebanon) with this advance. This seems most likely, since the first mold-blown glasses bear the signatures of Syrians. Also, their readily ductile soda glass was adaptable to this process.

More progress in manufacturing glass took place in the fifty years before Christ than in the preceding fifteen hundred. Blowing glass into a mold was a major occupation by 30 B.C. Glass coins with hieroglyphical markings were molded in Egypt, and jewelry was molded in Rome.

For a time, Rome was content to import glass from Sidon and Alexandria, but by the first century A.D. the Romans had achieved great skill in glassmaking. They cut shallow geometrical motifs on clear glass. By the fourth century A.D., Romans were engraving such pictorial scenes as chariot races and gladiatorial combats with the names of participants, as well as signatures of the cutters. They learned to roll glass into thin slabs, an early forerunner of plate glass for windows. They also applied mosaic techniques to form their famous *millefiori* vessels.

All glass in the first four centuries A.D. from around the Mediterranian is termed "Roman," made in the Roman world but not necessarily by Romans. Much common glass was made for daily use and was simply utilitarian, but some ornaments still dazzle us.

The First Cut Glass

Alexandrian shops began working glass upon a wheel, cutting facets and grooves. Later, they contrived to sculpture layered glass into designs with great artistry.

The best-known Roman specimen of sculptured glass, the Portland-Barbarini Vase, is 9⅝″ high, with white overlay cut to show white classical figures against a dark blue background. It is in the British Museum. It is supposed to have been made between A.D. 138 and 161 and was discovered in the tomb of the Roman emperor Severus (who was killed A.D. 235) during the course of excavations in Rome toward the end of the sixteenth century.

The vase was copied in a bone-paste, called jasperware, perfected by Wedgwood circa 1775. It was then copied in glass by John Northwood, with the carving requiring three years to complete. Thus, after fifteen hundred years, Thomas Webb & Sons, Northwood, and Stevens & Williams in England, as well as Gallé and others in France, revived this technique of carving cameo reliefs in glass. Cameo glass is now one of the most admired and expensive forms of cut glass. Whole books have been written on this subject.

The Spread Northward

With Roman conquest, glassmaking moved northward throughout Europe, especially to northern Gaul and to the valleys of the Rhône and the Rhine. With the conquerors there came changes in language, religion, and customs. In the case of Gaul, old gods assumed the names of new gods. Sometimes the changes were forced upon the vanquished, but sometimes, too, the conquered people imitated and admired superior methods and skills and eagerly adopted them. Glassmaking was one of these skills.

Rome and Venice constituted the fountainhead of this sophisticated art. Whole streets in Rome were given over to furnaces. Beautiful glass was no longer a luxury reserved for nobility.

In A.D. 200, Rome seemed to be stable. But by A.D. 300, the seeds of disaster were sown. Christianity became the religion of the Empire in 324, and the seat of government was transferred to Byzantium (Constantinople) in the year 330. Constantine the Great took with him famous artists and glassmakers of the Roman Empire. Rome was sacked by northern invaders in 410 and again in 455. The scarcity of specimens of glassware from the fifth to thirteenth centuries, however, is not a result of barbarian invasions. Rather, it is due to the fact that, under Christianity, people abandoned the practice of burying objects of value with the deceased.

The ebb and flow of power affected glassmaking in a most interesting fashion. The superstitious feared the massive cone-shaped furnaces with their fiery mouths, as well as the glassmakers, carrying what looked like balls of fire. Credulous country people around Venice spread the rumor that a fiery dragon lived inside a furnace there, and that he would come forth to destroy the unwary who ventured near the furnace. Certain nobles rode out to meet the monster.

Venice, a great trading nation between Western Europe and Asia, was making glass in the tenth century and had a flourishing glass industry by the thirteenth. Its finest period was from A.D. 1500 to 1550. The Venetians in the sixteenth century learned for the first time how to make glass that was almost clear. Toward the end of the thirteenth century, the Grand Council, in an effort to preserve their secrets and obviate the risk of fire in the city, had moved the furnaces to the island of Murano, where the glassmakers were marooned. On the island, three hundred glasshouses were lined up a mile long.

If a worker tried to leave or betray secret processes to a foreigner, his life was taken. In 1376, the Senate declared that all Murano glassmen were burghers of Venice, which meant that noblemen could marry the glassmakers' daughters. Children of such marriages were then considered nobility.

A second glass center at L'Altare, near Genoa, freely furnished men and methods to whoever requested them.

In a short time, the fragile glass of Venice became more fashionable throughout Europe than the beautiful Eastern wares from the Byzantine Empire. Many techniques that had been lost during the Dark Ages were rediscovered by the Venetians. They developed millefiori (colored rods cut and embedded in clear glass to resemble a "thousand flowers"), *latticinio* (milk-white threads in a clear background that resembled a net of lace, *vetro di trina*), and diamond point engraving. They also decorated blown and molded ware with enamel and gilding. Some believe these skills were brought by Grecian blowers who fled from Constantinople when that country was conquered by the Turks in 1453.

Other European countries decided that the same types of glass should be produced at home. Italian workers were persuaded to go to France, the Lowlands, Spain, Portugal, and to some extent to England, in spite of the threat of dire penalties.

In the eighteenth century, Murano's three hundred glasshouses dwindled to less than twenty. Venice tried to pry from the French their secret of making plate glass for mirrors, but France was as secretive as Venice had been.

Prague was more generous to the Venetians, who went there to study the processes that gave Bohemian glass its marvelous colors. The making of colored glass is a subject worthy of study for its own sake. Many types of colored glass were inspired by natural stones, such as jasper, onyx, agate, and chalcedony.

"Gilding the Lily"

From the beginning, artists were not content to simply change the shape of the objects. They experimented with numerous ways of "gilding the lily." These included carving, etching with acid, enameling, gilding, and even blowing a cup with gilding between two layers, called gold sandwich (in German, *zwischengoldgläser*).

Engraving was done with a diamond-pointed tool. Sometimes the incised lines were filled with black pigment. Engraving with copper or bronze wheels, of the kind practiced in Rome and by German cutters of the much-admired *Bergkristall* (rock crystal), was first done toward the end of the sixteenth century.

Wheel engraving was often done intaglio, carved below the original surface. Relief carving was sometimes shallow and flat, but the German *Tiefschnitt* (deep-cutting) is more elegant. The carving may have been left unpolished (matte) or polished (rock crystal).

Bohemian Glass

Bohemian glass had a great influence on the cut and engraved glass of our Brilliant Period. From the baroque designs to the Art Nouveau style at the turn of the twentieth century, Bohemian glass should be carefully studied for its role as one root of America's unique and distinctive glassware.

By the early nineteenth century, the Bohemians had developed a fine color technology, exploited in several ways. Two of the most popular were *cased* and *overlay*, in which one to several colors were laid over clear glass. Geometric and natural designs were cut through the colors to reveal the clear glass. The *staining* of clear glass with amber or red was another manifestation. A thin coat of color over clear is called *flashing*. Three of these processes were explained in the preceding chapter.

Vast quantities of this glass were exhibited at the 1851 Crystal Palace Exhibition in London, influencing English firms to copy these styles. Such wares, some of which were factory-made of a low quality, were also sent to America circa 1850, where they delighted those in the Victorian Era who loved colorful and ornate decoration.

Glassmakers from Bohemia and England, who were familiar with the techniques, were prepared to make these items in American glasshouses. One of the largest houses was the New England Glass Company, which employed about 450 workmen. A newspaper account published in the *Boston Transcript,* 16 June 1852, reported that many works "could not be surpassed in Bohemia or anywhere else in Europe." The Boston & Sandwich Glass Company and the Cape Cod Glass Company also produced glass in the Bohemian style. Some glass now identified as Bohemian may indeed have been made in America.

Bohemian glass in the first half of the nineteenth century also included heavy crystal ware with cross-cut diamonds, miter cuts, and fans similar to those made by the Anglo-Irish. But the heavy stems and feet only slightly resembled the American cut glass, which was so imitative of the Irish at the beginning of the century.

Much could be said of the exquisite engraving by Schwanhardt (1601-1667), a pupil of Caspar Lehmann, and his Nürnberg school of engravers. His work was characterized by delicate landscapes and scrollwork. The harnessing of waterpower circa 1700, together with the perfection of crystal-clear potash-lime glass, enabled engravers of the Bohemian-Silesian area to practice relief carving in the eighteenth century. German engravers did both relief and intaglio carving of the highest quality.

Other European Glass

Baccarat glass from France will be mentioned in Chapter 18, where we learn to discriminate between European glass and American.

In Belgium, the art of glassmaking has flourished since the thirteenth century, especially at Namur and Liége. The oldest continuous production has taken place at the Cristalleries du Val-Saint-Lambert at Liége. It began in 1825 at a monastery that had survived many tribulations since 1202. Quality is still the keynote in this father-son operation. Some families have spent their whole working life at Val-Saint-Lambert. A drawing, cutting, and engraving school is still maintained. Ten years of apprenticeship are required for a trainee to be considered proficient at cutting and engraving crystal, which is still mouth-blown and hand-cut. Some is blown into a mold. During the Art Nouveau period (1890-1910), the factory carved cameo glass, which now is greatly admired by collectors.

Before proceeding to England, let us look at a pair of decanters (fig. 7) made in the Pays-Bas (Low Countries) in 1842 or shortly thereafter. Holland and Belgium formed part of the Holy Roman Empire. The inhabitants were mainly of German stock, yet they were often under French rule. The two countries fell to Spain at the time of Philip II, were later joined to the French Republic, then were united into the Kingdom of the Netherlands, from which Belgium finally separated.

As the political influence changed, so did glassworkers and their methods. Throughout history, glass collectors and patrons have included Chinese emperors, Egyptian pharoahs, Roman caesars, doges of Venice, popes, kings, and other nobility.

The decanters with chains could never be mistaken for American. They are fairly typical of shapes made in Europe during the middle of the nineteenth century. They are cut and engraved in concave ovals (olivary shapes) and fleur-de-lis sprigs. Two intricately engraved wine jugs, executed by Hermann Miller in Mistrovice about 1875, photographed in Prague, and shown in plates 330 and 333 in the Vávra book, have the same proportions, but they have glass feet as opposed to the silver bases of these free-blown decanters.

The collars on the necks and stoppers, which are connected by chains, and the bases are punch-marked with such minute symbols that use of a jeweler's loupe is required to decipher the legend. It was necessary to buy a book on international silver marks, printed in Paris and written in French, to explain the 2H and a symbol resembling a sword with a bulging tip. The 2 is for objects from 5 to 10 grammes; H indicates "small works" whose silver content was .925-.833. Sterling is, of course, 925 parts per thousand, generally combined with copper. Note the steeple stoppers with flute cuts on the spire tops and on the long necks, and the row of punties around the bulging middle.

Fig. 7. Pair of decanters, 15″, made in the Low Countries (Pays-Bas) 1842 or later. Silver collars, chains, and bases are signed. Free-blown glass, cut and engraved.

Our English and Irish Heritage

Long before the Norman Conquest and even before the establishment of Christian monasteries on the islands and after the Romans conquered England in the first century B.C., Roman colonial settlements included glassworks. After the Romans left England, the paved streets and plumbing lines endured, but the glassworks fell into decay. Early Englishmen did not possess much aptitude for making glass.

Later, workmen from the continent, especially from Germany, came to England to ply their trade. From the thirteenth century, window glass was made in the small Sussex town of Chiddingfold. Bracken and beechwood provided the fuel.

During the reign of Henry VIII, attempts were made to attract Venetian glassmakers to England. These efforts were unsuccessful until 1549, when Joseph Cassilari brought eight glassmen from Murano and set up furnaces in London. The Venetian Senate demanded their return, threatening service on the galleys to death by trained assassins. Production ceased and the Venetians went home.

About the middle of the sixteenth century, glassworkers from Lorraine went to Surrey, then to London. They imported soda in the form of *barilla* from Alicante in Spain. Both lime and soda were produced by burning a plant growing in the Spanish salt marshes. Monopolies were granted to the immigrants, provided that Englishmen were taught the skills.

When French glassworkers proved to be unsatisfactory, Jean Carré (who had come to England in 1567 during the reign of Queen Elizabeth) imported six men from Antwerp in 1571. These experts in the Venetian craft were to be supervised by Giacomo Verzelini. Carré died a year later and Verzelini took over the project.

The delicate *cristallo* was made successfully for nearly a century before Ravenscroft introduced lead crystal, England's great contribution to elegant table glass and the direct ancestor of American Brilliant ware. Verzelini retired in 1592.

In 1618, Verzelini's last factory passed to Vice-Admiral Sir Robert Mansell, who secured monopolies giving him control of glassmaking in England. A 1615 edict had forbidden use of wood as fuel, but by then nearly all factories had adapted furnaces to pit-coal instead of charcoal. Domestic needs were served, while duty on Venetian and other continental glass limited imports to nobles and merchant princes only. Orders sent to Venice specified heavier glass to minimize breakage of the delicate ware. Mansell quit when Cromwell required forfeiture of monopolies.

English arts, suppressed during the Protectorate, enjoyed a rebirth following the restoration of the monarchy in 1660. Until the death of Charles II in 1685, English table glass was no longer a matter of monopolistic control, supported by royal patents. Still, many followers of Cromwell had acquired a taste for use of pewter on the table, and only a limited number dared enter the glass business until Ravenscroft's innovation changed history. English glass then gained a position of such prominence that there was no fear of renewing trade with Venice in 1664.

A gentleman named Ravenscroft opened a glasshouse in 1673. In 1674 he petitioned the king for a patent to make glass "in semblance of Rock Cristall" in a new way. His product contained calcined flint prepared from the Italian white marble river pebbles, which were crushed and sifted, and refined potash from Spain instead of soda. Unfortunately, his first glass was subject to *crizzling* (degeneration).

In 1676 he introduced a red lead formula, replacing vegetable potash flux with lead oxide. This glass is known as English *flint*. The lead increased weight and density of the metal and darkened the color, but it also increased the power of light refraction, throwing back showers of sparkles from a beam of light. It was not brittle, as was the glass made *à la façon de Venise* (in the Venetian style). The new flint glass was easier to work and more suitable for engraved designs and cutting. Due to its supremacy, England maintained her reputation for making the highest quality glass in the world for more than one hundred years. By 1695 there were twenty-seven flint-glass houses in England, employing about a thousand men.

In 1714, when George I succeeded to the throne, many artists still considered real rock crystal more refractive than flint glass. By 1740, glass was widely accepted. George brought German fashions with him. A great deal of commemorative engraving was done in Holland and was popular also in England during the reign of Dutch William and Mary (1689-1702), and especially from 1740 onward. Engraved work improved in quality and increased in quantity. Inscriptions represented peace treaties, battles, and emblems of trade and lodges. Supporters of the Stuart cause inspired the famous Jacobite glasses.

It might be helpful to review briefly the dates of English monarchial reigns to clarify the terms so often heard: Georgian, Regency, Victorian, and Edwardian.

Before the Georges were William and Mary, 1689-1702, and Ann, 1702-1714. George I, the first Hanovarian, ruled from 1714 to 1727; George II, 1727-1760; George III, 1760-1820. From 1811 to 1820, due to his father's insanity, George IV, Prince of Wales, acted as regent, then ruled until 1830 in his own right.

William IV reigned until 1837 when Queen Victoria began her long tenure, which lasted until 1901. Edward VII was King from 1901 until 1910, when he was succeeded by George V, grandfather of Elizabeth II. George V died in 1936.

Early English Cutting

From mid-eighteenth century to the end of the Regency in 1820, England excelled in the technique of glass cutting. Facet cutting or grinding, as distinct from wheel engraving, probably began in England with the manufacturing of looking glasses. Edges were finished with wide, shallow bevels decorated by floral and geometric engraving.

The first such cutting on vessels was done to the rims of sweetmeat glasses. Several references to "scollopt" rims are found prior to 1740, sometimes together with faceted stems on wine glasses. Early design often consisted of cutting the surface into pyramidal diamond shapes in low relief, elaborated by grinding down the pyramid to a flat table. The glass then was cut at the top at a right angle to the sides, producing the *strawberry diamond* made of sixteen diamonds on the field.

From about 1740 to 1805, similar cutting on a clearer and more refractive metal of thinner section produced more brilliant effects. Decoration of decanters began with light slicing and fluting, then progressed to all-over cutting in a variety of shallow facets toward the end of the 1750s. More deeply cut facets appeared in the 1760s on forms more delicate and tapering. In the 1770s we find engraved flowers and foliage, neoclassical swags, stars, and long flutes on the neck.

Until 1750, tumblers were made with a "kick," an arched base, to get the rough pontil mark off the table. After 1750 the base was flat with a ground pontil mark. About 1805, a radiating single star was cut on the bottom.

There was some diamond cutting after 1790, but this was not popular until the early years of the nineteenth century when deep cutting appeared, especially on the shoulders of decanters. Stoppers were elegant. At first, they were circular or pear-shaped. Then, they were in the form of a mushroom, at the end of the eighteenth century, fitted to squat, heavily ornamented decanters. The graceful, shallow-cut decanters and glasses that had been the ideals of the 1770s and 1780s gave way early in the 1900s to public demand for deeper cutting into thicker glass, resulting in ponderous, even pompous, pieces of great weight. This "all-over" cutting suited many but offended others.

English decanters, at first decorated in this manner, showed several variations within twenty years or so. There was a bulbous body with horizontal cutting, rings around the neck, and ball or mushroom stopper. Then came a form with vertical sides and *pillar* cutting. About 1850, some decanters were cut with pointed arches, a reflection of the fad for Gothic furniture.

It was John Ruskin (1819-1900) — writer, critic, and artist — who was mainly responsible for this revival of taste for Gothic architecture in public buildings, furniture, wood paneling in houses, and in pottery and glassware. He favored Gothic art as the norm of true art and moral value. John Ruskin was the archetype of manic-depressive. Precocious as a child, he was over-protected and highly educated by repressive, religious parents. He never fully matured emotionally. Unable to consummate his marriage, yet mad for young girls, he had frequent mental breakdowns and finally succumbed to mania.

Nevertheless, Ruskin used his great skill as a writer to fight social injustice and the *laissez-faire* philosophy of the government. He did more than anyone else to influence the public taste of Victorian England.

Simultaneously with the Gothic style, a reaction against heavy cutting on rounded shapes brought decanters and bowls cut with rows of shallow hollows, with or without engraving, similar to the Dutch decanters just described (fig. 7).

To illustrate Irish and English cutting circa 1800 to 1830, when sharp diamonds and horizontal step-cutting were so popular, we must use a 12″ Dorflinger vase made in America about 1880 (fig. 8), identical in design to a pitcher bearing the original paper label. It was cut in the Anglo-Irish tradition, similar to the "Old Irish" pattern of the Meriden Cut Glass Company during the Brilliant Period. Christian Dorflinger worked from 1852 until his death in 1915.

Fig. 8. Vase, 12″, by Dorflinger, in sharp diamond point and horizontal step cutting, resulting in great brilliance.

A Vicious Tax

In England in 1745 a vicious tax had been levied on the weight of materials in the crucible. This hampered development for nearly a century. To reduce weight, the glassmakers cut down the amount of lead and so diminished luster and quality.

To offset this, they resorted to excessive decoration. By 1835, half of their gross income was taken by taxation.

The excise tax was finally repealed in 1845, causing an expansion of houses. In Stourbridge and Birmingham alone there were twenty-two cutting shops.

At the Great Exhibition of 1851 in London, where a spectacular cut crystal fountain twenty-seven feet high was a main attraction, seventeen British glass manufacturers won prizes, none of which were for cut or engraved glass. Prior to the repeal of the tax in 1845, deep cutting had been a luxury few could afford. Now, at the 1851 Exhibition, a vast amount was on view. Thomas Webb's work received the highest praise. He was to go on to greater glory in the 1880s with his Cameo Glass.

Not every viewer admired the heavily cut glass. One aforementioned critic with an unusual ability to "paint with words" referred to the pieces as "prickly montrosities." This was John Ruskin's scathing denunciation of cut glass, which he characterized as "barbarous." It is said that he cooled the ardor of society for this luxury. From then on, cutting became less ornate. By the time of the 1862 Exhibition, public taste had swung back to engraving as the highest type of decoration. Cutting came back into favor late in the century, but English cutting was never again heavy and deep. Only Americans "went crazy" over deep, brilliant cutting.

On to Ireland

Since the tax was not imposed in Ireland until 1825, some English manufacturers transferred their businesses to Ireland. John Hill in 1785 moved from Stourbridge, England, to Waterford, Ireland, taking tools and fifty skilled workers with him. He came to manage the glasshouse built in 1783 by George and William Penrose, uncle and nephew. He earned an international reputation for fine glassware, but was disliked by William Penrose's wife. When Mr. Hill returned to England in 1786, Jonathan Gatchell operated the firm until 1823, the year of his death. Then, his relatives managed it until it closed in 1851. Both Penroses died in 1799.

Under the Gatchells, the quality of the glass was high and the cutting accurate, though shallow. The patterns consisted mainly of large fields of diamonds (large or small), flutes, and step cutting. Often the bowls had turnover rims and were on round, oval, or square pedestals.

There were also glasshouses at Cork, Dublin, Newry, Belfast, and Waterloo, but the technical knowledge, workers, and capital were English. Irish glass differed only slightly from English in that it was usually heavier. Early English glass was dark due to iron in the sand. From 1725 to 1730, nickel was used to decolorize the glass. Circa 1740, manganese was used, and by the end of the century, cobalt was popular. Control was needed not to turn the glass blue. It is said that most Irish glass had a bluish tint before 1810, that early Cork had a yellowish tint, and early Dublin — a shadowy black cast. Dreppard declares that Waterford (made from 1729 to 1851) never had a blue or smoky tint.

The well-known Irish decanters with basal fluting were blown into one-piece molds in the ordinary way, then insufflated by further blowing. The foot and stem of a vase or ewer might be formed in a four-piece mold.

Irish cut glass in general (and Waterford in particular) reached its greatest fame from 1790 to 1825. The dreaded excise tax was imposed on Ireland in 1825. As in England, when less lead was used to save weight, excessive cutting was employed so that a high price could be asked. This was the only way to make a profit.

If the period between 1780 and 1810 constituted the height of glassmaking in England, success lasted about fifteen years longer in Ireland. Twenty-five years of the excise duty, however, ruined the Irish branch of the industry. The only factory in Waterford closed in 1851. In 1948 a house opened in Waterford, copying some of the old designs of its forerunner. Information on the modern firm will be given in Chapter 18.

By 1810, our glasshouses were competing successfully with Irish imports. During the War of 1812, our future looked hopeful, but after the war ended on Christmas Eve, 1814, carloads of glassware, including cutware, were dumped on the American market by Irish and English dealers willing to sell below cost their large inventories built up during the war.

Coal and melting pots designed to protect the glass from the coal smoke revived American glass. (The New England Glass Company, established in 1818, was the first to use coal.) Also, many English and Irish blowers and cutters, discouraged by the economy in the "old country," decided to emigrate to America.

3

Cut Glass in America:
Early and
Middle Periods

American Cut Glass is generally divided into three periods: Early (1771 to 1830), Middle (1830 to 1880), and Brilliant (1880 to 1910, or even to 1917). At present, no records or specimens prior to 1771 have been found. Nevertheless, we shall begin our discussion with Wistar in New Jersey and Stiegel in Pennsylvania, neither of whom "cut" glass as we know it today. We close the Early Period in 1830 because federal tariff restrictions against imported glass at that time encouraged a great increase in domestic production.

As early as 1535 the Spanish conquerors were making glass at Pueblo de los Angeles in Mexico. A glasshouse was set up in 1592 in the town of Córdoba del Tucamán in the Territory of the Río de la Plata. Here broken glass, surely from Europe, was remelted and fashioned into various objects. Glassmaking was the first industry to be transplanted from Europe to the New World.

While Caspar Lehmann was working in Bohemia, the first permanent settlement by Englishmen was being established in North America at James Towne, Virginia. The year was 1607. Among the seventy passengers brought over in 1608 by Captain Christopher Newport were eight Dutch and Polish glassmakers. A glasshouse was built and some of its products were included in the first cargo exported from America in 1609.

The second American glasshouse was constructed at James Towne in 1620 by the London Company. Six Italian workers were sent here to make glass beads and marbles for trading with the Indians. Playing marbles was a favorite sport of these native Americans. The house survived the massacre of 1621 and was still in operation in 1623.

No further attempt was made in Virginia, but Massachusetts, New Amsterdam, New Jersey, and Pennsylvania were early in the field. Window glass was sorely needed; oiled paper and sliding wooden panels were poor substitutes. Therefore, window glass and bottles were the chief products at the beginning. In subsequent efforts at glassmaking, three outstanding names are Wistar, Stiegel, and Deming Jarves.

New Jersey

After acquiring capital by manufacturing brass buttons, Caspar Wistar (from the Netherlands) established the first successful glassworks in America in Salem County, New Jersey, in a community later known as Wistarberg. He imported Dutch glassmakers, started operations in 1739, and carried on until he died in 1752. Under his son Richard, the company survived the depression years of the Revolution until 1781. They made window glass and lamp chimneys, but also many useful and decorative containers, both colored and clear, classified as the South Jersey type. Wistar is said to have been the first maker of flint glass in this country, but he did no cutting. "South Jersey type" pieces were free-blown of bottle or window glass with hand-manipulated decorations. Pattern-molded glass was also made by Wistar and the other early glassmen. It was blown into a small mold, which established a pattern, then removed and blown to full size. Blown *three-mold* was added about 1812. This was blown into full-sized molds in several hinged parts.

Henry William Stiegel, a German immigrant, built a glassworks at Elizabeth, New Jersey, in 1763. He built two more at Manheim, Pennsylvania, in 1765 and 1769. He was highly successful for a few years, starting with bottles and windowpanes, then venturing into tablewares. The Revolutionary War brought to the "Baron" financial difficulties and even imprisonment for a few weeks in 1774 — a sad blow for an ambitious and ostentatious man who had lived in a mansion and whose comings and goings were announced by cannon reports.

According to research published by George L. Heiges in 1948, quoted by Carl Dreppard in *The ABC's of Old Glass*, Henry William Stiegel did not die in 1785 at the age of fifty-six as previously reported. In 1788 he was working for Henry Bates Grubb at Mt. Hope Furnace. The census of 1790 lists Stiegel as a resident of Warwick Township, Lancaster County. His glassworks did not cease operation when he was bankrupt and imprisoned for debt in 1774. Paul Zantzinger kept the plant going until 1780 or later.

Stiegel's colored and clear drinking glasses, cruets, salts, and other tableware were made in a great variety of styles (some were engraved and enameled), perhaps owing to the different nationalities of the men he employed. For engraved and enameled ware, he used a potash glass containing some lead, but not enough to make a true English type of flint.

N. Hudson Moore, in his book *Old Glass, European and American*, quotes an advertisement from the *Pennsylvania Gazette* for 27 June 1771, placed by an Alexander Bartram, enumerating the Flint Glass items obtained from Stiegel to be sold from his house. He added: "Wanted. A Glass-Cutter and Grinder; such a workman by applying will meet with good encouragement." Mr. Moore says that Stiegel himself hired cutters, grinders, and enamelers, but did not produce true cut glass. Perhaps he intended to copy fine English glass with prismatic cutting, as he had the less expensive Bristol, London, and Continental types of glass, but did not quite reach his goal.

Dorothy Daniel lists Stiegel as one of the early companies "known or believed to have produced cut glass."

In any case, Stiegel's efforts were not all in vain. He trained more than 130 men who moved on to work in Philadelphia, Pittsburgh, and Ohio.

Maryland

John Frederick Amelung came from Bremen, Germany, to Frederick-Town, Maryland, where he produced a superior quality of lightweight, soda-lime, wheel-engraved glass in the Bohemian style from 1784 to 1796. Cut and engraved initials, symbols, and emblems were done to order on the smoky or green-tinged glass.

In 1781, the Stanger brothers, former employees of Wistar, founded the Olive Glass Works, which made fine South Jersey pieces. Olive eventually became part of the Owens Bottle Company, a forerunner of the Libbey-Owens-Ford Glass Company of today.

In 1797, six of the Amelung craftsmen migrated to New Geneva, near Pittsburgh, to work in Albert Gallatin's glasshouse. Pittsburgh's coal, and later the natural gas, attracted several companies to this region.

Pennsylvania

At least four houses in Philadelphia should be mentioned. They are the Northern Liberties Glass Facture (1771-1820), purchased in 1820 by a group from New England Glass Company, who at the same time established the Union Glass Works (1820-1874), which made fine flint ware; the Kensington Glass Works (1772-1804), owned by John Elliott & Company, which produced heavy flint ware resembling Anglo-Irish cut glass; and the Schuylkill Glass Works (1780-1786), which probably made hand-blown decanters

Fig. 9. Wine bottle, 11″ to top of stopper, circa 1808, in style of William Peter Eichbaum. Has St. Louis diamond neck; shallow, simple engraving on shoulder; kugeln or bullseyes on body. Note double pouring lip, seen on an English oil bottle of 1825-1830 and on other bottles in America during this period.

and wine glasses of soda-potash glass and engraved them on a wheel.

Schuylkill is notable because this is where William Peter Eichbaum, descended from a family of glass cutters in Westphalia, found his first employment in America through friendship with Benjamin Franklin. He had worked for Louis XVI in Paris and is said to have been one of the founders of the glass village, St. Louis, named for the French king.

Eichbaum escaped to America after the fall of the Bastille. In 1797 he headed the new Pittsburgh Glass Works for O'Hara and Craig, but was not successful. In 1800 he left to open a hotel and tavern, but continued to cut tumblers and decanters to order. He used Robinson and Ensell (1807-1808) lead glass, which he preferred. Eichbaum introduced the German *kugel*, a round, concave cutting called bull's-eye (abbreviated to bullseye) into American glass cutting, and also the concave, hexagonal diamond motif, which he called the "St. Louis neck," on bottles. (*Kugeln* is the plural of *kugel*.)

The wine bottle pictured (fig. 9) may have been cut by Peter Eichbaum, although there are pictures of several bottles dated about 1840-1860 with similar motifs and proportions. These may have merely carried on his designs. This stopper was cut in hexagonal facets, which go well with the neck. It is doubtful that the original stopper was of this shape.

In 1796 two Revolutionary War officers, General James O'Hara and Major Isaac Craig, established a glasshouse in Pittsburgh, aptly called Pittsburgh Glass Company. O'Hara hired Eichbaum in Philadelphia, as well as the son of the famous New Bremen Amelung. This company had a long and interesting history under an assortment of names. It endured until 1890.

Benjamin Bakewell & Company, founded in Pittsburgh as Bakewell & Ensell, entered the cut glass field in 1809 and prospered until 1882. This firm also changed names many times. The last title was Bakewell, Pears, & Company. It also hired Eichbaum, who cut the first crystal chandelier in America, and Alex Jardelle, an expert French engraver. Bakewell was the first to make cut and engraved tableware commercially in our country; he also held the first patent (1825) on a machine to make pressed doorknobs.

With the aid of skilled English and French cutters, Bakewell produced fine lead glass tableware, such as decanters, compotes, champagne glasses, and tumblers. Table services were made for presidents Monroe and Jackson. President Monroe's set was completed in 1818 and was of *double-flint*, a glass high in lead content. President Jackson's set (in 1829) cost about fifteen hundred dollars — a fabulous sum in that day! It may have been a replacement for glass broken by unruly guests at a reception after Jackson's inauguration. Cut glass and china worth thousands of dollars were broken in the struggle for refreshments. Ladies fainted and men bloodied noses in the crush.

A pair of Bakewell vases was presented to the Marquis de Lafayette on the occasion of his historic visit to this country in 1824-1825. Lafayette also received a cut glass tumbler with his own likeness imbedded in the bottom. Bakewell advertised such tumblers with portraits of distinguished Americans, including DeWitt Clinton, Benjamin Franklin, and George Washington.

Bakewell's products were greatly admired by Deming Jarves. They won recognition at four exhibitions from 1824 to 1827 in the Franklin Institute. A London surgeon in 1818 expressed surprise at the excellent ware. He said the demand for these luxuries "lies in the western states, the inhabitants of Eastern America being still importers from the Old Country."

Bakewell metal was clear, although thinner than that made by New England or Dummer. Cut patterns were similar to Anglo-Irish, using the strawberry diamond, flute, prism, fan, star, blaze, and step cutting. They also resembled German motifs, such as the kugel, due to the influence of the Eichbaum family.

The Phoenix Glass Works (1833-1880) in Pittsburgh, founded by William McCully and others, made some of the finest cut and colored double-flint glass in America.

A Phoenix Glass Company was founded in 1880 at Monaca (formerly Phillipsburg) across the river from the site of the Rochester Tumbler Company and H. C. Fry. (The date, 1880, makes one wonder if this Phoenix was a continuation into the Brilliant Period of the Pittsburgh firm.) Andrew Howard and W. J. Miller made cased and flashed colored glassware of great merit. Green over white, as well as amber, blue, and red, were cut in new patterns, such as hobstar, cane, and notched prism. Solid pieces in amber, blue, and red included goblets with cut stems and St. Louis diamonds on the bowls. By 1891 the company began to make gas and electric shades that were cut, etched, and handpainted. Some sold for up to six hundred dollars each. (See fig. 83.)

Pittsburgh and other cities west of the Alleghenies were considered to be in the Middlewest. This area, opened up to settlement after the Revolutionary War, extended from Lake Erie to the Ohio River and included Michigan, Ohio, Kentucky, western Pennsylvania, and land later to be named West Virginia (1863).

Due to the expense of transporting glass from the East, there was a great need for glasswares made in the Middlewest. All of the necessary raw materials were found there in abundance, save one. The fine clay used in making the melting pots had to be imported from the East.

The great diversity of manufactured glassware included Stiegel and Amelung types, dip-molded, and free-blown, some of which were cut and engraved for the fashion-conscious people who prospered in their new homes. At one time, seventy glass factories were in operation in Pittsburgh.

West Virginia

Ritchie & Wheat (1829-1839) of Wheeling made fine quality lead glass in flute and panel cutting. Michael, Thomas, and R. H. Sweeney (1831-1867), also of Wheeling, produced high quality heavy lead glass. Plunkett & Miller (1839-1891) made fine clear and colored glass, cut and engraved, before 1863.

George and F. C. Dummer of Jersey City Glass Company (1824-1860) made heavy lead glass pieces with single star bottoms. They cut, engraved, and etched decanters, wines, pitchers, carafes, and tumblers. The Dummers sold most of their best cut glass to wealthy, fashionable people of New York City.

The claret jug (fig. 10, right), English in style, is typical of Dummer ware. (See p. 24, *Cut and Engraved Glass* by Daniel for comparison.) Some claret jugs without stoppers were made from mid-seventeenth century through the Brilliant Period to 1910. The heads of mushroom stoppers were pressed, then the shanks were attached. This jug came from the estate of an American heiress married to an Italian of high birth. They had homes outside of London and in America, according to the daughter-in-law, from whom we bought both pieces in the photograph. Judging by color and marks of wear, I have theorized that the handled jug was an antique (early 1900s) when purchased by the heiress, and that the Square Decanter was cut to order to match the claret jug, probably about 1880.

Square decanters with lapidary stoppers were sold in tantalus sets in the 1880s. Two or three square bottles with lapidary stoppers were kept safe from servants and children in a frame of mahogany or oak, which had brass fittings on the corners, a brass handle on top, and a lock at the end. Set No. 6960 in the "Renaissance" pattern, depicted in the 1902 Higgins & Seiter catalog, sold for thirty dollars for two bottles; forty dollars for three. These were cut in wide, vertical miters on the sides, broken by horizontal ogivals on the corners.

New York

John L. Gilliland established in 1823 a firm later called the Brooklyn Flint Glass Company Works. He produced heavy lead glass cut in lunar slices, diamonds, and crosshatching. John exhibited at the Franklin Institute at Philadelphia and at the American Institute in New York from 1828 onward. At the first world's fair, the Great Exposition at the Crystal Palace in London in 1851, Gilliland won the "best flint Glass" award. The company closed in 1868, having been owned since 1864 by Amory Houghton. Gilliland was one of the most important Middle Period glass factories.

Houghton moved to Corning, New York, in 1868 and established the Corning Flint Glass Works, which made fine blanks exclusively for the Hoare & Daily cutting shop at first. The latter was run by Thomas Hawkes. You will often hear a dealer say proudly, "This fine piece was cut on a Corning blank." Corning's decline was due in part to a flood and coal that was full of slate. The Glass Works went bankrupt in 1870. A Bostonian bought it in 1871, appointing Amory Houghton, Jr., as manager. Business improved, but real prosperity came with the Centennial Exposition in 1876 at Philadelphia.

The Long Island Flint Glassworks in Brooklyn (1852-1863) under Christian Dorflinger made fine lead glass that was clear, cased, colored, cut, and engraved. More information with examples will be presented in a later chapter on Brilliant glass.

Fig. 10. *Right:* Claret decanter, 12″, has a heavy mushroom stopper, numbered to match jug. A band of large, shallow relief diamonds encircles mid-section; concave St. Louis diamonds cover neck. There are half-flutes on shoulder and neck, panels around base, panel cuts on slice-cut handle. It resembles both an American claret jug with no stopper by George and P. C. Dummer (1825-1830) and English Georgian decanters of 1810. *Left:* Square decanter, 10½″, has a heavy, well-cut lapidary stopper. It has bands of large, shallow relief diamonds, with a wider band of St. Louis diamonds between these. It is more brilliant than its handled companion and resembles others circa 1880.

New England States

The earliest notable glasshouse in New England was erected near the Connecticut River in East Hartford by Richard Pitkin and Associates in 1783. The company raised capital by running a lottery. The plant was built to make window glass, but was converted in 1788 to make bottles and flasks. It thrived until 1830.

One of the most famous of the early glassmakers was Deming Jarves (1790-1869) who founded the Boston & Sandwich Glass Company on Cape Cod in 1825 after leaving the New England Glass Company, which he and three others had established in 1818 in East Cambridge. Experienced European cutters, using steam power, produced cut glass that won prizes in 1824 and 1837 at exhibits in Philadelphia and Boston. A brief review of New England's early history will be given in Chapter 14, devoted entirely to Libbey glass.

Jarves made pressed and blown ware in many colors, millefiori paperweights, and fine lamps. He made full sets of wines, goblets, finger bowls, and tumblers (plain, cut, etched, and engraved) after 1840. "Sandwich" usually brings to mind pressed *lacy glass* produced extensively in the 1830s, but the firm made both blown and cut glass as well. Mr. Jarves invented and patented numerous aids and devices. When the original Sandwich factory expanded from one eight-pot furnace to four furnaces of ten pots each, three thousand cords of wood yearly were required for fuel. He then invented a glass furnace that would burn coal.

Both firms lasted until 1888, when a labor dispute and the expense of importing coal closed them down after so many years of prosperity.

Jarves had chosen his location because land was cheap, pine trees were available for fuel, and because nearby beaches offered an inexhaustible supply of sand. Unfortunately, this sand produced glass with a strange yellow hue. Fine white sand from the Berkshires was then located across the state. It is also noteworthy that the company was first named the Sandwich Manufactory, but was renamed when expansion required taking in partners from Boston.

Deming Jarves started the Mount Washington Glass Company in South Boston in 1837. A large shop for cutting was run in connection with the glassworks.

Jarves remained with Boston & Sandwich until 1858. He quarreled with the directors and withdrew to found the Cape Cod Glass Works, taking many of the skilled men with him. He hoped his son John would take over the business some day. After John died in 1863, Deming lost interest. The factory was shut down shortly after his death in 1869. Later, a Dr. Flowers bought the factory and operated it until 1882, when it was permanently closed. Cape Cod never compared in size with Boston & Sandwich, but its products were equally fine.

Many of the earliest *blown-three-mold* patterns made to imitate cut glass were designed by Deming Jarves. This angered glass cutters, who felt he was encroaching on their work. His life threatened, Jarves was afraid to go into the factory for about six weeks. For six months, he did not venture out after dark.

Actually, the blown-mold pieces did not compete with cut glass, because the designs were smooth with rounded edges. Even though the company produced the "imitation cut glass," Sandwich cut glass received the Gold Medal at the Philadelphia Centennial Exposition in 1876.

Jarves was also instrumental in promoting *pressed* glass. He was anxious to find a faster way to make glassware so that it could be sold for less. With the help of a carpenter, he devised a wooden mold into which molten glass was poured, then pressed into the intricacies of the carved design with a tightly fitting plunger. When they found that the hot glass charred the wooden mold, distorting the pattern, the craftsmen changed to iron and brass molds, which could withstand the heat of the liquid glass. By the time Jarves secured his first patent in 1828, several other companies were using the new method.

The pressing machine of the late 1820s made possible a new type of American glassware called "lacy" (fig. 11), which was highly popular from 1825 to 1850. Though inspired by cut glass, as well as by French and Russian rococo designs with many curves, lacy was not a mere imitation. It had scrolls, acanthus leaves, and Gothic arches, as well as the diamonds and rays used in cutting. A stippled background is the chief identifying motif to look for in lacy glass. Strangely, the outside or pattern side is dull and matlike in appearance, but, viewed from the smooth inside surface, it sparkles. The proper heat in both mold and metal, the correct amount cut off into the mold, and speed of pressing were necessary for a good result. Usually a lead glass of fine quality was used for lacy glass, yet edges and joins were left rough and unfinished.

The cup plate pictured reminds us that drinking tea from a saucer was socially acceptable during the first half of the nineteenth century. These small plates were made specifically to hold the cup while the tea was cooling in the saucer. This prevented soiling the tablecloth. These work savers were highly ornamental in lacy glass and were produced by the thousands during the second quarter of the century by nearly every house.

Another Phoenix Glass Works should be mentioned. It was founded by Thomas and William Caines and William Johnston in South Boston (1820-1870). Fine flint glassware was cut and engraved there throughout the Middle Period.

Fig. 11. Sandwich Lacy glass: *Above right*, plate, 7″, with peacock feather border, scrolled eye center. *Above and below left*, cup plate, 4″, and plate, 5½″, both in "Roman Rosette." *Lower right*, salt, 3″, one of the rarest historical salts, shows a primitive steam engine pulling an open carriage; "H. Clay" on bottom. (Bert Hilby)

The Union Glass Company in Somerville, Massachusetts (1851-1924), is notable because Amory and Francis Houghton were there until 1864. It was one of the eight companies cutting fine clear and colored glass of all types in 1865. It also exhibited lamps and shades at the Centennial in 1876. One shade was five feet high.

Union filled orders from the greatest art establishments. Some orders were for colossal pieces, while others were dainty and delicate. One of their greatest feats was the forming of a giant two-piece punch bowl for Tiffany & Company of New York City. When cut, it was valued at $3,000. Many pieces made by Union were placed in palatial hotels and residences.

In addition to forming and cutting their own glassware, Union supplied blanks to other cutting shops. They were partly responsible for the fact that American glass was superior to Europe's.

The Middle Period

The time of 1836-1840 was one of deep depression. The molds for lacy glass were intricate and expensive. This may have induced the makers to change the type of design of pressed glass to simpler forms and motifs. Fire polishing had been introduced in England about 1834. It obliterated tool and mold marks and worked beautifully on the new designs of dignity and simplicity, but on lacy glass it removed some of the tiny stipples and low relief patterns.

New patterns with flutes and ovals were soon made in complete table settings. "Ashburton," named for the street where the New England Glass Company was located in East Cambridge, was produced in the late 1830s and as late as 1868. "Argus" of the same vintage is a related design. These are illustrated in the *cut* decanter and goblets in fig. 12. Wheel marks can be seen under a magnifying glass.

Pressed pattern glass was made in over three hundred designs, ranging from the simplest, such as "Ashburton" and "Flute" (fig. C.2) to the elaborate, such as "Actress" and "Westward Ho." From 1840 into the 1890s they were sold in increasing quantities. A cheaper substitute appeared after 1900, but it was of poor quality.

A later example of a design produced by both cut and pressed techniques is the famous cut "Russian" pattern, called "Daisy and Button" in the pressed version. Several pieces in "Russian" will be shown in subsequent chapters.

The popular "Ashburton" was sent in shipments around South America to San Francisco during the Gold Rush (1849-1851). Champagne glasses in green and cordials in gold were listed, although none are known to be extant. Popular patterns were copied by many houses. Both Sandwich and Bakewell made many of the same designs as the New England Glass Company.

Fig. 12. Decanter, 12½″, circa 1835-1840, in "Ashburton," probably by New England Glass Co. It has eight flutes on the neck and near the bottom with polished pontil mark. Flutes are like those on an Early Period decanter (pl. 6 in Daniel's *Cut and Engraved Glass*) and in the style of 1830 syllabub cups and whiskey tumbler from Ritchie glasshouse, Wheeling, W.Va. (pl. 49, Daniel). The exact stopper, blown, with a flat top, teardrop, and six flat side panels, is shown on a half-pint decanter of West Virginia glass (pl. 60, Daniel). The stopper plug and the opening into which it fits are frosted — a characteristic of the Middle Period. The goblets, 5½″, with short stems, nonagonal feet, and nine flat panels around the lower edge of the bowl, are cut in "Argus" — a sort of cousin to "Ashburton" and just as early. They are engraved with the initials *MG* in the fancy letters used in mid-nineteenth century. Two Bohemian-type goblets with ten-sided foot, of the same height and proportions, are shown in McKearin (Pl. 58A) and are attributed to New England Glass Co. (Matye)

Three pressed pieces are interjected here (fig. 13) for comparison with cutware. The "Vernon Honeycomb" celery vase in the middle and the fruit compote (or comport) on the left (with smocking above a closed tulip motif and a hexagonal stem on a round foot), are both made of heavy pressed flint. The compote rings like a bell when struck, exactly as cut glass does. Some pieces were so well-done, with sharp edges and the mold marks minimized or removed by fire-polishing, that they can easily be mistaken for cut. *Pattern glass* of pressed lead metal, not soda-lime, in simple, solid designs continued to be highly popular from 1850 to 1864 and is well worth collecting.

The jelly compote on the right in figure 13 is a fine example of the lime glass developed during the Civil War, when lead was scarce, by William Leighton of Wheeling, West Virginia. It copies the motifs of cut glass exactly, is clear and well-made, but is lighter in

Fig. 13. *Left to right:* Fruit compote, 7"×7", circa 1840, of "flint" or lead glass, has smocking above curved miters resembling a closed tulip. Celery vase, 10", in "Vernon Honeycomb" by New England Glass Company. Jelly compote, 8", is made of pressed bicarbonate of soda and lime, a leadless glass developed during the Civil War. Motifs are hobstar and notched prism flair.

Fig. 14. Pitcher, 8½", and tumbler, 3½", attributed to Dorflinger circa 1858-1868. Glass is relatively thin — another Dorflinger characteristic. The copper wheel engraving is shallow and flat. Oval flutes around base of jug are round at both ends. Base is cut in sixteen-point single star.

weight, blunt to the touch, and does not ring when struck. It is typical of the cheaper ware that drove some manufacturers of high quality lead cut glass out of business.

All three pieces in figure 13 have interesting histories. The compote on the left was inherited from the grandmother of Mr. Swan's adoptive mother, born in 1867 and married in 1889. This dates the compote used by her grandmother somewhere in the 1840s.

The celery vase came from a Mrs. Connell, the first white girl to enter Bellingham Bay in the present state of Washington. She was the granddaughter of Allen Francis (born 12 April 1815), the first consul of the United States to Victoria, British Columbia. He was appointed by Abraham Lincoln, his close friend, who often dined with the Francis family. The celery vase was taken with other household articles to the consulate in Victoria. (The source of this information: Mrs. Bert Hilby, whose sister's mother-in-law was Mrs. Connell.)

The jelly compote came from my maternal grandmother, married in 1888. This may have been a wedding present. My mother, born in 1890, always served homemade jelly for her biscuits or rolls in this pretty dish when we had company and for Sunday dinner.

By mid-nineteenth century, three-quarters of glass tableware were pressed and many were colored. Colored cut glass was most popular in the Middle Period, although some appeared earlier and some during the Brilliant Period (seldom listed in catalogs). Both single-flint and double-flint were used for pieces of one color (fig. C.1). Sometimes a solid red goblet, or one cased in clear, had a clear stem and foot. Or, a colored pitcher might have a clear handle. Cut motifs were generally simple, including bull's-eye, flute, flat diamond, or fringe (fig. C.2).

The pitcher and tumbler (fig. 14) are believed to be early Dorflinger, circa 1858-1868, with the honeycomb or St. Louis neck and highly arched handle on the jug. Compare the shape of the tumbler with Brilliant Period examples. It appears to be squatty by comparison and has only a polished pontil mark on the bottom.

In attempting to determine the age of the elegant decanter (fig. 15), one reads that early decanters, before 1820, had ground bottoms showing a round indentation where the pontil rod was cracked off. This one does. Plain-bottom decanters, however, were occasionally made after 1820. Flutes, grapes, and leaves were numerous in the Early Period. Steeple stoppers and faceted rings were often used in 1840 with flute-cut decanters. The clarity of the glass suggests that this one was probably made circa 1830-1840. It is most unusual and beautiful.

During the Early Period (1771-1830), Americans were struggling to establish their own industries and become independent of the mother countries. Still, it was natural at first to copy the styles brought from Europe. Indeed, our first artisans came to America from England, Ireland, and nations on the continent with mature skills learned in the "old countries."

By comparison with late-nineteenth-century cut glass, our early designs seem simple. From 1820 to circa 1835, fans, panels of strawberry diamonds, and semi-oval cuts on the upper part of tumblers and decanters were common, while flat panels and splits were used around the base. Horizontal step cutting was

Fig. 15. Wine decanter, 16¾″, with steeple stopper numbered to match. Intaglio engraved and polished grape design contrasts with flutes above and below. (Matye)

Fig. 16. Decanter, 13¼″, circa 1840-1850, cut in flutes, with engraved grapes on shoulder and stopper, numbered to match decanter. Notice teardrop. Bottom is plain.

often employed on decanter necks (fig. 22). Ribbed mushroom stoppers were favored on fine decanters (fig. 10, right). Pontil marks were ground off and the base was left plain or cut in a single star.

By 1830, tariffs protected our domestic crafts and industries and shut out foreign competition to a large extent. We developed, along with national pride, our own preferences in fashions and in glassware designs. When a wave of enthusiasm for pressed glass (first in lead, later in lime), as well as the deleterious effect on the economy of the Civil War, threatened to ruin the market for costly cut glass, some houses went along with the tide and made great quantities of the cheaper ware. Others, particularly in New England and Brooklyn, New York, developed the engraving of fine glass to "stay alive."

In the 1840s, the New England Glass Company had blown, cut into flutes, then engraved the flute surfaces in a further extension of design (fig. 16). John H. Leighton, superintendent of the house from 1849 to 1874, and his son Henry B. were engravers from Scotland. Their work was Germanic in style and subject (hunting scenes, for example). This fashion was shown at the 1851 Crystal Palace Exhibition of All Nations and subsequently spread from England to the United States.

Louis Vaupel, a German, was hired in 1856. His engravings are similar to old Bohemian, depicting landscapes, hunting scenes, animal groups, and flora. Henry S. Fillebrown joined the firm in 1860, skillfully engraving grape, wild rose, ivy, bird, and fish motifs. He worked here until 1880, developing a more American style.

Such fine engraving was the most significant crystal work up to the Philadelphia Centennial exhibition of 1876. Stock engraved glass was usually adorned with fruits, flowers, and initials.

At least three companies — New England, Boston & Sandwich, and the Brooklyn Flint Glass Company founded by John L. Gilliland in 1823 — engraved cased glass, made of two layers of colored glass or colored cut through to clear. This type reached its height of popularity in the 1850s and 1860s. Lamps for parlor or dining room were often cut or engraved from the 1830s to 1900.

Dorflinger and Gillinder were outstanding in the art of engraving. Dorflinger produced colored glass and is famous for green cut through to clear (figs. C. 3A and 3B). New England made much gold-ruby flashed glass, cut or etched through to clear, before 1830. Jarves started making a variety of colored blanks for cut glass between 1827 and 1830 at the Boston & Sandwich firm. Although his colored glass was outstanding until 1880, similar ware was made at Pittsburgh, Wheeling, and Cambridge.

Glass used for engraving in the Early Period was mainly soda-potash and was thin. American Middle Period was generally lead, while foreign engraved ware was usually of high grade potash (fig. 7). Our early engravings were in conventional patterns, such as "Greek Key" or "Swag and Rose," and not as refined as Middle Period work.

For a decade after the War of 1812, patriotic themes with ships and eagles found favor. Naval battles were commemorated by showing ships under full sail, with the enemy ship sinking into the sea. The Great Seal of the United States was a favorite subject.

Engravings of the middle years were skillfully sculptured in relief-like "paintings" of flora and fauna. Presentation pieces with a band of flowers and a name or message engraved in script or Roman block capitals were popular. Stems of goblets were still cut. Globular decanters were frequently cut with a horizontal band of diamonds combined with elaborate engraving.

Earlier pieces were usually slightly gray, except for those from Wheeling, which were always clear. Later pieces continued to improve with refinements in the formulae and in the methods of heating.

Growth of the Industry

By 1820 the country was prosperous and had nearly doubled in population since 1775. Only nine glasshouses were in operation, since we still depended on European imports.

Prior to 1820 the New England Glass Company of East Cambridge and Bakewell of Pittsburgh were the chief manufacturers, but by 1830 there were over forty and by 1840 there were 108. We had learned to depend on ourselves during the War of 1812.

By the end of the Civil War in 1865, only eight houses were producing fine cut glass. These were New England, Mount Washington, Bay State, Union, and Boston & Sandwich (all in New England); Dummer in Jersey City, Dorflinger in Brooklyn, and Gilliland's South Ferry Works in New York City. A few others still cut occasional pieces after going to pressed lime pieces.

A great deal of pressed glass, close to cut in appearance, was shown at the Great Exposition in London in 1851. Its popularity threatened to take over the market for the more expensive cut and engraved ware. Of course, there were always some snobbish Victorians who demanded only the finest, but the real salvation of the cutters and engravers depended from 1865 to 1870 on a sudden upsurge in sales of cut, engraved, etched, and sandblast decorations for lampshades and globes (fig. 6).

The Panic of 1873 nearly ruined the remaining cutting shops. Only J. Hoare, associated with Amory Houghton, Sr. of the Corning Glass Works in New York, survived as an independent cutting shop.

At the 1876 Centennial Exhibition in Philadelphia, few exhibitors were represented, but those who did demonstrate their skills started an unprecedented revival of this ancient art.

4

Brilliant Period Cut Glass

Most authors agree that the Brilliant Period extended from 1880 to 1910 or 1915. Actually, its inception was probably in 1876, the year of the Centennial Exposition in Philadelphia, where presentations by Gillinder & Sons, the New England and Mount Washington glass companies, and by Christian Dorflinger's factory excited public interest in "rich-cut glass," as it was called. This interest expired circa 1917, although a few companies produced fine ware at least until 1925.

An industrial and technological boom in the late 1870s and 1880s made millionaires of certain ambitious men. By 1890, one percent of the population owned as much as the remaining ninety-nine percent put together. Even upper-middle-class men could afford two homes. They gave their wives unheard-of amounts of money with which to entertain and decorate their homes. Cut glass, including punch bowls and salt dips in the dining room, vases in the parlor, and toilet articles in the bedroom were luxuries with which to dazzle visitors.

By its centennial, the United States had survived four wars and several political crises. The original population had grown tenfold. Many nations, such as France, at the crossroads of Europe, have absorbed segments of foreign populations over a period of centuries, but no other nation assimilated so quickly such a diversity of races and nationalities as our land. Customs, religions, languages, physical traits — all added to the richness of the social fabric.

The citizens were robust, bold, and extremely self-conscious of their achievement of freedom from the old, ingrown restrictions of their mother countries. In 1876 they chose to take stock of their accomplishments as a fledgling nation. To celebrate survival of the Union, the extension of geographical boundaries to the Pacific, and the transition from simple agrarian communities to a burgeoning industrial society, citizens planned various events.

The Centennial Exposition in Philadelphia

The major celebration was the Centennial Exposition in Philadelphia, which drew one-fifth of the population from May to November. Ten million people wandered through 180 buildings or traversed the 236 acres on a monorail car to see products from fifty nations.

The colossal Corliss steam engine, the biggest in the world, worked quietly to furnish power for the Exposition. This mechanical marvel was regulated by Miss Emma Allison of Grimsby, Iowa. She was highly educated in the theory and practice of engineering, and she set an example for male engineers in the neatness of her dress and the cleanliness of the engines and the engine room.

Inventors and industrialists displayed working models of the typewriter, telephone, continuous-web printing press, self-binding reaper, and many other machines. There were drawings of elevated sidewalks, skyscrapers, flying machines, trips to space, and similar fanciful daydreams. Every day was like the Fourth of July with parades, speeches, and fireworks.

Although relatively little cut glass was being produced in 1876, the American exhibits were the most outstanding in our nation's history. Subsequent exhibits at the fairs at Chicago in 1893, Buffalo in 1901, St. Louis in 1904, and New York in 1939 were never equal to those of 1876 in workmanship and brilliancy.

Dorflinger won the highest prize for its cut and engraved Centennial Set. Several books show photographs of this heavily cut, large (16⅝") decanter and thirty-eight footed wine glasses made at White Mills, Pennsylvania, especially for this display. The decanter had three engraved panels: the Goddess of Liberty, the U.S. Coat of Arms, the crest of the city of Philadelphia with the name of its mayor, and the date, 1876. Each wine glass bore the coat of arms for one state, the name of its governor, and the date, 1876. At the close of the fair, the set was presented to the city of Philadelphia. Today it is in the Memorial Museum in Fremont Park.

How exciting it would be to find one of the druggists' show bottles displayed at the fair by Dorflinger! Some had a smaller bottle that acted as a stopper for the main bottle. These must have been spectacular in cut glass.

Gillinder demonstrated the actual manufacture of glass in its own building. Thousands watched, then bought souvenirs made just for them.

The Boston & Sandwich Glass Company showed flint tablewares, flower stands, and colored perfume bottles that were cut, engraved, and etched.

The New England Glass Company displayed flint glassware, including the Daniel Webster punch bowl, and decorative pieces (cut, engraved, and etched). The glass tiles for mural decorations were in "fair taste," according to *The Reports and Awards,* Vol. 3, of the U.S. Centennial Commission. The firm received an award for its cut glass.

J.B. Dobleman, Green Point Flint-Glass Works of Brooklyn, New York, received a good report. La Belle Company of Bridgeport, Ohio, was said to have shown an ordinary quality of cut and engraved glass, but was commended for fine pressed glass.

Bakewell, Pears, & Company of Pittsburgh (1818-1882), whose cut glass had been so outstanding early in the century, presented only molded pattern glass of ordinary quality.

Mount Washington showed cut and richly engraved tableware, as well as chandeliers made to order to match furniture. A crystal fountain by Mount Washington was one of the most beautiful objects in the Main Building. It was forty-eight feet in circumference and seventeen feet high, and was made entirely of cut crystal prisms that reflected the changing light and split it into rainbow colors. At night it was lighted by 120 gas jets, concealed within, to turn the water and prisms into a fairyland spectacle. The fountain was surmounted by the largest crystal figure ever made: a 30″ Statue of Liberty.

Although comments by the judges contained such qualified statements as "cutting rich and tasteful; engraving in many cases very good, although in some instances rather too much elaborated" (concerning J.B. Dobleman's work) and "cutting rich and brilliant, in some cases perhaps overdone" (referring to Boston & Sandwich glass), the visitors were so delighted with the dazzling displays that their demands for these ornamental pieces gave rise to a great revival in glass cutting, which was to last well into the next century.

Victorian Inventions

One of the best ways to gauge the gradual transformation of our nation from an agrarian to an urban society is to go through the copies of the Patent Gazette in your public library. Here one can see drawings and specifications of everything from bottle caps and corsets to military forts and airships.

The first patent, issued to Samuel Hopkins for an improvement in potash production, was recorded in 1790. By 1836 only 109 patents had been issued. But by 1876, there were 14,172, or 15,595 including patented designs and reissues of original patents. The millionth patent was awarded in 1911.

In 1886 a "Medicine Spoon with Corkscrew Handle" was patented, as was a combined "Cigar-Lighter and Perfume Sprayer." The latter consisted of a statuette of a man holding a lighted lamp in one hand and a tray in the other. A perfumery-sprayer, connected by a tube which passed through the body to the mouth, ejected the spray when a bulb at the base was pressed. This was no doubt placed on the counter of a store to attract customers.

Victorians seemed to be fascinated by objects that folded and whose appearance was deceptive (*trompe d'oeuil* — "fools the eye," as the French would say). These included a combination playpen and clothes dryer and beds that were hinged to open at night, but folded up by day to resemble a piano, desk, or bookcase.

Our nation had emerged as a vigorous, resourceful country with a deep belief in freedom (freedom for men, that is). Although a Women's Pavilion, covering almost thirty thousand square feet and housing only women and their concerns, occupied a prominent place at the fair, women were still subservient to men and were under the same civil code as infants, criminals, and idiots. Most fundamentalist religious leaders preached that this was enjoined in the scriptures. They were opposed to the suffrage movement. Opponents to the vote for women argued that females were too busy bearing children and keeping the home to have time to study politics.

Those who derogated the creative ability of women overlooked the fact that out of the hundreds of inventions displayed at the 1876 Exhibition, seventy-four were by women. Most were shown only in the Women's Pavilion and were made to facilitate women's work in the home. But items that were also for men included a life-preserving mattress, telegraphic night signals, and a design for a combined desk and bookcase for use in public libraries.

Pity the poor women! A disproportionate number of corset designs were listed in the 1870s and 1880s. Even a nursing corset with a window-like opening on each side had a "wasp-waist." No wonder the ladies had so many "female troubles." It is said that some ladies of high fashion had their lower ribs removed surgically to achieve a tiny waistline. Vanity of vanities! In 1869, *Harper's Bazar,* a major fashion journal first published in 1867, not only showed a corset for the elderly lady, but a corset for girls from "12 to 14 years old," one for girls "8 to 10 years old," and even a corset for a child "1 to 2 years old." This passion for molding the female figure to fit the fashion ideal is reminiscent of binding the feet of girls in ancient China.

A mother's pain could be eased during childbirth if her doctor agreed. Queen Victoria had accepted chloroform for the birth of her seventh child, Prince Leopold, in 1853 and again for a confinement in 1857. This removed formal opposition in Great Britain, and to some extent in America; yet as late as 1921, the argument against ether for childbirth was that suffering was a strong element in mother love.

Baby carriages, walkers, hobby-horses (or rocking goats or geese), creeping dolls, and even a contraption to make Junior hold his pencil correctly while learning to write were patented in the 1870s. Of course, Junior could get back at the school by breaking windows with his Toy Catapult, a slingshot.

Designs for roller skates appeared in the 1880s, but the most enticing invention was published in 1905. This "Velocipede" (surely for rich boys) consisted of a two-wheel cart with pedals for propulsion. Ahead of the rider was a simulated life-size pony whose weight was supported by a single wheel.

In 1872 an apparatus "for preventing animal deposits in the streets" turned out to be a box under the horse's tail. Farm implements — plows, harrows, reapers — to be pulled by horses were constantly improved. Windmills, lightning rods, well and post-hole diggers, cider mills, cream separators, a machine for dehorning cattle, even a "cow-catcher" to move farm animals off the railroad tracks: all had to do with agrarian life, and many involved horses.

As industry developed in the cities, all sorts of inventions were patented: paper mills using wood pulp, spinning machines for cloth mills, printing presses, and, pertinent to our subject, glass furnaces, annealing ovens, molds, gadgets for finishing bottle necks, and glass blowers' and polishers' tools. A patent issued in 1884 read: "Applying Natural Gas to Glass Furnaces."

References to improved doors or wheelbases of "cars" referred to railroad cars. The railway was an important means of transportation during the last quarter of the century, as were steam-propelled canal boats. Several flying machines were patented, including an airship to be maneuvered by pulling ropes from inside.

By 1898, there were more than fifty automobile companies in existence in the United States. The first commercially successful American-made car was the three-horsepower Oldsmobile.

A race in Chicago "demonstrated conclusively the power of motor vehicles to cover long distances at high rates of speed." The winning carriage covered 726 miles at an average rate of nearly fifteen miles an hour!

Kerosene lamps and candles were used long after Edison patented his first "incandescing bulb" in 1879. Lamps caused many fires, especially in the shaky firetraps in the city slums. The 1871 Chicago fire, which leveled a swath a mile wide and five miles long through the heart of the city, is generally believed to have been ignited by a kerosene lamp set down on the barn floor by Mrs. O'Leary and kicked over by her cow. This holocaust burned for more than thirty hours and destroyed one-third of the city's property. An estimated 300 died and 90,000 were left homeless.

A fire extinguisher was patented in 1881. So was an electric table lamp, suggesting that electric lights would soon replace kerosene and gaslights. Electricity in houses was, however, slow to appear and hazardous at first. When Edison first installed electricity in New York City homes in 1881, he and his associates could buy no parts. They had to originate components with their own hands. The six dynamos installed in two old buildings on Pearl Street shook and vibrated so greatly that frightened workmen ran three blocks away and had to be coaxed back. Before Mr. Edison learned how to regulate the power, people would call and ask, "Our meter is red hot. Is that all right?" or "Our meter is on fire and we poured water on it. Will we still have electricity?"

As late as 1911 a tragic fire in the Triangle Shirtwaist Company in New York City took the lives of 140 people. About six hundred workers, mainly young girls of immigrant families who spoke no English, toiled long hours in this grimy sweatshop for a dollar a day. The owners had turned the plant into a deathtrap by making the girls file through narrow passageways to be frisked for stolen garments. All of the doors opened inwardly; some emergency exits were bolted shut. When fire broke out on the eighth, ninth, and tenth floors, exits were quickly blocked in the ensuing panic. Girls fled to the windows, where they clung to the sills until hair and clothing caught fire, then jumped to their deaths. Finally fire and building codes were overhauled and the trade union movement accelerated.

Among the inventions meant to improve the quality of life in the 1880s and 1890s were dentist drills and chairs, dentures, artificial limbs, and harnesses to straighten a crooked spine.

A 1908 *Ladies' Home Journal* magazine featured an article on "Sleeping Outdoors in the Home." The seeker of good health, using the Allen Health Tent, was to sleep with his head out of the window, protected by an awning. Another such invention was the Porte-Air Flexible Tube. It was made of steel rings and cloth, came through the window, and fitted over the head of the sleeper. This was a revolutionary theory, since many people believed that night air was poisonous.

Exaggerated claims for cures were advertised in all of the magazines and newspapers until curbed by the Federal Food and Drug Act in 1906. The 1900 Sears, Roebuck catalog listed "almost every known patent remedy" at the lowest wholesale prices to their retail, mail-order customers. In fact, Sears offered cases containing from twelve to forty-eight homeopathic remedies at prices from $.85 to $6.75, as well as the *New American Family Physician* — a $4.75 book for $1.65.

In spite of technological advances, the science of medicine in the Brilliant Period (sometimes called the Gilded Age) lagged behind for many years. The discoveries of Lister and Pasteur were slow to improve the public's health. Epidemics of smallpox, diphtheria, typhoid, yellow fever, and cholera decimated the citizenry periodically. As in the "old country," the rich fled from the cities, but were often overtaken by the disease they sought to escape.

The ignorance of most doctors was abysmal. Dr. Charles Eliot's demand for a final written examination of students at Harvard was rejected by the dean because the majority of students could not write well enough.

Surgeons, however, became quite daring. During the Civil War, it took forty seconds to amputate a leg without an anesthetic. When chloroform came into use, surgeons did more radical surgery on their unconscious patients than before, but they ignored Lister's advice to clear the operating room of germs. Consequently, many patients died of secondary infections.

So little was known about the effect of drugs that many innocents became addicts of alcohol, as well as of cocaine and morphine. The curse of alcoholism engendered a flood of religious tracts for the purpose of reforming the alcoholic. The author inherited an original pamphlet of twenty pages entitled "The Eventful Twelve Hours or The Destitution and Wretchedness of a Drunkard." It concludes with a poem thats first two lines are: "Oh, water for me; bright water for me; and wine for the tremulous debauchee."

"Bitters," used as a tonic to stimulate digestion and increase the appetite, as a mild laxative, or as a flavoring in mixed drinks, was a bitter herb, leaf, or root macerated in a spirituous liquor of 30 to 40 percent alcohol. Often the need for an alcoholic "tonic" became chronic and addictive. "Stomach bitters" or "nerve bitters" could be taken with impunity by those whose religious beliefs forbade drinking alcoholic beverages. One might even find an excuse for buying MELLISTON, advertised in 1905 as a "Cordial or Liquor Possessing Medicinal Properties."

The temperance movement, sparked by Dr. Benjamin Rush of Philadelphia in his "Inquiry into the Effects of Ardent Spirits on the Human Mind and Body," published in 1785, led to prohibition of selling liquor in Maine, 1851. Other states quickly followed. Bitters filled the breach with an increase in alcoholic content and bottles up to a gallon in size. A tax on alcohol which came with the Internal Revenue Act in 1862 further promoted the sale of bitters. Outlandish claims for curative powers were made. One MALT BITTERS, it is interesting to note, was prepared without alcohol and was recommended for delicate women, clergymen, brain workers, and children.

Ironically, temperance advocates went around the country preaching against the evils of drink, while using bitters to combat their depression, dyspepsia, nervousness, or some imaginary ailment.

Trademarks and labels are excellent indicators of how Americans lived between the wars. Often it is difficult to imagine how the designer received his inspiration. The label on LEUCORRHEA PILLS shows the representation of an angel. Perhaps this was meant to disguise the contents of the package. In 1896 "Remedies for Gonorrhea and Diseases of the Urinary Organs" were named SWIZZLE.

Mysterious and exotic names were akin to magic. In fact certain pills in 1894 were called MAGIC SEEDS, and a 1906 liniment was labeled MYSTERIOUS. HOPE OF THE INVALID; WARNER'S WHITE WINE OF TAR SYRUP; MRS. MOORE'S INFALLIBLE REMEDY (for "Cancerous Sores and Diseases of the Blood"); BALM OF GILEAD (a remedy for diseases of the throat); and RUDOLPH'S PHOSPHORIZED ELIXIR OF OATS are sufficiently vague to lull the patient. ZYMOTIC SPECIFIC No. 4 was both mysterious and impressive. There was also BEN-NETT'S HEALING DUST FOR HORSES, for man's best friend.

The use of Indian and physician's names seemed to guarantee efficacy. Consider THE SIOUX INDIAN ANTIDOTE; CREOLE (for diseases of the feet); KICK-APOO SPRINGS MINERAL WATER (from Stockton, California); DR. PRICE'S HEART REGULATER; DR. HEALY'S DANDELION TONIC; and DR. CAMP-BELL'S ARSENIC COMPLEXION WAFERS. DR. STRASSMAN'S EMMENAGOGUE fits both this and the previous categories.

Multipurpose remedies reveal more clearly the profound ignorance of the times. Consider DR. KUREM'S PAIN-EXTRACTOR, SYSTEM REG-ULATOR, HEADACHE-POWDER, PLASTER, AND POULTRY POWDER. It is impossible to restrain a smile as we see a "Medicine to Cure Tobacco Habit and Chronic Constipation." The label depicts a victorious gladiator with his foot resting upon the breast of a prostrate opponent (1895). Then there was "A Vegeta-ble Cure for Cancer, Tumor, and Ulcer" (somewhat related) and, from Germany, a "Medicine for Lung and Throat Troubles, Anemia, Scrofula, Phthisis, Indiges-tion, Nervous and General Debility and Rickets."

Fanciful and romantic labels, such as SWEET MOMENTS for cigarettes, AIRY FAIRY TOBACCO (1889), and GARLAND'S HAPPY THOUGHT SALVE (1896) were plentiful. An 1896 label for the CUPID HAIRPIN showed Cupid shooting a pin toward a lady's hair, using a large pin as a bow. In 1909 a trademark for an insecticide called DEATH DUST showed a skull blowing dust at insects lying upside down, dead.

Even patriotism was used to attract customers. In 1898 toy firearms were labeled MONROE DOC-TRINE, and in 1902 an ointment for rectal and skin diseases was named THE PRESIDENT.

What do euphemistic and fanciful labels have to do with our study of cut glass? Awareness of the grim realities of life during this period should help us to empathize with those who chose to block out the specters of a high rate of infant mortality, maternal deaths from "childbed fever," and epidemics of diseases for which there were no cures. This our ancestors attempted to accomplish by means of an elaborate life-style, if they could afford it. Blind faith in a patent remedy with an exotic name could sometimes help to quiet fear when illness struck a loved one and to keep hope alive for recovery, regardless of the economic class to which one belonged.

5

Social and Political Consequences of the Industrial Revolution

Industrial development had moved very gradually during our republic's first century. It gathered momentum so quickly at the beginning of the second that a revolution was in progress. New energy sources for fuel and power improved transportation by steamship and railroad; communication by telegraph. New agricultural machines, among which were the cotton gin and the reaper, freed millions of farm workers to migrate to the cities, where they obtained work in factories. Depending on where citizens lived and how they made a living, there was a much greater disparity in life-styles than there is today.

Life on the farm had always meant endless drudgery. The entire family toiled up to fourteen hours a day merely to sustain life. Little money was available for buying manufactured goods. A child often received only one gift at Christmas — perhaps a pocketknife, slate, or doll. During the depressed economic period from 1870 to 1900, many small and middle-sized farms were foreclosed.

Even if a man succeeded in enlarging his acreage, his wife's labor was just that much greater. She and her daughters had to cook for the farmhands and wash their dirty clothes, generally by scrubbing on a washboard with soap made at home from rendered animal fat and lye, then by boiling the sturdy garments in a washboiler. A few women had primitive machines activated by pushing and pulling a handle. In summer, laundry was often done out-of-doors to escape the heat of the steamy kitchen, or in the smokehouse (where hams were cured). An extra stove in this small, detached building could be used for boiling clothes, heating bath water, canning, and soapmaking. Of course, water had to be carried in from the well, and wood fed into a stove for both cooking and washing.

Needless to say, cut glass played a negligible role in the farm home, although occasionally a rich city relative sent a piece as a wedding gift. If a pampered city girl married a farmer, she required unusual stamina to survive, or she aged quickly and died young, often in childbirth.

Life in Small Towns

My father was a merchant. In our middle-class home in an Iowa town during the World War I years, we used two types of coal: anthracite, "hard" and more expensive, for the base burner in the living room (because it burned with a clean flame) and the cheaper bituminous, or "soft" coal, in the kitchen range.

Small towns did not usually have water and sewage systems. We drank water from a well that was pumped dry and cleaned annually by climbing down a ladder and scrubbing the walls. Once the water had a peculiar, unpleasant taste. A dead rat was found floating in the water. A second well, a cistern, caught "soft" rainwater from the roof. Free from minerals, it permitted soap to lather well.

I recall my father's digging a new hole and moving the outhouse whenever the old pit was filled. He simply covered the former location with dirt; nature did the rest. Unlike some careless people who allowed disease germs to seep into the well, he calculated drainage and distance properly. This type of sanitation was acceptable in country and town, but not in New York City in 1882 when 2 percent of the houses had water connections.

Bathing the baby was approved, but bathing adults was described by a Dr. Sargent as "a needless waste of time." Let us keep this in mind when we discuss perfume and cologne bottles of the Victorian era.

Life in the City

Turning their backs on the interminable labor and low earnings on the farm, thousands flocked to the cities, only to find themselves in another form of slavery. Employers hired and fired freely, since only 3.5 percent of the workers were unionized by 1900.

Garbage, rubbish, and barrels of ashes were piled on the sidewalks; pigs roamed the streets and were tolerated because they disposed of some of the garbage. The residue from fifty slaughterhouses in Cincinnati "drew a yearly mess of almost half a million pigs through the streets," according to Bettman.

Carriages, wagons, and streetcars were drawn by horses. Each horse produced daily about twenty-three pounds of malodorous manure that bred flies to spread disease. Stables with urine-saturated hay added to the stench. In dry weather, traffic turned the manure to dust, which was inhaled and drifted into the houses where it stung the nose and ruined the furniture.

Crossing the street was a game of Russian roulette. Before traffic lights were installed, there was never a halt in the flow of traffic. As if this were not enough, hundreds were killed crossing railroad tracks that ran through the center of town. The steam railroad owners preferred to save the construction costs of going around the civic centers. Early posters warned mothers to look out for their children and informed all citizens that the railroads were invading their beautiful streets.

The poor, trapped in the slums by casual jobs and ethnic ties, resided apart from, yet in close proximity to, the rich. The rich, in their brownstone mansions, had not yet fled to the suburbs. They inhaled sewer gas from poorly constructed drainage systems and clogged sewers as well as the soot and dust from their coal stoves. If an owner could afford a central steam heat system, the radiators hissed and hammered.

Mass production in city factories replaced much handwork. In addition to migrants from farms, over ten million immigrants from 1870 to 1895 swelled the work force potential. Desperate for a job, they were easily exploited by factory owners.

In the scramble for material success, the acquisitiveness of the newly rich industrialists fed on political corruption and the insecurity and poverty of the underpaid workers. Marshall Field, pioneer department store owner and philanthropist, was said to make $600 an hour, while his shop girls would have to work three years at $3 to $5 a week to earn that amount. Twelve-hour shifts in the mills, with machines set to the utmost speed that men could endure; exposure to heat and poisonous gases in factories and mines; accidents that killed and maimed, with no compensation for the victims (although some companies did pay for burial), were the order of the day.

Child labor in factories was a national disgrace. Some parents complained that New York would not take workers under eight years old! Certain textile mill boys and girls had to stand on boxes to reach the whirling spindles. Often their hands were caught and maimed. Children were shipped from one state to another like animals. An 1870 census put the total of child workers at 700,000, not including vendors and shoeshine boys. One-third of all mill workers were children. In 1900, four of every hundred nonagricultural jobs were held by children ten to fifteen years old.

It was not until 1904 that the National Child Labor Committee was formed to put an end to this practice. Even as late as 1916 and beyond, it is clear that laws for compulsory school attendance and age limits for work were not yet effective.

The states were on the way to establishing public schools for all children, but progress was uneven and slow in coming. Rural schools with pupils ranging in age from five to sixteen or older were often taught by a young person who had passed a test given by the school board.

A Miss Barstow of Canton, Massachusetts, was stoned to death in 1870 by four unruly boys to whom she had given a slight reprimand. Often a strong young man was chosen to teach because he was big enough to break up fights among ruffian older boys.

Salaries in 1888 averaged $42 a month for men and $38 for women, plus free board and room with various families. Teachers seldom stayed more than one term, often barely twelve weeks because children were farm workers. The teacher had to build a fire, clean the building, and submit to scrutiny of every phase of living. My father taught country school one term in 1906, then quit.

City schools were no better. They were overcrowded, dirty, and poorly supplied with books, since political bosses often ransacked educational funds. Teaching methods were humorless, mechanical, stultifying. Many children came to school hungry and exhausted from factory work done to help support the family. Finishing eighth grade was often an impossible goal.

This is one of the things about the "good old days" that many people have forgotten or never learned: the same wide gulf between rich and poor existed here as in the "old country," whose social and economic conditions the immigrants believed they had left behind. Only the affluent could afford to buy luxuries such as cut glass.

There was an exception to the rule. Workers in the glasscutting factories often set their relatively humble tables with "rejects," gifts from the proprietor, or pieces they were allowed to make on their own time after hours. Rejects were pieces that did not pass inspection for sale. Some companies permitted workmen to buy these for a small sum; others threw them into the cullet bin.

"Pork barrel" politics were common. Federal jobs were bestowed on certain individuals, who were then expected to contribute generously to the incumbent official "for the good of the party." Secret deals were made with wives as a reward for influencing their husbands in government to make appointments. The Republicans carried all but two of the nine presidential elections between 1868 and 1900. In every case their candidate was a military hero.

Religious revivals have appeared periodically in our nation's history. A great temperance revival had covered the country early in the nineteenth century. Camp meetings for the saving of souls, principally sectarian in nature, still flourished every summer under tents in nearly every town.

During the post-Civil War period, the newspapers, burgeoning in number after the improvements incorporated in the rotary-web printing press, sensationalized every scandal. They illustrated accounts of rape, murder, sex, and violence with consummate bad taste.

Upon this scene appeared an evangelist with a magic gift of oratory, Dwight L. Moody, and his unattractive, fleshy singer, Ira Sankey, whose voice mesmerized the ladies in his audience. Moody frowned upon Holy Rollerism as being undignified. His respectability appealed to the industrial lords of mining, railroads, and finance.

Billy Sunday was another influential evangelist. It is noteworthy that gaffer Emil Larson, who had started with Dorflinger, made a vase for Billy Sunday at the Durand factory in New Jersey. Sunday returned the favor by giving Larson a "plug" at his tent meeting.

As America dealt with minorities, it was agreed that something must be done for the Indians. *Life* magazine in 1891 ran cartoons condemning our treatment of the Indian, comparing ours to Russia's policy concerning Siberia: starve or shoot.

A start was made on the long journey toward equality of blacks. In 1890, only 20 percent of all black children received any education at all. Their lifetime average was one hundred days in school.

Between 1882 and 1903, at least 3,337 people were lynched, according to the *Chicago Tribune*. Most were blacks killed without trials and many without cause.

Drawings of blacks depicted as amiable clowns were used on labels. In 1902 Black Satin stove polish had a label showing the face and head of a laughing black boy with shiny shaved head. The smiling woman on Aunt Jemima's Self-Raising Flour appeared in 1906.

Other ethnic jokes ridiculed Jews and Italians. The flood of aliens filled many with alarm. The condescension of established Americans toward the immigrants can be found on labels, strange as it seems. In 1905 a washboard label showed Uncle Sam, an eagle perched on the back of his chair and a washboard on his knee, as he explained the use of the product to two oddly dressed aliens.

On the literary scene were such lasting names as Whittier, Longfellow, Bryant, Lowell, and Oliver Wendell Holmes. Bret Harte was foremost in depicting the new West; Mark Twain was a popular speaker on the lecture circuits.

Harriet Beecher Stowe was the best-known of the women writers. Helen Hunt Jackson was the most famous woman poet, and Mrs. E.D.E.N. Southworth, deserted by her husband and left with two small children, was queen of the female novelists. Her first novel was aptly named *The Deserted Wife*. Her magazine serials were bestsellers and made her wealthy.

To placate the clergy, who set the code of morals for the middle class, publishers of the "story paper" accepted stories whose heroes refused to drink wine or use tobacco, and who opposed gambling, adultery, blasphemy, and dueling. *The Ledger* in Philadelphia hired the Reverend Mr. Henry Ward Beecher as a contributor, but dropped him after his trial for adultery with the wife of Theodore Tilton.

Although the end of the Civil War saw some three hundred women doctors in practice, tradition worked against them. The Pennsylvania State Medical Society forbade its members to consult with female colleagues. Dr. Mary Walker had received her certificate as a physician from Syracuse College in 1855. She found few patients, so was forced to turn to schoolteaching in New York City. When the war began, she volunteered as a nurse. Dressed in trousers and a long-tailed coat, she served on the battlefields. After the war, she worked as a newspaper reporter briefly, thus opening this new field to women. After another try at medicine, she became an active suffrage leader.

In the West, women plowed, broke horses, built claims on homesteads, even held up stagecoaches! Remember Belle Starr? In Milwaukee a young lady bankrupted several scions of wealthy families in an all-night poker game. Ten women competed in a rifle match and won. Miss Maria Spelterini, wearing tights and carrying an umbrella, walked across Niagara Falls on a tightrope. Girls began chewing gum and smoking cigarettes and cigars. Some even chewed tobacco and used cuspidors (fig. 147) — dainty and ladylike spittoons, of course. A group of young women formed an opium club in Nevada.

During the 1840s, Susan Anthony, Lucretia Mott, and Elizabeth Stanton had fought for the freedom of slaves. After the slaves were freed, these women championed the Fourteenth and Fifteenth Amendments. Their version of legislation would have given women, as well as former slaves, the right to vote.

These forceful women faced another half century without the vote, with one notable exception. In Wyoming, where frontier women had proved to be as rugged and resilient as men, Mrs. Esther Morris persuaded candidates of opposing parties to support women's suffrage in 1869. To embarrass the Republicans, the Democrats passed the bill, sure that the Republican governor would veto it. The governor surprised his political enemies and the rest of the Union by signing it.

The average American considered himself to be a self-made man, so he admired the robber barons such as the Vanderbilts, Goulds, Carnegies, and Rockefellers, whose names are now honorably stamped on foundations and universities. The average man saw no reason for government control over the new empires of steel, petroleum, railroads, and manufacturing. Only the man on the lowest rung of the industrial ladder saw the need for change, but was helpless to act.

Fig. 17. A typical retail store in 1907. The girl with dark hair (*right rear*) by the stove was my mother.

In President Grant's annual message to Congress early in December 1875, he noted the coming centennial year and reviewed the nation's one hundred years of progress: from four to more than forty million people, from thirteen to thirty-eight states. He reviewed the changes from an almost totally agricultural society to one in which two million people earned their livings in factories.

All of these changes transformed the physical environment. They also led to changes in family relationships, ideals, morals, and religious convictions, which had seemed secure and serene, and to which many people now looked back with nostalgia.

Compensations for the Spartan Life

Having presented a somewhat negative perspective of life in the last quarter of the nineteenth century, let us admit that there were compensations for the simpler life of the times.

Excepting the industrial workers at the very bottom of the scale, many of the poor in worldly goods did not realize that they were poor. Compared with our time in history, their expectations were not high. They accepted hard work, long hours, and low wages as their lot in life. A strong religious faith helped them to accept sickness and death with calm resignation.

Children were taught the skills needed in their future roles as mother/housewife or father/provider. The girl who planned to break out of the mold was exceptional. My mother escaped an unhappy life with a cruel stepmother by working in a store at seventeen (fig. 17). After two years as a clerk, she moved to another town where she trimmed hats for a milliner. She married at twenty, uncertain as to whether she was doing the right thing in giving up her freedom. Father was very persuasive.

As a small girl, when her own mother was still living, she was required to make quilt blocks or sew rags together for a rug for an hour after school before she could go outside to play. Her brother had to cut kindling for the fire and to carry in water from the well before he could play with his friends.

Old people were not put away in "rest homes," but were kept with the family where they shared their wisdom with the children. When they became bedfast, the entire group helped to keep them comfortable and to show love and respect.

Fig. 18. Individual cream and sugar set, 1¾″, in checkered diamond and fan. Design resembles that of a Hawkes jardiniere in October 1909 *Ladies' Home Journal*.

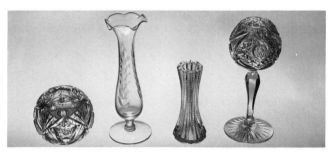

Fig. 19. *Left to right:* Violet globe, 2⅜″, fully cut in star, fan, and zipper. These were often sold with a small mirrored plateau. Bud vase, 6″, dainty, light cutting on thin blown blank. Bud vase, 3¾″, in notched prism, probably a Bohemian import. Rare footed violet globe, 5⅝″, called a "Violet Holder on Pedestal" in one catalog, is cut in hobstar, zipper, fan, and star.

Fig. 20A. Tumble-up or boudoir set in "Brazilian," patented 28 May 1889, #19114. Tumbler, 4⅛″, and carafe. 7⅛″, are signed with the trefoil. Pill bottle, 3¼″, has HAWKES in capital letters. Neck is fluted. Fans, single stars, silver diamond, and miter cuts constitute this popular design. Only the top of an eight-point hobstar shows around the low edge of the sides. Carafe has a low foot.

Poems were published praising the patience and fortitude of invalids; paintings portrayed sad deathbed scenes showing of family gathered about the bed of a dying person, old or young. The paintings had inspiring or maudlin titles (depending on the opinion of the viewer) suggesting that he or she was about to join the angels. Some depicted the family doctor seated by the bed, chin on hand, staring at his patient, or gazing dejectedly out of the window, deeply concerned, but helpless.

Ladies' magazines published many hints on how to care for the sick. In the 1880s, *Good Housekeeping* ran a monthly column, "In and About the Sick Room." There was a column called "Hints for Convalescent Children" in a 1910 *Ladies' Home Journal*. It told how to make a bag to pin on the bed. This was for necessary items, as well as for an occasional "little surprise."

Among the suggestions were directions for making the tray of food attractive with dainty accoutrements and with fresh flowers. Small cut glass items were adapted to this use. They included the cream jug and sugar bowl (fig. 18), the tiny bud vases and violet globes (fig. 19), and the individual salt and pepper shakers (fig. 216).

The tumble-up or boudoir set in "Brazilian," a water bottle or carafe with pill bottle and matching tumbler (figs. 20A and 20B), all signed Hawkes, was particularly useful for the invalid, although many were

Fig. 20B. Pill bottle fits into neck of carafe; the tumbler is placed over both. "Eye-Opener #1490" in catalog.

Fig. 21. Invalid's jug, 7¼″, ideal for bed tray, but could be used for buttermilk or cereal cream at the table. Design is transitional from old motifs to new in early 1880s. Includes relief diamond, hobstar, beading. Triple-notched handle. (Gerritse)

standard bedside equipment for anyone who drank water at night or took pills in the bedroom. This was especially true in homes without bathrooms or any running water in the house. This tumble-up and the invalid's jug (fig. 21) are rare. An article in an 1889 *Good Housekeeping* magazine, in describing fashion in cut glassware, stated that "the old-fashioned carafes with glass cup covering the mouth are no longer seen." They were temporarily out of style. A much plainer water set was advertised in 1914.

For those who remained on the farms or in small towns, the old values of family closeness remained to a large extent.

Fig. C.5. Red overlay pane, 23″ × 13″, came from an inn, called the Miller House, near the railroad station in Sandwich, Massachusetts. It was installed in 1848. It is now in the permanent collection of the Sandwich Glass Museum. (Courtesy of Sandwich Glass Museum)

Fig. C.2. Green cut-to-clear 12″ decanter in Dorflinger's "Heavy Flute," now called "Prince of Wales" because the Canadian Pacific Railway ordered it for use on Edward VIII's private train when he visited Canada in 1919. Red wines 4¾″; green 3⅞″.

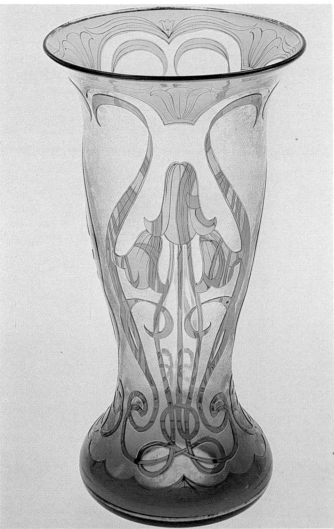

Fig. C.4. Acid-etched cameo vase, 11″, cased green-to-clear, produced by Carl F. Prosch, expert in etching and gold decoration. He operated a factory, called the Honesdale Decorating Company, built by Dorflinger in Seelyville, Pennsylvania. Vase signed "Honesdale" in gold on polished pontil. (Conkling)

Fig. C.1. Pair of candlesticks, 7½″, in apple green, circa 1860 or earlier. Bases are heavy; holes for candles are much larger than those after 1876. (Photograph by Conkling)

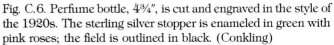

Fig. C.6. Perfume bottle, 4¾″, is cut and engraved in the style of the 1920s. The sterling silver stopper is enameled in green with pink roses; the field is outlined in black. (Conkling)

Fig. C.9. Living room shows Gundy-Clapperton lamp in "Hob Star" beside red chair, and umbrella stand in the hall. (Gordon)

Fig. C.10. Living room view shows pair of Pairpoint Daisy and Butterfly lamps ("Daisy" design), footed rose bowl by Hawkes in "Kensington," large basket on piano, two bonbon baskets, and an ashtray with silver mounting near a lamp. (Gordon)

Fig. C.11. Living room view: Pairpoint lamp, several pieces under painting, on and under piano. (Conkling)

Fig. C.20. Green room: Renaissance couch, Handel lamp, cast iron bench (silver-plated), and eight-foot showcase filled with cut glass. Pottery pieces on top are Amphora (1890s) from Austria. (Gordon)

Fig. C.15. Upstairs hall, where cabinet pieces are displayed on shelves of a Governor Winthrop desk. (Conkling)

Fig. C.16. Upstairs hall shows corset vase on small table, and decanter set, tray, and candlesticks on card table. (Conkling)

Fig. C.19. Green room (formerly a solarium) with cane chair and Art Nouveau china closet. (Gordon)

Fig. C.17. Dining room with case lined with red, table set with glassware, etc. (Conkling)

Fig. C.7. Detroit Electric Brougham, 1914 model, with an 86-volt system, is powered by fourteen six-volt batteries — seven at each end. Motor is under the floorboards in the center. Owner is Karl Jernes. (Conkling)

Fig. C.8. Cut and engraved bracket vase in 1914 Detroit Electric Brougham. This type of body was named after Lord Brougham (1778-1868), an English statesman. (Conkling)

6

Nomenclature of Motifs and Patterns

As we discuss the use of cut glass in social intercourse and its importance as a symbol of prestige during America's Gilded Age, we shall employ a specialized vocabulary. We shall examine changes in taste concerning styles of glass cutting and engraving, which paralleled changes in architecture, home furnishings, and fashions in clothing.

Photographs of pieces from my collection and items borrowed from generous friends will be shown to illustrate the text. The reader may have to look ahead or backward for a few illustrations. It will simplify the task and clarify the descriptions if we first agree upon terminology.

Terminology

Before illustrating changes in styles, we must agree upon names for each *motif* (separate figure). Several motifs comprise a *pattern* or *design*. Strictly speaking, "pattern" may mean the paper form cut by the creator of shapes for glass blanks. "Design" is used in the Patent Gazette, where drawings were recorded. A chart could be drawn for reference, but the best way to learn to apply the terms is to see actual examples. Often it is difficult to equate a drawing with the real piece.

Each motif is composed of one or more elemental incisions into the surface of the glass. Even those figures that seem to stand out in relief are produced by cutting (or, more precisely, by grinding) into the surface. With the exception of the *pillar* (fig. 133), every motif is made of straight or curved miter cuts, or a concave hollow in the glass. Even the pillar started as a prism between two miter cuts. It was then ground down to a convex curved surface.

A *miter* cut was produced by a wheel with a sharp, V-shaped edge. The angle of the V and the size of the wheel enabled the cutter to make a great variety of motifs. The following are motifs produced by miter cutting.

Blaze or *Fringe*. One of the simplest miter cuts, borrowed from old Anglo-Irish patterns, consisted either of shallow, parallel cuts, possibly of the same length, used around the base of a decanter, or of graduated unequal lengths used around the top of a bowl as a border (fig. 107).

Silver Thread was a fine-line cutting to fill in the background and give brilliance, used by Sinclaire in some of his floral engravings (fig. 155).

Fine-line Bands were used in Hawke's "Sheraton," "Millicent," and "Gracia" patterns in combination with engraved medallions (fig. 311). These fine parallel lines were accomplished by means of a *gang wheel* in which grooves had been cut by a diamond-point stylus. It was introduced in 1913 by the Norton Company of Worcester, Massachusetts, maker of cutting wheels. The gang wheel was also used by cutleries in making serrated knife blades.

Horizontal Step is a prismatic cutting, also used often in the early nineteenth-century Anglo-Irish pieces. See the Dorflinger vase (fig. 8), the flower center (fig. 22), and the compote (fig. 204, right) whose base is cut in horizontal steps.

Fig. 22. Flower center or tulip bowl, 12″ d × 9½″ h, weighs 13 lbs. Step or horizontal prism cutting on neck; Harvard or Chairbottom design. It closely resembles a covered jar by Kellner & Munroe, a small factory in Brooklyn, New York (1908-1918). At its peak, the firm employed twenty-one cutters and two acid dippers or polishers. It made pieces of high quality and sold through such retail stores as Tiffany & Co. and Weinburg's in New York City. It used crystal blanks from Belgium. This blank is clear, but the color differs from fine American, suggesting that it may be Belgian.

Fan. By radiating miter vanes from a focus in a half circle, a figure resembling an open fan was achieved. One of the most common early patterns in America was "Strawberry Diamond (a crosscut diamond) and Fan." Early glass used the fan as a border for bowls and vases. Brilliant glass continued to do so (fig. 23, left), but in more dramatic ways. It also used the fan as a secondary motif to fill in uncut areas.

Flashed Fans had small fans between the spokes or vanes.

Single, Flashed, Radiant, and Pyramidal Stars

Single Star. By continuing the radiant miter cuts completely around the focus point, a single star was made. This is the most common decoration on the bottom of vases and pitchers and the least expensive to

Fig. 23. *Left to right:* Ice cream saucer, 5″, in "Emblem" by J. D. Bergen differs from the catalog illustration of a handled nappy, in that it has tips of the star cut in trellises instead of silver diamond. Ice cream saucer has flashed eight-point hobstar "drawn" with double lines. All stars in this well-cut saucer are clearly defined hobstars.

cut. Some refer to it as a "rayed base." Figure 24 shows three bonbon, olive, or sauce servers with a single star on the bottom.

Flashed Single Star. The single star can also be flashed, as in the sauce bowl on the left (fig. 25). This has been called *Shooting Star* or *Snowflake* by some.

Radiant Star. Hawkes, as well as Dorflinger, made this more interesting single star by altering the length of the rays to make a six- or eight-point star, as in the "Flutes and Greek Border" bowl by Hawkes (fig. 312). His rare tray (fig. 320) not only uses this in the center, but the designer has devised a beautiful border by encircling the radiant star with the brilliant cuts usually employed on the outer edge of the finest hobstars.

Pyramidal Star. This was made by cutting triangular prisms that radiated from a central focus. It was frequently used in the center of the button of the hobstar (fig. 36). It was also one of the two principal motifs of the famous Russian pattern (fig. 293).

Split; Curved Miter Split

Splits are deep miter cuts that often separate elements of the pattern. John S. O'Connor is supposed to have introduced the *Curved Miter Split* in his "Parisian" pattern assigned to Dorflinger in 1886.

Vesica, Split Vesica (and Square), X-Cut and Double X-Cut Vesica

Vesica. The vesica is a pointed oval made by curved miters.

Split Vesica and *Split Square.* In some cases a vesica filled with diamonds may be split down the middle by a straight miter cut. Figure 171 shows split squares of silver diamond on a stunning punch bowl.

Fig. 24. Pair of bonbon, olive, or individual sauce servers, 5⅝″ 1 × 2⅛″ h, in a cradle shape; hobstar on each end, miter cut and zigzag star on opposing sides, single star on bottom. Larger bonbon, 6¾″ 1 × 2⅝″ h, has a pinwheel at each end (unusual center hob) and a short chain of hexagonal fields on sides. May have been used with a small ladle for serving sauce. (Matye)

X-Cut and *Double X-Cut Vesicas* are vesicas divided into sections by curved miter splits that pass through the vesicas in the process of forming ovals or some other configuration. Separate parts of the vesica are then cut in different patterns (fig. 96).

Center Radiants. These are cuts that radiate from the center of the bottom of a piece. Figure 26 illustrates five of the last six terms nicely. The bonbon dish on the left shows both straight and curved splits; the smaller olive or almond dish has four double X-cut vesicas that meet in the center with different cuttings in each section. Both dishes have center radiants.

Ladder, Trellis, Zipper, Kite, Lozenge (Diamond), Pentagon

Straight miter cuts can form motifs resembling common items. Figure 27 shows a bowl with four *Ladders*. It also demonstrates the use of splits for separation of motifs. Figure 23 shows an ice cream saucer on the left with fans that join the scalloped edge and the *Trellis* motif consisting of a fan crossed by parallel miter cuts. The rose trellis can have any number of vanes.

The *Zipper* defines a configuration of parallel lines at right or acute angles to a split that cuts them in two. The finger bowl on the right in figure 25 has two zippers in each figure between the pinwheels. A crosshatched *Kite* is above the hobstar in the bonbon on the left in Figure 26.

Kite is my term for a kite-shaped field of silver diamond (or some other small, repetitious motif) — a quadrilateral figure with two equal angles in opposition, as well as two adjacent sides that are equal but shorter than the other two equal and adjacent sides. It resembles an old-fashioned kite.

A *Lozenge*, according to the dictionary, is a "four-sided equilateral figure whose opposing angles are equal," hence a diamond. It has two acute and two obtuse angles. This term has been used loosely by others.

A *Pentagon* is a polygon having five sides and five angles.

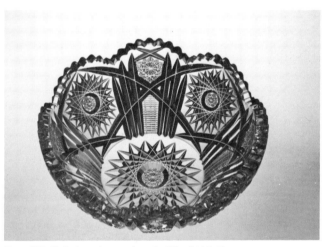

Fig. 25. *Left to right:* Cranberry or applesauce, 6¼″ d × 2¼″ h. Flashed star in center; six flashed stars alternate with panels of two eight-point hobstars with crosshatched buttons. Edge notched, not scalloped. Finger bowl, 4¾″ d × 2¼″ h. Three pinwheels alternate with three geometric devices featuring crosshatching (silver diamond), zippers, and fans. Clear blank, nice ring, good weight and polish. Design closely resembles J. D. Bergen's "Golf," which has a single star instead of the square of silver diamond, and lacks the crossed miter cuts at the foot of the device. Pitkin & Brooks also cut a similar design, #3913, called "Venice." (Both from Matye)

Fig. 27. Salad or berry bowl, 8″ × 3½″. Large twenty-point hobstar base; four twenty-point hobstars on sides, separated by panels consisting of a small flat star above a grid resembling a ladder. Deep vertical cuts and crossed curved splits give fair brilliance, even though this late Brilliant Period piece was cut on a figured ⅜″ blank.

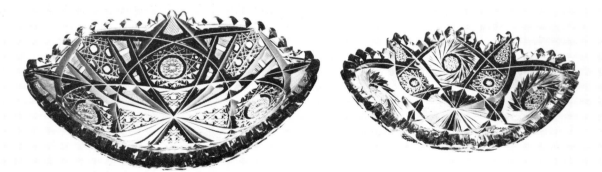

Fig. 26. *Left to right:* Bonbon, 7½″ l × 5¾″ w. Acute triangles are filled with hobstars, cane, silver diamond, and parallel cuts. Fine work on good blank. Olive or almond, 6¼″ l × 4⅜″ w. End pinwheels have unusual hobs with sixteen sides. This is a small gem. (Matye)

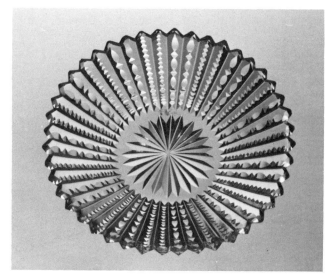

Fig. 28. Lemon dish or pin tray, 4½″, in "White House." Following the advent of the "Nautilus" design by T. G. Hawkes in 1896, W. C. Anderson of Libbey Glass created a pattern in 1897 (later modified as "Prism") called "White House." Labor costs of cutting beads were far less than making hobstars, so many companies used this motif far into the twentieth century.

In 1947, President Truman ordered a new service to replace the old "Russian" service. The new "White House" (adapted from an older one), cut by Hawkes, had a small central, single star encircled by radiant bars of notched prisms. (See Daniel, p. 277.) Dorothy Daniel considers any variation of this standard to be "White House," provided it has no larger figure, such as bullseye or hobstar.

This small dish, with nearly straight, sloping sides, differs in that the notched prisms are arranged in pairs cut in small, even notches, alternating with pairs cut in a long and a short. Pitkin & Brook's "Prism" had this arrangement combined with a chain of hobstars and silver diamond.

Block. One of the simplest applications of miter cutting is the block, in which apparently raised, flat-topped squares are made. This was an early pattern (circa 1880) in imitation of the Anglo-Irish, but it was too plain to appeal to many Americans. The tumblers in figure 62 exemplify this cutting perfectly.

Notching or Beading

Notched Prism or *Beading* could be varied in several ways. By placing miters close together, either parallel or closer at one end and slightly apart at the other (as when decorating a round bowl or tray), a dramatic design could be achieved by notching. Notching or beading meant cutting the prism between the miter cuts to make a pattern resembling a string of beads. Length of notches was varied deliberately to produce different sized "beads" (fig. 28).

Notched Vertical Prism, alone or combined with simple bull's-eyes, sometimes constituted the entire pattern. The clear cream and sugar set (fig. 29), believed to be unsigned Straus, is a fine example of a simple design cut on a superb blank.

Notched Horizontal Prism. Beading was also cut on the edge of horizontal prisms, as in the "Senora" carafe by Libbey (fig. 254) and related pieces in the chapter on Libbey glass.

Notched Prism Flares are a further extension, done by spreading the miter cuts and inserting fans at one end, sometimes at both, as demonstrated clearly in the Pitkin & Brooks bowl (fig. 30). This was a favorite motif of theirs and also of J. D. Bergen.

Bull's-eye or Punty (sometimes called *Roundelet* in England, *Printie* or *Punty* in Ireland, and *Kugel* in Germany. When written *Kugeln,* it is plural.) This is a

Fig. 29. Cream and sugar set, 3″, in "Prism and Bullseye," attributed to Straus, is in the exact pattern for patent #28733 designed by Benjamin Davis, assigned to L. Straus & Sons, 31 May 1898. A single sixteen-point star is on the bottom; handles are double-notched. (Matye)

concave or hollowed out circle made by the round-edged fluting wheel (fig. 29). Some call it *Round Thumbprint*, since the thumbprint is olivary in shape. Used as an allover design in pressed glass, it was known as the "Mirror" pattern. (See fig. 319 for example in cut glass.)

Sunburst. A sunburst effect was made by encircling a bull's-eye with prism flares, as in the pitcher (fig. 31). Some sunbursts had a hobstar in the center. A Libbey sunburst consisted of a bull's-eye with single radiant cuts around the center.

Feathering or Flashing. Sometimes leaves were outlined by means of small, miter cuts, as in the luncheon plate (fig. 4). Hobstars were often dramatized by flashing. In figure 23, the ice cream saucer on the right has three flashed hobstars. In 1889 William C. Anderson patented design #19053 for Edward D. Libbey, showing a flashed hobstar whose points were cut in silver diamond. The company named it "Florence Star," said to be named for Libbey's bride. The Meriden Cut Glass Company used this type of star often (figs. 351 and 355).

Diamonds: Silver (Crosshatching, Strawberry); Crosscut; Large Shallow

The diamond came in many forms, and is also the product of miter cutting. Since there is much confusion, due to use of various terms to describe the same thing, let us be very precise. Strawberry diamond is a case in point.

Silver Diamond. In the Anglo-Irish tradition, copied by Americans in our Early Period, the *English Strawberry Diamond* was a field of small diamonds, usually sixteen, produced by making small parallel cuts in one direction, then by crossing these at right angles. The field was a flat-topped pyramid (usually one of many, covering a large area) made by dividing the glass surface into squares by means of larger miter cuts at right angles to each other (like the Block).

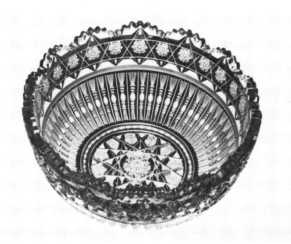

Fig. 30. Berry bowl, 8″ × 3¾″, in "Border" by P&B (1904-1905 catalog). Chain of flat stars is especially Bergenesque, but prism flairs with broom-like ends were almost a trademark of P&B. (Matye)

Fig. 31. Jug, 8¾″, in a Sunburst design. Large 24-point hobstar on front under lip; triangles of silver diamond, fans, and flashed leaves. Pouring lip is fluted and handle triple-notched; thirty-two rays on bottom. Heavy and brilliant. Sunburst is like those made by P&B circa 1907, and Enterprise, 1910. Tumblers do not match pitcher, but are related. Their sunburst is a flashed single star. They have crosscut and silver diamonds, no feathered leaves. Of finest quality, also, they were shown with the jug. The dealer said nothing. We had not yet learned to distinguish fine differences in patterns.

Some authorities now refer to all fine diamond cutting as *Strawberry Diamond,* regardless of the shape or size of the area it covers; others call it *Crosshatching.* To avoid confusion, I shall call it *Silver Diamond,* borrowing a term used by Dorflinger in his catalog descriptions.

Crosscut Diamond. American Strawberry Diamond consisted of a somewhat larger diamond with a cross cut into the flattened tip. The "Strawberry Diamond and Fan" pattern was common early in our Brilliant Period. (See fig. 461, right — an early Brilliant syrup jug.) It clearly referred to the *Crosscut Diamond,* as I shall call it from now on. In England, this was called *Laced Diamond.* Some use the terms, *Crosscut* and *Chequered,* interchangeably, but the latter is slightly more ornate (fig. 18).

Large Shallow Relief Diamonds were common in Early and Middle American glass, as shown in the handled claret decanter and the square decanter in figure 10. They were seldom seen during the Brilliant Period.

St. Louis Diamond or Honeycomb refers to concave hexagons or quadrilateral diamonds cut into the glass, covering an area such as the neck of a carafe or pitcher. Dorflinger was fond of wrapping the throat of a pitcher with this motif (fig. 14). A Dorflinger catalog shows a cigar jar covered with hollowed-out diamonds, the stopper cut to match the jar. The pattern was known as "Honeycomb." Early American cruets and castor bottles were often cut this way. The dainty cologne bottle in "Prism" by J. Hoare (fig. 32) shows this motif clearly. It was obviously named for the lower motif.

The work of William Peter Eichbaum was discussed in Chapter 3 on Early American glass. It was he who introduced the German kugel or bull's-eye in America and also the hexagonal diamond panel cutting on bottles, which he called "St. Louis neck," probably in honor of the glass village which he had founded for King Louis XVI of France.

Sharp or Relief or Nailhead Diamond. This was a sharp, pointed diamond with four pyramidal sides (but it can have three). Since I cannot imagine a nail with a sharp head, I shall call this *Sharp Relief Diamond* and perhaps comment on its size. See the Dorflinger vase discussed previously (fig. 8).

The Hobnail or Button is a raised hexagonal or octagonal form, seen in the "Russian" cut design and its pressed counterpart, "Daisy and Button," and in the centers of hobstars and pinwheels. The hobnail was aptly called *Hexagonal Diamond* in the Mount Washington catalogs. The banana bowl (fig. 191) shows fine, sharply cut hobnail as an effective secondary motif. The spoon tray (fig. 33) has kites of hobnail at the ends. Small triangles of hobnail form the points of a six-point central star. Early in the period, hobnail, larger in scale, sometimes covered the whole piece. This appealed to those with simpler taste.

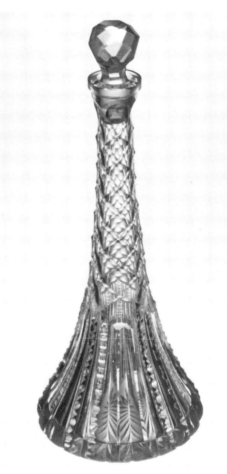

Fig. 32. Sauce or toilet water bottle, 8½″, in "Prism," shown in J. Hoare's 1910 catalog. The St. Louis or Honeycomb neck, topped by a lapidary stopper, rests on a body cut in notched vertical prism. Bottom is rayed. A bitters bottle like this, with "Sterling Silver squirt" top, priced at $4.50, was called "Albany" in an original catalog from Higgins & Seiter, a wholesale house, circa 1903. (Do not confuse this with Meriden's "Albany," consisting of bullseye and notched prism.)

Fig. 33. Spoon or olive tray, 6¾″ l × 4⅝″ w. A long ellipse down the middle holds three unusual six-point hobstars with a small replica, a star of David, on the button. Four hobstars, six fans, and triangles of fine hobnail complete the design on this versatile piece. (Matye)

Hobstar, called Rosette if exquisitely done, is a complex figure with many versions. It seems to have been the salient feature of Brilliant glassware, although it appeared occasionally during the Middle Period. The hob or button in the finest examples stood high in relief above the intersecting miter cuts around it. These cuts met at the outer edge to form points, each cut giving the hobnail just one more facet on its side in passing. The points generally varied in number from eight to thirty-two, but a few rare items had forty-eight-point stars, such as the ice cream tray by Libbey (fig. 250) and the 10″ bowl by Hoare (fig. 375). A rare punch bowl in the Wiener-Lipkowitz book (p. 77) has sixty points!

The button was often decorated by means of a pyramidal star with its own small miter-cut system around it. In some cases, when eight or ten points were formed on the hobstar, the points were large and kite-shaped and were cut in silver diamond. Meriden featured a flashed star made this way as the principal motif, combined with secondary figures. Hawkes, Dorflinger, and others used a small eight-point hobstar in many patterns, such as "Middlesex" (fig. 288).

Zigzag or Flat Star. I have coined this term to describe the nearly flat star made by cuts similar to the continuous line we learned to make as children when drawing a five-point star, the pentagram. (This was done without lifting the pencil from the paper.) It was devised after 1900 and used more frequently as time went on to decrease the cost of labor. It was not always symmetrical, but was sometimes lengthened at one end. A chain of these may be seen around the top of the bowl in figure 30.

Pinwheel or Buzz. The *Pinwheel* looks like a child's toy pinwheel revolving in the wind. Doubtless the word *Buzz* occurred to someone who visualized a buzz saw. The vanes were miter cuts, straight or curved, spinning off from the central hobnail. They often had fans between them, giving a flashed effect. The terms, pinwheel and buzz, are used interchangeably, although I prefer the first. I feel inclined to apply "buzz" to late, inferior cuttings.

The first pinwheel patent appears to have been #30267, 28 February 1899, by Patrick H. Healy, assigned to the American Cut Glass Company of Chicago, a subsidiary of Libbey that used Libbey blanks. Clark is so noted for use of this motif that some authorities believe he originated it. Figure 390 shows a fine plate by Clark. We just passed over a pinwheel (fig. 25) on a finger bowl of good quality. The jug or pitcher shown here (fig. 34) illustrates several of the cuts we have described: pinwheel, band of hobnail, silver diamond, hobstar, and a column of flat or zigzag stars.

In trying to save labor costs, many companies adopted the buzz and zigzag star motifs to produce showy pieces in less time than the more intricate hobstar required. Late in the period, during the war years, many buzz designs were done on figured blanks of inferior quality. We have seen several vases and bowls cut on lightweight, "muddy" blanks that we would not accept as a gift. Be careful; examine closely before buying, but do not automatically reject all pinwheels. When we first started to collect cut glass, we were warned to avoid this pattern. In our initial ignorance we sold a 12″ tray, inherited from Earle's mother, to "upgrade" our collection, only to regret it later. Now some of my most unusual pieces have pinwheels, as you will observe as we go along.

Flute, Panel, and Pillar Flute.

Flute. Finally, among the basic motifs is the *Flute* — a hollowed-out, vertical surface — most frequently used on necks of carafes, bottles, and decanters. It is also found near the top and under the lip of vases and of pitchers (usually called "jugs" in the old catalogs), sometimes on bowls.

The *Panel* is like the flute, except that it is flat. The plain, Colonial-revival Libbey pitcher (fig. 264) has both: flutes on the body and two flat panels on the handle.

The *Pillar* (fig. 133) is the reverse of the concave flute. It is convex, rounded out from the surface, and produced by grinding down the sharp edge of a prism or a wider surface between miters.

Fig. 34. Jug or pitcher, 9⅛″. Handle double-notched. Note that the size is small for a tankard shape. (Matye)

Motifs Employed as Patterns

Certain arrangements of motifs grew into well-known patterns, which could either be used to cover the whole surface (often true early in the period) or to act as a motif combined with other motifs (later in the period).

Cane or Chairbottom, Hexad-of-Buttons-and-Star, Cane-on-Cane, and Harvard or Chairbottom

Cane (or *Chairbottom*) resembles the woven cane found in chair bottoms and backs. It consists of eight-sided buttons in alternate squares formed by vertical and horizontal cuts. Double diagonal cuts cross the remaining squares at right angles to each other. The bonbon, olive, or spoon tray (fig. 35) shows triangles of cane with clear buttons very distinctly.

Hexad-of-Buttons-and-Star is a term I have coined to describe what others call a *Cane or Russian Variant.* "Hexad" means "a group or series of six." In this motif a group of six buttons surrounds a pyramidal star, then each hexad becomes a part of the next six. It seems to be related to "Russian," where four buttons are arranged around the pyramidal star. This cutting is found on some of our finest pieces: rather large on the rare Libbey vase (fig. 252) and extremely small on the finely cut bowl (fig. 122) seen among the rarities in Chapter 11.

Cane-on-Cane. Another rare use of cane is manifest in the water goblets, wines, and finger bowl (figs. 142 and 143). On each button in the cane pattern is found an incredibly small replica of a section of the design, including four tiny buttons.

Harvard (also called *Chairbottom*) for most companies described a variation of cane. (Libbey's "Harvard" is entirely different, as we shall see in Chapter 14 on Libbey glass.) In some cases, alternate rows of buttons were starred and crosshatched; in others, a different treatment of each hob alternated in the same row, like a checkerboard.

Early in the period, Harvard was a dominant motif, as shown in the massive flower center (fig. 22). The vase's neck is cut in Horizontal Step, as previously described. I believe this, however, to have been made circa 1908-1913. Cutters often reverted to an earlier style to be different from current fashions.

Harvard was frequently combined with other motifs. The bowl in figure 36 is a fine example of equal emphasis on three large hobstars and three equally large areas of Harvard. This would have been made in the 1890s.

Harvard was also used with floral cutting late in the period. This footed rose globe (fig. 37) has many of the characteristics to be found circa 1915-1918: fair quality of glass, the design, and a less expensive floral cutting. The cookie jar (fig. 217), about 1913, is a good example of transitional design, also.

Fig. 35. Bonbon, olive, or spoon tray, 8″ × 4½″. The large flashed "Florence" hobstar (with silver diamond points) at each end is the principal motif. A large, regular hobstar in the center, fans, four smaller hobstars, large triangles of cane, and smaller ones of silver diamond complete the design. Cut on a pressed blank, but a clear one, and cut accurately. (Matye)

Fig. 36. Bowl, 8″ × 4″, in Harvard and Hobstar, circa 1890-1900. Base is cut in a smaller hobstar, with six points finished in silver diamond. Finest glass, precisely and sharply cut. The touch of fingers causes it to ring. When we first saw it, we thought scallops were chipped. They are not, but look so because the design goes off the edge into infinity. Note depth of cutting of hobstar on the side facing the reader.

There was a great disparity of quality in Harvard cutting. Some items have been so badly done that they would seem to have been practice pieces for apprentices; others were superb, such as the Canadian lamp and the matching tray (figs. 417 and 416).

Russian. Probably the most famous pattern was *Russian.* It was designed by Philip McDonald and assigned to Hawkes, 20 June 1882. It consists of the pyramidal star and hobnail combined in an intricate fashion. Figure 38 shows a spoon tray in Hunt's "Royal" with Russian covering the bottom and "Arcadia" on the sides. If viewed so that rows of pyramidal stars alternate with rows of hobnails (buttons), the Russian seems simpler.

As stated in the original patent, the hexagonal button may be left clear, or decorated in several ways. Through the years, the variations have acquired names that are helpful in visualizing a piece described verbally or in writing:

1. If clear, we call it "Cleveland."
2. Cut with a single star, it is "Canterbury."
3. Cut in silver diamond (crosshatched), it is "Ambassador."

4. Cut with a small hobstar, it is called "Persian." This is the most expensive and ornate.
5. A very small hobnail combined with a large pyramidal star has been dubbed "Polar Star."

Many pieces were cut almost entirely in Russian, like the jug in figure 39, but others were decorated by a combination of Russian with another design. This spoon tray (fig. 38), with its border in an Arcadian pattern, exemplifies the latter premise.

Fig. 37. Footed rose globe, 7½″ h × 8″, in Harvard and Floral, circa 1915-1918. Three feet; rayed bottom. Harvard buttons are cut alternately in silver diamond and fine hobnail; panels have flowers with fine-line petals, centers of silver diamond, and miter leaves. The feet and unusual treatment of the Harvard are similar to a rose bowl (Revi. p. 453) by Washington Cut Glass in Seattle, Washington, shown in their catalog circa 1915. There is no guarantee that this piece was cut by the Seattle firm, but such similar features help us to arrive at an approximate date. Note fine-line notches around edge. (Matye)

Fig. 39. Cereal cream or juice jug, 6″, in Canterbury Russian. This size was often used in the sick room. (Rice)

Fig. 38. *Left to right:* Spoon tray, 7¾″ × 3½″, in Hunt's "Royal," patent #41555, 11 July 1911, by Harry S. Hunt, shown in 1911-1912 Marshall Field Catalog (Chicago). "Russian" (twelve facets on button) covers bottom; six hobstars on sides alternate with crossed bars containing silver diamond and a star-cut button at the intersection (as in "Arcadia" by the Sterling Glass Company of Cincinnati, Ohio). Blackmer's "Sultana" (New Bedford, Massachusetts) utilized same Arcadia motif with pentagons of fine diamond alternating with hobstars, but without Russian (Revi, p. 65). Bonbon or almond dish, 3¾″ sq, has a twenty-point hobstar on the bottom. The button is cut as an eight-point Middlesex hobstar in miniature. Sides have fans and crosscut kite shapes. (Matye)

Fig. 40. Jug, 8″. The flashed single star seems to be a stylized flower, identical with the main motif on a tumbler made by Unger Brothers of Newark, New Jersey (1901-1918). This proves nothing except a possible date, since so many designers used like motifs at this time. Under the fluted spout, one sees a pyramid of notched vertical prisms, topped by crosscut diamonds and fans. Handle is triple-notched; half flutes encircle base. Quality is good. "D" by Fry.

Cut/Engraved and Wholly Engraved Designs

To be consistent, this section should simply point out the different ways in which designs inspired by nature were interpreted in glass decoration. Later, we can explain the changes and the reasons behind them, although inferences can be drawn as we proceed.

Geometrically or Miter-cut Flora. A flower-like effect could be produced entirely by use of miter cuts, as shown in the pitcher (fig. 40). The flashed single star seems to be a flower on a long stem; the diagonal cuts on each side can be interpreted as leaves and grass. This could be a stylized daffodil. This is a floral cut design called "D" by Fry.

Light, Inexpensive Cutting. My mother's fern dish (fig. 41) shows the least expensive cutting of floral decoration. The leaves are miter-cut and left gray; the flower petals are fine-line, shallow-cutting, and the centers — silver diamond. This type of flower was common circa 1917. The piece does not belong in a collection of cut glass, but is included to make clear that, while the design is technically cut, it is "beyond the pale."

The vase inherited from Earle's mother (fig. 42) is more complex. The stems and leaves are rather deep; the blossoms hollowed by a round-edged wheel. Both

Fig. 41. Fern dish, 8″ × 4″, pressed in a three-part mold, has lightly cut flowers placed over seams above each foot. One flower is cut on the bottom. Miter leaves, stems, and flowers are left unpolished.

Fig. 42. Vase, 10½″, has fine-line blossoms and leaves with veins left unpolished. Petal cuts and starlets are also matte. Rayed base.

were polished, then veins were cut in the leaves and fine lines on the petals and left unpolished. The starlets are also matte finish. It cannot be classified as intaglio, but is charming. The style, identified by the notched edge, seems to be of 1908-1917 vintage, yet the glass has a lavender cast. Upon close inspection, swirls and eddies can be seen, as in some older glass. Could it be pre-Brilliant Period?

Fig. 43. Berry bowl, 8¼″ × 3¼″, in a floral and vertical prism cutting, has scalloped edge similar to that of a celery boat (Revi, p. 386) cut at Vetter Cut Glass Manufacturing Co., Cleveland, Ohio, in 1915. Vetter "produced a superior grade of cut glass." This bowl is skillfully cut on an excellent blank of medium thickness and weight.

Fig. 44. Fruit bowl, 9″ × 4″, circa 1909; 5 lbs.; large capacity. A six-point star of geometric motifs covers bottom. Six corn flowers with polished hobnail centers, petals of matte, fine-line cutting, and polished miter stems and leaves occupy nearly vertical sides. A patent drawing, #40051 by Robert H. Pittman for T. B. Clark, 15 June 1909, shows blossoms like these, thus helping to date the bowl.

Transitional. The berry bowl (fig. 43) is a fine example of combined geometric and floral cutting. It was probably made near the end of the period (1908-1915), when some excellent and some poor items were manufactured. The smooth, scalloped edge is a feature of the "Floral" phase of the period, as opposed to the serrated edges of geometric, Brilliant ware.

Fig. 45. Fruit bowl, 9″, in a Fruit pattern, with stone-engraved grapes, pears and plums. The owner believes it to be unsigned Tuthill, but the fruit is not as realistic as that of Tuthill. Note serrated edge on scallops, typical of Fry, and swirls of sharp hobnail for contrast. (Gerritse)

The deep, heavy fruit bowl (fig. 44) is another excellent example of the transition from geometric to floral after 1905. It fulfilled all of the requirements: it reduced labor costs by using miter-cut leaves on a fairly large area; it appealed to customers who sought something new, yet continued to satisfy those who appreciated the deep, geometric brilliant style.

Look back at the footed rose bowl (fig. 37) to see another example of transitional cutting; and ahead to figure 217, where a cookie jar is predominantly Harvard, yet has clear panels cut in flowers.

Intaglio Engraving; Gravic. Figure 45 depicts a perfect example of intaglio engraving, the crowning glory of naturalistic design! This fruit bowl has swirls of sharp hobnail for contrast.

Intaglio engraving was deeper than mere surface engraving done by means of small copper wheels. It was like a realistic painting with delicate nuances and attention to faithful reproduction of nature. We have already described the mechanical means, but would be reminded that this sort of sculpture in glass, whether by means of stone or copper wheel, required more than a skillful artisan. It required an artist who could cut freehand figures — sometimes by looking at a drawing or a model for guidance, sometimes from an outline on the glass made by painting or by scratching with a steel stylus. The creator of the "picture" often composed at the wheel.

Gravic was a trade name patented by Hawkes to label some of their finest quality intaglio engraving, often in combination with geometric cutting on the same piece. To be correct, we should not use "Gravic" to describe the intaglio work of other companies.

Fig. 46. Whiskey shot glass, 2¾″, signed Libbey-in-a-circle, in "close-up" to show rye grain engraved on a pinched-in, pentagon-shaped area on three sides of the vessel. This is dramatized by a double row of miter cuts. Bottom is rayed. The matte rye design is only ⅞″ tall.

Fig. 47. Vase, 10″, in "R.C.155," attributed to Sinclaire. In *H. P. Sinclaire, Jr., Glassmaker,* Vol. I, photo 762 of 1917 inventory, one sees a vase of this shape, 12″ high, in "R.C.155" at $4.69 each. It appears to have the cuts at the top and the swirling leaves near the base. The blossoms are too dark to match with these. If only their lighting had been better!

The subjects of engraving were numerous: flowers; grains (fig. 46); fruits; vegetables, such as celery and corn; animals such as birds (fig. 5), butterflies (fig. 75), fish, horses (fig. 144), dogs, cows, and deer. Tuthill, Hawkes, Sinclaire, and Pairpoint are famous for intaglio work, but Libbey also did outstanding engraving (fig. 277).

Portraits of people were sometimes engraved by special order on presentation pieces. One of the finest was that of the double portrait of President William McKinley and his wife, used in his 1900 presidential campaign. It was carved in 1901 by master engraver Hieronimus William Fritchie of Corning on the front of a tankard pitcher. The busts, each on a clear oval area, are framed by ornate, rococo scrolls. The back of the jug and the handle are engraved in dainty, realistic flowers and leaves. The Dorflinger pitcher, green cut to clear (fig. C.3), is in a similar vein. This would seem to be a revival of the intricate, florid designs of fifty years before in Europe.

Another beautiful and effective form of pictorial cutting, unlike the realistic flora and fauna we have described, is illustrated in the "Shagbark" pattern, cut by Hoare, and a similar design by Libbey, called "Libbey" (fig. 275). The flower petals were produced by miter cuts, parallel or nearly so, in a slight hollow; the centers were fine hobnail, also cut in a hollow so that a raised, rounded effect was produced when looking down into the piece. All were polished, yet the silvery illusion of depth is remarkable. Three examples will be shown with the Libbey pieces.

Engraving on Thin Glass. Copper wheel engraving was done on thin glass, either in flowing leafy designs or in dainty stylized flowers arranged in precisely formal configurations. These were left in matte gray, were partially polished, or entirely polished, in which case the technique was known as *Rock Crystal.* Sinclaire and Pairpoint were its greatest exponents, but Hawkes and Steuben did similar work. This vase (fig. 47), attributed to Sinclaire, shows Rock Crystal engraving on a relatively thin blank. Hawkes used the *fishscale,* seen at the bottom, in his "Classic" design; Pairpoint used it in "Hampton." (Both are illustrated in Pearson's *Encyc. II,* pp. 90 and 164.) Of course Sinclaire worked for Hawkes before going into business for himself.

Greek Key Fret (a separate category of engraving). Greek Key continuous border designs were engraved in a shallow manner on a flat-edge, copper wheel. They may be polished or matte (figs. 313 and 312). They are not all alike (fig. 339). A fret is an ornament consisting of small, straight lines or bars, intersecting one another in right or oblique angles, often of solid filets or slats intersecting each other.

Learning To Identify Motifs

If you have methodically matched each description with the designated photograph, you should see cut pieces with "new eyes." What might have been a blur of design will be sorted into identifiable motifs. The novice collector may wish to go back over this chapter several times. Later on, we shall give further directions on how to identify American glass as opposed to European, old versus new, and how to recognize high quality that is worth the investment.

7

Evolution of Pattern Styles, Patented Designs, and Trademarks

Now that we are more aware of the tenor of life in America during the years between the Centennial and World War I and we speak the same language of cut designs, let us examine pattern styles of cutting, discover who made "rich Cut Glass," and learn how it reached the privileged segments of society able to afford it. In this chapter, we shall trace the evolution of glass design and explain how makers tried to protect their creations by means of design patents and trademarks.

Evolution of Styles in the Arts

In music, a limited number of degrees of pitch can be combined to produce an infinite variety of melodies and harmonies. Within this endless flow of recorded music, as well as in unrecorded folk songs, many distinctive styles have evolved.

Glass cutting can be traced through similar phases. Compare the chaste and restrained design of a Dorflinger bowl (fig. 284) with a Tuthill intaglio bowl (fig. 333). Some designers combined geometric with naturalistic motifs to produce striking contrast between the two. The "Vintage" bowl by Tuthill (fig. 332) and the Hawkes Gravic "Fruit" celery dish (fig. 314) are fine examples of this marriage of styles.

Some glass firms entered the market with something new, but continued to make old patterns to satisfy conservative customers. Smaller companies followed the new trend after being assured that there would be sufficient demand for the new patterns.

As shown in the review of the Centennial Exposition of 1876, a few American companies exhibited deep-cut brilliant glass of marvelous quality. Dorflinger's "Centennial Set" is a case in point. Dorflinger also exhibited a plainer set of stemware that was thin, with flutes around the base of the bowl, engraved with animals and foliated scrolls. On page 245 of *Two Hundred Years of American Glass* by McKearin, one can see a cordial with an eagle and a horse, and a wine with a horse and a rabbit.

Another example of exquisitely engraved glass is the famous pair of blown, cut, and engraved globular bottles ordered by a New York banker as a gift for his niece, Miss Ellen Rogers. The bottles were made circa 1890 by the Corning Glass Company and decorated by J. Hoare. Each has a galloping horse and hound on one side and a group of stable buildings below the initial "R" on the reverse.

Most of the American *cut* glass from 1876 into the 1880s, however, continued in the Anglo-Irish tradition with English strawberry diamond, large sharp relief diamond, fan, flute, and block — all cut in a fairly shallow manner. Some fine-line cuttings of crosshatching (silver diamond), done by means of a triple-miter wheel, were cut through on a fluting wheel to make clear flower forms in a field of diamonds. This may have been an effort to combat pressed-glass imitations of cut glass, since it was impossible to reproduce fine-line cutting on a press. The square nappy with four such flower forms (fig. 197, left) illustrates this technique, although the piece was advertised in a 1903 catalog.

Copper wheel engraving was still highly favored in 1876 and into the 1880s. Some engravings, such as two Gillinder goblets shown at the fair, were exquisite. One was thick and deeply cut like the Dorflinger Centennial Set, but with panels engraved with "Virtue, Liberty and Independence." The other had birds and flora on a thin blank. True copper wheel engraving was more expensive than cut glass. The best pieces were seldom listed in catalogs, but were commissioned by jewelers and rich individual customers.

Corning, New York, had fine engravers, many of whom were Bohemians who came fully trained as master engravers. Such men often lived at the home of a friend for a year or two until they had saved enough money to send for wife and children. Then, even when working in a factory, they would establish a shop at home (in a barn or attic) and work there during slack seasons. Some did all their work at home on consignment.

The engravers' most common subjects were monograms, floral designs, inscriptions on presentation pieces, and coats of arms. But some outstanding work included portraits, public buildings, and scenes from classic mythology.

From 1880 until about 1906, deep brilliant cuttings on heavy, clear glass were "the rage" with the general public. An article on "Home Furnishing and

Decoration" in *Good Housekeeping*, 11 May 1889, declared that "a table glittering with prismatic, diamond-like hues, lending its brilliancy to deeply tinted flowers, and contrasting with the fair white of the linen covers and napkins" was the most beautiful sight a hostess could desire to display to her guests. The writer recalled that "only recently all our cut glass was brought over from England. Now we have perhaps a dozen factories...in which glass is equal in quality and superior in brilliancy and whiteness to the imported ware." Popular patterns in 1889 were "hobnail, strawberry diamond and fan, Russian, Maltese, prism and bead, Phoenix, and old English."

The writer also described how the glass was arranged on mirrors in sales rooms to "dazzle the eyes of the purchaser." She said that several large tables were crowded with globes for gas and electric lights, both etched and cut, "but the most beautiful are full cut...For electric lights the display is unusually fine. Drop an incandescent burner into one of these sparkling cones of glass and your room is fairly ablaze with the reflected and multiplied lights. The cutting is every bit as fine as that of the choicest table ware." This is certainly true of the light bowl shown in fig. 83.

Natural gas as fuel facilitated rapid fusion of the metal, production of a crystal clear glass, and a more consistent annealing, since the heat could be better regulated. Applying electrical power to the cutter's lathe permitted the faster-spinning wheels to cut more deeply. The new pieces were so prestigious that orders were placed from the White House as well as by foreign dignitaries from Cuba, Mexico, Sweden, China, and Russia.

The improved, perfectly colorless glass was blown into heavy blanks, then cut deeply. Early Brilliant period glass often featured one motif or pattern, such as block, hobnail, Russian (fig. 39), or cane. It might use two rather sedate figures, such as American strawberry (crosscut) diamond and fan (fig. 437, right).

From about 1890 to 1895, two dominant motifs were often employed, as shown in the sharply cut, brilliant bowl (fig. 36) in Chapter 6.

Circa 1895 to 1905, designs featured the hobstar, curved split, cane, and notched prism, often combined with older and simpler motifs, such as hobnail, fan, diamond and block.

Although the height of this "cut glass mania" lasted from 1885 until 1905, many well-cut brilliant pieces were made as late as 1915 and beyond. "Rex" by Tuthill won a gold medal at the Panama-Pacific Exposition at San Francisco in 1915. Described as resembling a magnificent diamond, this pattern has cane vesicas that radiate from the center, with fans between the points and a chain of hobstars around the sides.

An original 1911 catalog of Thomas J. Jusek & Company of Elgin, Illinois, a wholesale jeweler, included sixteen pages of cut glass — all geometric cuttings, with not one floral design.

Meriden's "Alhambra" (fig. 339) was patented in 1910. A huge punch bowl (to be cut with 6″ hobstars) with sterling silver band and matching cups was specially ordered from Hawkes and Gorham by John Jacob Astor IV in 1911. A beautiful bowl in typically brilliant styling was photographed in the inventory of the Sinclaire factory in 1917 (fig. 357).

Harper's Bazaar, in a 1905 article on "New China and Glass Ware," described "an interesting difference this year between the favored styles in glass and in china. In china the preference seems to turn to low effects. Dumpiness is sought for in most small pieces and in many large ones. In glass, on the contrary, there is a soaring tendency and nearly all the novelties are high. Even the old-time épergnes are in vogue again." Tall tankard pitchers, celery dishes, and nappies were raised on a stem and foot. The rare banana bowls on a standard probably were introduced at this time.

The writer stated that "the good old stand-bys in cut-glass dishes of every sort are still selling steadily, and there are new dishes to be seen in the conservative hob-nail and strawberry cutting." Comments were made concerning an exception to the general trend: "...exquisite rock crystal, which is as beautiful as it is expensive." The new fruit designs "are very rich and heavy and hardly suitable to any table save that of the plutocrat." These would have been the stone-engraved Gravic by Hawkes and similar engraving by Libbey and Tuthill. "The shapes in this are rather low and not at all eccentric." There were many new styles in candlesticks and candelabra. "To the exclusive soul one of the charms of the new glass is that thus far it has not been imitated in the cheaper ware."

One must admit, however, that after 1905, although well-integrated patterns such as Hawke's "Queens" (fig. 307) continued to be made, some weird designs appeared. Too many motifs were combined in the same pattern. Odd shapes were devised in an effort to hold on to the trade that had flourished for so many years. Even the great Hawkes designers went too far in searching for new ideas (fig. 48). The vase in figure 49 may also fall into this category. The flared top, with unusual contours cut in hobnail; the combination of so many motifs — hobnail, hobstar, Gothic arch, diagonal and horizontal miter cuts, and flutes — on such a small piece must have offended those with conservative taste. But with its twenty-four point hobstar on the bottom, it doubtless excited the buyer looking for something new.

A design for a "Glass Dish," patented by Heisey in 1906, had a rim with exactly the same contours. Some cutting shops bought Heisey pressed pieces (good and inexpensive), ground off the raised signature (an H in a diamond), then cut them in their own designs. Could that be the origin of this vase? If not, we can at least use the shape of the rim as a clue to the age of the vase.

Decline of the Brilliant Period

In September 1913, *American Homes and Gardens* ran a piece called "The Decorative Value of Glass" by George Crane, who wrote a monthly column, "Within the House." Mr. Crane was forceful in his defense of old English and Irish glass with simple cutting. He was disdainful of Brilliant American glass. He wrote:

> Elaborately cut glass seems a waste of time. It is neither artistic nor does it leave any room for imagination, and that, after all, must be part of one's scheme in the placing of decorative glass. Cut glass immediately suggests a big shop, where long tables fitted with it invite the passer-by to pause and look at some fearful piece that at one time was expensive, but has since been cut down so as to be most tempting in price. The unwary passer-by falls, the piece is purchased, and a fine cut glass punch bowl, with all the little punch glasses hanging by hooks, graces the highly polished golden oak sideboard! Plain glass, with its graceful forms, is so much better that one often wonders why one does not see it more.

Such fashion arbiters as Mr. Crane were instrumental in inspiring the lady of the house to put away her treasures, some of which were appreciated by her daughters and granddaughters, and some of which found their way into a Salvation Army barrel.

Fig. 48. Hawkes vase, advertised in *Ladies' Home Journal*, April 1905.

Fig. 49. Vase, 9⅝". A multitude of motifs on such a small piece!

The decline was not entirely due to a change in public taste. Makers of cut glass had to contend with workers who pressed for higher wages. The trade of glasscutting was an exacting one, requiring an apprenticeship of from four to ten years. One had to be strong to hold a heavy blank steadily against the grinding wheel. At O'Connor's shop in Goshin, New York, a wassail bowl of ruby and crystal was cut for the owner's home. The bowl was so heavy that a leather halter had to be devised to support it.

Until John S. O'Connor invented a vacuum machine to suck up the ground glass, the cutters inhaled the lethal particles. Even after the invention, most of the shops continued to work without it. Cutters, like mine workers, suffered lung disease. New unions contended that emery or carborundum powder was also injurious to health. The use of lead powder with felt-lined brushwheels gave a high polish, but it caused death from lead poisoning. Its use was banned in the early 1920s in England and possibly in the United States.

Changes in Style

After about 1906, owners tried several methods of stabilizing their business. The most obvious was to save labor costs by cutting less time-consuming motifs. Although the "Nautilus" design by Thomas G. Hawkes in 1896 was expensive to make, it did introduce the inexpensive notched prism cut. Many designs combining the notched prism with bull's-eye or another simple cut were subsequently used for this reason. The pinwheel was used from 1900, and more often after 1905, partly because it cost less to cut than a hobstar (fig. 50).

The *figured blank,* in which the largest incisions were pressed into the blank by the mold, not only saved cutting time, but also saved material. As much as one fourth of the glass might be ground away during the cutting of a plain blank. Prestigious companies in Corning seldom used the figured blank, but firms elsewhere did, bringing about a monotony of design that bored discerning buyers. To these customers, engravings, which could not be mechanically produced, became more desirable. These included both the polished copper wheel engravings and the less expensive, though often attractive, stone engravings.

Some took another tack. There was an effort to change the public taste by advertising. Such suggestions as "Let's go back to the simple designs of our grandmothers" were made. An advertisement in an August 1908 *Ladies' Home Journal* showed a plain goblet with an engraved monogram. "Start with the goblets and complete the set gradually." In April 1909, a plain low pitcher was illustrated by Hawkes:

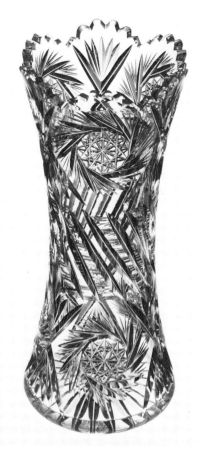

Fig. 50. Vase, 12″, in pinwheel or buzz design. Excellent example of simplified cutting circa 1906 or later. Diagonal miter cuts occupy "waistline" of piece and cost little to execute. Quality of glass is good, not superb. It would have been a handsome vase for a middle-class home.

The highly prized *perfect white* of Hawkes Cut Glass gives to the new monogrammed pieces a beauty unshared by more elaborately wrought glass. The personal completion of a set so marked is an artistic pleasure.

A 1910 *Ladies' Home Journal* showed a plain paneled candlestick and rhapsodized:

A chaste design of exquisite beauty, yet of almost Puritanical simplicity. This beautiful candlestick, like all Hawkes Cut Glass, is a chef-d'oeuvre of an artist who loves his work. In crystallene clarity and perfection of cutting there are none to compare.

Libbey's pitcher in "Plain Flute" (fig. 264) and Hawkes's creamer and sugar bowl in "Flutes and Greek Border" (fig. 313) are perfect examples of this phase.

The *American Home and Garden* magazine of June 1911 printed an article on "Decorating the Summer Home Cheaply." It recommended pressed glass colonial reproductions. More expensive cut pieces could be used in the city home (fig. 426).

Fig. 51. Vase, 10″, circa 1912-1919, in floral cutting. Blossoms in matte finish with silver diamond centers, miter leaves and stems polished, rayed base, simply notched edge. Reminiscent of some of McKee's work.

Another attempt to save the business was a change to naturalistic floral cutting (fig. 51). Three issues of *Good Housekeeping* in 1909 carried advertisements touting the new "Rose" pattern by Clark. The first, showing a picture of a heavily cut, brilliant bowl with thirty-two point hobstars and sections of hobnail, reminds the reader that "Clark Cut Glass is notable for the depth of cutting, high polish and water color, assuring rich and delicate effects." It then states (to prepare the reader for *next* month's advertisement):

Cut Glass stamped "Clark" — a standard brand among highest class dealers and connoisseurs for the past quarter century — may be had in new and beautiful patterns — masterpieces of art and craftsmanship. The latest, "Rose," is of unusual charm.

The next two advertisements show a footed vase and a tulip-shaped vase with an ordinary blossom whose petals are of fineline cutting and whose centers are crosshatched. The leaves are simple and miter-cut. The tulip vase has five bands of fine hobnail to separate the five panels, the "petals" of the vase. The propaganda calls the "Rose" pattern a "wide departure. It is of exquisite grace and workmanship, and so brilliant, so attractive in design, that it at once commands attention." The other notice says it is of "striking beauty, rich

in its delicacy; one of the most impressive ever made." To us, this is one of the ordinary, shallow floral cuttings.

In many cases, the company continued brilliant cutting on part of a piece, but left clear panels on which to cut or engrave floral decorations. This *transitional* style saved labor costs and re-educated public taste. The large fruit bowl (fig. 44) has a deeply cut hobstar covering the bottom and better-than-average floral cutting around the sides. The flower centers of tiny hobnail required skill and time, but the miter-cut leaves and stems saved many hours of cutting and polishing. Skilled cutters and good blanks were still obtainable in 1909 and beyond.

Several types of naturalistic cutting and engraving were for sale after 1900. Hawkes advertised Rock Crystal Glass in the *Ladies' Home Journal* in 1905, saying that it "differs from Hawkes Cut Glass, resembling more the ancient Intaglio or Cameo cutting of glass and crystal. It is made in diversified shapes, decorated with flowers, figures, or any form of freely playing ornament."

Of course, engraving was not new in 1900, as our study of the past has revealed. Styles in all forms of art are cyclic in character. Even while Brilliant Geometric cutting was at its height, some designers preferred to copy nature. H.P. Sinclaire, Jr., the leader of this movement toward graceful engraving, began in the late 1880s while he still worked for Hawkes. The several firms who made the finest intaglio-engraved pieces found them expensive to produce, so they limited output to those customers who could afford a high price. The pocketbook of the consumer determined the degree of excellence he purchased.

One economic solution for the problem of declining sales and rising overhead was substitution of the acid bath for wood-polishing. The smoother had spent hours polishing every cut on a wooden, cork, or walrus-hide wheel. Sometimes a brush wheel was used. This was invented by Dan Forbes of West Meriden, Connecticut, in March 1880. It consisted of "sections of brush-fiber with intermediate disks of fabric and paper" (patent #226,054). The new acid-polished ware sparkled, but on close inspection it had a pebbled look when held to reflect the light.

The first patent record for acid polishing was #220,137, 20 July 1880, by George F. Lapham, Sandwich, Massachusetts: "In combination with the ordinary hand or wheel cutting and polishing of an article of glass, the subsequent treatment of it by acid." About 1890, acid-dipping did it all for those who abandoned wood polishing for the faster method. This was a risky process for the workman. He had to dress in protective clothing, wear a mask, then time the immersion in acid on a stopwatch to prevent overexposure before dipping the glass in water to stop the action. Disposal of the waste was a secondary problem.

R. Wilkinson of Stourbridge, England, took over his brother's glassworks after Frank's death in 1927. He maintained that inhaling poisonous fumes from hydrofluoric and sulphuric acids so weakened the lungs that Frank died of pneumonia after a four-day illness.

Conscientious "old-timers" deplored acid dipping, which often smoothed the edges of the cuts so that they resembled common pressed glass to the touch.

Early in 1878, William Fox of Wheeling, West Virginia, patented a method of fire-polishing pressed glass to remove mold marks.

This information helps us to judge both age and quality of cut glass, as well as to learn how to discriminate between cut and pressed.

The Art Nouveau (New Art) movement was at its peak in France and England between 1890 and 1910. It's a wonder that this turning away from stiff, formal design toward free-flowing natural forms (fig. 407) did not sweep away the American taste for Brilliant cut glass altogether. Evidently the States were drifting farther and farther away from the countries of origin.

When World War I began in 1914, potash and other ingredients could no longer be imported. Lead, which was absolutely essential for production of fine glassware, was needed for ammunition. In 1917, when the U.S. entered the war, patriotic citizens turned their attention toward defeating the enemy under the hated "Kaiser Bill." Lavish entertainment was considered frivolous, even unpatriotic. Gone were the days of preoccupation with elaborate dress and rituals.

Colored Cut Glass

Many glasshouses had produced fine colored cutware during the Middle Period. These included Page & Bakewell, Mulvaney & Ledlie, and Fort Pitt Glass Works of Pittsburgh; C. Dorflinger & Sons of White Mills, Pennsylvania; Hobbs, Barnes & Company of Wheeling, West Virginia; New England Glass Company of Cambridge, Massachusetts; the Boston & Sandwich and Cape Cod Glass firms of Sandwich, Massachusetts; Jersey City Flint Glassworks in New Jersey; Brooklyn Flint Glass Works of Brooklyn, New York; and Joseph Stouvenal & Company of New York City.

Colored cut glass from the Brilliant Period is scarce and expensive. The Phoenix Glass Company, Monaca, Pennsylvania, founded in 1880, made a great deal of it. In fact, it specialized in cut glass of all colors, in solid as well as cased and flashed glass. In the cased glass, the colored layer was thick and of a brilliant color.

Gillinder & Sons of Philadelphia also made colored cut glass, but Dorflinger's is better known. Dorflinger's cased green glass, cut through to clear, is a fine, bright color, often blown thinner than average, sharply cut, and beautifully engraved (figs. C.3A and 3B, Cover).

Other companies (Bergen, Fry, Libbey, Hoare, Hawkes, Mount Washington, and Clark) found colored glass too expensive to manufacture beyond 1900, except on special order. According to Louise Boggess, co-author of *American Brilliant Cut Glass*, only certain pieces were made in color. Wine sets, punch sets, bowls, nappies, water carafes, vases, and plates were the most common. Few were advertised. The Weiner-Lipkowitz book, *Rarities in American Cut Glass*, shows outstanding items in turquoise, cranberry, green, blue, gold, and rainbow, which blended three or more colors. Few were signed.

Although colored cut perfume bottles were plentiful at the time of the Centennial Exhibition in 1876, they are seldom for sale.

We had in our collection only a pair of solid color candlesticks in rare apple green (fig. C.1), a green decanter with red and green wines (fig. C.2), and a green/clear, acid-cut-back cameo vase signed Honesdale (fig. C.4). When my husband and I started to buy in 1967, we passed over a low, 10″ bowl in green/clear, which I am now sure was by Dorflinger. We knew then that much new European glass has similar motifs, so decided to wait until we became more knowledgeable before buying anything in color. Now the few beautiful pieces for sale are extremely expensive, and the less costly are unattractive.

Presentation pieces of finest glass were often fitted with silver mounts, on which were engraved monograms, dates, and/or special occasions. Boxes, bottles, and cruets had silver fittings, also. Some fine specimens of silver/glass combinations will be shown in Chapter 10.

Pattern Names

Searching for pattern names is fascinating, but often frustrating. Among the thousands of designs are some that are easily recognized and are called by names familiar to everyone associated with interest in cut glass. "Brunswick" and "Queens" by Hawkes are two examples (figs. 306 and 307).

Some patterns are difficult to identify, if the design has been adapted to fit different shapes. "Lotus" by Egginton looks different when applied to a whiskey jug as opposed to a dish (figs. 367 and 366). Others are so complex that they can barely be deciphered.

Then too, not all patterns were given names by the manufacturer. Many catalogs listed some patterns by names and others by cutting number. Sinclaire may have called a pattern "RC 155," with the RC standing for Rock Crystal.

Dealers and writers have christened certain designs. Revi referred to a Libbey pattern (fig. 267) as "Star and Feather," citing Catalog #24. Boggess found it in a 1909 catalog, labeled "Star and Feather."

Pearson, in his first book, showed a reproduction of patent drawing #38,000, 8 May 1906, and decided to call it "Stalks and Stars" for "reference purposes and calculated to help recall the design." In later books, he gave it the catalog name.

As if this were not enough, two or more companies might cut the same pattern. Dorflinger and Hawkes both cut "Brazilian." Sometimes two or three companies collaborated in filling a large order. Hoare's "Monarch" (fig. 384) is identical to O'Connor's "Napoleon." The wholesale house, Higgins & Seiter, illustrated it in their 1899 catalog as "Napoleon," so we may assume they were selling O'Connor glass. Nevertheless, they also listed the O'Connor "Princess" (patented 19 February 1895) and sold it under the name "H.&S." They sold Dorflinger's "Renaissance" under its correct name, but did not identify *any* maker of the glass they handled. Who could imagine at that time that this ware would be collected and appreciated as art objects? Who could foresee the vexation caused in years to come by these oversights?

Design Patents

Throughout the last quarter of the nineteenth century, many patents for improved furnaces and tools and methods for putting bubbles into glass or decorating the surface appeared. The first evidence of "Decorative Cutting of Polished Glass Globes" was patent #243,579 in 1881. This was not cutting as we know it. "Glass is cut to resemble diamonds by coating with glue and causing the glue to contract so as to tear out pieces of glass."

Wheel-cut patterns appeared in a minor way on such items as "a radiant flower, a dahlia" cut on the side of glass globes for lamps in 1871. A pressed-glass clockcase engraved on the front was also registered in 1871.

It is difficult to locate registered cut glass patterns because copies of the design drawings were not shown in the Patent Gazette until April 1892. Yet we know

that "Russian" was patented by Hawkes 20 June 1882.

The design patent relates only to the appearance of the article, not to its construction or composition. Only the actual creator could apply for the patent, but he could assign it to his employer, as designers often did. The patent's duration was for three and a half, seven, or fourteen years, depending on the fee paid at the time of filing. At its expiration, the design lapsed into the public domain if not renewed.

The reason for patenting a design is obvious. The maker wished to prevent others from imitating it. Unfortunately, rival firms frequently "broke" the pattern by changing just enough of the design to avoid prosecution in a United States district court. In fact, some designers were hired because they were experts in

Fig. 53. Catalog illustrations of J. D. Bergen's "Caprice," 1904-1905, and P&B's "Bowa," circa 1907, closely resemble the Libbey celery dish in Figure 52.

Fig. 52. Celery tray, 12″ × 5″, signed Libbey/circle. Elongated figure-eight on base is formed by curved double splits (with notches on the prism), that cross in the middle and at ends where fans lie between the splits. A band of hobstars crosses the middle; smaller bands divide the notched prism sides halfway to the ends. Vesicas contain zigzag, prism-centered stars.

plagiarism. The celery tray signed Libbey (fig. 52), compared with two catalog drawings from other firms (fig. 53), is an excellent example of the slight changes that could be overlooked by the customer.

Trademarks on Cut and Engraved Glass

The Trademark Act of 1946 defines a trademark as "any word, name, symbol, or device, or any combination thereof adopted and used by a manufacturer or merchant to identify his goods and to distinguish them from those manufactured or sold by others." According to Dr. Arthur G. Peterson's scholarly study (1968), "over two hundred companies in the United States have used four hundred or more trademarks on blown, pressed, cut and engraved glass."

The use of trademarks as signatures on glassware began to a small extent in the early 1860s. The first registration of a trademark for glass tableware was the word "CENTENNIAL," by Thomas G. Cook of Philadelphia, #1201, 8 April 1873. Trademarks in the 1870s were used chiefly by lamp makers. Under the Act of 1881, new registrations were good for thirty years. But since 1905, continual protection of a trademark can be provided by renewal every twenty years. (Patents on inventions expire in seventeen years with no provision for renewal.) A trademark may be transferred and renewed as long as the mark is used in interstate or foreign commerce.

Some trademarks were never registered, but those that were are an indication of pride in a good product and a cherished reputation. Some were registered after being used for many years. J. Hoare & Company registered theirs 12 May 1914, stating that they had used the mark on cut glass since early in 1895.

Trademarks or signatures pressed in the glass (such as the embossed Heisey H within a diamond) have an advantage over etched or engraved signatures, and especially over the paper label, which was usually washed off at once. Etched marks are sometimes worn away after long usage.

We were fortunate in finding two pieces with original paper labels: the berry bowl in "Diamond Poinsettia" (called "Starflower" by Revi), signed MORECROFT CUT CRYSTAL (fig. 54), and the "Old Colony" Dorflinger Bowl (fig. 284), shown later with other Dorflinger pieces. The Morecroft label was glued near the edge, as shown in the photograph, while the Dorflinger sticker may be seen as a black spot in the center of the bottom. Discovery of such labels is thrilling to the serious collector.

Libbey's cut glassware was also marked with a paper label until 21 April 1896, when the company registered the name "Libbey" over a curved saber, to be etched or engraved "on every piece." A greatly enlarged signature is shown here (fig. 55). The earlier paper label depicted an eagle with spread wings, holding three arrows in each claw.

Fig. 54. Berry bowl, 7″ × 3½″, in "Diamond Poinsettia," signed MORECROFT CUT CRYSTAL on original label, ⅝″ l, which has a silver border and letters on a blue background. No signs of wear on the clear glass. A butterfly is on the bottom; miter-cut leaves and stems in three sprays flow gracefully around bowl. Flower petals were left gray. The center, made of a hobnail with six points, resembling a jewel, is polished.

Fig. 55. This Libbey-over-the-saber mark, used from 1896 to 1906, at the height of the Brilliant Period, was acid-etched on a flat portion of the fluted neck of a carafe (fig. 254) in the "Senora" pattern. The tails of L and y are not connected. The mark measures ⅜″ from handle to tip of blade of the sword.

Companies did not always adhere to the registered symbol. Straus, for instance, registered a circle with a diamond cutting in the center, STRAUS printed above and CUT GLASS below the faceted center. The etched mark on the glass has always been a five-pointed star within a tiny circle. Perhaps the former was used on a paper label and on letterheads, since the registered legend reads "on glass or label."

Farrar and Spillman, in their authoritative book on Corning glass, say that when a designer changed companies, it was customary for him to take his patterns with him. The former employer would drop these designs from his line.

The Ideal Cut Glass Company was founded in Corning in 1902 and closed in 1933. It was moved to Canastota, New York, in 1904. Frederick Morecroft held two positions in the firm: secretary in 1908 (when W.B. Hitchcock, a wholesale jeweler of Syracuse, bought the company), and president after the owner's death. "Diamond Poinsettia," the firm's most successful design (fig. 54), was created by Tom Burns, foreman, but was registered under the name of "Frederick L. Morecroft, Syracuse, New York," filed 27 May 1912, granted 11 November 1913. Only the starflower is shown in the patent drawing. This registered flower exemplifies perfectly how a patented, simple motif could be combined with other motifs. My bowl has a butterfly, while the vase-lamp of a friend has stems and leaves with starflower. Both pieces were cut on fine blanks, but a vase and two bowls on wavy, inferior glass (probably cut during World War I) were seen at shows.

Ideal had no trademark, so why the "Morecroft Cut Crystal" label? Did Morecroft own a separate shop of his own? We know he was still with Ideal as late as 1927 when he registered a ship design, called "Constitution" by Revi.

Although the trademark or signature generally indicates the origin of manufacture, the *private brand mark* may not. A dealer may have purchased cut glass from one or several companies and placed his own mark upon the glass. A jeweler may have bought the glass, then marked his silver fitting, as did Shreve & Company on the martini pitcher (fig. 110). Or a jeweler might add his mark to that of the maker of the silver fitting, as did C. D. Peacock in the pair of decanters (fig. 106).

Sometimes a retailer, who stamped his own mark upon the glass, requested that the manufacturer withhold his signature. The sauce bowl (fig. 56) is signed T.M.J., the private brand of T. M. James & Sons of Kansas City, Missouri, agent for Libbey cutware as early as 1893.

Canadian dealers often stamped their marks on unmarked glass or added the dealer's name to that of the maker.

Fraudulent signatures, incised or stamped with hydrofluoric acid, can be added at any time after the glass has cooled. We have seen false signatures:

TUTHILL on large, paneled twin vases, which looked modern and European; CLARK on a huge two-piece punch bowl of poor quality; and FRY on a modern basket, made recently in Europe (fig. 420). The latter has a spurious FRY scratched with a stylus into the side of a miter cut on the bottom. Forgeries are not common, but have been perpetrated.

Novice collectors who hear that glass is signed might logically imagine the cutter's or engraver's signature somewhere on the glass. Sometimes the artist *has* signed his name on the glass, but generally the signature is the trademark of the company.

A signature can be difficult to spot. Take the item to a window in the daytime, then tip it away so light glances off the surface. The mark should not be opaque, for that would call attention to it and blemish the surface of the piece.

Some marks are so prominent that one can look directly at them and see them at once. Others are worn or were not well imprinted in the first place. Many Clark signatures are faint and hard to find.

A shopkeeper once asked me to find a signature on a celery tray. She said the seller had assured her it was marked HOARE, but neither she nor her husband could locate the mark. I spent all of five minutes, tilting the piece this way and that, until finally a complete, but very faint, signature came into view. We marked the spot with tape to avoid losing it again.

After finding a Hawkes advertisement showing my syrup jug (figs. 97A and 97B) and advising the reader that every Hawkes piece is marked, I looked many times and found nothing. While explaining the situation to a visiting collector, he picked it up and exclaimed, "Here it is! A tiny trefoil at the base under the handle."

Fig. 56. Sauce bowl, 6″ × 2½″, is signed T.M.J., the private brand of T. M. James of Kansas City, Missouri. Bottom is cut like a hobstar within a hobstar. Bands of hobnail cross to create an expanding six-point star, covering the entire piece. Between points lie pinwheels with eight vanes and zigzag centers. (Seymour)

He had held it just right so that reflected light disclosed a faint mark. This location proves that the top has not been removed and resilvered. If it had, chances are that the silversmith would have replaced the fitting in such a way that the signature would be rotated away from the customary location directly under the handle.

Another collector/friend wrote recently to say that, after looking at an ice cream plate for four years, she has finally found a smeared Egginton mark.

Bowls are generally marked on the inside, in or near the center of the bottom, or near the top edge. Creamers, sugars, and pitchers are signed either on the top flat surface of the handle or on a clear surface beside or under the handle. A carafe may be signed on a flute on the neck or on a side surface near the base. Plates may be marked in the center inside, or near the edge, inside or outside. A few pieces, so finely cut that there were no clear areas, have been signed on a side of a deep miter cut. Keep looking! You may be happily surprised.

On one occasion, my husband was holding a beautiful tray up to the light. Suddenly he exclaimed, "Come here, Louise. Look what I found!" Near the edge was a tiny Libbey-in-a-circle, which even the dealer had overlooked. We agreed that if she had known it was there, she would have charged at least $25 more for the tray.

We have read that perhaps 10 percent of all cut glass pieces were signed. At one time, we calculated that 18 percent of our collection was signed, although we never let the signature influence a purchase. Most dealers charge more for signed pieces, which is understandable. New buyers perhaps are safer in buying signed items until they acquire sufficient knowledge to discriminate wisely. Hopefully this can be accomplished in a few months through study of this text and observation of good pieces at shows, in shops, and in private collections. Remember that a signature does not guarantee fine quality.

Some say that the earliest signatures were placed only on outstanding pieces by certain companies. This has not yet been verified. Although some firms declared in advertisements as early as 1891 that every genuine piece was signed, this was not true. Many times, only one piece in a set was marked. (See figs. 386 and 391 in the Clark section.) Hawkes and Libbey seem to have made the best effort in this direction, but even their stampers or engravers may have missed a few. We have a signed Hawkes Gravic celery and a matching nappy (fig. 314), the latter of which omits the word "Gravic" from the mark for no apparent reason.

8

Advertising, Distribution, and Prices

Before 1890, too many people regarded our glassware as inferior to that of Europe. Wholesale and retail dealers often represented American-made glass as European to their clients, actually showing inferior European ware to customers who asked to see American glass.

Advertising

The fact that dealers pretended that fine American glassware was European so enraged American manufacturers that they launched an expensive advertising campaign in the 1890s to change the situation. Now we realize that American rich cut glass outshone European products. Strangely, American cut glass was recognized abroad as a superior product. In an advertisement in *Life* and other magazines in 1891 and thereafter, Hawkes kept reminding Americans that Hawkes cut glass had "gained the award of Grand Prize, Paris 1889". Many companies included the words "genuine American cut glass" in their descriptions.

Manufacturers, cutting shops, wholesalers, and retailers often published illustrated catalogs. Catalogs of any sort of item were first issued in the 1850s, giving names or numbers to the products. Those for glassware, first printed circa 1880, identify cut patterns and their makers, if the catalogs were published by the manufacturer.

Some companies issued catalog pages, which they gave to jobbers and wholesalers. From these, the jobbers made up their own catalogs with their names on the covers. Often wholesale firms invented pattern names for pieces bought from several firms. This makes it impossible for the collector to learn the true origin of his piece, even when he locates it in the catalog. Higgins & Seiter of New York was in this category, as were many wholesale jewelers.

Fig. 57. Slide, 3¼″ × 4″, including black passepartout paper frame, made to flash on the screen of the local theater, advertises Libbey Cut Glass, sold by Simmers & Freitag, "Baker City's Only Exclusive Jewelers." This mark, with tails of *L* and *y* joined, was used from 1906 to 1913. When etched on glass, the motto, "The World's Best," was omitted.

Some factories advertised in periodicals. Hawkes placed an advertisement in 1910 in *Ladies' Home Journal*, testifying that Hawkes Cut Glass was still cut from the solid blown blank:

The difference in the finish is unmistakable. The pressed blank is dull, lustreless. Its appearance is that of a cheap, molded article. Glass cut from a pressed blank may be easily detected by passing the fingers lightly over the inside of the article. Wherever the cutting on the outside is deepest, a slight swelling on the inside will be noticeable to the touch. Hawkes Cut Glass is genuine...absolutely flawless...perfectly smooth. It has a brilliance, a beauty only equaled by that of a diamond. When held to the light Hawkes Cut Glass is as clear as crystal.

Here we have the best criteria for judging good cut glass.

A few companies made slides of glass products to flash on the screen in local theaters (fig. 57). These early "commercials" were shown with business notices between the newsreel and the feature picture.

Some factories had their own showrooms, to which retailers came to choose merchandise. Some had retail shops as well. Dorflinger had both in New York City. The 1895 *Ladies' Home Journal* carried an advertisement saying, "The only store in the world exclusively devoted to CUT GLASS. For those who cannot come we have prepared a pamphlet, to be had for the asking." The Ohio Cut Glass Company had showrooms in New York City, Chicago, and St. Louis.

Some sent salesmen "on the road" with samples. These men either rented a hotel room to display samples (carried in special trunks padded to prevent breakage) or called upon retail stores to take orders. Wholesale catalogs were sent across the country to retail outlets too widely scattered to visit.

Distribution

We often hear that cut glass was sold by jewelers. This is true of the highest grade. Some makers, such as M. J. Averbeck of New York City and Honesdale, Pennsylvania, boasted that they "sold exclusively to the retail jewelry trade." Averbeck claimed that all their cut glass was "as good as it can be made;...all, whether low or high in price, is cut deep and highly polished...ranks with the best." As manufacturing jewelers, Averbeck sold diamonds, gold jewelry, and sterling novelties in New York City from 1892 to 1923. In the mail-order catalog (circa 1900-1909) listing cut glass, they declared that it was made and cut at Honesdale "in our own factory," and that every piece was marked with their trademark. The banana bowl pictured (fig. 58) is precisely like the "Oval Bowl or Dish" in the "Genoa" pattern, priced at $14, but is unsigned. Perhaps they used a paper label, as well as an etched trademark.

Some prominent jewelers who published catalogs listing cut glass (as shown in Ehrhardt's *Price Guide*, 1973) were M. Bazzett, A. C. Becken, and Gordon & Morrison of Chicago; S. F. Myers of New York City (manufacturer and wholesaler); and Wm. Volker of Kansas City. Studying the designs for sale in a particular year is helpful in tracing the evolution of design.

Fig. 58. Banana bowl, 10″ × 7″ × 4″, in "Genoa" by M. J. Averbeck. Large thirty-two-point hobstar on each end; smaller twenty-point hobstar on each side; four "new moons" of cane; notched prisms and fans. Clear buttons and areas of fine glass left uncut produce a dramatic effect.

As will be seen in the chapter on silver fittings, some jewelers attached their own silver mounts, then stamped them with their *personal brand*. The most prestigious names were Tiffany, Shreve & Company, Gorham, and Reed & Barton. C. G. Alford & Company functioned as a retail jewelry outlet in New York City from about 1872 to 1918. They did not manufacture glass, but did stamp ALFORD in a lozenge on the cut glass they sold.

Good department stores also handled cut glass, from the finest to the average grade. I was going mad trying to find "C. D. Peacock," stamped on the silver stoppers of a pair of decanters (fig. 106). Looking back through photocopies of magazine advertisements, I found the name in a May 1906 *Ladies' Home Journal.* There was a cream and sugar set cut in pinwheels, to be "sent to any address, charges prepaid, for only $3.50." The store offered free "the great Peacock shopping guide, containing 6,000 photographs of suitable gifts for all occasions." C. D. Peacock was established in 1837, "the oldest store in Chicago."

The Peacock advertisement was typically persuasive, reminding the reader that "cut glass is always in good taste. It is to the table what diamonds are to the evening toilet — The Finishing Touch. It beautifies the table as nothing else can. Silver shines, but real Cut Glass sparkles." It is easy to see how the public could be swept along with enthusiasm for this luxury.

T. B. Clark & Company of Honesdale, Pennsylvania, whose flowery advertisements were quoted previously, offered to send a booklet to the customer who could not find Clark Cut Glass at his dealer.

Crown Cut Glass Company of Pittsburgh sold directly to the public. A 1903 advertisement in *Ladies' Home Journal* describes a special offer ". . . to introduce to you the richest, most brilliantly beautiful cut glass ever made in America. For June weddings, is your pocketbook limited to a $5.00 present? Here is a beautiful Cut Glass Bowl — delivered free to any point East of the Mississippi for $5.00."

Colonial Cut Glass Works at Trenton, New Jersey, also sold by mail order, "saving you the middlemen's profits, half the price asked by the dealer." A sugar and cream set for $3.50, express prepaid, was offered in 1903 "with privilege of examination. We refund money promptly and pay express charges both ways on any purchase which may not suit."

Liberty Cut Glass Works of Egg Harbor City, New Jersey, in 1902 offered at "a saving of at least 40 percent" a two-piece sugar and cream set for $3.75 with a free catalog. In 1903, a 5″ footed violet vase "designed from the newest French model" sold for $1.50. "A dealer would have charged $5.00."

In 1904 an advertisement showing a club-shaped bonbon at $3.50, cut in hobstar and cane, was run by the Lackawanna Cut Glass Company of Scranton, Pennsylvania, to be ordered directly from the maker.

At least one company gave free samples. The Enterprise Specialty Company of Wheeling, West Virginia, in 1906 offered free a cream pitcher or a jelly stand. One had only to cut out the picture and send it with ten cents "to defray expressage." The offer was limited.

Some makers sold straight to the consumer by mail order, while others sent their ware to wholesalers for distribution, in which case their identity was often lost. Some large outlets sold cut glass from many manufacturers to retailers and also to consumers by mail.

Among wholesalers who handled cut glass and other gift items were Lewis & Conger of New York City. They also sold etched and gold-banded glass, and the "very finest English China."

Wanamaker's of New York City published a gift and toy catalog in 1910 for "Christmas Gifts by Mail." Their December advertisement in *Ladies' Home Journal* depicts the 8″ "Wanamaker Christmas Fern Dish" with silverplated liner and three feet, geometrically cut "on the sides and on the bottom," placed on a mirrored, 10″ footed plateau of white metal base, quadruple-silverplated. It sold for $5.

Abram French & Company of Boston sold "a full line of tableware and ornamental goods in china, crockery, and glass." *Life*, in 1891, showed a beautiful pottery jardiniere on a pedestal in one issue and a 9″ cut glass bowl in "our own pattern" in another. The bowl weighed over four pounds and was cut in English strawberry diamond and large fans. Its price was $10 — a month's wages for many in that year.

William Volker & Company of Kansas City, Missouri, handled art goods — paintings, pedestals, pottery, and china — in addition to cut glass. Reprints of a 1909 wholesale catalog appear in Ehrhardt's cut glass *Price Guide* of 1973.

Pitkin & Brooks Company, a large wholesale glass and china distributor, was formed in 1877 in Chicago by Edward Hand Pitkin and Jonathan William Brooks. They owned and operated a factory in Chicago and controlled and operated two more there. They also owned a cutting shop at Bowling Green, Ohio (called Ohio Cut Glass Company) and the Pitkin & Brooks Cut Glass Factory in Valparaiso, Indiana, established in 1911.

Pitkin & Brooks was the only company to sell three grades of glass: *P&B*, their finest, hand-finished grade: *Standard*, "superior to 75 percent of cut glass manufactured in this country"; and *Imported*, made abroad in large quantities to Pitkin & Brooks specifications, "superior to the product of some American manufacturers."

The trademark shown in the 1907 catalog was P&B on a fleur-de-lis with DIAMOND above and CUT GLASS below, within a circle. Marks actually seen on some of their glassware consist of P&B within a diamond-shaped frame. Only the finest grade was signed. The punch bowl and cups (fig. 59) illustrate their "Korea" design, so named by Revi, patented by W. P. Feeney for the company, 21 October 1913. Two signed cruets (fig. 464) may be seen in Chapter 18. An individual berry bowl in "Athole" is also pictured (fig. 447).

Marshall Field & Company in Chicago set up separate areas for wholesale and retail trade in the 1880s. In 1887, Mr. Field constructed an entire building to serve the wholesale division, encouraging retailers to come there to choose jewelry and fashions. He had only a few "general salesmen" to visit retail stores. My father, who managed a store selling dry-goods, shoes, and clothing in Kirksville, Missouri, from 1918 to 1927, used to "go to market" twice a year to either St. Louis or Chicago.

Field's 1896 jewelry catalog also contained cut glass, eyeglasses, clocks, and lampshades. This was soon after the depression of 1893, when relatively few could afford luxuries. Yet many fortunes had been made during Chicago's rapid growth as a railroad center

Fig. 59. Punch bowl, 12″×6″, and cups, signed P&B, in "Korea" (named by Revi). Chain of hobstars around top, flower motif #44753 altered to fit size of piece. Five motifs in bowl, one in bottom of cup. Polished miter-cut stems and leaves complete transitional design. Clear, heavy blank. (Bowl courtesy of Taylor's Treasures)

and due to its fame as the site of the World's Columbian Exposition in 1893-1894. The 1896 trade catalog displayed fine merchandise not found anywhere west of Pittsburgh. Small-town merchants could not afford to carry a stock of the more expensive items for the relatively few members of social aristocracy, so they would show the catalog to their customers, then place an order for them.

The reproduction of this Field catalog (by the Gun Digest Publishing Company in 1970) shows nine pages of Rich Cut Glass, a line of "American Cut Glass at popular prices." It does not identify the manufacturer, but features two of "our own Special Designs," the "Cayuga" and "Owasco" patterns. Other patterns have only catalog numbers. "Our prices are always the lowest."

Ehrhardt's *Price Guide* reproduces thirty pages of Marshall Field's 1911-1912 catalog. We hear so much about floral designs at this time, but the majority shown here were geometrically cut. There were some Buzz designs, some transitional, and some floral engraving, but there were still many of the traditional brilliant patterns. Of course, there is no way to tell how many were on figured blanks or by which method they were polished. No pattern names or manufacturers are listed, although we do recognize several well-known companies' designs.

Sears, Roebuck & Company, also of Chicago, bore this name for the first time in 1893, having passed through many transformations. By 1900 the company sold everything for the home, surely at the lowest prices in America. Mr. Sears, who wrote most of his own promotional materials, addressed himself candidly

to merchants. He declared that they would not get one cent off the retail price for any amount of merchandise, but that they could afford to send orders for customers (most of whom would not make the effort to order for themselves), make a profit, and keep the trade that might go elsewhere for items not stocked in local stores. If the merchant wished to buy for resale, he could be assured that the Sears name would not appear anywhere on the merchandise. At this time, 1900, Sears carried only a pressed imitation of cutware. "Your neighbors will pronounce it genuine cut glass." Thirty-nine pieces sold for $2.75!

The 1908 catalog showed similar imitation cut glass. Forty-eight pieces sold for $3.39. If truly cut, they could have retailed for "not less than $150.00." A small section showed genuine cut glass in six designs, one of which was a "Heart" pattern — an 8″ bowl on a mirrored plateau for $5.98. A salt and pepper shaker set with sterling silver tops was $1.25.

By this time, the postal system was becoming increasingly reliable, so the farmer could beat the high margin/low inventory disadvantages of the local store by means of mail order from Sears, or from Montgomery Ward, also based in Chicago.

New York's Higgins & Seiter, established in 1887, had by 1899 become the largest mail-order company in glass and china in the United States. The firm sold to anyone (if reached by freight or express lines) "at 25 percent less than usual prices" the finest products "of the world, in variety beyond precedent or competition," with a money-back guarantee. Illustrations show clearly some of the best cuttings by renowned manufacturers, but unfortunately, pattern names were often changed and the makers not identified.

The rare matching whiskey bottles or decanters pictured (fig. 60) are identical with those in the 1899 Higgins & Seiter catalog. The pattern is "Georgia." The search is still on to discover the maker. The same decanter, without a handle, was sold in tantalus sets with either two or three bottles at $30 and $40. The same set with three bottles and twelve matching tumblers sold for $59. With two bottles and six tumblers, it was $40.50. This pair of decanters is now valued at well over $2,000, but sold then for $10 and $12 apiece!

The *tantalus* was a frame of mahogany or oak with brass trim at the base and a brass handle on top. It was fitted with a lock to protect the master's liquor from larcenous servants and curious children. Cigar jars came similarly protected by an elegant frame. Some frames were silver-plated.

Higgins & Seiter advertised in family magazines, offering, besides the 25 percent discount, a free book "on request only" — a book called "Serving a Dinner" by the prestigious Oscar of the Waldorf.

Fig. 60. Pair of whiskey bottles, 13″, one with handle, in 1899 Higgins & Seiter catalog as "Georgia." Stoppers shaped like corks cut in chain of lozenges cut in silver diamond, properly called "English Strawberry Diamond." Top of each cork has a sixteen-point single star and a notched edge. The lapidary-cut ring lip is unusual. Neck is fluted with beading and quadruple horizontal cuts. Handle is double-notched with double crosscuts at intersections. Principal design consists of three hobstars, hexagons and pentagons of cane with clear buttons, and vertical columns of bullseyes. Bottles are sharply cut on brilliant blanks and are wood-polished.

The catalog is an excellent source for identification of old china (English, French, German, and Austrian); plateaux and handled mirrors used as trays; Russian copper and brass novelties; electroliers (table lamps) in the Art Nouveau style; marble busts and pedestals from Italy; hall clocks; teakwood pedestals from the Orient; Dutch pottery; and other art goods. At headquarters there was an art gallery for selection of paintings.

Also illustrated are satin-lined boxes of white leatherette containing sets of china or cut glass. Under the satin lining were indentations made to hold each piece in its place. This was a practical plan to enable the breakable ware to arrive safely, then to serve as storage in the home. A china chocolate set, an ice cream set, or a dozen plates (hand-painted and all different) made a

lovely wedding gift. As highly or more highly prized was a boxed set of a dozen cut glass tumblers at $7.50 to $18.50; a salad, fruit, or berry bowl in its own case at $5.50 to $16.50; a whiskey decanter with six matching glasses at $19.50; a dozen punch cups at $11.50; or a celery tray for $5. Ice cream sets also came in gift boxes, although none were shown in the 1899 catalog. Remember these prices when we discuss workmen's wages.

Cut Glass in Advertising Other Products

As a sign of the times and as proof of the prestige and popularity of cut glass, advertisements of various products featured illustrations showing those products served elegantly in cut glass vessels.

In December 1897, *Life* depicted two alcoholic products of G. F. Heublein & Brother of Hartford (Connecticut), New York City, and London. An illustration of a formally dressed *bon vivant*, seated in a wicker chair next to a table with a bottle of Heublein Cocktails and a lamp, shows him with an arrogant mien, lighting a cigarette. A long exposition follows, touting the superiority of the bottled mixed drink, as compared with an uncertain product mixed at the bar. Then a hint of female emancipation:

> In the past, the male sex were the only ones privileged to partake of that daintiest of American drinks, the "Cocktail." With the innovation of Club Cocktails it has been made possible for the gentler sex to satisfy its curiosity in regard to the concoction about which so much has been written and said, and which has heretofore not been obtainable by them.

Below is shown an enormous punch bowl with large hobstar, fans, and other motifs (and with matching cups) advertising Heublein's Club Punch, "as delicious to drink as it's easy to make." The invention of the cocktail led to two new pieces of cut glass: the cocktail shaker, fitted with a silver top, and stemmed cocktail glasses, which were wider at the top than wines.

Even Puffed Wheat and Puffed Rice, advertised by the Quaker Oats Company (December 1910 in *Ladies' Home Journal*, used a beautiful floral bowl, cut in the same style as Hoare's "Shagbark" pattern, to serve fruit and cereal. "Serve the crisp grains in a separate dish, and let the folks scatter them over the fruit. The blend is very enticing and it modifies the tart of the fruit." As to the cereals, "People are eating fifteen million dishes a month." By 1913, Puffed Wheat was shown in china bowls.

Fig. 61. Advertisement in July 1912 *Ladies' Home Journal* (p. 34) for Welch's Grape Juice, showing brilliant-cut punch bowl and cups, in addition to lemonade pitcher and tumblers.

The Charles B. Knox Company (in the same magazine) offered a booklet with recipes for making candy with Knox Gelatine. The illustration is a cut glass compote full of candy cubes. The compote is different from any seen today. It has a zigzag edge, about 1″ deep, in clear glass. Below are diamond fields cut in silver diamond, separated by fans pointing up and down. The foot is similarly cut, and the stem is cut in lozenges and prisms.

Welch's Grape Juice (*Ladies' Home Journal*, July 1912) gave recipes for Welch's Grape Punch and Lemonade, served in elegant vessels of cut glass (Fig. 61).

Products for Care of Cut Glass

The care of cut glass led to concoctions for cleaning it "to restore the original fire and brilliancy." In 1902, Bevy Brothers of Detroit advertised in *Ladies' Home Journal* their "Colonial Spirits put up in sealed packages only" for this purpose.

In 1907 the same magazine ran an advertisement for Pearline. "Stop using Soap — and Wash all Glass with PEARLINE. Nothing so mars the Beauty of Choice Glassware as the Filmy Cloud that remains after Washing with Soap in the Old-Style-Way." A demure maid in uniform and cap is shown washing five items of brilliant cut glass in Pearline.

This was in direct competition with the Ivory Soap factory, which as early as 1893 had offered prizes for the best twelve pieces of verse suitable for publication, praising the use of Ivory for washing cut glass. An advertisement in *Ladies' Home Journal*, January 1912, still advised using Ivory on cut glass so that "it will sparkle like stars on a winter's night."

To counteract advertisements for special glass-cleaning products, Ivory stressed its mildness. Philosophically, the Victorian work ethic was opposing the new instant, effortless life-style. "Reject any soap or washing compound that will cleanse without an expenditure of time and labor. Ivory will do the work as quickly as it can be done with safety (*Ladies' Home Journal*, 1897)."

Ownership of "rich cut glass" serves as a tangible link with that life that now seems to have been simpler, more romantic, and less hectic than the present.

9

Evolution of a Glass Factory: Mount Washington/ Pairpoint

Of the companies that were noted for cut lead glass in the Early and Middle Periods, only a few survived past 1876. Bakewell of Pittsburgh lasted until 1882, but its fine cut and engraved ware declined in quality toward the end to become a commercial pressed product. Phoenix Glass Works, also of Pittsburgh, made some of the finest cut and colored flint glass in America before it closed in 1880. The New England and the Boston & Sandwich lasted until 1888. New England then became the famous Libbey Glass Company of Toledo, Ohio. Mount Washington, organized by Deming Jarves, became part of the Pairpoint Corporation in 1894.

Among the firms overlapping the Middle and Brilliant Periods was the Corning Glass Works in New York, 1868-1964. Amory Houghton, Sr., operated Union Glass Works in Somerville, Massachusetts, in 1852. He bought John Gilliland's Brooklyn Flint Glass Works near South Ferry, New York, in 1864, then moved to Corning in 1868, where he and his brother-in-law, Henry P. Sinclaire, set up the Corning Flint Glass Works. There he made superb glass exclusively for cutters Hoare and Daily, who set up a cutting shop on the second floor. Later he sold to other shops, mainly Hawkes and Sinclaire. Several of his descendants sat on the board of the First National City Bank, headquarters of the William Rockefeller branch of the Rockefeller network of financiers. The Houghtons still owned 30 percent of Corning Glass Works in 1975.

Glasshouses of the Brilliant Period

There were a thousand cutting shops during the Brilliant Period, but many did not turn out high quality pieces of lasting value. Some cut figured blanks, while others operated for a short time or left no record of their work.

Some manufacturers had cutting shops and, in addition, sold to other cutters. For example, Pairpoint made, cut, and engraved glass, but also sold blanks to Meriden Cut Glass Company in Connecticut and to Hope Glass Works in Providence, Rhode Island. Hope Glass Works in turn supplied cut glass to Gorham to combine with their silver fittings. Some of the factories engaged cutters and engravers to decorate glass in home workshops.

Mount Washington/Pairpoint

As one of the prize winners at the Centennial Exposition, Mount Washington/Pairpoint of New Bedford, Massachusetts, helped to launch the Brilliant Period. Its interesting history can actually be traced to the present time. The physical plant was one of the most substantial and complete in the country.

Comments by some cut glass aficionados (and even some dealers) imply that many people recognize only pieces engraved in butterflies, mitered leaves, and flowers as being Pairpoint in origin. On the contrary, many geometrically cut designs were made there. An undated Pairpoint catalog contained 138 patterns for engraved glass, several transitional pieces, and thirty-three designs of the Brilliant style. George C. Avila, writing *The Pairpoint Story,* divided production of American glass into these periods: Early, 1771-1830; Middle, 1830-1880; Brilliant 1880-1905; Pairpoint, 1905-1939; and Gunderson, 1940-1956.

One forerunner of Pairpoint was the New Bedford Glass Company. It was founded in 1866 by several workmen who left the Sandwich Glass Factory after a dispute with the management. The new company was financed originally by merchants of this Massachusetts city, known as the whaling capital of the world. Whaling reached its peak in 1857, when 329 whaling ships were registered. Decline set in with a shifting of hunting grounds, and especially with the 1859 discovery of petroleum in Pennsylvania. Petroleum displaced whale oil as an illuminant in lamps and as a lubricant for machinery.

The name of another forerunner, Mount Washington Glass Works, came from a factory built in South Boston in 1837 by Deming Jarves, agent for the Boston & Sandwich Glass Company. Established for his son George (twelve years old at the time), the business was conducted by a Captain Luther Russell until Russell's death in 1855.

In 1839 Labree & Jarves (John D. and George D., respectively) was listed as a glass factory and maker of lamps and chandeliers. From 1840 to 1860, it operated under the name Jarves and Cormerais. When George died of consumption in 1850, Henry Cormerais carried on the business. He was joined by William L. Libbey as bookkeeper in 1851 and Timothy Howe as clerk in 1856. The glass factory was first listed as the Mount Washington Glass Works (the firm's generally accepted name) in the Boston City Directory in 1856.

The business closed in 1861, then was taken over by Howe and Libbey. When Mr. Howe died in 1866, his interest was purchased by Libbey. By 1869, dissatisfied with the old run-down plant, Libbey bought the aforementioned New Bedford Glass Company for $35,000 in January 1870. This plant had had a short life due to financial problems.

Having moved to a new location, Mr. Libbey used the original South Boston name, Mount Washington Glass Works, even though the firm name of record was then the W. L. Libbey Company. Captain Henry Libbey joined the company when an increase in business required more capital.

Libbey's newly acquired factory in New Bedford was well-designed. A commodious glasshouse, twenty by thirty feet in area and three stories high, had been erected in 1866-1867. It was fireproof, with brick walls and floors, an iron door, and corrugated iron roof. It had a ten-pot furnace (sixty-two feet square) in the middle of the main building, annealing ovens or kilns (fifty feet long), a selecting room, a mold room, and an office on the first floor. Large machine and cutting shops, as well as an office for the designer, were on the second floor. Stock and chandelier rooms occupied the third floor. The basement contained a mill room for grinding and mixing clay, a sand room, a cinder pit, an ashery for purifying alkalis, engine rooms, and a carpenter shop. The building was heated by steam and had two elevators.

Aside from the main factory, there were other spacious buildings. A decorating shop for Art Glass had three large kilns for firing the ware. A cooper shop provided space for making the packages to be shipped.

There were also a storage building for packed goods, clay and pot rooms, a blacksmith shop, and a boiler shop. Stables were located on an adjacent lot. Supplies were delivered to and from an extensive water frontage nearby.

The making of glass was begun in the basement by mixing ingredients in a large trough. Fine white silica from the Berkshire mines in western Massachusetts was the principal ingredient. To the silica was added potash, soda, alumina, oxide of lead, lime, and other substances to produce silicates of these bases, called fluxes. Waste glass, or cullet, added to the mixture promoted fusion and chemical union of the elements.

The furnace, in which ten pots rested, was twenty-two feet wide. Five tons of coal, fed through a flume, was consumed every twenty-four hours. The intense heat was regulated by an arrangement of drafts. The fires were seldom allowed to go out, because the pots would crack if allowed to cool and would have to be replaced. Fires burned continuously during eight years prior to 1874.

Another furnace for reheating the glass burned oil. Its heat was intensified by using a super-heated steam blast. Its nose holes, into which the glass was inserted, were called glory holes.

The melting pots were made of a special clay imported from Stourbridge, England. Barefoot men and boys trod upon the clay while preparing it for the pots, which measured about four feet high and the same in diameter. Each pot held about a ton of glass.

Each pot was built by hand. Great care was taken to avoid imperfections, because extreme heat or action of the ingredients could cause leaks. Even when perfect, pots lasted from only a few weeks to seven or eight months. In case of breakage, new pots kept hot in a furnace were substituted, and as much glass as possible was bailed out of the leaking pot and saved.

In the pot, ingredients were heated to a white heat, then the temperature was raised as rapidly as possible to the point where the material was perfectly fluid. It was held there for from ten to thirty hours while the bubbles disappeared, impurities were skimmed off, and insoluble matter settled to the bottom. The furnace was not allowed to cool until the metal became viscid and could be removed and worked.

Among the categories of employees in the factory were foot gatherer, knob gatherer, warming in and bit gatherer, tube alley gatherer, knob gaffer (blower), servitor, mold boy, drawing out tube-rods with gaffer, middleboy, presser, doorknob cutter, perfume stoppers, and taking-in boy.

Working conditions would not be acceptable to most "blue collar" workers of today. Men were divided into gangs, or shops, of six and worked two shifts (called *moves*) a day. One gang worked from 1 a.m. to 6 a.m., then again from 1 p.m. to 6 p.m. The second gang worked from 7 a.m. to noon and again from 7 p.m. to midnight. A *knocker-upper* was hired to walk along the streets knocking on windows of the tenements to wake the workmen in time to get to work promptly for their allotted shifts.

Skilled foreign workers were induced to work in New Bedford. Homes were prepared for them in advance so that they could start to work the day after they arrived.

One notable workman from Europe who "made good" was George Thomas Thatcher. In 1873, nearing the end of his apprenticeship in designing and engraving, he left England because of difficulties with his employer. At first he worked at the Boston & Sandwich Glass Company, then he came to Mount Washington as designer and cutter. During a strike in 1883, he went to work for the Smith Brothers in New Bedford, where he was made foreman. In 1886 he bought out their cutting department. In 1891 he sent for his brother Richard, who worked for Corning Glass Works. Their partnership lasted until the panic of 1907.

Master glassmakers started young to learn their trade. Robert Gunderson, long associated with Mount Washington/Pairpoint, was born in 1872 in Hadelands, Norway. He started work at age seven as a *glasspustere*, cleaning blowpipes and gaffer's tools. He was then elevated to *carry-in-boy.* He mastered the art of glassblowing by the age of fourteen and finally became one of the three best glassblowers in America.

His boyhood friend, H. "Gilly" Gulbranson, a top glassblower in his employ, was also born in Norway in 1878. He started his apprenticeship at six and a half years of age!

Two other famous names should be mentioned. One is Albert Steffin, head designer at Mount Washington from 1885, who stayed on after the company was absorbed into the Pairpoint Corporation. He was responsible for many original patterns, one of which is a Butterfly and Daisy design, shown later in this chapter (fig. 68). When he retired in 1914, he persuaded Floyd Francis Cary to leave the Pittsburgh Glass Company (where he had attained a national reputation) to come to Pairpoint. Previously, Cary had designed silverware for Alvin Sterling Silver Manufacturers of Long Island. Floyd married Anna Tripp, the manager's daughter. He was able to change with the public's taste. He designed special presentation pieces,

such as a vase in the "Federal" design for Franklin Delano Roosevelt.

Generally, workers moved from factory to factory in an effort to make more money. Often they moved when a venture failed. Some worked steadily for years in the same plant; others were like the fur traders of the Far West, who "blew" all their season's earnings in one big celebration on gambling, drinking, and women. These less stable glassmakers often worked furiously ten to twelve hours a day in two shifts, made enough money to take a vacation from the hot, uncomfortable labor, broke their contract, and went hunting or drinking until their funds were exhausted.

As a rule, the large glass companies often were paternalistic in caring for their sick and destitute workers. Describing working conditions at the Boston & Sandwich firm in 1832, the *Daily Evening Transcript* of Boston noted that the company had "erected two houses of public worship and a large schoolhouse, where a school is kept through the year — the only public school in the town that is kept over four months in the year."

As an indication of capital needed for such a venture, let us use the stock company formed in 1871, to whom the Libbeys sold out for cash and mortgages totaling $60,000, thus making a $25,000 profit on the original investment. Capital was at first $100,000 and later increased to $150,000. W. L. Libbey was appointed agent, and Captain Henry Libbey superintendent.

In 1872 W. L. Libbey left to become the agent for the New England Glass Company in Boston. Management of Mount Washington passed to Captain Henry Libbey. The now internationally famous company declined rapidly during the Depression of 1873 and closed in 1874.

That fall, the company was revived by Frederick S. Shirley, an Englishman. It was completely reorganized in 1876. The name was changed to Mount Washington Glass Company. An additional eight-pot furnace in a new glasshouse was added in 1881. In the 1880s, 250 persons were employed. Mr. Shirley began to produce ornamental pieces in White Lusterless glass with hand-painted decorations.

Among the many innovations in Art Glass for which Mr. Shirley was responsible are Lava Glass, Burmese, Peach Blow, Rose Amber or Amberina, Acid Etched Cameo, Royal Flemish, Albertine, Crown Milano, Napoli, Mother-of-Pearl Satin, and Iridescent.

Mount Washington also filled the demand for a new line of electric globes. As many as five thousand a week were shipped to plants controlled by the company, some as far away as Australia, or Egypt. Bulbs for Edison lamps were blown by the thousands. Crystal chandeliers, which sold from $30 to $5,000, were completely manufactured here. Most of the mansions of the newly rich were decorated with these magnificent chandeliers of cut crystal pendants. The doors opened by means of Mount Washington glass doorknobs, some of which were cut.

Enter Pairpoint

The Pairpoint Manufacturing Company (a small Britannia metalworks), organized in 1880 with capital of $100,000, was named for its first superintendent, T.J. Pairpoint. Its first building was 120 by 40 feet in area and had three floors. In 1881 a second three-story building, 120 by 30 feet, was added. And in 1882, a four-story building, 260 by 40 feet, was built. All three were of brick. Power was supplied by a hundred-horsepower steam engine.

Business increased gradually. Mr. Pairpoint resigned in 1885, to be succeeded by Thomas A. Tripp. Another four-story building, 40 feet by 80 feet, was added in 1890. Still another, 260 by 40, was built in 1891. The firm employed three hundred hands in the factory and had nine traveling salesmen. Annually, two hundred young men from the schools of New Bedford were trained and hired.

Pairpoint made gold and silverplated ware, including holders for pickle casters and tops for biscuit jars; table flatware; hat, hair, and clothes brushes; wine coolers and ice pitcher sets; jewel and cigar cases; candlesticks and épergnes; and casket hardware. The base of most of the ware was of Britannia metal (tin, copper, antimony, and zinc), although German silver, which was much harder to work, was used for tableware sold to hotels, railroads, and steamships, since it could tolerate rough handling. (German silver consisted mainly of copper, zinc, and nickel.)

In 1894 Pairpoint purchased the Mount Washington Glass Company. Until the date of purchase, the two companies had "operated as cooperative neighbors," according to George C. Avila in his definitive work, *The Pairpoint Glass Story.* Many beautiful articles collected today are combinations of Pairpoint silver and Mount Washington glass.

In 1897, when New Bedford celebrated its semicentennial, the Pairpoint Manufacturing Company had twelve hundred employees, of which one hundred were glass blowers, and three hundred were glass cutters. The rest were paper goods or silver workers or those with related duties. The New Bedford Paper Company, established in 1890 and the largest maker of paper tubes for textile mills in the United States, had also joined the corporation.

According to Leonard E. Padgett, author of *Pairpoint Glass*, the corporation kept a force of traveling salesmen who covered the United States and Canada, and maintained sample showrooms in Montreal (Canada), Sidney (Australia), San Francisco, Chicago, and New York City. Its products were placed in the foremost jewelry and department stores in our nation. Its reputation was for products unexcelled by any other manufacturer anywhere.

The Pairpoint Manufacturing Company advertised itself as the owner of Mount Washington Glass Company, the latter bearing its own name until well into the twentieth century. In 1900 it ran into financial difficulties, reorganized, and changed its name to the Pairpoint Corporation — a name it held until 1938.

The corporation enjoyed twenty years of prosperity. But at the forty-first annual national convention of the American Flint Glass Workers Union held in New Bedford in July 1917, notes of warning, were sounded by a speaker, Arthur N. Harriman. He praised the past fifty years of production in New Bedford of cut glass of the highest quality by workers "who have tasted the benefits of organization," then he impressed upon his audience that the majority of the city's workers were still "underpaid, underfed, and discouraged." He asked his colleagues to work for "freedom of the working class from industrial slavery and political inequality." He reminded the convention that involvement in the war was affecting the industry adversely. Potash, essential to the glass business, was almost impossible to get, while coal and other necessaries were increasingly costly. Had the "writing on the wall" been made even clearer, he would have foreseen the demise of many fine glasshouses during and following our participation in World War I.

Pairpoint continued to make some brilliant patterns between 1900 and 1917, as exemplified by the cheese and butter set (fig. 65) in "Nevada." From 1910 into the 1920s, the company produced vases, compotes, and other footed pieces in a distinctive style. These were engraved or pictorially cut. Some had a "bubble ball" knop in the stem (fig. 78). Steuben of Corning and Dorflinger of White Mills also used "controlled bubbles" to some extent.

During the 1920s and until 1938, Pairpoint produced fine colored ware, but also continued to cut and engrave crystal, often combining matte with Rock Crystal in the same engraved design. The discovery of King Tutankhamen's tomb in 1922 served as inspiration for engraved glass with Egyptian motifs. Designers also derived concepts from old Stiegel and Venetian ware, and they copied early nineteenth-century Anglo-Irish motifs in a revival of geometric cutting.

The country-wide depression of 1929 nearly caused a cessation of production at Pairpoint. In the early 1930s, however, a Pairpoint School of Glassmaking was initiated in an endeavor to persuade young men to learn glassblowing and engraving. An apprenticeship of at least four years was required before a decorator could work at the bench. "Soft" American students were unwilling to accept low wages during the long period needed to learn the skills.

In 1932, a boy apprentice in engraving earned from 21 to 27 cents an hour; cutters received from 31 to 75 cents (for the boss), with most cutters getting 55 to 74 cents. The top man, O. Carl Banks, got 99 cents an hour! A lowly clerk earned 25 cents hourly.

Competition from cheap Japanese products was causing grave concern by 1934. Business volume continued to decrease. In May 1938, the glass and silverware departments were sold to J. and B. Kenner, Inc., a salvage firm, but work never actually ceased.

In 1939, Isaac N. Babbitt bought the glass factory from Kenner. The new owner announced that he would resume operation of the glass department under Mr. Robert Gunderson, one of the foremost glassmakers in the world. O. Carl Banks, probably the best cutter and engraver in the nation, headed the cutting department. Every piece bore a round silver label (showing a figure in black of a man blowing glass, a goblet on the left, and a vase on the right), inscribed with the words, "Gunderson Masterpiece." The plant was now called the Gunderson Glass Works, Inc., and was greeted with enthusiasm and orders by such famous companies as Tiffany and Marshall Field. Mr. Gunderson was chosen by the glass manufacturers of this country to take charge of their exhibition at the New York World's Fair in 1939.

From 1888, when Gunderson left Sandwich to work at Mount Washington Glass Works, until 1952, when he passed away, he saw the transition from heavy cut and engraved ware to finer, lightly engraved pieces, and finally to his masterful style of glowing designs and shapes of clear or "bubble" crystal, whose beauty needed no further decoration.

After his death in 1952, the factory became part of the National Pairpoint Company. Its name was changed to Gunderson-Pairpoint Glass Works, and it continued to produce both fine crystal and colored ware, plain and engraved, called "Pairpoint Heirlooms." Robert Bryden had joined the firm in 1950 as a trainee. He was made sales manager in 1952.

Tariffs on glass imports were lowered under presidents Roosevelt and Truman, causing unfair competition. In the summer of 1956, the plant's two chimneys were condemned by insurance underwriters, and other equipment was declared decrepit. Mr. Bryden made the last batch of Burmese and shut down the furnaces in December. A further revival, "Pairpoint of Wareham" by Bryden, who moved operations to East Wareham, Massachusetts, in 1957, ended in 1958. The last employee who remained to finish odds and ends was John Souza, born in St. Georges, Azores. He had come to New Bedford as a boy. A cutter, smoother, and polisher, he started to work at Pairpoint in 1913 when he was twenty, at a starting wage of ten cents an hour. His final wage was $2.76 an hour.

The old buildings burned in October 1965. In 1968, at the time Mr. Avila's book went to press, only "diggers" remained. They were the people who found fragments dating back to the Mount Washington period, which verified history of the famous company. These shards showed lemon yellow under black light, proving that the formula was the same as that used in early Sandwich glass, brought to New Bedford by workers in the 1860s.

In February 1958, Mr. Bryden leased facilities in Spain and continued making Pairpoint Glass for twelve years. Occasionally, one finds a piece with a paper label marked "Pairpoint — Made in Spain."

A new factory was built in Sagamore on Cape Cod and began making glass in January 1970 with Robert Bryden as manager. New master craftsmen from Scotland again blew glass "off-hand" as of old.

A 1977 brochure lists the company's products, including a dozen varieties of colored Art Glass, in addition to clear, full lead crystal. According to Mr. Bryden, they had spent "a number of years making special order Pairpoint Glass in Europe before returning to this country to build the Sagamore factory. At present we are working on plans to return to New Bedford where a new glassmaking facility will be erected not far from the new Glass Museum there."

This has now been accomplished. The Pairpoint name, like the phoenix bird of mythology, has arisen from the ashes of past discouragements, to again create beautiful glassware in New Bedford. Mr. Bryden also said that "because of the cost, heavy cutting is usually done only to order. Engraving is carried on daily."

Factories Descended from Mount Washington/Pairpoint

The complexities of the glassmaking industry, which resemble the shifting sands of the desert, can be further exemplified by listing factories initiated by former Mount Washington/Pairpoint employees.

Blackmer Glass Company in New Bedford (1894-1916)

Crystal Palace in Scotsdale, Arizona, by Joseph Cummings

Edward Koch & Company, Chicago (1899-1926)

Gibbs & Kelley in Honesdale and elsewhere (1895-1928)

Keystone Glass Company in Hawley, Pennsylvania (1902-1918)

Libbey Glass Company, Toledo, Ohio (1888-)

Ohio Cut Glass Company, founded in Bowling Green, Ohio, by Pitkin & Brooks (1904?-1912)

Skinner Glass Company, Philadelphia (1895-?)

Smith Brothers, New Bedford (1874-1899)

Thatcher Glass in New Bedford (1886); in Fairhaven, Massachusetts (1893-1907)

Whaling City Glass Company, New Bedford, by David Dexter (?)

Smith Brothers

Of these "descendants," Smith Brothers should be sketched briefly, if only because much of their work is indistinguishable from that of Mount Washington.

Fig. 62. Tumblers, 3¾", circa 1875-1885, attributed to either Smith Brothers or Mt. Washington, whose catalog describes the design as "Block Diamond fine" at $24 per dozen. They are clear and elegant and still appeal to those who prefer simpler patterns. Dorflinger's was "Block Diamond."

Their father, William L. Smith, came from England in 1851 to work as a decorator for the Boston & Sandwich Glass Company at the request of Deming Jarves. He did outstanding work in the decorating of Art Glass, gilded lamps, and apothecary ware. William trained his sons, Alfred and Harry. After a few years, he moved to Boston, where he founded the Boston China Decorating Works.

In 1871 William Libbey established a decorating shop at the Mount Washington Glass Works and placed Harry and Alfred in charge of it. After three years, they bought their department, leased the shop, and operated under their name, Smith Brothers — Fine Decorated Glass Ware. They worked for themselves, as well as for Mount Washington. By 1876 they occupied their own building, decorating blanks purchased from Mount Washington and other firms here and abroad. This shop decorated opal glass shades, lamps, vases, and tablewares, producing beautiful pieces by gilding and applying colors to glass.

When cut glass became "the rage," they opened a cutting shop, using Mount Washington blanks. Their patterns greatly resembled those cut at Mount Washington for obvious reasons. Tumblers in a block pattern are shown here (fig. 62). The celery vase in Revi, page 62, from the collection of descendents of Alfred Smith, looks exactly like #19, plate 5, in the 1880s catalog of Mount Washington. Therefore, the tumblers could have been cut at either firm or by Dorflinger. New England had patented a similar design in 1875.

After many successful years, the business declined. The brothers filed for bankruptcy in 1899, sold the remaining stock cheaply, and separated. Alfred returned to the decorating department at Mount Washington, while Harry went to Meriden, Connecticut, to work.

Examples of Mount Washington/Pairpoint Glassware

It is common knowledge that the Pairpoint mark, a P in a diamond, is found on silverplated ware of merit. It is less well-known that the company ran the gamut in cut and engraved crystal from the heavy, geometric designs of the 1880s and 1890s to delicate engraving on thinner blanks as late as the 1920s.

Frederick F. Shirley registered a trademark, RUSSIAN CRYSTAL, with a two-headed eagle, 30 January 1883. It was used for several years on a paper label. Few articles are found today with the label still attached. Unfortunately, neither Mount Washington nor Pairpoint ever had an acid-etched mark for lead glass. When a silver mount bears the Pairpoint mark, one can assume that the glass is from the home factory.

Perusing a catalog of the 1880s, one sees one or two motifs covering all or nearly all of the surface of a piece. Among these are block, Russian, crosscut diamond (then called strawberry diamond) with or without fan; hobnail (then called hexagon diamond), and cane. The "Old Colony" pattern found in a catalog of the 1920s was one among several that revived the early Anglo-Irish style of cutting at this time. It featured a silver diamond band above sharp relief diamonds and closely resembled the Dorflinger Bowl in Chapter 15 (fig. 284).

There are many unusual shapes in the early catalog. Serving trays with up to six pieces were made. Some had triangular parts. Others were in three pieces, looking like a bird in flight, composed of body and wings.

Beautiful stemware came in matched sets. These included water goblet, saucer champagne, claret, port, sherry, and cordial. Lemonade (which we now call punch cup), half-quart tumbler, half-pint tumbler, champagne tumbler, and finger bowl were cut to match the stemware. Imagine the elaborate, formal dinners at which these services were used!

Pitchers (or jugs) and liquor containers came in a great variety of shapes. Vases included cornucopias suspended by silken cords, crescents, épergnes, and flower globes. Although most articles were heavily cut, a few were engraved with flowers and animals.

The rectangular tray (fig. 63) cut in traditional "Strawberry Diamond and Fan" is a good example of a style popular in the 1880s. The square nut dishes (fig. 438) and the syrup jug (fig. 461, right) in the section on cabinet pieces, both cut in this pattern, also seem to be Mount Washington products. The syrup resembles the egg-shaped sugar shaker shown in an original catalog circa 1890 (in the Corning Museum of Glass).

Fig. 63. Rectangular ice cream tray, $14\frac{1}{2}'' \times 7\frac{3}{4}'' \times 1\frac{7}{8}''$, is sharp, brilliant, heavy. Because of quality and accuracy of cutting, and resemblance to a bonbon server in an 1880 catalog, it is attributed to Mt. Washington. (Serres)

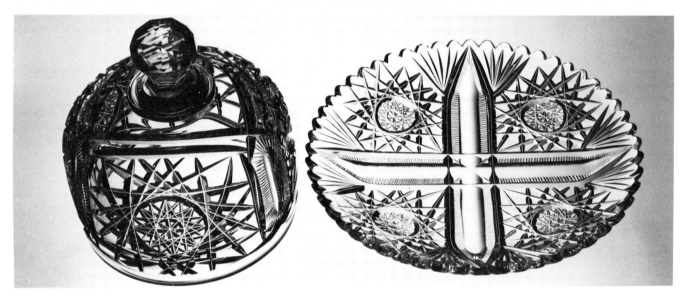

Fig. 64. Cheese dish, $6\frac{3}{4}''$ to top of knob, with cover resting on $9\frac{1}{4}''$ plate, in "Nevada." Butter dish, $5\frac{3}{8}''$ h, plate $8''$, is identical, but smaller. On plate, crossed flutes with notched edges give a sunburst effect. Domes have three large hobstars and three oval sunbursts. Excellent quality.

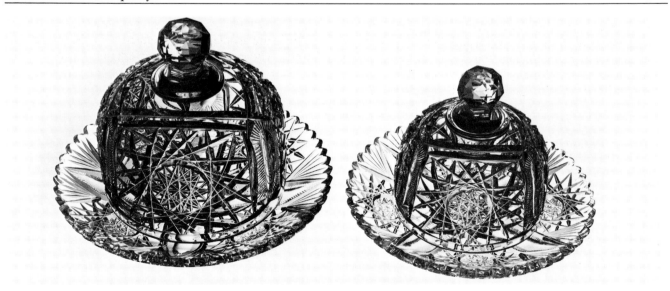

Fig. 65. Cheese and butter set in "Nevada."

Nearly every company cut this pattern in crystal; some cut it in red, green, and yellow. Thus it is easy to acquire a complete set. Examine carefully before buying, however, because young apprentices were often started on this design. Their lack of experience sometimes shows.

Passing now to the years between 1894 and 1915, pictured is a cheese dish in "Nevada" (fig. 64). The "Nevada" design is illustrated in a Pairpoint Corporation catalog (at the Corning Museum of Glass) in the form of a 7″ plate selling for $42 per dozen, or a 12″ plate at $12 each.

A matching butter dish in "Nevada" is shown with the cheese (fig. 65) to aid the reader to recognize each by size.

The mismatched butter dish (fig. 66) has a "Nevada" plate. Until the above cheese dish was purchased, we thought parts of this butter dish were meant to go together. The dome had a fan, doubly notched split, and hobstar as elements of design. The quality and color of the glass was identical in both sections. Comparing the dome and plate of the cheese dish, however, one finds that they match perfectly, while the parts of the butter dish are slightly different. Both domes have similar knobs, fluted at the neck, and have the design repeated three times around the sides.

In conclusion, this butter's dome must have come from Pairpoint, but was accidentally switched in the retail store. It is unlikely that two different domes were designed to go with the same "Nevada" plate. This is one of the mysteries that make collecting glass such a fascinating hobby. While this chapter was being written, a butter dish was purchased that does match the cheese. It was bought from the same dealer who sold the cheese dish several years ago. Word was left at the time for him to contact the author if he ever found a "Nevada" butter. Three years later a letter arrived with welcome news.

The glove box (fig. 67) in "Daisy" was considered to be typical of Pairpoint glass by Mr. Bryden in 1977 when photographs were sent to him for identification. "If the metal is not stamped with the Diamond P trademark, it would have been made and cut at Pairpoint as far as the glass goes and then sold to one of the many silver companies that used Pairpoint glass parts." This box is stamped only with "77." It would have had to have been blown into a mold to achieve the shape, then cut and polished. Glove boxes in mint condition are scarce and expensive.

Patent #39982, 11 May 1909, by Albert Steffin for the Pairpoint Corporation, showed a drawing of a bowl on which "daisy flowers reach the top of the rim of the vessel, the rim taking the shape of the outer edge of the flowers." Simple miter-cut leaves completed the design. Revi named this "Late Daisy." Pearson calls it "Butterfly and Daisy."

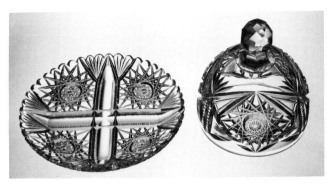

Fig. 66. Butter dish, 6½″ to top of dome, 8″ plate. Plate is "Nevada"; mismatched dome, probably a "cousin." Undoubtedly from Pairpoint.

Fig. 67. Glove box, 10¾″ × 4¼″ × 3½″, in "Daisy." Chain of small bullseyes, with a row of contiguous, ½″ vertical cuts above the chain, goes around lid's edge. Two rows of oval thumbprints, with triple crosscuts at their junctures, embellish sides. A forty-eight-point star, with vanes reaching to the ends of the box, creates a sunburst on the bottom.

As in the case of the Morecroft bowl (fig. 54) whose "Diamond Poinsettia" flower was patented, stylized butterflies were added to the basic daisy design by Steffin. The cream and sugar set (fig. 68) clearly shows the adaptation of a pattern to fit the shape of the piece. The creamer has the overlapping daisies reaching the top of the rim and one butterfly seen from a side view under the lip. The sugar bowl separates the daisies and shows two butterflies with outspread wings, one on each side.

The puff box in the same design, with glass lift-off lid (fig. 69), is heavy for its size, and the glass is perfectly clear. Four butterflies, two with open wings and two seen from the side, appear on the sides of this jar.

Fig. 68. Cream and sugar set, 3″ h, in "Butterfly and Daisy" (Pearson) or "Late Daisy" (Revi). Each has a sixteen-point hobstar on bottom, with flashing resembling tufts of grass around the star. Superior, heavy blanks, excellent cutting. All motifs polished.

Fig. 69. Puff box, 5½″ × 3¼″, in "Butterfly and Daisy." Four butterflies alternate with four daisies, whose centers are slightly concave.

Fig. 70. Cracker and cheese, 9″ d × 2½″ h. Top is 4½″ d, in "Butterfly and Daisy." Dish for holding cheese is attached to plate. Thick base enhanced by a forty-eight-point radiant star.

Fig. 71. Fruit bowl, 9″ × 3⅝″, in "Arbutus." Flower petals and butterfly wings left in matte finish. Highlights, butterfly's body and antennae, and leaves and stems are polished.

Fig. 72. Jewel box, 7½″ × 4″, in "Arbutus." Sides have two rows of thumbprints with triple-X cuts where they meet (like those on glove box).

Fig. 73. Cologne, 5⅛″ in "Arbutus" features a close-up of the butterfly. Blossoms are there, but cannot be seen.

The cracker and cheese server (fig. 70) depicts another adaptation of this design. It is also of the finest workmanship. The concept of a piece for this purpose was new in 1909. The form of the blank was filed 19 January 1909 by William H. Krebs of New Bedford, #41027, but published 6 December 1910, nearly two years later. A similar article in porcelain was inherited from Mr. Swan's mother.

The bowl (fig. 71), jewel box (fig. 72), and cologne (fig. 73) have a more realistic butterfly. The pointed scallop, the reverse of the early rounded scallop, was sometimes used on the edge of bowls after 1907. The dainty design was called "Arbutus" in Pairpoint's catalog. The blossoms must be stylized, since an arbutus flower has five petals and is tubular. The large blossoms look like polyanthus; the tiny ones resemble forget-me-nots.

The jewel box was bought in Oregon when we first started to collect. About a year later in California, the matching bowl was found in a private home. Four years later, we found the perfume in a shop in California. If you're limited to a small collection, trying to assemble as many examples of one design as possible is a good plan. For lighthearted beauty, nothing is superior to butterflies! Since the silverplated fittings are not marked with the Diamond P trademark, one must assume that the glass for the jewel box was made and decorated at Pairpoint, then sold to a silver company.

Speaking of butterflies, not even Tuthill can surpass those on the flower center in Butterfly and Thistle (figs. 74A and 74B) and on the pair of table lamps in "Daisy" (figs. 75A and 75B). The Butterfly and Thistle pattern is illustrated in another book, but marked "not identified." The verified "Garland" butterfly is exactly like those on our flower center and lamps. Fortified by Mr. Bryden's opinion in 1977 that the lamp "shade is undoubtedly from this factory," all three pieces are declared to be Pairpoint work. Now that Mr. Padgett's book, *Pairpoint Glass*, is out, there is absolute proof for origin of the lamps. An Electrolier in "Daisy" is shown on page 146 with a lovely butterfly in flight.

We found the first of the pair in a shop in 1969. In 1972, I was thrilled to find its mate down the valley in a home shop. The lamps are identical except for the prism drops hanging from the silverplated frame. Both sets are old, but slightly different.

The vintage and floral engraving on the two marmalade or jam jars (fig. 76) was done on thin blanks, requiring a delicate touch. Pairpoint grapes were lined up in rows, as opposed to more random arrangements by other firms. A 1920s catalog listed many items cut through colored glass to clear in "Grape." Colors were amethyst, blue, chrysopas (gold), auroria (a reddish amber), canaria, and green.

The centerpiece or footed bowl (fig. 77) in the "Chelsea" pattern was sold with matching candlesticks for the dining table. The Rock Crystal design of stylized

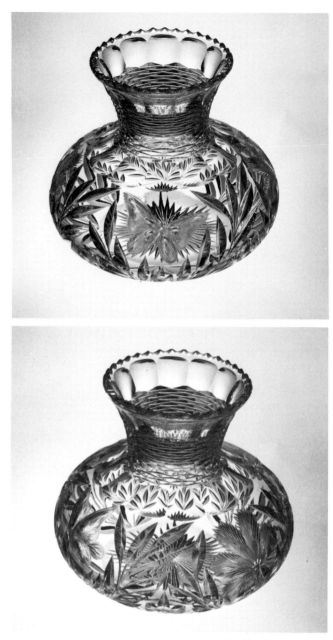

Figs. 74A and 74B. Flower center, 10″ d×8½″ h, in a Butterfly and Thistle design. Butterfly is shown on opposite sides. Two large thistles are also in opposition amidst miter-cut, polished leaves. Thistles and butterflies were left gray for contrast. Half flutes above and below a collar of convex, but short, diamond cuts complement the intaglio engraving. On the bottom is a radiant forty-eight-point star.

Figs. 75A and 75B. Electrolier, 17½″×12″, in "Daisy." One of a pair. A row of concave circles appears an inch above silver-plated frame, which holds the globe. Between daisies on the base are notched flutes. Vertical cuts encircle base. Two bulbs are lighted by means of pull chains. The black speck, visible by a leaf on the dome (fig. 75B), is an unmelted grain of sand or a bit of clay — the only imperfection in any of our Mt. Washington/Pairpoint pieces. We photographed this dome to show one type of flaw that was largely eliminated in Brilliant Period glass.

Fig. 76. Jam or marmalade jars, 4″. Engraved "Grape" jar has a glass lid, with a notch for a spoon, and a rayed base. Floral jar has a sterling silver notched lid, engraved with a fancy *T*, and a plain bottom with polished pontil mark.

Fig. 77. Centerpiece, 12″ × 5¼″, in "Chelsea."

Fig. 78. Footed vase, 13″, in "Chelsea" with controlled bubble ball knop or connector in stem. (Voorhees)

Fig. 79. Footed vase, 13″, in "Victoria," exquisitely engraved on fairly thin glass. Trellis and blossoms on clear glass were left gray. Rosebuds were cut through a satin-gray or matte panel, then polished to clear.

flowers and swag, resembling a pearl necklace, was similar to Sinclaire designs done at the end of the Brilliant Period and into the 1920s. This footed bowl or compote for fruit or flowers is fairly thin, clear, and has a nice ring when tapped.

The footed vase (fig. 78), also in "Chelsea," has the "bubble ball," often used by Pairpoint.

The dealer who sold this lovely vase (Fig. 79) in the "Victoria" pattern had marked it "Tuthill." The design was engraved on plates made in 6″, 8″, 10″, 14″, and 16″ sizes, on vases of several shapes, on compotes, on cream and sugar sets, and perhaps more. It is difficult to comprehend that a hand-engraved design of such

delicacy and accuracy was actually cut to order on so many items. It is also hard to believe that Pairpoint glassware, comparable to or better than imports from Europe or Asia, was sold at affordable prices.

Less than ten years ago, few buyers appreciated this type of copper wheel engraving, so prices were much lower than for heavy, brilliant glass. In 1968, such a vase as the "Chelsea" (fig. 78) might have sold for $50. In August 1978, a pair of vases similar to the "Chelsea" was advertised in *Hobbies* for $500 — a dramatic increase in a short time. Perhaps there is still time to find a "sleeper" in this post-Brilliant glassware.

10

Life-Style of the Rich

The Industrial Revolution afforded an unheard-of opportunity to rise from rags to riches in a short time. A flood of immigrants and displaced agricultural workers provided a labor force for the burgeoning machines of commerce and industry. Some capitalists trampled their workers; others were paternalistic and did their best to be fair to employees while building enormous fortunes. No matter how kindly disposed they felt toward their workers, however, the owners considered them to be biologically inferior by nature of their position on the ladder of achievement.

Why were the poor so poor? According to the thinking of the time, they were the products of natural selection. The rich rose to the top because they were superior. Herbert Spencer (1820-1903), an Englishman, eliminated all feeling of guilt concerning the vast disparity of wealth. He coined the phrase "survival of the fittest," and advocated a philosophy of Social Darwinism. According to this theory, free meals were detrimental to those who got them, since they stifled ambition. But they were good for the self-righteous givers, increasing their self-esteem.

Architecture of the Splendid Age

The rich built palatial private homes and justified the extravagance by saying the poor could learn by example. Opulent mansions symbolized the success of the new class of business tycoons created by the Industrial Revolution. The *noveaux riches* desired palaces equal to those of European royalty, whose wealth they matched or sometimes exceeded. In an era of unrestrained free enterprise, there were few taxes. A temporary income tax, which had been imposed in 1861 due to the Civil War, was lifted in 1872. Andrew Carnegie, whose mills brought him $25 million in personal wealth, paid no income tax.

At mid-century, the States had no graduate architects. Most were self-taught. Those who studied the subject in college had French professors. Consequently, they went out into society to create copies of European palaces. Public buildings were greatly influenced by this learning. The Cincinnati Chamber of Commerce resembled a French château with Romanesque arches. A monument to President Garfield was a German pseudo-Gothic tower. And the principal hotel in Selma, Alabama, resembled an Italian villa.

A style purporting to be English "Queen Anne" was spawned at the Centennial. The British Government Building had Jacobean high chimneys and gables and neoclassical details indoors. From this evolved a style for private dwellings that included Elizabethan half-timber, pressed brick, fancy shingles, and pressed tin cornices and ceilings. All sorts of variations appeared in residences, which were adorned with multiple gables and towers, balconies, and balustraded verandas. Even the interiors of elegant Pullman sleeping cars had frettings and groovings, alleged to be Queen Anne.

Stone buildings resembling medieval fortresses might be suitable for armories, asylums, prisons, and even railway stations, but as private homes they were dark and depressing. An architect named Henry H. Richardson used cut stone to build impressive structures, but he also employed naturally water-rounded cobblestones to erect some hideous houses.

Stone had been desirable when nails were cut by hand, but with the advent of a machine-made cheap product in the 1840s, wooden buildings could be braced and fastened together by a liberal use of nails. The "Carpenter Gothic," with gingerbread décor applied in thin slats and fanciful curlicues, was an outgrowth of the power-driven saw and lathe. Knobs and spindles adorned every porch, while scallops outlined the roof edge. There is a parallel to be drawn between the housepainter who had to painstakingly renew all of these surfaces, and the housewife or cook who spent most of her time in the kitchen preparing every kind of food "from scratch." Those were the days of long working hours, accepted as a matter of course.

The Vanderbilts had a French Renaissance château of fabulous elegance built at a cost of $4.1 million near Asheville, North Carolina, between 1890 and 1895. *The Guinness Book of World Records* of 1978 calls it the largest private house in the world. It has 250 rooms. With its twelve thousand acres, it was valued at $55 million in 1979. It is presently owned by grandsons of George Vanderbilt II.

Another Vanderbilt constructed the famous *Breakers* at Newport, Rhode Island, from 1893-1895. This seventy-room rendition of a sixteenth-century Genoa *palazzo* was found to be too small for its owner, Cornelius Vanderbilt II, so an extra story was added to accommodate the domestic help. William H. and sons, William K. and Cornelius II, spent over $15 million on a suite of mansions on Fifth Avenue in New York City. It is incredible that William H. employed seven hundred artisans to decorate one of his houses, and, of these, 250 did marquetry and carving. The Vanderbilt houses were the work of Richard Morris Hunt.

Samuel Colt, between 1855 and 1862, built a mansion in Hartford, Connecticut, which was somewhat like an Italian villa, but with Turkish pinnacles and domes. It was said to be English in feeling, however.

Frederick Eaton Church (1826-1900), famous landscape painter, began construction of *Olana* in 1870. This Persian palace was located on a hill overlooking the Hudson River. As a world traveler, he brought home priceless furnishings of Oriental, Islamic, and European origin, and enjoyed ornamenting his home for many years.

Many rich interiors featured at least one room (a den or library) in the Moorish manner, with oriental rugs on walls and floors, Turkish water pipes (hookahs), brass trays, and inlaid tables and ceilings. The Turkish Bazaar at the Centennial inspired many to desire such items as a round, tufted ottoman on casters and upholstered chairs with fringe and tassels. Relaxing in such a setting of fantasy provided relief from the tensions of the business world.

In 1865 Legrand Lockwood of Norwalk, Connecticut, Wall Street broker and railroad magnate, ordered the interiors of his mansion embellished with Egyptian porphyry and Florentine marble. (Porphyry is a hard stone having a dark, purplish groundmass containing small crystals of feldspar.) The woodwork was of dark oak, brazilwood, black oak, rosewood, satinwood, ebony, boxwood, and cedar of Lebanon, which was carved, gilded, and inlaid. The dwelling had fourteen bathrooms, two billiard rooms, a bowling alley, art gallery, theater, and library. Much of the furniture was French, massive, and ornate.

We must mention Christian Herter, a handsome, multi-talented artist, born in Germany and educated in Stuttgart and Paris. In a scant ten years (1870-1880), he decorated some of the homes of the richest tycoons in America. He retired at forty, returned to Paris to paint, and died of tuberculosis at forty-three. In California his clients included the railroad magnate, Mark Hopkins, who died before his mansion was finished. Quoting from the *American Heritage of Antiques:* "The master bedroom. . . was designed with a Venetian décor: the walls of ebony inlaid with precious stones and ivory marquetry, the doors padded with blue velvet, and a ceiling painted with amorous cupids at play."

In New York, Herter's last commission was for William Henry Vanderbilt. Herter was both architect and interior designer for Vanderbilt's block-long brownstone, a jewel box which cost $1.75 million. It was in the Italian Rennaissance style, with such wonders as gold-encrusted doorways and red velvet walls, intricately embroidered and studded with cut crystals of every hue. A Japanese parlor was done in a lacework of bamboo with enormous jewelled dragonflies.

Mansions were often fitted with windows of stained glass in geometric shapes studded with jewels (semi-spherical pieces cut in facets). Some had pictorial windows by Tiffany that were breathtaking in their beauty. A few had cut glass windows, colorless or colored cut to clear.

The Sandwich Glass Museum now owns a cut Red Overlay Pane (fig. C.5), 13″ × 23″, which came from an inn called the Miller House near the Sandwich railroad station. The inn was remodeled in Greek Revival style in 1848 when the railroad came to town. The museum also owns a colorless Lacy Pane, 8″ × 10″, circa 1830, used in a corn shed in Sandwich. These are Middle Period examples.

In the November 1968 *Spinning Wheel,* Mr. Albert Christian Revi reported that a cut glass door panel (fig. 80) had come to light while he was seeking information on the Laurel Cut Glass Company of Jermyn, Pennsylvania. It was made circa 1907 for the residence of Homer D. Carey, president of the firm, and had been removed from the door frame and stored for safekeeping by Carey descendants at the time Mr. Revi wrote the article. Old photographs show that the 31″ × 46″ panel was colorless and cut in Laurel's "Pineapple." Large blossoms were cut in a pinwheel fashion, and buds

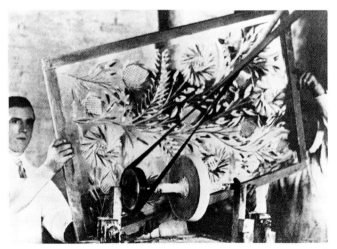

Fig. 80. "A contemporary photograph of the cut glass panel taken on the day it was completed in 1907. James Penrose, left, and Melvin Dunlop, right, are holding it in the frame in which it was bound during the various cutting and polishing processes." (Photo and legend by permission of Albert Christian Revi from his article in *Spinning Wheel* magazine, November 1968, p. 58)

were in the old Strawberry Diamond motif, with curved flashing resembling thistles. Butterflies were placed among the flowers. "The men who made it were Melvin Dunlap, designer and rougher, William Haffner, smoother and foreman of the cutting shop, and James Penrose, polisher."

Glass doorknobs, curtain tiebacks, and furniture knobs embellished house interiors. Great mansions were often fitted with cut glass knobs and pulls, but upper-middle-class homes were more likely to have blown or pressed pattern-molded knobs. Pressed knobs were most popular from 1826 to 1850, but continued to be made during the Brilliant Period.

As explained in Maude Eastwood's excellent book on collecting doorknobs, many ornate knobs were finely wrought of brass, bronze, and iron. Imported porcelain knobs, hand-painted and signed, were purchased to decorate the finer houses. Plainer porcelain knobs were made in this country.

Most glass knobs were poured or pressed into iron molds, cooled in the lehr, and finally sent to the grinding wheels, where rough edges were removed and the surface polished. These were made of soda-lime glass, containing fine white sand, soda ash, lime, and nitrate. A few contained lead and were cut by experts. Illustrated are two such doorknobs from Mrs. Eastwood's collection (figs. 81A, 81B, 82). Some cut knobs were spherical, faceted like a cologne bottle stopper. A lapidary-cut doorknob sold for $13.50 in 1904.

Among companies that manufactured cut glass doorknobs were Yale & Towne Manufacturing Company and Mount Washington/Pairpoint. The latter made free-blown, pattern-molded, cut and engraved knobs — many in the factory's colors. Opalescent, blue, amber, and canaria knobs have been excavated from under their building erected in 1880.

In addition to the sparkling chandeliers with prism-cut drops for which Mount Washington was famous, the finest mansions were graced with cut globes and stalactites covering bulbs next to the ceiling. Cut bowls suspended by means of chains also added to the scintillating interiors.

This preoccupation with light reflections may have been a reaction to emergence from an era of dim candle- and lamplight. If you have ever tried to read by a kerosene lamp, you may appreciate the thrill of electric lighting. The dimly lighted home accounted partially for the custom of "early to bed and early to rise" in the "good old days."

How exciting it was to find this rich cut bowl (fig. 83), as it would have been labeled in the old catalogs, hanging in the shop of an eighty-year-old lady! Such shades are indeed rare. We theorize that many precious cut shades were destroyed by wrecking crews during the first half of this century, while razing old houses and hotels to make way for "progress." This lampshade, cut in cane and other familiar motifs, rests in a

Figs. 81A and 81B. Cut glass doorknob from two aspects, cut in English strawberry diamond and fan with faceted sides. (Photographs courtesy of Maude Eastwood)

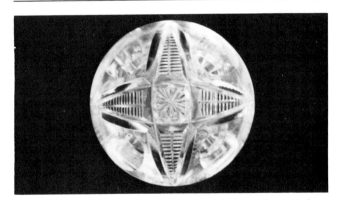

Fig. 82. Cut glass doorknob cut in central single star, four zippers, and four bullseyes. (Eastwood)

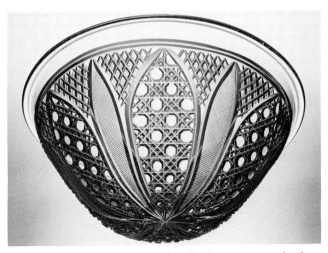

Fig. 83. Bowl light shade, 14″ × 6½″, in cane and silver diamond vesicas, miter separations, and triangles of crosscut diamond.

nickel-plated rim, suspended from a ceiling canopy by three chains. It is of lead glass, hand-cut and polished, and it rings like a bell when tapped.

There is no proof that the bowl was made by the Phoenix Glass Company of Monaca, Ohio (a small Ohio River town northeast of Pittsburgh), yet it closely resembles in shape and size a 14″ rich cut bowl that sold for $60 in 1893. A 16″ rich cut ball, cut in "Star and Hobnail," sold for $112.50, which was a high price in 1893. Phoenix, founded by Andrew Howard in 1880, was noted for its fine colored glass. Commercial success led to development of an even more lucrative line of cut and etched globes and shades. The firm also produced elaborate hand-painted and stained shades, some selling for several hundreds of dollars. Phoenix sponsored a brilliantly lighted exhibit of domes, globes, stalactites, balls, and bowl-shades at the Chicago Fair of 1893.

The Life-Style of George W. Childs

Good Housekeeping, "a family journal," featured articles on the life-style of George W. Childs in 1886, 1890, and again in 1894, the year of his demise. He was said to be "among the few rich and noted men of the world whom none envied and all loved."

He had come to Philadelphia as "a poor, friendless boy of fourteen" and had won his way to wealth and recognition "without other help than that given by unflagging energy, industry, persistence and honesty." According to the adoring reporter, Hester Poole, "the desire for riches in generous souls is not for the hoarding of bonds and stocks, or of broad lands." The best ends for which the home is established are to make it "the center of good influences, to secure its permanence and attractiveness, to embellish it with objects of enduring loveliness, and to gather choice and noble minds around the hearthstone. . . It is that the inmates may give benefits and receive culture."

Mr. Childs was publisher of the Philadelphia *Ledger* from 1864 to 1894. He married Emma Bouvier Peterson, whose father was Child's first partner in publishing. Emma was a "tiny brunette of a nervous and highly wrought organization" who attained the dignity of a fine art in housekeeping.

The articles describe two of his three exquisite homes: a mansion in Philadelphia, and *Wooten*, the summer home with a dairy and springs, situated on 120 acres at Bryn Mawr. Fresh milk and spring water were sent twice daily to Philadelphia or to the third home at Long Branch.

Mr. and Mrs. Childs were noted for their hospitality. They entertained titled aristocrats from South America and Europe (such as the Emperor and Empress of Brazil and several English lords), as well as authors (Dickens and Longfellow) and prominent military commanders (generals Grant and Sherman).

In one interview, Mr. Childs gave samples of his menus (written in French), which were nine courses, as a rule. He described the etiquette of invitations and the formal dress and service; declared he never used tobacco nor drank alcoholic beverages, but served wines (a different wine for each course) to his guests; and expressed his opinion that a small dinner party of ten or twelve was more successful than one of a large number of guests. He required quick changes between courses in order to limit the time for eating to two hours. Guests who had arrived at seven were expected to leave by eleven.

At this time, formal dinners were the most important of all social functions. Consequently, a great deal of money was spent on the accoutrements for entertaining guests by feeding them lavishly. Reference was made in *Good Housekeeping* to the Childs's famous $40,000 dinner set:

> Above the sensuous pleasure of partaking of appetizing food, there is the esthetic enjoyment derived from its concomitants. Fine porcelain, gleaming silver, iridescent crystal, soft light, fragrant flowers, low tones, the hum of conversation, the bright dresses of the ladies, the sense that each is giving of his best for the delectation of the others, all stimulate the faculties and produce a delightful exhilaration.

Mme. Poole's elegant style of writing, couched in florid, romantic phrases, epitomizes the Victorian ideal of life with the "beautiful people" of high society. In order to visualize the use of cut glass in even the finest homes of the era, and to comprehend its place as a status symbol, we must borrow a few more words from her eloquent descriptions.

Although she rhapsodizes concerning the dining room, "in which the body is daily refreshed and fortified," she also mentions adjacent areas traversed by guests. As one advanced through the vestibule, he looked down a vista terminating in a full-length mirror set in a door frame at the extremity of a smaller hall leading out of the dining room and on one side of a butler's pantry.

Separated from the dining room by carved and gilded pillars was the music room, with two grand pianos. Heavy hangings of tapestry could convert the room into two apartments whenever desired. Beneath a massive mirror at one end of the music room stood three large vases from the Royal Berlin manufactory, "which kings coveted in vain." We should mention the Prometheus vase, shown by Minton at the Centennial. It was of ovoid shape, 30″ high, of a sky-blue color. A short neck was capped by Prometheus bound to the rock, while the vulture tore at his heart. In addition, vases by Crown Derby and Royal Worcester were displayed here. The music room opened into the drawing room, separated only by pillars. Under gaslight, ornamental mirrors produced an endless succession of vistas.

The dining room measured thirty by fifteen feet and had a sixteen-foot ceiling. It was entered by a broad doorway at the end of the spacious hall. The door frames were of marble. Its woodwork was of oak, highly polished and trimmed with amaranth of a darker tone. The wainscoting, about 30″ in height, was surmounted by walls hung with "Japanese paper, having an embossed ground of gold with birds of Paradise and grapes in natural colors."

A built-in cabinet housed fifteen plates of Royal Vienna procelain, all different, which had once belonged to the Ex-Queen Caroline of Naples. They were "worth their weight in gold." On the opposite wall, a built-in buffet, eight feet wide by thirteen high, held pieces of glass and silver.

The dining table of solid oak was long enough to seat twenty-four persons. The chairs were upholstered in dark green leather. Aubusson carpeting corresponded "exactly with that in the music and drawing rooms with tints of crimson, ivory, dull green and old gold." The other rooms were brilliant with crimson, ebony, and gilding. A large central chandelier in porcelain and gilt, two side candelabra with mirrored backs, and two drop candelabra before the end mirrors lighted the dining room.

The butler's pantry contained cupboards filled with porcelain and crystal, sufficient for lavish hospitality. There were complete services of Minton, Royal Vienna, and Copeland. There were also sets of fish plates, no two alike, and "a special compartment devoted to after-dinner coffee cups and saucers, and their larger cousins made for the Chinese herbs." Stairs at one side of the pantry led to additional storage on the floor above.

When not in use, the dining table was covered by a scarlet spread of Oriental cashmere embroidered with bullion thread. Figure 84 shows the table covered with a white damask cloth, set for one of those famous dinner parties. In the middle of the table on a mirror lake, there rests "a center piece in richly chased silver gilt, vasiform, and finished at the top with eight burners, though it was used for flowers instead." The end pieces, silver and gilt candelabra, are supported by winged griffins.

> Standing by the candelabrum at one end of the table is a silver and gilt water cooler... The corresponding article at the opposite extremity is a crystal bowl, fifteen inches in diameter and nearly as high, used for flowers. This and its companion in another city are the finest pieces of glass yet made by any American manufacturer, and for beauty and perfection of cutting they are unexcelled by the best

Fig. 84. Dining table in Philadelphia home of George W. Childs, set for lavish dinner party. Note large cut glass bowl by Thomas Hawkes and other cut pieces, as described in text. (*Good Housekeeping*, 15 May 1886, pp. 1-5)

Baccarat ware. The work was done by Thomas Hawkes, the great-grandson of the Mr. Hawkes who first introduced cut glass into England. The profusion of crystal upon the table in the shape of exquisite carafes, compotes, fruit and bonbon stands, low and high, and with or without silver bases, are a revelation of the stage to which glass-cutting is carried in the United States.

Here is proof positive that the affluent leaders of society valued the finest American glass as highly as the famous ware from Bohemia or France. There were some snobs, unlike Mr. Childs, who still felt that only European imports were worthy. Some dealers met this foolish belief by representing their American pieces as Baccarat, or from some other foreign maker. Obviously these ignorant, though rich, customers were unaware that most of our finest artisans were transplanted Europeans.

Lavish Entertainment

On land, the moguls had private railway cars, used both for business trips and pleasure excursions. The cars were richly decorated in palatial fashion. Even if one did not own a private car, he could travel in Pullman dining and sleeping cars, which were marvels of comfort and décor. At the World's Columbian Exhibition of 1893 in Chicago in the Transportation Department, a model dining car was shown, "finished in the finest of vermillion wood imported from South America, with windows of stained glass in delicate hues, seats elaborately carved, and kitchen which is a model of cleanliness and condensation of space."

In Bancroft's *Book of the Fair*, Volume II (published in 1893), an enormous volume, there is an excellent view of this dining car. Tables for four are set for a meal with white linen cloths, silverware, and articles of richly cut glass. Clearly visible are a large three-ring decanter and a handled decanter, both with faceted ball stoppers, and a tall tankard pitcher, footed goblets and wines, and a water carafe (fig. 85).

> The Sleeping-cars are marvels of comfort finished in Pompeiian red, and satinwood, artistically carved and polished to a mirror-like brightness, each of its compartments a miniature boudoir, and with separate design and color scheme...all with upholstery of silk brocade. All compartments are provided with toilet appliances, and with water, hot, cold, and iced. The electric lights are shaded with silken fringe; the entrance ways paved with mosaic, and vases placed on stands remain undisturbed by the motion of the train, so smoothly run these palace cars, the very embodiment of the luxury of modern travel.

Fig. 85. Model dining-car shown at World's Columbian Exposition of 1893 in Chicago. (Bancroft's *Book of the Fair*, Vol. II, p. 553)

Fig. 86. Yacht decanter, 8″×8″, cut in bullseyes and notched prism; similar to "Albany" by Meriden. Base is covered by twenty-point hobstar; handle is double-notched. Many companies cut a version of this design, but style and quality suggest Meriden or Dorflinger. (Hamstreet)

On water, the yacht was the home-away-from-home. Cut glass was a part of the décor here, also. In fact, yacht glassware was designed specifically for moving vehicles. In 1898 Dorflinger ran an advertisement in *Harper's* magazine showing such ware. Near an open porthole (through which one sees a ship on the horizon) is a table with a carafe, drinking glasses in several sizes, and a decanter — all cut in a simple, miter design, and all very wide at the base to prevent tipping. A humidor containing cigars is fluted around the base and has bull's-eyes on shoulder and stopper. Against the wall are shelves that support rows of stemware hung upside-down by means of slipping the stems into notches on the shelves. A yacht decanter (fig. 86), now often called Captain's Decanter, is in the same bottom-heavy style.

Cut glass, the symbol of prosperity, was everywhere. Even the horseless carriage had wall brackets into which were inserted pointed vases for fresh flowers (figs. 325A, 325B; figs. C.7,8).

Not all rich men were as circumspect as the righteous Mr. Childs. The Astors, Morgans, and Rockefellers spent fortunes on parties to entice the cream of society into their Fifth Avenue mansions. Sometimes hostesses, such as Mrs. Vanderbilt and Mrs. Astor, engaged in snobbish feuds.

Christmas parties were "the thing." A typical Carrie Astor Christmas party offered a twelve-course meal with roast pheasant, truffles, caviar, trout, oysters, ten wines, and champagne. It would cost as much as $65,000.

In 1884 a party cost Mrs. Cornelius Vanderbilt $70,000, according to a newspaper reporter. The array of glass, silverware, and food was so heavy that each table had its legs reinforced with steel struts. The 340 guests each drank over a quart of Moët et Chandon champagne. Flowers alone came to $11,000, because they were out of season and were shipped from the South. Only rare and unusual vases were worthy of such expensive flowers. These vases (figs. 87, 88) are of sufficient grandeur and size for such occasions. Both are rarities.

The latter vase in "Empress" by the Quaker City Cut Glass Company (1902-1927) of Philadelphia is 24″ high. It was shown in an undated catalog, probably 1904-1905, selling for $61 wholesale. It was also made 30″ high for $90; 36″ for $125. These so-called "Revolving Vases" were described as "positively the newest and most unique Vases ever offered, composed

Fig. 87. Rare vase, 14½″; ½″ thick; 8½ lbs. Four large hobstars, four small flat stars, and four areas of cane decorate bulbous top. Narrowed portions cut in honeycomb; chain of alternate lozenges of silver diamond and flat stars encircle middle bulge; similar chain in kite fields goes around base. Bottom has a twenty-four-point star.

Fig. 88. Three-part "revolving" vase, 24″, in "Empress" by Quaker City. Double rows of cane (with hobstar on each button) in columns are separated by notched vertical prisms. Principal motifs at top, on center ring (fitting over metal parts that screw together), and on base are three pinwheels with intricate centers. Silver diamond, hobnail, and fan complete design of this elegant vase, fit for an empress.

Fig. 89. Champagnes, 4⅜″, attributed to Quaker City or Averbeck. Bowl cut in cane, fan, and hobstar; stem has teardrop. (Photograph by Conkling)

Fig. 90. Punch bowl on standard, 14″ d × 15″ h, in "Majestic" by Quaker City has four thirty-two-point hobstars around top with smaller twenty-four-point hobstars below them. These alternate with large vesicas with curved splits, chains of graduated hobstars with clear buttons, beading, and two smaller vesicas of hexad-of-buttons-and star, always a mark of quality. Stub, cut in a twenty-four-point hobstar, fits into a collar cut in hexagons of fine diamonds and zigzag stars. Pattern is inverted on the base. Extremely brilliant; weighs 32 lbs. This size was listed at $162.50 wholesale in the 1904-1905 catalog. (Miles)

of three parts, put together with Solid Silver Mountings." The catalog also listed three-part punch bowls joined in the same manner. The 15″ size in "Roosevelt" sold for $375. Motifs on a tulip-shaped bowl included the pinwheel and hexad-of-buttons-and-star, a cutting found on finest ware.

Quaker City knife rests were unusual: "Something new in Knife Rests, Centers of Heavy Metal, Quadruple Silver Plated, Square, Sextagon and Round." These are worthy of a search.

The three champagnes (fig. 89) are cut on unusual blanks with a stem resembling a knife rest. Illustrations of stemware on blanks identical to these appear in a 1905-1910 catalog of Empire Cut Glass Company (Flemington, New Jersey), in the 1904 Quaker City catalog, and in a 1904-1905 catalog for M.J. Averbeck, manufacturing jewelers of New York City. Averbeck cut glass was made at Honesdale, Pennsylvania, "in our own factory" and was "never advertised" (fig. 58). Doubtless all three companies had access to the same blanks.

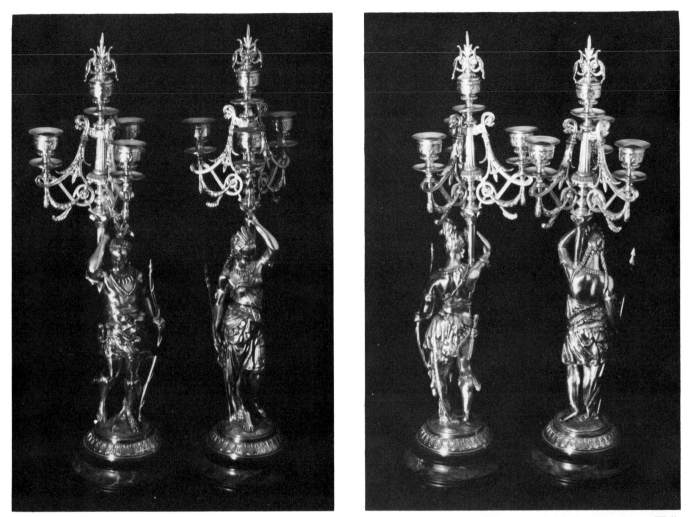

Figs. 91A and 91B. Indian figural candelabra, 24″, front and back views. Each weighs 9¼ lbs. — not as heavy as bronze. Well-proportioned figures cast in some metal containing silver. Experts have been consulted, but no two agree on country of origin. Some feel, as I do, that they were created for the Columbian Exposition in 1893 to honor the New World by a European artist (German?) who viewed American Indians as exotic and glamorous beings. Only the female is marked *EO* under the base.

Unfortunately, the Quaker City trademark — a drawing of William Penn and the words "Quaker City" and "Hand Finish" — was applied to the glass by means of a paper label. The Averbeck trademark, a stylized monogram of MJA, was probably on a paper label, also. The Quaker City champagnes sold for $5 each; the Averbeck sold for $37.50 per dozen, "exclusively to the retail jewelry trade."

One can easily imagine this spectacular, globular punch bowl on a standard (fig. 90) at a Vanderbilt banquet. Made by Quaker City in the "Majestic" pattern, it is similar in feeling and size to the 15″, two-piece "Aztec" punch bowl by Libbey, advertised in the *Saturday Evening Post,* 21 September 1901, which sold retail for $300. "Presentation pieces should be beautiful and durable, of such design and execution as to class them among works of art." This bowl is as finely cut as the "Aztec" and is surely a work of art fit to grace a mansion.

Victorian Silverware

Silver and gold, mined in our western areas, were in such abundance that there were limitless amounts for commercial purposes. Candelabra (up to three feet tall), silver table services (sometimes gold-trimmed), elaborate fruit bowls, silver statues and figural candelabra, such as these Indians (figs. 91A and 91B), were *de rigueur* in the homes of the rich. Gorham and Tiffany were cited for a variety of original designs in various treatments — chased, repoussé, inlaid, and niello — with real artistic merit.

The finest flatware was sterling silver, but most was silverplated. Some knives had plated blades and pearl handles. Table flatware came in a bewildering array of shapes for every conceivable use, some of which we cannot discover without consulting an old catalog.

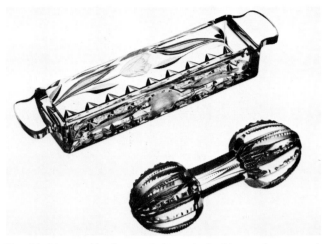

Fig. 92. Unusual knife rest, 5½″, with double teardrop signed HOARE in block letters. Few were signed. Domino sugar tray, 8¾″, is design #3888, aptly called "Tulip," by Gundy-Clapperton of Toronto, Canada. Bottom is cut in a chain of hobstars; glass is best ever seen in a sugar tray.

There were table knives for dinner, a smaller edition for lunch, plus fruit, orange, and dessert knives. Some were designated for bread and butter, and others for fish.

Besides dinner, luncheon, salad, and dessert forks, there were individual forks for fish, oyster, crab, and lobster. There were also fruit forks with three tines.

Spoons were made for bouillon, soup, tea, dessert, and ice cream. Some were pointed, with deep bowls, for eating oranges and grapefruit.

Carving sets, often made with horn handles and a sterling or German silver ferrule where handle joins blade, came with a steel for sharpening the blade. The knife blade, after use, was rested upon a cut glass knife rest (fig. 92) to keep meat grease off the tablecloth.

Serving pieces included cheese knives and scoops, spoons for serving ice cream, berries, salad, salt, sugar, and jelly; ladles for bouillon, soup, oysters, gravies, sauces, and bonbons. There were pierced spoons to sift sugar or serve vegetables (leaving juice in the bowl). There were serving knives for butter, fish, and even those with tines on the tip for melon and cheese. Fancy serving forks were used for salad, fish, cold meat, sardines, and bread. There were special serving pieces for cucumbers and sliced tomatoes. Most dramatic were the serving utensils with cut glass handles, such as fork and spoon sets for salads, berry spoons, and ladles for punch (fig. 289).

One item that would seem ridiculous today (when houses are so warm that one can wear summer-weight clothing indoors in winter) was a spoon warmer. Just as we preheat the teapot, our forebears heated the cereal and beverage spoons at the table in a boat-shaped, covered vessel containing hot water. Any reader old enough to remember arising in an ice-cold house can appreciate this preoccupation with warmth.

Other contrivances included a butter pick, sugar tongs for serving cubes of sugar (fig. 92), and a silver or nickel-plated "nutcrack." The latter came with six or twelve picks, neatly boxed, making a useful gift for newlyweds. Even the poorest family could enjoy cracking nuts and picking out nutmeats on a winter's evening.

Coating base metals by electrolysis was practiced as early as the 1840s, but became a large commercial business at the time of the Civil War. Sterling silver pieces, which could be afforded only by the wealthy, could now be reproduced at prices most people could afford. Napkin rings with attached figures of animals, cherubs, and fruits became popular with everyone, regardless of wealth. We inherited a plated toothpick holder, with a baby chicken beside a broken eggshell, inscribed "Just Picked Out."

The three Rogers brothers of Hartford, Connecticut, are generally credited with establishing the silver-plating industry in America. In 1862 they joined the Meriden Britannia Company, which made great quantities of Britannia ware, a refinement of the earlier White Metal. Britannia could be silverplated. Elaborate centerpieces with exotic figures and attached glass bowls for fruit or flowers graced many tables.

Although it was originally listed as a fruit or berry bowl, the item shown (fig. 93) came to be called a Bride's Basket because so many were given as wedding gifts. The bride's basket succeeded the épergne (fig. 153) in popularity in the 1880s, and remained in favor until the 1920s. This one is marked "Meriden Silverplate Company" (which in 1898 joined with Meriden Britannia and many other independents to form International Silver Associates). It is also marked "Quadruple," indicating a thick plating. Meriden quit stamping wares "Quadruple Plate" in 1896, thus dating the basket not later than that year.

The inserted bowl is a replacement that happens to fit nicely, obviously cut in the Floral or Transitional Period after 1906. Many bride's baskets were of colored glass of various types, and many had ruffled edges, such as the lovely Hawkes bowl in figure 318. Cut glass inserts were exceptional.

Meriden Britannia made condiment and pickle casters (or castors), teapots, and coffeepots. We were unable to find a condiment caster in American cut glass and had to settle for one made in England (fig. 404). By 1879 Meriden was offering a tilting ice water pitcher with matching goblet on a frame in forty-five different styles!

Fig. 93. Bride's basket, 8″ d × 3⅝″ h. Bottom of bowl cut in eight hobstars. On sides are six panels of engraved matte flowers and buds (stylized carnations) with polished miter leaves. Bars of relief diamonds with flat tops separate panels and decorate edge. Frame is typical of Meriden Silver Plate Company, whose name and "Quadruple" appear in a circle around a lion, with #743 below. Embossed scene of leaping deer, mountains, a tree, a lion with one foot on a small deer, hills, a large bird in flight, a palm tree, a stag with horns, etc., repeats itself around base. Applied leaves decorate legs and handle. Most baskets have a ring to hold bowl; this has a solid base. (Matye)

Silver-mounted Cut Glass and Presentation Pieces

Since Anglo-Saxon times, rare and valuable objects have been made more precious and beautiful by adding gold and silver mounts. This tradition carried on through the splendid age of which we speak. Only the finest blanks, expertly cut, were given this treatment. Some pieces are still sold at reasonable prices, but will doubtless increase rapidly in value.

Such prestigious silversmiths as Gorham and Reed & Barton, both of New York, published illustrated advertisements in magazines. In 1892 Gorham showed in *Life* "Silver Mounted Crystal," along with such accoutrements as "Silver Mounted Umbrellas, Canes, and Whips." In a Reed & Barton representation in an 1898 *Life* issue, we see a tall, cut glass martini pitcher with ornate sterling silver collar and spout, a tall jar, an inkwell, and a puff jar for milady's dresser — the last three with sterling lids. "Our goods are for sale by all the leading jewelers."

Fig. 94. Coasters. *Left to right:* One of eight with silver rim and a cut star, four marked MB Co. (Meriden Britannia Company) and four — MSP Co. (Meriden Silver Plate Company). One of four with nickel rim and small cut star, signed STERAUWARE, N.Y.

Fig. 95. *Left to right:* Puffbox, 4½″d x 2¾″h. A hobstar with two fans alternates with three blazed thumbprints (resembling flower buds) and miter cuts (simulating stems and leaves). Three complete designs encircle jar. Lid marked "STERLING, a dagger through a B, 1208 Pat. 1904." This is the early mark of R. Blackinton & Co., founded in 1862 in North Attleboro, Massachusetts. It has an Art Nouveau type of embossed design; two male lions stand with front feet resting on a shield; engraved *CT.* Interior of lid is gold-washed. Blackinton's products consisted mainly of sterling silver and 14K gold novelties, flatware, holloware, dresser-ware, and a small amount of costume jewelry. Pomade box, 2″d x 1⅝″h, is cut in notched prism. Beaded silver top with engraved monogram *MJT* is marked "STERLING, a large C enclosing a T and P, followed by a small o." Probably Tucker Parkhurst Co. of Ogdensburg, New York. Their sterling silver manufacture was listed as out of business before 1904 in a *Jewelers' Circular.*

Many small items, as well as bowls and pitchers, were made with sterling or plated silver fittings and were so listed in catalogs. The most elegant and unusual pieces, however, were often prepared on special order for clients to whom price meant nothing. They might even have been designed exclusively for the customer. These were often engraved with a message, a name, and sometimes the date. Presentation pieces are especially intriguing to the advanced collector.

Except for a few items in group photographs, or those withheld for a special reason, all cut glass with silver in this volume will be presented in this chapter. Some exemplify types which were plentiful; others are rarities, which proves that not all rarities are in museums.

109

The coasters (fig. 94) were used in Earle's home. There are eight with silver rims and four with nickel. They are cut simply, but were photographed to show how practically every glass item in the house was decorated by cutting or engraving. Dresser and card trays were also made in this fashion. The card tray rested on a console table in the hall as a receptacle for "calling cards" left by visitors. This was a requirement in polite society.

The first coasters were small trays with wheels, used for passing a decanter around the table to avoid breakage or spillage. The root word "coast" refers to its synonym, "slide." Later, stationary coasters (of all sorts of material) were used to protect wood surfaces and linens from drinking glass stains. A stationary wine caddy (or coaster) for a wine bottle will be shown with other rarities in the next chapter (fig. 140).

The puff box (fig. 95), with the initials CT on a shield between two lions on the sterling lid, is a reminder that monograms were a popular form of decoration all through this period and beyond Stationery was monogrammed, and letters were sealed with wax pressed to form one's initials. When a girl became engaged, she was thrilled to embroider her new initials on towels and pillowcases for her "hope chest."

The small jar (fig. 95) was called a pomade, vaseline, or ointment box in the catalogs. It is also monogrammed.

The square trinket box (fig. 96) may have held cuff links, shirt studs and collar buttons, or perhaps stick pins for the ties of the master of the house; it may have been a repository for pins and brooches for milady. The edges were silver-bound to protect them from chipping and to facilitate attaching a hinged lid.

The syrup jug (fig. 97A) is signed "Hawkes" so faintly that one might easily miss the mark This exact piece was shown in the February 1907 Ladies' Home Journal, page 40 (fig. 97B). Note the declaration that every piece was signed. Design is "St. Regis."

Among smaller items fitted with silver, we should mention here the syrup jug (fig. 461) in the old "Strawbery Diamond and Fan" pattern of the 1880s. This can be seen under cabinet pieces, photographed with an all-glass syrup jug.

The sugar sifter (or shaker, dredger, or duster) was called a muffineer in England. This one (fig. 98) has a silverplated, screw-on top. Its design is typical of the early days when we were still imitating Anglo-Irish styles. These shakers were often used for cinnamon toast, being filled with a mixture of cinnamon and sugar. Cut glass examples are rarely for sale. Late last century they were made in a great variety of materials, including silver and many types of art glass.

Fig. 96. Trinket box, 5½" sq, with silver fittings. Double-X-cut vesicas radiate from center of lid. Design nearly identical to that on a jug in a Heinz Bros. advertisement in a 1905 newspaper. (Jo Frazier)

The unusual oil cruet (fig. 99) is signed HAWKES on both silver and glass. In 1912, Hawkes began to make its own silver mounts and marked them HAWKES STERLING. Previously, silver fittings had been supplied by Gorham. The Wreath and Flower type of design, stylized flowers with string-of-pearls swag, sometimes with hanging tassels, also was used by Sinclaire and Pairpoint, late in the Brilliant Period, now referred to as the Flower Period.

The graceful claret decanter (fig. 100), signed GORHAM STERLING, may have been on the borderline between Middle and Brilliant Periods. The fluted neck, the body shape, and the form of the silver fittings resemble an engraved English claret jug, dated 1855, in James Norbury's book on Victoriana. The English version had a human mask under the pouring spout, similar to those in our chapter on foreign glass (fig. 403). Glass is attributed to Hoare.

Fig. 98. Sugar sifter or muffineer, 5¼″ Diagonal, double-miter cuts divide surface into squares containing small flat-topped diamonds and split diamonds. These alternate with old English strawberry diamonds and two tiny fans. Larger fans are cut at top and bottom. Base rayed.

Syrup Jug

Hawkes Cut Glass

The smaller pieces of Hawkes Cut Glass are distinguished by the same exquisite skill in cutting and the originality of design that marks the more elaborate ones.

No piece without this trade-mark engraved on it is genuine. If your dealer does not sell Hawkes Cut Glass, write us for address of one who does.

T. G. HAWKES & Co., Corning, N. Y.   HAWKES

Fig. 97A. Syrup jug, 4½″, signed HAWKES under a tiny trefoil on a small space near base, under handle. No mark on silver. Fig. 97B. Syrup jug, as illustrated by Hawkes in February 1907 *Ladies' Home Journal.* "St. Regis" design. (Photograph by Conkling)

Fig. 99. Oil cruet, 7″, signed Hawkes on both silver and glass, lightly engraved in a "Wreath and Flower" design, even on handle and bottom. Novel ball stopper swings open when cruet is tipped for pouring, then drops back to close opening.

Fig. 100. Claret decanter, 10″, signed GORHAM STER-
LING, cut in three fields of crosscut squares, silver diamond, zigzag stars with rayed buttons, and fans. Bottom
plain with polished pontil mark.

The banquet mustard pot (fig. 101) is truly a rarity,
suitable for use at a large dinner party. The simpler
cutting allows the clarity of the superb glass to be seen
to best advantage. Its design appears to have been
inspired by the architecture of a Russian cathedral with
pointed dome.

The lady's flask (fig. 102) enabled the lady who
tippled to carry her alcoholic refreshment with her
wherever she went. The honey pot and tooth powder
dispenser (fig. 102) are two more useful items combining silver and crystal.

The cigar jar (fig. 103), as it would have been
designated in a catalog, is often called a humidor, since
it kept tobacco moist and fresh. Such jars had a hollow
knob for inserting a damp sponge. This one, marked
Wilcox Sterling, would have been one of the superior
products of a company that joined many others in 1898
and was called International Silver Company. Jedediah
and Horace C. Wilcox formed the Wilcox Britannia
Company in 1865, changing it to Wilcox Silver Plate
Company in 1867. Meriden Cut Glass Company provided cut glass inserts for the work of the silversmiths,
most of whom continued to use their own trademarks.
The jar is cut in Meriden's "Zipper."

Fig. 101. Rare banquet mustard pot, 8″, with bone paddle,
rough at the tip, shows discoloration from mustard. Paddle
has a sterling handle, beaded to match lid. Elegant piece cut
in bullseyes and concave ovals. Arches under four feet meet
in center; handle is triple-notched. Lift-off lid marked with "a
cross, STERLING 894 U 925-1000 FINE," and has gold-
washed interior to prevent pitting of silver. Lower edge, which
slides down over a ⅝″ silver band around opening, is beaded.

The bitters bottle (fig. 104) on the left is also a
product of Wilcox and Meriden Cut Glass in Meriden,
Connecticut, home of many prestigious firms. Collectors look eagerly for bitters bottles, but seldom find
them in cut glass.

The barber bottle (fig. 104) on the right would have
been found in a barber shop catering to well-to-do
business and professional men or in a wealthy home.
Sometimes, by request, a barber would order a set of
two or three bottles for a customer for use in his home.

Barber bottles came in all sorts of glass: clear and
colored, cut and pressed in many patterns; in Bristol,
amethyst, and hobnail. Many were enameled by an
artist with scenes or paintings of people or flowers.
Each contained hair tonic, shampoo, or after-shave
lotion that smelled so strong that, for some time after a
gentleman's trip to the barber shop, the air about him
was redolent of bay rum or some more odoriferous
lotion.

Personalized hair tonic bottles and shaving mugs
were kept on the shelf for patrons who came daily or
every other day. The bottles were bought empty from

Fig. 102. *Left to right:* Lady's flask, 4¾″, cut in rows of hexagonal buttons alternating with rows of pyramidal stars, signed STERLING E.I.R. on the cap. (Author) Honey pot, 4½″, has sterling knob on stopper marked *WSW* for Wilcox. Fine-cut motifs include hexad, eight-point hobstars, silver diamond, fans, and beading. Handle triple-notched; neck cut in flat panels; base rayed (Dolan) Tooth powder dispenser, 5″, cut in concave diamonds in hexagonal shape. Lid with dispenser (which turns to reveal a hole) marked with a cursive *L* and STERLING 8647 — trademark of LaPierre Manufacturing Company of Newark and New York City. (Dolan)

Fig. 103. Cigar jar or humidor, 8″, repoussé lid marked WILCOX STERLING. Glass cut in alternate columns of plain and patterned beading in Meriden's "Zipper." (Gerritse)

barber supply houses and filled with barbers' own concoctions to remove dandruff or "cure" baldness. The Pure Food and Drug Act of 1906 banished refillable bottles in barber shops, resulting in the disappearance of these colorful vessels, as well as miniatures used as samples by traveling salesmen.

The covered butter dish (fig. 105) can be considered rare because of the monogrammed sterling silver knob signed Wilcox. This knob is *not* a replacement for a broken glass knob, as suggested by a visitor who had never before seen a silver one. Doubtless the dish was made to order as a gift, and most likely by Meriden. When the edge of the dome is tapped, it rings like a bell.

This pair of decanters (fig. 106) is rare, since the sterling stoppers with embossed poppies were made by special order and engraved *M* for the Masterson family in Canada, according to the dealer. Here is an excellent example of the use of a personal brand. They are marked "C.D. Peacock STERLING, a cross, 1357 AM 925-1000 FINE." In the chapter on advertising and distribution, we mentioned C. D. Peacock, "the oldest store in Chicago," established in 1837. It sold expensive silver items, watches, jewelry, and cut glass.

On page 52 in Rainwater's American *Silver Manufacturers*, the cross shown on these stoppers is depicted as the trademark for J. F. Fradley & Company of New York City, established in 1869. This firm made "14K gold and sterling silver cane and umbrella handles; 14K dresserware and novelties; sterling photo frames, vases, desk accessories."

Fig. 104. *Left to right:* Bitters bottle, 8″. Tiny screw-on cap tops Wilcox sterling stopper with cork inside. Glass is brilliant — typical of Meriden Cut Glass Company. Pattern: diamond-shaped areas of cane and those split horizontally by a prism with tiny fans above and below. Barber bottle, 8¾″, unsigned Hoare or O'Connor in "Monarch" or "Napoleon," has silver-topped cork stopper. "Monarch" is characterized by vesica with crossed splits, dividing it into two large and two small areas. Top large area has a star; lower is silver diamond with one split that starts at bottom and goes three-quarters of the way up through the fine cutting. These vesicas alternate with large hobstars around the piece. Fans complete the design.

Fig. 106. Pair of decanters, 11¼″ with sterling stoppers, engraved *M.* Silver signed C. D. Peacock. Numbered stoppers are not interchangeable, since they were ground to fit perfectly into necks of hand-blown bottles that varied slightly in size. Necks fluted with fine notching. Chief elements of design are hobstar in a kite-shaped field and a lozenge of silver diamond above an inverted fan.

Fig. 105. Butter dish, dome 5⅜″ d × 5⅞″ h. Plate, 8″, has beaded silver knob signed Wilcox, engraved with monogram *AS.* Design reminiscent of "Corinthian," cut by many companies in various ways. Note the hexad, found on many Libbey and Meriden pieces. Fine quality, wood-polished.

Fig. 107. Salad bowl, 9″×4″. Silver rim with beading; engraved monogram in fancy script, *TGC*. Trademark is "lion passant gardant, anchor, *G* STERLING S2806, followed by Neptune's trident" — Gorham. Cut by Hoare in 1897.

One can reconstruct the origin of these decanters by assuming that C. D. Peacock, jeweler, obtained the cut bottles from a high-grade source and ordered the stoppers to be fitted by Fradley. Either Fradley or Peacock engraved the M; Peacock then stamped his personal brand on the silver. The embossed poppies suggest the Art Nouveau period (1890-1910), a time of rebellion by artists against formal, classical design. The New Art preferred free, flowing forms copied from nature. L. C. Tiffany was a foremost exponent of this style.

The salad bowl with silver rim (fig. 107) is subdued and dignified in a tailored style reminiscent of Dorflinger's "Miter and Silver Diamond." It would please a critic of the "overdone" cuttings at the height of the period. This was cut by J. Hoare in 1897. The lion, anchor, and capital *G* was adopted for all sterling articles by the Gorham Corporation of Providence, Rhode Island, in 1868 — the same year that they abandoned the coin silver standard, 900/1000, and adopted the sterling standard of 925/1000 fine silver.

Fig. 108. Fruit bowl, 9″×4″, has silver rim in Vintage design marked Gorham. Glass cut in "Tiffany," identified by dealer. Central rosette has forty points around a center consisting of an eight-point star with a sharp jewel with eight facets. Each of the thirty-two-point hobstars around the sides has an identical center. Projections are so sharp that they hurt the hand when bowl is held. Weighs over five lbs.

The fruit bowl (fig. 108), with heavily embossed "Vintage" sterling silver rim by Gorham, is truly a masterpiece fit for a museum. It was purchased at Tiffany's in the 1880s. The design is planned so that the sharp-pointed jewel in the center of the bottom rosette does not touch the table's surface. Such creations were naturally cut on the finest blanks.

This berry bowl (fig. 109), with embossed roses on a sterling rim, monogrammed *HLS*, came from Shreve & Company, San Francisco. Cutting is striking and unusual. The star in the bottom resembles one seen in a bowl signed HAWKES. Shreve was a fine jeweler (on a par with Tiffany) who supplied the very best to those who could afford the best.

The elegant martini pitcher with sterling spoon (fig. 110) has a beautiful embossed silver collar. The dates "1877-1902" indicate that this was a silver anniversary gift for someone in the Ross family, "Ross" being engraved on both collar and spoon. It is also marked with the personal brand of Shreve & Company of San Francisco, where Dorflinger, Hawkes, and Libbey glass pieces were fitted with silver mountings. Founded in 1852 as a jewelry store, a silver factory was opened in the early 1880s. The firm prided itself on the quality of its monograms placed on special-order presentation pieces.

The wine carafe or water bottle with sterling collar (fig. 111) is also a presentation piece, a trophy, awarded to a polo championship winning team called the "Reds." It is precisely dated "1900," and the place is designated as the Sacramento State Fair. Team members seem to be of Irish extraction, judging by their names. A true specialist might make a collection of nothing but cut glass trophies. That would take some searching!

Two views (figs. 112A and 112B) of an extraordinary ashtray show another presentation piece, doubtless a gift to a retiring officer of an Elks Club in Everett (Washington?). His initials were E.A.P. The lodge number was 479 and the date — 8 September 1906.

The perfume bottle (fig. C.6), cut and engraved, has a sterling silver stopper enameled on top in green with pink roses, the field outlined in black. The shape suggests the 1920s.

Cut glass and silver candelabra (fig. 113) are truly rare. The plated silver is unmarked, but these candlesticks are identical to a pair signed WILCOX, sold without the arms, but with bobèches, so we may assume that the cutting was by Meriden on Mount Washington blanks. The quality is superb.

The other candelabra shown here (fig. 114) are smaller, the glass cut in horizontal steps with an "Arcadia" border around the base. Of the few examples shown in books, most appear to be all glass.

Fig. 109. Berry bowl, 8″; 9″ with rim, signed "Shreve and Co, San Fran. STERLING" with engraved initials *HLS*. Fine blank.

Fig. 110. Martini pitcher, 13″, with spoon, 14″, presentation piece signed Shreve & Co. on both jug and spoon. The name "Ross" and "1877-1902" engraved on sterling collar, decorated with flag lilies. Glass design consists of hobstar, notched vertical prism, and a brilliant sunburst of miter cuts. Handle double-notched with kite of silver diamond below it; bottom cut in a twenty-four-point single star. Spoon with twisted stem has a deep bowl and a floral design on the handle.

Fig. 111. Wine carafe or water bottle, 7½″. Collar marked "STERLING G, a cross, 922T 925-1000 FINE," plus a minutely scratched RX. The cross indicates that Fradley of New York City made the collar. Engraved in cursive writing is:

Polo Championship
Sacramento State Fair
1900
Won by Reds
No. 2 T. A. Driscoll, Capt.
No. 3 Charles Dunphy
No. 4 Joseph Tobin, Jr.
No. 5 Francis Carolan

The cut pattern is simple and masculine in effect.

Figs. 112A and 112B. Ashtray, 5½″ d, with sterling rim and attached matchbox holder: a presentation piece. Outside of holder is engraved "EVERETT LODGE PBOE 479 9. 8. 06." Initials *EAP* in cursive writing on inner side not visible in the view taken to show glass design. Four crossed ovals, resulting in an eight-point expanding star with hobstar center; kites and bands of silver diamond; flat stars and fans.

Fig. 113. One of a pair of candelabra, 17½″ with three silverplated branches in place; 9½″ base for one candle — a rare find. A twenty-four-point hobstar covers bottom of scalloped foot. Beaded and plain prisms, with bands of crosscut diamonds around narrow "waist," enhance beauty of candlesticks with two teardrops. Quality flawless. When removable top is in place, one may use three candles in the arms with twisted stems, or four by removing flame-sculptured snuffer. Each holder has a removable bobèche to catch wax drippings. Bases identical to a pair signed Wilcox.

Fig. 114. Pair of candelabra, 12″, cut in eight panels of horizontal steps below silver-plated mount. Bases cut in "Arcadia," the name listed in catalogs of Sterling Glass Co. of Cincinnati, Ohio. Similar patterns were cut by others — Hawkes, Bergen, Blackmer, and Hunt among them. Hunt cut a table lamp in "Royal" (patented 11 July 1911), composed of Arcadia and Russian. The lamp's "trunk" was cut in horizontal steps, suggesting that these candelabra came from Hunt in Corning, New York. They are unmarked. (Dolan)

From an historical standpoint, the candelabrum was a natural outgrowth of the single candlestick. With its graceful arms and flexibility as to the number of candles, it was the decorative table lighting source of the 1700s and 1800s. In the late 1700s, massive candelabra were made for the great houses and churches of England and the Continent.

The Sheffield plate candelabrum generally had two branches and a central socket with removable finial, into which a third candle fitted. Victorian dining tables featured twisted and removable branches, providing a change from a single candle to a choice of up to seven light units. The examples illustrated here provided one, three, or four.

The 20″ vase (fig. 115), engraved and polished in the Rock Crystal style, is attributed to Hawkes by comparison with a signed cream and sugar set. Collar and base are of sterling silver; the four embossed cherubs on the base are typically Victorian. The hallmark of Wm. B. Durgin of Concord, New Hampshire, is on the bottom. This firm was purchased by Gorham in 1905.

Finally, we have a lightly cut picture frame (fig. 116), identified as Sinclaire by comparison with a verified frame. The silver is marked STERLING; the glass is not signed. The photograph is of Earle.

Decline of the Gilded Age

With the introduction of personal income tax in 1913, followed by the Great War and its overtones of patriotism and practical simplification, came an unwillingness of succeeding generations to live as their parents had. Maintenance of such vast establishments became a burden, rather than a triumph. This has led to ruthless destruction of most of the great mansions of the Gilded Age. Only in the last few years has an effort been made to preserve the relatively few remaining examples. Some have been preserved and restored by historical societies; others have been converted to quarters for architects, lawyers, or other professionals.

Fig. 116. Picture frame, 12″ × 14″, marked STERLING, attributed to Sinclaire. Rock Crystal border of blaze or fringe with floral accents lies within sterling frame. Corners decorated by a classical figure in silver, repeated on the four heads of screws that go through the glass to secure black velvet mat on which photograph is placed. An easel backrest, also black velvet, holds frame upright. Such cut glass frames are scarce.

Fig. 115. Rare 20″ sterling silver-mounted vase, engraved; attributed to Hawkes. Silver signed Wm. B. Durgin of Concord, New Hampshire.

11
More Cut Glass Rarities

Extraordinary pieces, now called *rarities,* were not usually listed in catalogs for the ordinary customer. Enormous vases and punch bowls, made in scale to fit the large rooms of mansions, as well as replicas in cut glass of articles normally made of some other material, were generally made by special order. Unidentified but exceptional pieces are shown here; identified rarities will be shown in sections categorized by maker.

Whether the "Tiffany" pattern bowl (fig. 108) in the previous chapter is the same as the "Tiffany" design used on a 150-pound punch bowl cut by John S. Earl of Brooklyn is unknown. At any rate, Earl's $3,000 punch bowl, whose pedestal was 16″ high, was blown by the Union Glass Company for Tiffany & Company of New York in 1904. It held thirty gallons. With the bowl suspended by pulleys, thirty workmen took part in executing the design over a period of 210 days. While one cutter was at work, two men steadied the bowl.

Farrar and Spillman, in *The Complete Cut & Engraved Glass of Corning,* report that Diamond Jim Brady saw and admired it, but wanted an even larger bowl. Union and Earl again collaborated and sold the masterpiece to Brady for $5,000. Union Glass Company specialized in making large blanks for others to cut.

Examples of Cut Glass Rarities

Walking sticks or canes evolved from wands or staffs, which were carried as a symbol of authority by dignitaries of European courts as far back as the fifteenth century. Doubtless they could be traced even further to the symbolic crook and flail held by the pharoahs of Egypt, and to the staff held by Moses when God opened the Red Sea for His people's escape from Egypt.

There was a great vogue for walking sticks for both men and women during the Victorian Age. They were plain sticks with gold or silver heads, although in the 1890s there was a revival of porcelain crutch handles and even some heads of faceted colored glass. Some ladies' umbrellas and parasols featured gold plate, sterling silver, or inlaid mother-of-pearl. Some had engraved name plates to facilitate their return if owners absentmindedly mislaid them.

Beautiful umbrellas and parasols were an accessory of milady's costume when she went outdoors, partly as a fashion and partly to keep her "schoolgirl complexion." To be desirably feminine, ladies had to have a "peaches and cream" skin. A tan and/or freckles were anathematic to the ideal image of a lady.

When I was four, my mother insisted that I wear a sunbonnet when playing in the yard. I hated it and threw it out on the road. I was scolded and made to put it on again, so I threw it into the well, hoping to lose it forever. Dear Mother, thoroughly frustrated in her attempt to raise a beautiful, marriageable daughter, spanked me and put me to bed.

In Italian, *ombra* means shade; *ombrella* — little shade. The Latin is *umbra,* hence umbrella. The folding umbrella, invented in France, had ribs made of whalebone, then of oak, and finally of grooved steel. The covering material was glazed cotton cloth, paper, or silk treated with oil to shed rain. Alpaca as a covering came into use circa 1850. The umbrella was used for rain or sun, but the word generally applied to use against rain.

Again in Italian, *parasole,* from *parare* (to ward off) and *sole* (sun) became parasol in English. It was a "light, portable sunshade. . .used especially by women," a definition found in a 1911 dictionary.

Umbrella stands of some sort were in every front hall during the Brilliant Period. One piece of furniture, the combined hatrack and umbrella stand, had a hinged seat that could be raised to reveal a metal-lined box for overshoes and rubbers. Holes in a shelf about two feet from the base were made to receive umbrellas, whose tips rested in another metal-lined box to catch the rainwater drops. If this was not used, there may have been a free-standing "tree" for hats and coats, and a separate umbrella stand of brass or glazed pottery. Built-in closets in the hall or bedchamber were few. *Armoires* or cupboards, still common in Europe, were used for hanging clothes.

A few of the elite had cut glass umbrella and cane stands. Some of these had silver mountings; some did not. Either way, they were so expensive that only the wealthy could afford them. In addition to dainty umbrellas and parasols, ladies also carried canes for a time. A smaller stand, especially for ladies' canes, was made by a few companies. To cushion the tip of a cane or umbrella, a piece of felt was placed in the bottom.

The full-sized umbrella stand by Sinclaire or Hawkes, with Bow and Festoon engraving and undulated edge (fig. 117), seems appropriate for the ladies. This is attributed by an expert to Sinclaire, although Hawkes, Pairpoint, and Steuben also made wreath patterns.

The other stand (fig. 118), with beading, bull's-eyes, and stars, a Fry pattern according to the dealer in rarities, is more masculine in design. The quality and boldness, however, leads us to believe that it may be an elaboration of #28133 by Benjamin Davis for Straus & Sons of New York, registered 3 May 1898. Both are conversation pieces and would be excellent showcases for a collection of canes and/or umbrellas and parasols.

This rare whiskey jug (fig. 119), which holds one gallon, was sometimes called a demijohn or carboy. (Ordinary glass carboys held from one to ten gallons and were enclosed in wicker work, having two wicker handles.) It was doubtlessly made to order for a wealthy individual who entertained lavishly or for a hotel. Attributed to Hoare.

The bulbous pitcher (fig. 120) may have been described as a "wide mouth jug" in a catalog of the period. The shape is unusual. The 28-point hobstar that covers the bottom, the triple-notched handle, and the brilliance of the glass are marks of high quality.

The finely cut punch bowl with matching cups (fig. 121) must indeed be rare, since a matching 14″ tray is shown in the Weiner-Lipkowitz book on rarities. It is described only as "an extremely well-cut tray." The angle of the double flashing around the triple-X vesica is noteworthy.

The fruit or berry bowl (fig. 122) is also a rarity. Four lovely rosettes on a clear field contrast with complex cuts, filled with incredibly fine motifs, to make an unusual piece of the most delicate artistry. Only a master cutter could have executed this design.

The large orange bowl (fig. 123) contrasts nicely with the three pieces previously discussed in that it is heavy and bold in concept. The arrangement of motifs is unique and cleverly devised — probably Straus's "Corinthian" altered to fit the shape of the bowl.

Fig. 117. Umbrella stand, 23″, with undulated edge engraved in "Bow and Festoon" (our name for identification) in matte finish, probably by Sinclaire. Four chains of lozenges, alternately cut in hobstars and crosscut diamond, encircle piece. Between these are three chains of concave ovals, 2″ in length vertically. Flutes, 3½″ h, around base; bottom cut in large 36-point single star. Heavy but graceful and feminine.

Fig. 118. Umbrella and cane stand, 24½″. Chains of zigzag stars, with silver diamond triangles above and below, encircle stand at four places. Between bands, columns of beading alternate with clear panels, each cut in four bullseyes. Motifs offset. Bottom, cut in a thirty-six-point single star, shows much wear. Attributed to Fry by dealer.

Fig. 119. Whiskey jug, 16½″. Neck cut in horizontal steps; triple-notched handle; rayed base. Body sharply cut in hobstars and curved miters enclosing eight-point hobstars, cane, and silver diamond. Attributed to Hoare. (Wilson)

Another piece, important in scale and suitable for a large dining room, is this rare fruit compote (fig. 124). The tripartite form of the compote (or "comport" from the English, a term also used in many American catalogs) is unusual. Pitkin and Brooks used this shape, as well as the pinwheel and the fan of prism

flairs. This dramatic treatment of the pinwheel within the Gothic arch was surely from the first decade of the twentieth century. Many companies, including Averbeck, Bergen, and Clark, used the pinwheel after Patrick Healy registered design #30267, 28 February 1899, for the American Cut Glass Company of Chicago.

Fig. 120. Jug, 8″ h × 7⅜″ d, has unusual eight-point stars that alternate with flower-like device, consisting of four cross-hatched vesicas separated by fans and kites of silver diamond. Two deep miter cuts separate body from fluted neck. (Bob and Fran's Antiques)

Fig. 121. Punch or lemonade bowl, 12″ × 6″, with matching cups in an exquisite design, consisting of four thirty-two-point rosettes and four notched and double-flashed vesicas radiating from bowl's center. Vesicas triple-X-cut, each containing three hobstars and triangles and kites of silver diamond. Cups match bowl, but design simplified. A hobstar occupies a square area on the bottom.

Fig. 122. Fruit or berry bowl, 9″×4″. Four thirty-two-point hobstars alternate with vesicas, sub-divided into seven sections filled with minutely cut motifs, such as Russian and hexad — the smallest we have ever seen. All cuts hand-polished.

Fig. 123. Orange bowl, 13″×7½″×5″; 6½ lbs. Unusual arrangement of motifs. Three large twenty-four-point hobstars alternate with three fan-over-cane devices, so that a hobstar appears at one end of the oblong bowl and a fan-motif at the other. Silver diamond points of hobstar on base are twisted, not symmetrical. Figured blank, but well cut.

Fig. 124. Fruit compote, 12″ d × 10″ h; 9 lbs. Dramatic use of pinwheel within a Gothic arch. Fan of notched prism flairs. Notches on edge are two shorts and a long, often used by Dorflinger.

Fig. 125. Jelly compote, 7″ d × 9½″ h. Bowl's design employs hobstars, cane, and fine hobnail, as well as triangles of even finer hobnail and silver diamond. Foot, scalloped with vertical parallel cuts on its edge, divided by double splits into four squares, each containing a hobstar.

Although the previous compote is striking in appearance, this elegant piece (fig. 125) more surely deserves the accolade, "Rich Cut Glass," so often used in advertisements. The intricately cut bowl (7″ wide) was used for serving jelly, jam, or sweetmeats. Its unusual stem, with teardrop and knop cut in three hobstars, raised it to a height of 9½″ above the fully cut foot. No single star here! Whereas some items heavily cut with various motifs bordered on the ludicrous, this compote is harmonious and worthy of admiration.

Although the cutting is not as detailed, this compote (fig. 126) divided into four compartments is rare and of excellent quality. One could serve four different jams or jellies, relishes, or candies in this practical piece.

Cut in the old American "Strawberry Diamond and Fan," common in the 1880s, this two-piece butter dish (fig. 127) is truly a rarity. The stub, which fits into the opening of the lower part with two handles, has five holes drilled through the glass. Butter pats were placed on a bed of cracked ice in the upper part. As the ice melted, water dripped into the lower vessel. Dishes like this were also made for serving cress.

This charming sauce boat with matching tray (fig. 128) reminds us that meals were then replete with rich sauces and gravies. No one seemed to worry about calories.

Fig. 126. Compote, 9″ d × 8″ h, with four compartments; 5 lbs. Stem has unusual knop with a tear.

Fig. 127. Two-piece butter dish, 6″ d × 4″ h, in early "Strawberry Diamond (crosscut) and Fan"; triple-notched handles. (Dolan)

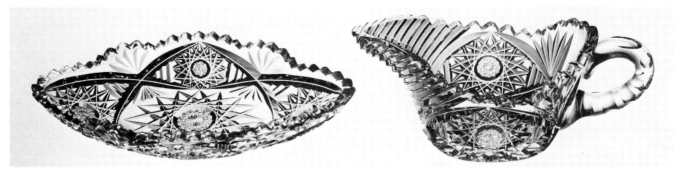

Fig. 128. Sauce boat, 7½″ 1×3″ h, with matching tray, 8¼″ 1×1½″ h. Lip in steps; handle double-notched. (Dolan)

Fig. 129. Canoe spoon boat, 11⅝″×4⅝″×2¼″. Design consists of a cluster of six hobstars around a central hobstar with six points of silver diamond, lately identified as "Plaza" by P&B.

Fig. 130. Bonbon dish, 8¾″×7½″×2¾″, cut in hobstars and cane, is rare in shape and design. Glass brilliant; cutting perfect (Matye)

Fig. 131. *Top to bottom:* Bonbon dish, 9″ l × 2¼″ h, inverted to show design clearly. Principal motif, a large hobstar, is dramatized by band of zigzag stars, miter cuts, and fans. Stick bonbon, 5″ d × 3¾″ h, has a tear going up the faceted knob. Such dishes were also used to serve butter balls. (Both from Dolan)

While canoe-shaped spoon boats are not exactly rare, they are seldom for sale, and some are mediocre in quality of glass and accuracy of cutting. Irving made canoes, labeling them "Spoon Boats." This one (fig. 129) is deeply cut on an excellent blank in "Plaza" by P&B. It may also have been used for olives, bonbons, pickles, or celery.

The variety of shapes in bonbon dishes was great. An interesting collection could be assembled of these alone. This one (fig. 130) seems to be a variant of a Meriden design, registered in 1900, named "Bysantine" by Revi.

The resemblance of this bonbon dish to a brassière (fig. 131) seems to be too close to be coincidental. Even the hobstar buttons are strategically placed. Surely the cutter smiled as he worked.

The round stick bonbon or butter ball dish (fig. 131) would be a ring tree without the faceted knob on the handle. Such a piece was made to hold finger rings, and would have been part of a dresser set.

Heart-shaped nappies were often given as Valentine's Day gifts. The triple-heart nappy with double-notched center handle (fig. 132) would truly have thrilled milady! It can be used for relishes, candies, nuts, or three varieties of jam. Revi (p. 304) shows a double nappy of the same size and handle by Irving Cut Glass Company, Honesdale, Pennsylvania. Irving sold superb glass all over the United States and in many foreign countries. This server may well be an Irving showpiece.

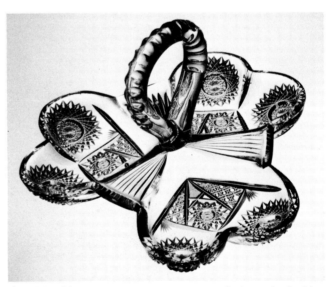

Fig. 132. Triple-heart nappy, 11½″ w × 6″ h, with double-notched center handle cut in hobstar, cane, silver diamond, and fan.

The 14″ decanter (fig. 133), cut in pillar and cane, is footed and has a matching stopper. Note how the cane buttons graduate in size.

The dainty condiment slipper (fig. 134) is indeed rare. The "Block" pattern was used in the early 1880s by several companies. Ruth Webb Lee's *Victorian Glass Handbook* (p. 189) shows a slipper of similar form that holds two perfume bottles.

Fig. 133. Footed decanter, 14″, in cane and pillar. Pillars on matching stopper can be aligned with the four on the decanter.

The book paperweight (fig. 134) is well cut in "Harvard" — a fine cabinet piece or useful desk accessory.

Napkin rings (fig. 135) were often made of silverplated metal, but were also found in cut glass. Glass rings are rarely seen today and have quintupled in price during the past ten years. In the richest homes, napkins were changed after every meal. In middle-class homes, as well as in boardinghouses and college refectories where the same people ate regularly, the linen napkin, thrust through the ring, was left at the place for use during several meals. Some schools

Fig. 134. *Left to right:* Slipper condiment holder, 5⅜″ l, cut in old "Block" pattern, probably by Mt. Washington, Smith Brothers, or New England. Salt, mustard, and pepper containers rest on steps cut in slipper. Superb glass. (A dealer/friend believes it is English.) (Author) Book paperweight, 4⅝″ × 3¾″ × 1¼″, cut in "Harvard" on front and miter elsewhere to simulate binding and leaves. Clear blank; expert cutting. (Dolan)

required the student to bring his own ring. A different pattern on each ring (or the name engraved on a silver ring) helped the diner to recognize his own, in case rings were switched while "crumbing" the tablecloth.

This tea, dinner, or call bell (fig. 136) is cut in Libbey's "Corinthian." It was used by the mistress of the house to summon the maid or butler. After electricity was installed in the house, a call button or buzzer was set into the floor near the chair at the foot of the table. The lady had merely to press down with her foot to ring a bell or buzzer in the kitchen. Old cut glass bells are scarce and expensive. Yes, it really rings! Learn to discriminate between old and new in Chapter 18.

One seldom finds complete, matching sets of any kind. This berry set (fig. 137) so closely resembles designs #33909 and #33910 by William Marrett for Libbey, 15 January 1901, that either it was designed by him or it is a plagiarized variant by a rival company at that time. The owner has two more individual dishes, which are obviously made-to-order replacements. They are not as brilliant or well cut.

In the colored glass section of the Weiner-Lipkowitz book (p. 157), there is an amethyst cut-to-clear decanter in this exact design (fig. 138). The colored version is not footed, but it does have a stopper cut in the hobstar design to match the bottle. At first a sense of alarm arose to suggest that the stopper does not match the colorless decanter. After noting that the stopper not only fits perfectly, but that it also has seven flutes that correlate with seven on the neck, one must conclude that the company cut the clear version in this fashion intentionally.

Fig. 135. Napkin rings, 1¾" l, have notched edges. Were bought together and look related, although patterns differ. Rings twice as long were used for large dinner napkins. Ring on right identical to one signed HAWKES.

Fig 136. Tea, dinner, or call bell, 5⅜", in hobstar, silver diamond, and fan — Libbey's "Corinthian." Faceted clapper hangs from a chain, the top end of which is embedded in glass at base of handle.

The wine goblets (fig. 138) do not match the decanter, but look attractive with it. They are of fine quality, cut in a complex design.

The round tray in "Cane" (fig. 139) is the perfect size for holding a wine decanter and stemmed wine goblets, or a whiskey jug and small shot glasses. Its use prevented drops of alcoholic liquor from damaging the varnished surface of table or buffet. It may also have been used at bedside to hold a tumble-up (fig. 20) or a small jug and tumbler.

This wine caddy (fig. 140) was made to hold a wine bottle, serving the same purpose as a coaster. It protected the tabletop from damage by alcohol. Another rare coaster is shown with Libbey glassware (fig. 251).

A wine washer (fig. 141) was at each place setting in certain homes for the purpose of rinsing the wine goblet between courses. You may recall that the renowned dinners for celebrated guests at the Philadelphia home of George W. Childs were often comprised of nine courses with a different wine for each course. Rather than use nine stemmed glasses at each place, the wine washer could be employed. It is doubtful that many households had them, however, for wine washers are rarely seen.

The water and wine goblets are cut in the rare "Cane-on-Cane" pattern (figs. 142A and 142B). These are one each of a dozen. There are eleven finger bowls (fig. 143), since one was cracked during shipment to the dealer. These are attributed to Hawkes without proof. Finger bowls originated in Europe, where fresh fruit often was and still is eaten as a final course. As proof that these bowls are hand-blown, they are slightly different in height and shape. One can play a tune by tapping the edges lightly, as each bell-like tone is of a different pitch.

129

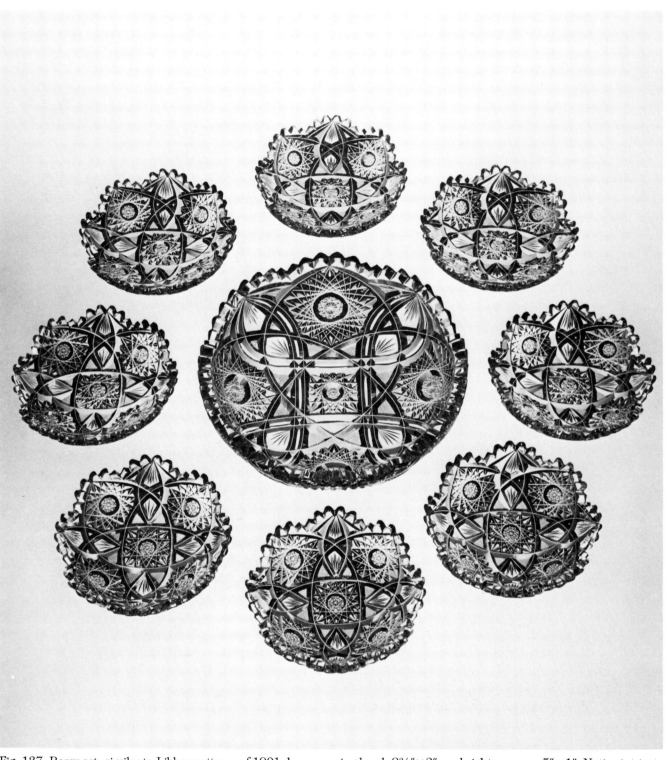

Fig. 137. Berry set, similar to Libbey patterns of 1901, has a serving bowl, 8¾″ × 2″, and eight saucers, 5″ × 1″. Notice intricate design featuring curved miter cuts that intertwine. (Hoglund)

Fig. 138. Footed decanter, 13½″; 16⅝″ with stopper. Three large hobstars with oval buttons made to fit deeply cut vesicas alternate with three smaller vesicas cut in pyramidal squares, with fan and two triangles of silver diamond above and below. Scalloped foot cut in a hobstar. Fluted stopper has large teardrop; neck fluted with beading. Wine goblets, 4¼″. A fan above a fan in a shield-shaped area, enhanced by beading, alternates with a fan above a hobstar, underlined by beading. Small flutes and lapidary cuts on knopped stem, plus a hobstar with clear center on the base, made these wines more interesting than ordinary vessels.

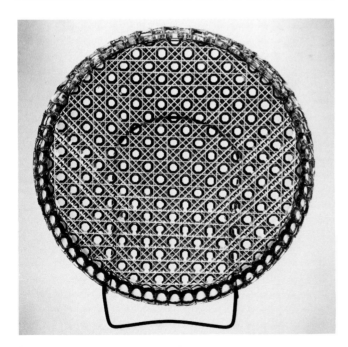

Fig. 139. Round tray, 11″, in "Cane" with clear buttons has a gallery, 1¼″, cut in vertical flutes. Such trays were used in place of a mirrored plateau for decanter and wines.

Fig. 140. Wine caddy, 4½″ d × 3½″ h, has rayed base over ½″ thick. Cut in buzz, fan, crosscut diamond, and miter. (Nash)

Fig. 141. Wine washer or ice tub in "Iceland" by Hawkes, 7″ w × 5″ h. Tabs cut in horizontal steps; base in a twenty-four-point hobstar. Around sides, six hobstars alternate with small sunbursts, with kites of silver diamond above and below. Various miter cuts complete fine cutting on an excellent blank. (Dolan)

Fig. 143. Finger bowl, 5¼″ d × 3″ h, in "Cane-on-Cane." Although "Harvard" is a form of "Cane" or "Chairbottom," its double cuts are usually diagonal and the single cuts horizontal and vertical. In this "Cane-on-Cane," directions are reversed.

Figs. 142A and 142B. Water goblet, 6½″, and wine, 6⅛″ in "Cane-on-Cane." On each button of the basic cane pattern is cut, in miniature, a section of the design, including four tiny buttons or hobnails. It is amazing to see the size decrease as one looks down the bowl. Each stem is fluted and faceted with a teardrop. Foot cut in a typically Hawkes radiant star.

Since affluent Americans emulated royalty from the "old countries," it is interesting to learn that King Edward VII was the first monarch to popularize cigar smoking in the English Court. Custom decreed that no one smoke unless the king gave permission. Edward enjoyed a good cigar and allowed members of the court to smoke in his presence. He assumed the throne in 1901 and died in 1910. In 1918 an American cigar (or "segar") named for the king made Edward's name a household word in the United States.

After a lavish dinner in Victorian or Edwardian society, the men often adjourned to the library or game room for brandy and cigars. There they were free to tell "manly" stories without offending the ladies, or to

Fig. 144. Cigar ashtray, 7¼″ × 2″; 4 lbs., is beautifully engraved in a horse's head. It has notched prism flairs on lower sides and a row of miter cuts around the top. It may have been made in Europe for P&B to their specifications. Prism flair was often used by P&B, who did some engraving in America.

discuss business, a subject too complex for mere women to understand. This handsome ashtray (fig. 144) is a fine example of those placed beside the heavy, leather chairs in a somber, masculine setting.

Meanwhile, the ladies would go to the drawing room for after-dinner coffee and gossip. The dainty demitasse cup and saucer (fig. 145) by J. Hoare is truly rare and would have been found in only the great mansions of the rich. As to how such glassware could

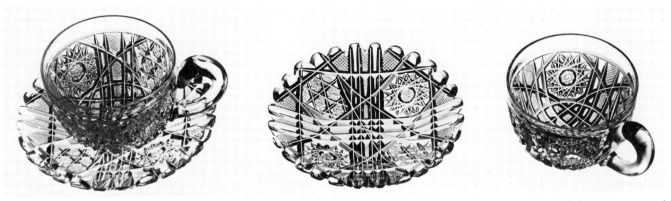

Fig. 145. Demitasse, 2⅝″ d × 2″ h, and saucer, 4″, by J. Hoare in an intricate pattern containing cluster and hobstars separated by miter cuts. Tiny saucer has a scalloped edge. Cup's rim and the quality are comparable to those of the fine "Cane-on-Cane" pieces (figs. 142, 143). Design is "Elfin." (Author and Dolan)

Fig. 146. Lady's cuspidor, 10″ × 2¾″, with rolled edge, in a Daisy pattern. The radiant star is typical of Hawkes, as is the undulating edge, yet Dorflinger, Pairpoint, Diedrich (Monaca, Pennsylvania), and others cut similar daisies.

Fig. 147. Lady's cuspidor, 9″ × 5¾″ h, attributed to Steuben, has undulated edge. It is engraved in Rock Crystal style. Between six applied, curled "handles" are bands of engraving that resemble a woven grass mat. Stylized flowers, tiny bullseyes, and bands of fine miter cuts complete decor. Bottom has polished pontil mark. (Photograph by Conkling)

withstand the stress of hot coffee, one can only conjecture that a demitasse spoon placed in the cup while pouring helped to dissipate the heat. We are not about to try it! Design is called "Elfin."

Doubtless the ladies who used these rarities during their after-dinner sojourn talked of the latest fashions, how difficult it was to find competent help to staff their several homes, whether to hire Irish or Chinese servants, problems with nursemaids and governesses for the children, and how to entertain visiting royalty from abroad.

Men used tobacco in all forms, requiring both ashtrays and spittoons, more elegantly referred to as cuspidors. The word cuspidor is derived from the Latin *cuspir,* meaning "to spit." Cuspidors for men were standard equipment in stores, courtrooms, and other public establishments. They were also found in homes, where daily cleaning fell to the servants. Most were made of steel, brass, plated nickel, or heavy tin. Some were of heavy ceramics, including stoneware.

Some ladies smoked, while others used a pinch of snuff inside the cheek and found it necessary to expectorate. Whereas the hillbilly grandmother smoked a corncob pipe or chewed a quid of tobacco, using her man's spittoon, the social butterfly employed a dainty, enameled Bristol glass cuspidor or an elegantly cut or engraved crystal vessel, such as this one engraved in daisies (fig. 146) or the cuspidor or spittoon (fig. 147) attributed to Steuben. Few of these have survived. Either they were stumbled over, kicked, and broken, or were thrown away when no longer socially acceptable.

The footed ice cream tray (fig. 148) is the only one we have seen. The design is interesting to examine.

One rarely finds a complete bridge set (fig. 149). Four ice cream saucers or bonbon dishes, shaped like the emblems on bridge playing cards, came in a silk-lined box to give as a prize. Design is "Whist."

Fig. 148. Footed ice cream tray, 12½″ × 8½″ × 2″, in X-cut vesicas and beading. One end of each vesica is left clear to reveal the round lee under tray. Four large, sharp relief diamonds mark intersection of double cuts in the center.

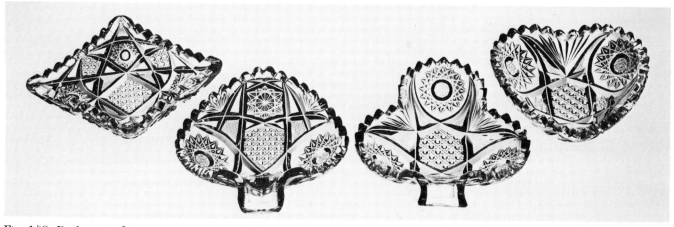

Fig. 149. Bridge set of ice cream saucers or bonbons, cut in hobstar, cane, silver diamond, and fan. "Whist." (Nash)

Opinions differed on the purpose of the object (figs. 150A and 150B) shaped like a mug with scalloped edge. Is it a shaving mug for the round bar of soap that produced lather for the shaving brush, or is it a spoon holder to be passed by the maid? Finally, it was found in a Quaker City catalog as a flower mug in "Eden."

The decanter in "Cleveland Russian" with the plain button (fig. 151) is one of a pair. Shown with a water goblet, a wine, and a saucer champagne drawn from a set, the decanter is distinguished by a tear the full length of the panel-cut handle. Judging by the narrow, pinched lip, the notch at the top of the handle, and the manner of attachment of the handle, one could estimate the date to be in the early 1880s. It closely resembles Mount Washington examples. Note that the neck of the decanter and stems of champagne, wine, and water goblet are cut in St. Louis diamond. The goblet is quite large and its stem thicker than those of the lighter-weight wine glasses.

Victorian delight in dual-purpose furniture carried over into cut glass. The rare reversible compote-vase (figs. 152A and 152B) is an excellent example of Libbey engraving. The beautifully sculptured fruit is of the high quality for which both Tuthill and Libbey are noted. Very few of this type of novelty were made. The 1917 catalog of Oskamp Nolting in Cincinnati, a wholesale house of jewelers, shows a 10″ footed punch bowl. The bowl may be lifted off to use as a separate bowl, while the foot may be inverted to serve as a compote. Its wholesale price was $21.

Figs. 150A and 150B. Flower Mug, 3¼″ d ×4″ h, in "Eden" by Quaker City. Base has twenty-point hobstar. Glass exceptionally clear; cutting sharp. (McKaig)

Fig 151. Decanter, 9″, 11¾″ with stopper, in Cleveland variety of Russian. Base rayed. Water goblet, 6¾″, saucer champagne, 4⅞″, and wine, 4⅞″ — each has six flutes at the bowl's base.

Fig. 153. Epergne, 9″ d × 13″ h, is relatively small when compared with some. A superior pinwheel is main motif. Secondary motifs: fans, hobstars, and triangles of silver diamond. Some vases were joined to base by means of a threaded, metal joint. This one is solidly joined, glass to glass.

In 1905, *Harper's Bazaar* reported that "even the old-time epergnes...are in vogue again" as center-pieces on the dining table. Some were in cut crystal, but they were also made of vaseline and other colored glass. Some had three vases bending gracefully away from the vertical position of the taller, central vase. In this rare épergne (fig. 153), either fruit or floating blossoms were placed in the lower bowl, with cut flowers in the upper vase.

All lamps cut geometrically on fine blanks are rare. They usually have faceted pendants. This one (figs. 154A and 154B), probably by Hawkes, shows the base to better advantage without them.

This exquisite bowl (fig. 155), which I attribute to Sinclaire, could have been cut by Tuthill or one of the independent shops in Corning. The "silver thread" background was used a great deal by Sinclaire. His six-panel bowls, however, were mainly of thinner glass and had smooth top edges. It is heavy and sharply cut.

One can assume that the unsigned footed bowl (fig. 156) in the "Persian" type of "Russian" was made by Hawkes, Dorflinger, or more likely by Mount Washington, whose catalog showed Russian-cut bowls with this same edge.

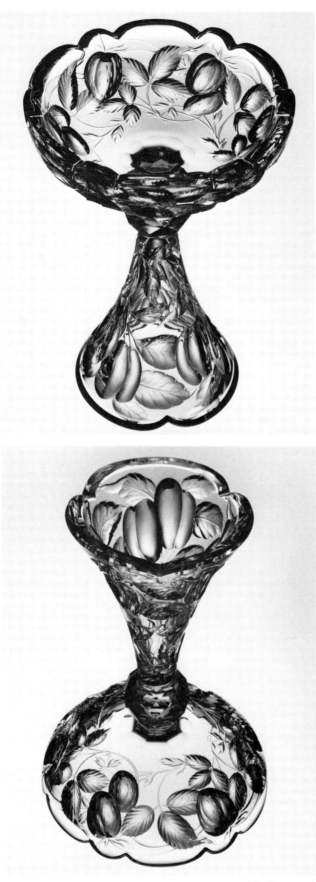

Figs. 152A and 152B. Reversible compote, 9″. Unsigned intaglio fruit by Libbey. All engraving work completely polished. Inverted, base becomes a vase. (Gerritse)

Fig. 155. Bowl, 8″×3″, cut and engraved, has six panels with sixteen-point hobstar on each, set off by fine-line flashing. Each line cut individually — not on a gang wheel. Base has engraved blossoms, buds, and leaves, partially polished. A prism flair lies between panels. (Weir)

Fig. 156. Footed fruit bowl, 10″×5″, cut circa 1885 in Persian type of "Russian." (Button cut as an eight-point hobstar.) Note clear 5″ circle, through which is seen the 5″-wide foot. Plateau, 14″, was listed in the 1899 Higgins & Seiter catalog in either gold or silver. This is silver.

Plateaux came from 8″ to 18″ in diameter at 2″ intervals. This one (fig. 156) was sold for $4.20 by Higgins & Seiter in 1899. They are seldom for sale by dealers now because most plateaux are retained for display purposes. The rococo design on the silver-plated base is typical of that on many household articles in the 1890s, such as lamp bases and especially the nickel-plated trim on base burners (parlor stoves) and kitchen ranges.

A fabulous punch bowl, measuring 24″ in diameter by 12″ deep, was made by Hawkes as a special order for John Jacob Astor IV in the year 1912. The brilliant Steuben blank was cut deeply in a unique design, while matching cups were proportionately adorned.

Figs. 154A and 154B. Table lamp, 21″ h × 14″, with three bulbs. Cut in hobstars, bands of single stars, and silver diamond. Finest quality. (Photograph by Conkling)

The bowl was being fitted with a 4" embossed sterling silver band by Gorham at the time of the sinking of the *Titanic,* the "unsinkable" ship that struck an iceberg in the North Atlantic. Mrs. Astor, grieving over the loss of her husband, never claimed the bowl. It was sold to another family, where it remained until 1970 when it was offered for sale to the public.

The Sinking of the *Titanic*

The *Titanic* was a symbol of progress. It was more than a gigantic liner, longer than the Woolworth Building is tall (750 feet) and much longer than the Great Pyramid is high (451 feet). The *Titanic* and its sister ship, the *Olympic,* built by the prestigious British White Star line, were 882.5 feet long by 92.5 wide. The *Titanic* was eleven stories high and weighed over 45,000 tons. It had tennis courts, golf courses, and even a herd of cows.

Although we are awed by such statistics and impressed by descriptions of luxurious staterooms with adjoining rooms for servants, the stained glass windows in the smoking room, and other signs of wealth, we must take note of several important facts, some of which were fatal.

The floating city was taking the ice-plagued northern route, yet six warnings by wireless concerning icebergs were ignored. Phillips, first operator, was giving personal messages from passengers to Cape Race in Canada when the liner *Californian* tried to warn him. He snapped, "Shut up, shut up! I am busy." An hour later, at 11:40 p.m., 14 April 1912, the *Titanic* sideswiped a berg which cut a 300-foot gash in her side.

When Captain Edward J. Smith finally realized that the "unsinkable" behemoth was indeed sinking, he ordered the lifeboats uncovered. This was about twenty-five minutes after the collision. He also ordered a call for help. The *Californian* was only ten miles away, but the annoyed operator had closed down his set. Later, men on the *Californian* stood watching as rockets were fired from the *Titanic,* reported this to their sleepy captain (who took no action), and continued to watch as the *Titanic's* lights sank into the sea. They supposed the ship to be moving away. The steamer *Birma* heard the call, but was a hundred miles from the scene. Others answered, but were also too far to help.

There were only sixteen lifeboats and four collapsible canvas boats. Altogether they could carry 1,178 people, yet there were 2,207 on board. There had been no drills. Loading was haphazard, some boats were only partially filled. Class distinction was clearly evident, as steerage passengers were mainly ignored. Few escaped.

Although the rule was "women and children first" and many upper-class men gallantly placed their wives in boats, then stayed behind, the end result was that, of the crew, 139 were saved; of men passengers, 119; and of women and children, 393: a total of 651. Figures on lives lost differed from 1,503 to 1,635.

There were many heroic actions among the passengers and crew. The band members played ragtime until the water was over their feet. None were saved. It was suggested that Isador Strauss, member of Congress and multi-millionaire banker, who had built Macy's into a national institution, might go because of his advanced age. "I will not go before the other men," he replied. His wife refused to be rescued without him. "Where you go, I go." They smiled and sat down on a pair of deck chairs.

The Astors

It was fashionable for members of high society to be the first to cross the Atlantic in such style. A deluxe suite on the *Titanic* cost $4,350 for six days. (Harold Bride, second wireless operator, made $20 per month. It would take him eighteen years to earn this passage fee.)

Because of our knowledge of the Astor punch bowl, unclaimed by the widow, we have chosen the Astors as prototypes of the "beautiful people" who made that aborted voyage.

Mr. Astor's great-grandfather, John Jacob Astor, emigrated to America at the age of twenty from Heidelberg, Germany, in 1763. His American Fur Company was the first American business monopoly, but the greater part of the family fortune was made in New York City real estate. Astoria, Oregon, is named after him.

John Jacob Astor IV, a Harvard graduate, built, among other edifices, four of the largest hotels in New York City. He organized and equipped a battery that served in the Cuban campaign. At his death at the age of forty-eight, his fortune was estimated to be over $87 million. According to Walter Lord's fascinating book, *A Night to Remember,* Mr. Astor had once observed, "A man who has a million dollars is as well off as if he were rich." Think about that.

The Astors were a handsome couple. They came aboard with a manservant, a maid, and their Airedale, Kitty. Many dogs of the rich were as glamorous as their owners.

When the ship hit the iceberg, Mrs. Astor heard a noise and concluded it was some mishap in the kitchen. She lay back in bed. As the ship glided to a stop, the silence alarmed some of the passengers. Mr. Astor went up to investigate. He returned to report calmly that they had struck ice, but it did not look serious.

Deep below, the steerage passengers had heard a tremendous noise, which sent them tumbling out of bed. No bells sounded an alarm, but word passed quietly all over the ship that it was serious. Passengers were incredulous and reluctant to get up.

Going on deck, "Mrs. Astor looked right out of a bandbox in an attractive light dress." The Astors whiled away time in the gymnasium while the lifeboats were swung out. They sat side by side on a pair of motionless mechanical horses. They wore their lifebelts.

When the captain ordered people into the boats, Astor ridiculed the idea. "We are safer here than in the little boat." The boats had to drop seventy feet to reach the ocean. Now there was no more joking. As Mr. Astor helped his wife into the boat, he asked if he could join her, as she was "in a delicate condition."

"No, sir. No men are allowed in these boats until the women are loaded first."

Astor requested the number of his wife's boat, then stepped back and stood alone quietly. Other social luminaries stood about in clusters as they watched and waited for the end.

When the captain relieved the crew from duty, some jumped, but most stayed with the ship. A man later reported that his last glimpse of the captain was in the water with a child in his arms. One rumor went around that he had shot himself; another that he declined to be saved and went down with his ship. The final wireless message for help was sent at 2:18 a.m. The lights failed two minutes before the massive liner foundered at 2:20 a.m., 15 April 1912.

April 16, the *New York American*'s lead article was almost entirely devoted to John Jacob Astor. At the end, it did mention that eighteen hundred others were also lost. Mrs. Astor was met in New York by two automobiles carrying two doctors, a nurse, a secretary, and Vincent Astor. Mrs. George Widener and Mrs. Charles Hays were each met by a private train.

End of the Golden Age

We must remember that there were no movies, radio, or television stars then for the common people to adore. The 190 families in first class on the *Titanic* were attended by twenty-three handmaids, eight valets, and assorted nurses and governesses, not to mention hundreds of stewards and stewardesses who served them. To enjoy this luxury vicariously was a sort of substitute for worship of royalty, now lost to the American people.

Never again did wealth serve as a god to such an extent. Some ministers preached that the disaster was a heaven-sent lesson to punish people for faith in material possessions. A hundred years of peace, improved technology, and countless inventions heretofore undreamed of had inspired too much self-confidence. The *Titanic* disaster woke people up. It was a stunning blow.

Several practical changes were adopted to prevent another tragedy. Ocean liners advertised that henceforth they were taking a southern route, the American and British governments established the International Ice Patrol, wireless operation on a twenty-four hour basis was mandated, and requirements for lifeboats were updated. Class distinction in filling lifeboats was also ended, at least officially.

We entered an era of uneasiness and even of fear. Two short years later came the realities and insanity of war. Emotions were whipped up for patriotism, hatred of the enemy, and self-sacrifice. There was little room left for the frivolities associated with excesses in dress, manners, and entertainment.

Cut Glass in the White House

Visiting diplomats and royalty were often caught up by the enthusiasm of their wealthy hosts, or viewed our glass creations at a fair, then ordered American cut glass in preference to that made in Europe.

Although Hoare supplied cut glass to the White House during Grant's administration, Dorflinger and Hawkes seem to have been the chief sources of this tableware.

Christian Dorflinger served eight presidents, from Abraham Lincoln to Woodrow Wilson. Some of this ware was produced in his glasshouse in Brooklyn, New York, and some later at White Mills, Pennsylvania. His Lincoln service, delicate and thin, with the United States coat of arms above a band of silver diamond, is considered by many to be the most beautiful of all services ever used at the White House. Mrs. Mary Todd Lincoln personally selected it and signed the bill for $1,500. Part of the set consisted of goblets with colored bowl, but with stem and foot of clear glass. This may account for reference to "Bohemian" stemware at state dinners mentioned by journalists.

Mrs. Lincoln was criticized for her extravagance and her low-cut gowns, one of which cost the incredible sum of $5,000 in 1865. An 1861 photograph shows her in a full-skirted dress. She wore flowers in her hair and a set of Tiffany pearl earrings, necklace, and bracelet. She carried an ivory or lace fan.

The Lincoln service was used by Andrew Johnson (1865-1869), Ulysses S. Grant (1869-1877), Rutherford Hayes (1877-1881), James Garfield (1881), Chester Arthur (1881-1885), and for a time by Grover Cleveland (1885-1889) until he ordered the "Russian" pattern from T. G. Hawkes in September 1885. This brilliant design, created by Phillip McDonald, was patented 20 June 1882, but as soon as Hawke's seven-year patent term expired, it came into public domain and was cut by several other companies.

An order was filled for President Cleveland for six hundred pieces to be used for state dinners. The White House version of this design (fig. 156), soon to be called "Russian," was set with an engraved, shield-shaped cartouche of the United States coat of arms and was signed, "Hawkes."

In 1886 President Cleveland was married in the White House. At state dinners given by Cleveland and his wife, rare wines and liquors were served, but none were available at their private dinners. Even at state banquets, Mrs. Cleveland and the president's sister, Rose, had only glasses of water at their plates. A journalist described the first state banquet to honor the cabinet. At each plate were six Bohemian wine glasses, a cut glass carafe, tumbler, and champagne glass. Salt cellars of cut glass with golden shovels and silver pepper stands were beside these. Resting on each plate was a large damask napkin, and on this was a corsage of roses and ferns for the lady guest or a boutonniere for the gentleman.

A complete banquet service was purchased for the Russian Embassy in Washington. Shortly thereafter, the American Embassy at St. Petersburg ordered a complete service, hence the name, "Russian," for this famous design.

President Harrison ordered "Russian" from Christian Dorflinger & Sons, paying $6,000 for 520 pieces in 1890. Cleveland used it in his second term (1893-1897) and William McKinley used it, too (1897-1901). Theodore Roosevelt (1901-1909) added a highball or ice tea glass in "Russian" (but in 1902 ordered a copy of the Lincoln set, replacing the shield with an engraved "R"). William H. Taft (1909-1913), Woodrow Wilson (1913-1921), Warren G. Harding (1921-1923), and Franklin D. Roosevelt (1933-1945) continued to use "Russian" until 1938.

During the Prohibition era (1920-1933), alcoholic beverages were not served in the White House. Wine glasses were used again after repeal, but Russian-cut pieces were considered to be too expensive for large official entertaining. Besides, skilled glass cutters were now "few and far between." F. D. Roosevelt ordered a pattern from Hawkes called "Paling," since it resembled a fence paling. It had a simpler engraved coat of arms.

"Paling" was used by Harry S. Truman (1945-1953) and Dwight D. Eisenhower (1953-1961), but when John F. Kennedy came to the White House, Mrs. Kennedy decided she preferred a tulip-shaped, plain crystal with a long, plain stem. Crystal for "The President's House" was ordered from the Morgantown Glassware Guild in West Virginia.

Except for the days of Prohibition, most first ladies served wine and alcoholic punch at dinners, receptions, and musicales. During Tyler's tenure (1841-1845), "Daniel Webster Punch" was a favorite. It consisted of Medford rum, arrack menschino, brandy, champagne, strong green tea, lemon juice, and sugar.

Grant's successor, Rutherford B. Hayes never served liquor in his Ohio home, and Mrs. Hayes took a strong stand against serving it in the White House. Nevertheless, her table always "groaned with delicacies." She earned the nickname of Lemonade Lucy and was the cause of the expression, "Water flowed like wine." She had to bow to protocol, however, when the two Grand Dukes of Russia, Alexis and Constantine, made a state visit, 19 April 1877.

White House banquets during the last quarter of the nineteenth century began at seven o'clock and lasted up to three hours. They consisted of twenty-nine courses, sometimes broken in the middle with frozen punch. The table resembled a flower garden, with vases or baskets of flowers every few feet and festoons of vines and flowers around the edge.

A photograph in Robert's *Table Settings* shows an 1899 White House table setting with a central hedge of greenery — smilax and asparagus fern — down the middle. It would have been difficult to see who was sitting on the other side. A 1902 state dining table is also shown with "Russian" stemware clearly visible. "Huge clumps of plants dominate the table." Remember this mania for decorating with fresh flowers and greenery as we view the great variety of cut glass flower containers in this volume.

12

Life-Style of the Middle Classes

Just as monarchs in Europe copied Louis XIV's Versailles château with its *Galerie des Glaces* (Hall of Mirrors), so did socially minded families down the economic ladder, at least to the middle rung, attempt to imitate the "Elegance, Taste, and Art in the House" of men like George W. Childs (to borrow the title of the 1886 article on his homes in *Good Housekeeping*).

Middle-Class Houses

American homes were relatively simple until 1860 when the newly rich began to symbolize their material success by means of flamboyant styles in house construction. This orgy of palaces continued for forty years. Efforts by the less affluent to emulate the rich resulted in some weird and wonderful creations, characterized by critics as "steamboat Gothic" and "aggressively frightful."

Thanks to the new, ingenious woodworking machinery, such embellishments as ornate towers, spindles, and portholes filled with colored glass filtered down in some degree, even to lower-middle-class homes. Mansard roofs gave a French appearance to some. Knobs, curlicues, and scallops (called "gingerbread") trimmed others.

Interiors of comparatively modest homes were garnished by beautiful woodwork around doors and windows, and by wainscoting in the dining room (fig. C. 17). All were made possible by the new woodworking machines.

As glass factories recruited foreign workers, so did such furniture factories as Berkey & Gay of Grand Rapids, Michigan. Out of 255 employees, only eighty-two were born in America.

The first two-thirds of the nineteenth century saw revivals of styles: classical (with Greek and Roman motifs), Napoleonic Empire, English Regency (coarsened for public consumption), Gothic, Elizabethan, Rococo, and the French fashions of Louis XIV, XV and XVI — all successful in varying degrees.

During the 1830s, massive furniture with S and C scrolls was derived from the French restoration period. About 1850-1860, John H. Belter created a rococo style with lacy floral designs of laminated wood. "Renaissance" generally describes furniture with divergent elements from Europe, mainly from the French, which featured the broken-arch pediment, applied medallions, the tapering baluster leg, and inlaid burled panels. Notice the green settee (fig. C.20).

In the post-bellum years (1865-1876), the historical revival reached its apex There were curvalinear rococo ornaments on some pieces, animal heads on chair arms, and deeply carved fruit and flowers on chair backs. A substyle of Louis XV was a parlor set, produced *en suite* from the 1850s onward, with medallion-back settee and chairs, often with carbriole legs. My husband's home had lion heads in the music room and medallion backs in the parlor.

The last thirty years experienced an incorporation of many historical sources in the same piece of furniture. Many pieces were ponderous and overdone. Even Grand Rapids furniture became monstrous, "an array of vulgarity," albeit of fine workmanship.

Some designers broke with revivalism around the middle of the century and used materials other than wood, such as wire, iron, *papier-mâché*, cane, rattan, or animal horns. Fads included Turkish designs with fringe and embroidery, chairs constructed of steer horn (circa 1885), tables and chairs made of tree branches with their bark intact, and bamboo with an oriental look. The Art Nouveau style, with its delicate flowing lines, influenced furniture as well as Tiffany glass, lamps, and other items from about 1890 to 1910. (See china closet, fig. C.19.)

Previously we mentioned the Victorian penchant for folding furniture. A Madame Récamier type of couch had a concealed bathtub, revealed by lifting off the top. It had to be emptied by dipping out the water. A bathtub patented in 1881 resembled a Murphy wall bed. Standing on end, it was recessed into a wall, or was installed in an existing closet in any room. The tub was hidden behind a door that, when opened, permitted the tub to be lowered into the room.

The ritual of the bath did not generally take place in a room specifically for this purpose until about 1900. Especially in the lower classes, a portable round wooden or galvanized metal tub was filled in the kitchen or smokehouse. It was comfortable for children, but for adults, feet hung over the side. In poor households, a bath was taken weekly on Saturday, with several members using the same water.

Mass-produced furniture for the common people assumed only a semblance of the styles made for the rich.

Mechanization eliminated jobs previously done by hand. It standardized designs, making handwork more precious to those who could afford it. Machine-made items, especially such articles as lamp bases and kitchen ranges, were covered with ornate, embossed designs, some of which were attractive. The parlor heating stove was a thing of beauty, with isinglass windows through which one could see dancing flames. It was trimmed with nickel-plated bands and rested on an insulating board with a zinc surface.

The Patent Gazette, circa 1895, shows many patterns for wallpaper and carpets. The paper generally had formal tapestry-type patterns with a border next to the ceiling. Many Whittall Anglo-Persian rug designs were patented. Made in Worcester, Massachusetts, they were the first "American Oriental" rugs, machine-made, and wore for generations. Wall-to-wall carpets were floral or geometric in design.

Rooms were "busy," with an excess of patterns and a clutter of mass-produced knickknacks, such as waxed flowers and peacock feathers, often kept under a glass dome. John Rogers statuary groups in plaster, depicting soldiers in the Civil War and ordinary happenings in family and social life in America, were made between 1859 and 1892. A few were cast in Parian, probably by Copeland and Garrett in England. They were popular and modestly priced at $6 to $30. Rogers was the Norman Rockwell of that era.

The 1895 Delineator magazine printed articles on "Artistic House Furnishings and Decorations." They show incredibly complex draperies, with swags and tie-backs, in more than one material on the same window. Doorways were hung with draperies, partly to conserve heat.

Kerosene lamps and candles are seen in an 1896 illustration, as well as a hanging Moorish lamp. "Above a cherry secretary is fastened a bracket which supports a marble bust that stands out white and clear from a novel background — a dried palm leaf."

A 1905 article in American Homes and Gardens shows a simpler treatment of windows, but potted plants and statues still abound. "The Decorator's Last Word on the Dining Room" shows a cut glass footed punch bowl on the oval table and several pieces of cut glass on the buffet. From this time onward, designs of furnishings became progressively simpler and less pretentious.

Ferromania

A sort of "ferromania" seized American society near the advent of the Brilliant Period. In 1857 the United States was second only to England in the production of iron. The tensile strength of the metal permitted designs to be executed that were impossible to do in stone or wood.

Consequently, such public items as the light posts in Union Square, New York City, and in the Ladies' Pavilion in Central Park became works of art. Columns and façades of buildings, and even a new dome over the Capitol, were cast of iron. After the terrible Chicago fire of 1871, when it was found that iron structures crumpled from intense heat, the use of stone was revived for safety's sake.

Nevertheless, all through the 1860s and 1870s, iron was used for girders and stairs, decorative columns in Greek designs, garden furniture, radiator shields when steam heat was used, and for some indoor furniture. Note the green, velvet-covered stool (fig. C20) cast by W. H. Howell Company of Geneva, Illinois, circa 1903. Its cabriole legs are silver-plated. Metal "finishing plates," pressed into formal designs similar to those in cut glass were also used extensively to decorate ceilings.

The Horseless Carriage

For those who could afford the best in pleasure carriages, drawn by one horse or a pair, an advertisement of broughams in Life (1891) quoted Seneca:

> Per quae luxuria di tiarum ludit [The caprices of luxury which would escape the tediousness of riches] All of these caprices of luxury are to be found in our Broughams: Toilet Box, Card Rack, Umbrella Holder, Cane Slide, Cigar Ash Tray, Pneumatic Signal Tube, French Indicator Watch, Stable Shutters, Sliding Third Seat and noiseless gear... They cost no more, for we include them all as a part of the necessary equipment, just as the wheels or shafts are necessary.

The Latin quotation reminds us that the educated man of culture had a firm grounding in the classical languages. This advertising symbol of snobbery, directed to the cultured customer, is another "sign of the times." Only by accumulating wealth could one climb over the barrier to a higher class. Even then, old families of wealth were often reluctant to accept the newly rich. Orientals and blacks were never welcome in society.

A 1905 article in Suburban Life predicted that the automobile was destined to play a conspicuous part in the development of suburban districts. Men who could not afford a motor car in the city could do so by moving up to twenty miles away in the country, where living expenses were lower. At the same time, they could escape congested city streets and "flats." According to the article, the

> Average man of sedentary habits...suffers from a lack of sufficient exercise. Automobile riding furnishes a large amount of helpful exercise without danger of causing strains or injury. The work of steering, gear changing, managing the foot pedals, together with the jar, swaying and jouncing of the car all work toward this end. Riding in a motor car may be compared in many ways to horseback riding, although the exercise is less violent.

For one who could afford an automobile in 1905, a Model C Buick Touring Car, open to the elements, had two cylinders, sixteen horsepower, and cost $1,200. In 1907 a Craig-Toledo sport model was $4,000 F.O.B.!

Advice in a 1910 issue of *American Homes and Gardens* suggested that if one already owned an open "touring" car, he could purchase an extra closed body for winter use. "During the months the new body is in use, the touring body can be renovated and made as good as new for use again next spring."

Various fittings, including a cone-shaped vase for flowers, were "found on all well appointed limousine cars." Such a vase was often of cut glass, pointed at the bottom to fit into a holder (fig. 325A and fig. C.8). "A speaking tube leading from the inside to a point beside the chauffeur's head is indispensable." Even less luxurious cars were fitted with vases. Victorians and Edwardians loved flowers!

We were permitted to photograph a 1914 Detroit Electric automobile (fig. C.7), restored to new condition by its owner, Karl Jernes. As we rode to the park to meet the photographer, he remarked that Henry Ford and Thomas Edison each bought one. It originally cost $3,000 and was made by the Anderson Electric Car Company of Detroit. Its top speed is twenty miles per hour.

We sat on a bench seat while he steered by pushing a lever. Dials on the dashboard were some four feet away. A seat facing the main bench was on one side by the door, so that an extra passenger would ride backwards. I placed fresh carnations in the bracket vase for the occasion.

Family Entertainment

Families of both upper and middle levels owned cottages by the sea or on lakes. The "cottages" ranged from Newport (Rhode Island) palaces to three- or four-bedroom houses. Servants were taken along to do the work.

Earle's parents owned five cottages at an exclusive beach in Connecticut. They lived in one in summer and rented the other four furnished. While helping my bridegroom clean up the mess after the 1938 hurricane, we found that Mother Swan had left a cut glass, handled nappy and a small Wave Crest box with hinged lid — both of which we "rescued." To her, they were of negligible value.

In the time between the wars, outdoor recreation included rides in the country to visit friends and relatives, for picnics, or to reach lakes for boating, fishing, and swimming. Cut glass was actually used at picnics (*Ladies' Home Journal* July 1902). A small carriage, called a dogcart, was used for paying calls in summer. It required a coachman and horses with cropped tails to keep up the correct social image.

There were fox hunts across farmers' fields in the fall and hunting in winter. Tennis and cricket were fashionable sports at social clubs. Young men of middle income often played baseball in uniform on the home team.

The author was surprised to find that the July 1897 issue of *Munsey's Magazine* carried an article, "The Modern Swordswoman," describing fencing as "a fad of the hour among American society women." It was said to be picturesque, valuable as exercise to develop "the finer lines of a woman's figure," giving her "perfect poise and ease of bearing." The announcement that Mrs. John Jacob Astor was one of the best fencers in the metropolis caused a perceptible increase in the demand for foils and fencing outfits, and doubled the classes of certain *maîtres d'armes*. In some upper-middle-class homes, the billiard room was taken over by the ladies for fencing. "It will add to her strength ...but it cannot make a man of her."

Even more surprising was an article in a 1911 *American Homes and Gardens*, entitled "Flying as a Sport for Women."

Older men belonged to elegant clubs, where banquets were held for any reason at all — perhaps to celebrate the opening of one's stables or in honor of a racing dog. At one of these, a capitalist and horseman, C.K.G. Billings, gave a dinner where half the guests on horseback ate at tables attached to the pommels of their saddles. At the end of the meal, the other half, the horses, were served at oat-filled troughs.

Middle-class businessmen were usually not quite this silly, but they did participate in such events as bicycle parades, where a silver loving cup was awarded for the best decorated cycle (fig. 157). Bicycles generally had a large front wheel and a small rear wheel until 1890, when a patent was issued for one with wheels of equal diameter.

Christmas parties, masquerades, and social *début* balls, called "coming out" parties, were ideal situations for husband hunting, every girl's chief occupation after secondary school. Any unmarried woman over thirty was an "old maid." Prospects grew dim after twenty-six.

Easter parades and weddings were fine places to display one's taste in clothing. Since the zenith of any *débutante*'s ambition (or at least that of her mother) was to marry a titled European or a rich American, the most prestigious feather in one's social cap was an invitation to a rich wedding. A girl might meet an eligible bachelor there.

Fig. 157. Studio portrait showing trophy won by Tom Mullen, *left*, and Calvin Swan, *right*. Award was for best decorated bicycle in 1909 parade celebrating 250th anniversary of the founding of Norwich, Connecticut.

While the rich usually served liquor and danced, many less affluent families were strictly religious and considered both pleasures to be sinful.

In the absence of television and radio, people created their own entertainment. In 1894 the *Delineator* magazine printed an article, "Recitation and How to Recite, Social Evening Entertainments." After Edison's invention of the "talking machine," a hand-cranked model in 1877 and a motor-driven type in 1888, people enjoyed recorded music at home.

The piano or organ was a status symbol, and learning to play and sing were valued accomplishments for young ladies. The J. Hardman Autotone Player Piano was advertised in a 1907 *Ladies' Home Journal* for $550 and up — "a great joy for people with melody in their hearts but not in their hands." Young men often learned to play a mandolin, banjo, or some band instrument.

Card games were a source of home entertainment. In 1905 trademarks for at least the following games were registered: Strange People, Birds, Indians, Wild Animals, Words, Addition-Subtraction.

Magazines played an important role in the dissemination of knowledge at a time when travel was limited, and in the absence of the instant communication of radio and television. Among literary periodicals, *Century* magazine imparted an amazing array of information, written with impeccable sentence structure and broad vocabulary. The avid reader could secure a higher education in his own home. Subjects included biography, studies of foreign cultures, science, history, and fiction. Compared with this, the abbreviated *Reader's Digest* and the recent *Life* and *Look* are "child's play." The author perused copies from 1881 to 1900 and was astounded to find such erudition for popular consumption.

Magazines were also a source of entertainment and advice: " A set of false teeth will sometimes remove dispeptic troubles of long standing. The teeth with metal plates (platinum or gold), although more expensive than rubber or celluloid, are to be preferred." A *Ladies' Home Journal* article on health in 1911, entitled "The Most Dangerous Animal in the World," warned that the housefly often flew from decaying fish or from cuspidors to the nipple on a baby's bottle.

Titles of magazine articles are clues to the place of women in society and to their interests, if we exclude those few who entered the business world and the daring young ladies who shocked their elders by using tobacco and dressing like "show girls." For example:

The Poetry of Dish-Washing
The Morality of Cooking
The Mistress of the Broom
House Decoration Rich and Bare
Concerning Tears — Their Sacredness and
    Blessed Influence
The Abused Mother-in-Law
Cholera Infantum
How Elnathan and I Went to Housekeeping
Rose Leaves for the Jar of Memory

In 1891 a piece on "Beauty Care" in *Life* gave directions for making face cream of vaseline and cucumbers. In a 1903 *Ladies' Home Journal*, a detailed description of the causes of unpleasant body odors was given with advice on how to prevent them. "Unhappy is the girl who is afflicted by malodorous perspiration." Causes listed were hysterical excitement; certain diseases; medicines and foods, such as onions and garlic; tar, turpentine, alcohol, coffee, truffles, iodine, and valerian (a sedative). In the case of men, caring for horses and working as tanners or as butchers caused lasting body odors. Home remedies were described, with an admonition to see a doctor if they failed.

Articles gave advice to parents on training their children and offered lessons in good manners to young people. It was not good form to stand with arms akimbo, feet wide apart, or elbows on knees.

Housekeeping hints, such as how to dry-clean lace, were plentiful to aid women in their chief work in life. There were even suggestions for Christmas gifts, such as a new carriage or saddle horse for the pastor (a cooperative gift, of course).

Magazines for ladies usually contained a page of paper dolls to cut out for little girls, and some had directions on how to make a toy for boys. *Ladies' Home Journal* published a continuing feature for children called "Brownies 'Round the World" by Palmer Cox. It was narrative verse in rhymed couplets — educational and entertaining.

The Art of Cooking

Foremost was the art of cooking. The prinicpal way to entertain friends and relatives in any kind of home was to feed them. Even if a lady had a maid-of-all work, she often cared for the china and glassware, parlor, and bedrooms and did the daintier cooking herself. Periodicals were filled with advice for the homemaker. Such advice was given in the first issue of *Good Housekeeping*, 17 October 1885, by Christine Terhune Herrick. Here is a "simple dinner" for the woman who does her own work or who has only one maid:

The Art of Dining: a Company Dinner
Raw Oysters (in their shells)
Clear Soup
Boiled Cod with Smelts, Tomato Sauce
Lettuce Salad
Crackers   Cheese   Olives
Ice Cream   Sponge Cake
Fruit   Bonbons   Salted Almonds
Coffee

Concerning finger bowls used at the end of the meal: "A dainty addition is that of a carnation or a bit of geranium, or citron aloes floating in the finger bowl. It is less stereotyped than a slice of lemon and preferred to any perfumed waters."

The dessert *par excellence* during the Golden Age was homemade ice cream. "The smoothest, most delicious ice cream, a water ice, or a frozen dessert is quickly made and adds to the fun, festivity, and feasting when the wonderful triple motion White Mountain Ice Cream Freezer is one of the party." Advertised in *Ladies' Home Journal* in 1909, this freezer allegedly required four minutes of turning a crank to make ice cream. This favorite dessert was heaped in a mound on a long, oval tray before the hostess. A stack of small, individual dishes were to her left. As a scoop was placed in each saucer, it was passed around the table to her left. Since refrigeration consisted of an icebox, or sometimes a cave in the yard or a cellar under the house, there was no way to keep the cream frozen. It had to be completely eaten each time it was made.

The menus of that era, the many courses, and the frequent use of fish are much closer to meals still served in Europe. Choice of foods seems strange nearly a century later. When did the reader last eat braised oxtails and cauliflower, or sheep's kidney and rice?

The "Art of Dining" is not an idle phrase. Food preparation was time-consuming; serving the food was ritualistic.

Fashions

France was the fountainhead of fashions in the nineteenth century. Fashions should be studied correlatively with home furnishings and the political scene. For example, during the French Revolution, republican ideals were expressed by all things Greek. Corsets were abolished, and fewer and simpler garments were made for women. Under Napoleon, Empire furniture had Egyptian motifs; precious fabrics were made to please the Emperor, and the *chemise* with waist raised to just below the bust was worn by women.

Under Napoleon III, fashion decreed the crinoline, a petticoat of haircloth or other stiff material to bell out the skirt. Hoops were another means of achieving the bell shape. Special furniture had to be devised to enable a lady to sit. Counters in stores slanted backward toward the base to make room for the hoop skirt. Women followed Empress Eugénie's vogue until 1870, when the Franco-Prussian War put an end to the Second Empire.

Fashions were now inspired by those worn in the theater or shown in paintings from earlier centuries. Gowns were lavishly trimmed with artificial flowers, ribbons, ruffles, and fringe. Layers of skirts, with the outer layer caught up in poufs and flounces, defy a brief description; they must be seen to be believed. Evening gowns were "off the shoulder." Day or evening dresses had trains.

Patents for such items as a "Combined Breast and Skirt Supporter and Shoulder Brace" and a "Combined Hoop-Skirt and Bustle" (1884) give some indication of the complexity of ladies' gowns. In the 1880s, however, there was some toning down of the extreme silhouette, especially in yachting and tennis costumes. Still, ladies wore their corsets and bustles at play. By 1889 the rear extension began to recede, but the bustle gave way to enormous sleeves. These varied from "puff" to "mutton leg."

An 1896 Marshall Field catalog presented a section of illustrations of coming creations by European designers, nearly all of which were court costumes.

In 1895 a syndicate of the greatest drygoods houses in America had sent a representative to Europe, carrying a small fortune and powers of persuasion. Consequently, such designers as Félix of Paris and Emilia Bossi of Florence, who designed costumes for such royalty as the Queen of Italy and the Princesses Lobanoff, Radziwill, and Obolinsky of Russia, sent drawings. All costumes were dramatic, with huge sleeves, but they could serve as inspiration for simplified versions for American ladies.

Fig. 158. Portrait of a "liberated woman" in 1910. This young lady had her own millinery shop. She hired my mother to make hats — each one an original creation. Note that an entire bird decorates her hat.

A lady during this time had a great variety of costumes. Periods of mourning were rigidly observed. Weddings and honeymoons required sumptuous bridal gowns, going-away costumes, and second-day dresses. There were costumes for traveling, for walking, and for the racetrack. It is now easier to visualize the multitude of cut glass pieces made to hold powder, "toilet water," gloves, wigs, handkerchiefs, jewelry, and parasols.

The "wasp waist," required by fashion, inspired some women to have the lower two ribs removed surgically to achieve a tiny waistline. The "hourglass" figure was popular 1891-1898, yet an interest was developing in rather masculine-looking, tailored suits.

The American Girl, as depicted by Charles Dana Gibson, illustrator, was now often working for a living in business establishments and graduating from high school, seminary, or college.

After 1900, corsets changed from exerting a downward pressure on the abdomen to being straight-boned in front, thus emphasizing bosom and hips. In 1902 clothes still dragged on the ground; by 1905 they cleared the shoe tops.

Quoting from *Américas:* "The years between 1890 and 1914 saw great ostentation and extravagance in fashion. Women wore hats everywhere, and hat designers used flowers, mercury wings, ribbons, plumes, and even entire birds (fig. 158) to decorate their often enormous creations. Besides the rage for heron wing feathers, or aigrettes, ostrich plumes and bird of paradise feathers were popular adornments."

The huge hats of *La Belle Époque* or Edwardian Era were an encumbrance in buses and railway carriages and in the streets. The need for long hatpins led to a need for hatpin holders (fig. 435).

Flowers were everywhere: on dresses, on furniture, and in architecture. Bead fringes adorned lampshades and screens, and were sewn on women's clothes. The latter were also decorated with cascades of laces and masses of embroidery.

Just as a lady was not fully dressed to go out unless she was wearing gloves and a hat, without a parasol her ensemble was incomplete. A single parasol would not do, if one wished to follow the vogue of owning several that matched or complemented the color she was wearing. These accessories called for a cut glass glove box (fig. 67) and an umbrella stand (fig. 117).

World War I put women into men's jobs. They drove ambulances and trains, became plumbers and electricians. Clothes became practical and austere. Toward the end of the war, the "boyish look," with short-cropped hair, flattened breasts, and dropped waistline, came in. A "Bust Reducer Brassière" was sold. Large hats were discarded. One saw only an occasional plume.

Men's clothing also went through many phases, as interesting as those of women, though not as varied and flamboyant.

Children's clothes in the Victorian period reflected adult styles; they were less complicated, but were clumsy and impractical. Little boys wore skirts until the age of four or five, then went into long pants and bowler or straw hats. After 1900 both boys and girls wore more childlike clothing.

It is easy to draw a parallel between styles of furniture, ornaments, fashions, and cut glassware. The entire life-style was well integrated.

13
Cut Glassware in the Home

Let us imagine that we are not as wealthy as Mr. Childs, but we do have a substantial home in the city and a summer place in the country or at the beach. We select cut glass of the highest quality to embellish the various rooms, to provide sparkling highlights here and there among the colored art glass, bronzes, marble busts, and cloisonné; perhaps even a stuffed peacock on the newel post on the stairs. Our pieces may not be as massive as those used in the grand mansions, but the quality is just as high. We find them in jewelry and expensive department stores.

Assuming now that we are a middle-class family, where the head of the household is a doctor or a well-to-do merchant, our moderately expensive cut glass may be bought in stores or ordered by mail.

Now let us pretend that the father is lower middle class, economically speaking. The nearest we can come to emulating our ideal life-style is to buy less dear glassware cut on pressed blanks or cheap imitation cut glass like that sold by Sears or Butler Brothers. It is pressed in motifs copied from cut glass. This is somewhat like wearing costume jewelry when one cannot afford real gems.

The Many Uses of Cut Glassware

Cut glass, "the gift that never fails of a welcome," was either purchased directly for the home, or it was received as a gift, perhaps by "someone just entering upon fresh and rosy young girlhood" or by "one with whitening hair — your mother or some dearly loved old friend." A 1909 Libbey advertisement in *Pacific Monthly* deemed it appropriate for "the man of affairs or the boy at college."

Tobacco and cigar jars or humidors (fig. 159) made elegant gifts for men who smoked, or who tolerated guests who did. They came with a recessed lid for insertion of damp cotton to keep the tobacco moist.

The bitters bottle and the barber bottle (fig. 104) were appropriate gifts for men, as were liquor and wine containers of all types. Marshall Field advertised in the 1906 catalog three elaborately cut glass pocket flasks. Two were rectangular and flat, about 6″ high, and one was a heart-shaped flask. Two heavily cut flasks,

Fig. 159. *Left to right:* Tobacco jar, 6″, for pipe tobacco. A sixteen-point hobstar covers heavy lid; concave ovals encircle shoulder. Sides have lozenges of crosscut diamond, fans, and zippers. Cigar jar, 7″, for cigars standing upright. Stopper fully cut to match jar, decorated in hobstars and splits. Both bases rayed.

shown in H. L. Cohen's book on silver, have hinged silver caps. The flattened bottles are seated in embossed silver bases. One is decorated with an Indian chief's head in full feather regalia, the other by an Art Nouveau lady's head and shoulders.

A new awareness of hygiene in the time between the wars brought patents for commercial toilet tissue (some medicated), many odd-looking toothbrushes, and "Tooth Soap" or powder of various types. A full-page advertisement appeared in magazines advocating the use of Ivory Soap as a *dentrifice.*

My mother's grandfather made a tooth powder of ground charcoal and salt, to be rubbed over the teeth with a clean cloth.

There were cut glass containers for toothbrushes and tooth powder (fig. 102), suitable as gifts for either sex. These were placed on the washstand in the bedroom with the washbowl, large jug for cold water, small jug for hot water, soap dish, drinking glass, and a

Fig. 160. Inkwell in "Cane" with clear buttons, 3″ sq × 3½″ h, has a sterling hinged cap by Gorham. Base rayed. (Photograph by Conkling)

double-lipped waste jar. There was usually no running water in the house at this time and no drains for waste. Later, the holders for brush and powder were in the bathroom near the lavatory.

Cut glass inkwells (fig. 160) were used by both sexes. This one has an embossed, monogrammed cap by Gorham in sterling. Stands in silver plate were made to hold one or two ink bottles. These had a trough in front for penholders. Another desk accessory was a mucilage or paste jar with a brush anchored in the silverplated lid. A stamp-moistener/paperweight will be shown with Dorflinger glass (fig. 288).

The engraved and cut collar box (figs. 161A and 161B), in which to keep the separate celluloid or stiffly starched collars worn by men is a rare find. The notched prism flairs are typical of Pitkin & Brooks, who also did some engraving.

While we are in the bedroom, let us look at a remarkably fine piece: a comb and brush or dresser tray (fig. 162). It was for comb and brush or for hair receiver at one end, powder box at the other, and cologne or perfume bottle in the middle.

The puff box and hair receiver (fig. 163) are typical of pieces set on the tray, except that these do not match. Unhappily, the author rejected a puff box to match the hair receiver because it was greatly overpriced. The latter is signed HEISEY and is pressed.

Figs. 161A and 161B. Collar box, 8″ × 4¼″, with intaglio fruit and notched prism flairs, both in matte gray. Although Tuthill made a grape and pear design in intaglio, this is different. Tuthill grapes are enhanced by a polished highlight on each one; leaf veins follow nature more faithfully. Here, veins are too straight and cut across curved sections of the leaves, as if hastily done. Also, the curled tendrils are different. These stutter along like dotted lines. We do not mean to downgrade this rare piece, but to point out differences.

Fig. 162. Comb and brush tray, 15½″ × 6¾″. End designs are of the "Arcadia" type: silver diamond pentagons and square within a square. These squares alternate with squares containing a hobstar. Central figure is a cluster of hobstars around a pyramidal star. Remaining areas filled with fine, unpolished diamond, proving that acid dip was not used. Inch-high gallery scalloped and cut on outside in thumbprints.

Fig. 163. *Left to right:* Puff box, 5″ d × 3″ h, has a twenty-four-point hobstar with prominent hob center on the lid. Four sixteen-point hobstars alternate with X-cuts containing notched prism in lower quarter and a zigzag star above. Base rayed. Hair receiver, 4¾″ d × 2¾″ h, signed on inside center with Heisey's "H-in-a-diamond" and "Pat'd 1/25/10." Engraved pears, grapes, cherries, and single star on base all left gray.

The engraved fruit is so like that of Tuthill that one might suspect that a Tuthill engraver, after retirement, purchased a plain Heisey piece and engraved it for pleasure. Heisey, however, did a limited amount of intaglio engraving.

The hair receiver was a receptacle for hair caught in the brush when a lady brushed her long hair "a hundred strokes" at night. This hair was accumulated, then placed in a piece of net and shaped to form a "rat." She would comb her hair forward down over the face, place a rat just above the hairline (sometimes over the ears, also), then comb the hair back over it, forming a pouf. The rest of the hair was rolled in a knot or bun at the top or back. A wide-brimmed hat, called a "Merry Widow," sat atop all of this circa 1910. The long hair

saved in the receiver could also be recycled into a "switch" by the hairdresser. This looked rather like a horse's tail and was used to add bulk to one's coiffure. Some ladies used the hair to stuff ornamental pillows or to make "hair pictures."

When I was six, my baby-sitter, Miss Zorra Mock (an old maid at thirty), stayed overnight in the guest room. When she stood, her hair touched her ankles. It had never been cut. Upon retiring, she draped her hair over the arms of a rocking chair next to the bed. When Zorra complained of headaches, the doctor suggested she cut her hair to the waist, reducing the weight that was pinching the nerves in her neck. She compromised by thinning it. How did she wear it? By braiding it and wrapping the braids round and round her head. Hair was indeed her "crowning glory."

Fig. 164. Puff box, 5″ × 3″, in "Harvard" has a lift-off lid and a thirty-two-point single star on the base.

A round covered puff box (fig. 164) like this one (except that the Harvard cutting was larger) was listed in the 1911-1912 Marshall Field catalog. It sold for $8 then and was valued at $125 in Ehrhardt's 1973 price guide. Made for bath powder, it could also have been used for bonbons in the parlor.

An article in *Good Housekeeping* (June 1893), entitled "What to Do in My Lady's House: The Sleeping Room," recommended that toilet articles in silver and glass "grace the delicate scarf that enhances their beauty on the dressing case. The vinaigrette, pin tray, button hook, and pin cushion find a resting place in my lady's sleeping chamber."

The vinaigrette was used originally to relieve offensive odors in hot, crowded rooms. In the 1780s, a Dr. William Henry devised an aromatic vinegar solution intended to prevent contagion of disease when sniffed. In the late nineteenth century, the vinaigrette contained smelling salts or other aromatic substances, such as ammonia and lavender-scented crystals or medicinal vinegar, and was used to revive milady when she felt an attack of the vapors coming on. These vinaigrette bottles were usually cylindrical, from 2″ to 5″ long, with hinged or screw caps that fit over the bottle's matching glass stopper. They hung either from a chain attached to a tiny finger ring or to a bracelet, or were suspended from a châtelaine around the waist. Sometimes they were carried in a glove, purse, or muff, or in a small compartment in the top of a gentleman's walking stick.

From the châtelaine at the waist hung other "personals," such as buttonhooks for gloves, watches, folding scissors, dog whistles, et cetera. *Châtelaine* is French, meaning "lady of the manor" or "wife of the Castellan." She carried keys for the many rooms of the castle attached to a chain worn about the waist.

The fascination felt for flowers and perfumes by the Victorians was well-founded in history. In pragmatic terms, one might say that the complex clothing, together with the lack of facilities for easy bathing and laundering, made pleasant odors desirable.

The use of sweet odors by early physicians, especially in nervous diseases, was taught as science in 1893. Certain flowers were found to ward off pestilence and develop ozone. The spirit and soul of the flower have been wafted as incense to the gods from ancient times.

The preoccupation with flowers and perfumes in the latter nineteenth century was not new. It was a resurgence of ancient customs in a time when certain classes had the money and leisure to indulge, even revel, in such sensual pleasures. After the American Civil War, menial servants replaced slaves in the time-consuming tasks of exchanging wilted flowers for fresh and washing the vases daily along with the lamp chimneys.

The small perfume (fig. 165) is similar in form to a vinaigrette. It was often carried in a muff — a sort of cylinder of fur or cloth into which a lady or girl thrust her hands for warmth. If of fur, the muff might be trimmed with the animal's head and hanging tails or ribbons. It usually had a ribbon or strap to slip over the wearer's head for support. A muff often came with a matching stole. Many glove colognes tapered to a rounded point and so could not stand on end. A tiny chain from bottleneck to screw-on cap prevented dropping the stopper.

This atomizer (fig. 165) for perfume has a rubber bulb hidden in the tassel of fringe.

The shoe perfume (fig. 166) would have rested in the middle of the dresser tray. A Chinese antiquarian (according to Carl Dreppard) cited ladies' shoes carved from rock crystal in the Celestial Kingdom. Glass shoes were "all the rage" in the Victorian era, but few were cut. (See also fig. 134.) Some American companies sold small objects, such as perfume bottles and knife rests, made to their specifications in Europe. This may have been a Bohemian import.

The oval trinket box (fig. 167) could have held cuff links, shirt studs, or tie stick pins for the man of the house, or pins and other small items for the lady. Veils were an essential element in dressing. Often a new veil revived an old hat. The costume veil matched the ensemble in color. Some veils covered hat and face or were draped about the hat and were caught at the back of the hat by a large veil pin. Such pins were kept in a trinket box.

A ring tree was often used on the dresser. It was like a shallow bowl with a small post rising from the center, on which to keep one's rings. It resembled the stick bonbon dish (fig. 131), but without the knob on the handle.

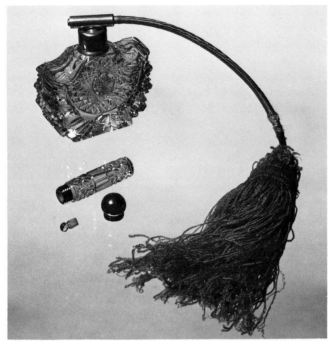

Fig. 165. *Top to bottom:* Perfume atomizer, 4″ w, cut in hobstar and prism. Fittings silver-plated; 11″ rubber tube has a bulb covered by a Victorian pink silk tassel. Glove, purse, or muff perfume, 3″, with screw-on cap has inner, ground, push-in stopper to insure retention of contents. Design consists of a chain of diamonds at each end, then a band of diagonal prisms and eight panels in the middle.

Fig. 166. Shoe perfume, 6″ l, is cut in shallow Russian, horizontal steps, and hobstars. Smooth edges indicate acid polishing or import. Rod for applying perfume is intact.

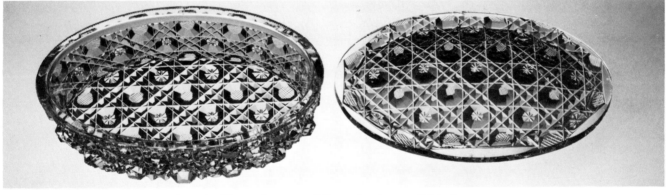

Fig. 167. Oval trinket box, 5½″ l, in the Harvard variety of Cane; deeply cut. (Matye)

The hatpin holder (fig. 435), most often made of porcelain, was a familiar article on the dressing table. To distinguish these from look-alike salt shakers, muffineers, and sand-sprinklers (for blotting ink), remember that most hatpin holders have solid bottoms, with from six to twelve small holes in the top to hold the pins. Tops are solidly attached and are either slightly raised or are concave. Bud-vase-type holders, sometimes sold now as open-top hatpin holders, are actually toothbrush holders. Long hatpins were made to keep the hat from blowing off in the wind. This was accomplished by pushing the pin through hat and chignon of hair in the back and out again through the hat. Often a second pin was used in front. A "nib" or guard was then put on the sharp point for protection.

Hatpin holders were not in common use in America until after the 1860s. They were at their zenith during the 1880s and 1890s. During the first quarter of the century, fancy hairstyles had required high crowns and small brims, but no pins to keep the hat in place. Subsequently, bonnets with ties under the chin were in vogue until after the Civil War. Tired of resembling southern belles, the ladies topped off their new fashions with large, heavily decorated hats that required pins. The extra long pins for the enormous hats of the 1890s were kept in tall holders. The turn of the century brought smaller hats and pins with holders measuring 5″. Height helps one to date the holders.

The Merry Widow hat expired after 1910, much to the relief of theater-goers. The war in 1917 changed hats to the *cloche* (a bell-like, close-fitting hat), obviating a need for hatpins. Pins came in novel forms, and so are delightful to collect. Heads might be set with stones, or be of French enamel with delicate flower designs. An article in a 1911 *Woman's Home Companion* described a little owl head made of real feathers and one whose top opened to reveal a tiny powder-puff and mirror.

The hatpin was effective as a weapon. Some states made it a crime to carry one concealed in a purse or on one's person. My mother accepted an invitation for a Sunday carriage ride in the country with the banker's son when she was seventeen. Used to having anything he desired, he made advances and would not desist. She took out her hatpin and jabbed it into the top of his thigh and felt it hit bone. The next day his irate father came to Grandfather's store to protest that she had probably crippled his son for life. Grandfather replied forcefully that the boy might have ruined the girl's life if she had not had the spunk to defend her honor.

The small clock (fig. 360) to be shown with Sinclaire pieces was used in the bedroom.

These miniature kerosene night lamps (fig. 168) were for the sick room or nursery and are rarely seen. They make interesting cabinet pieces.

Bedroom lamps (fig. 169) were smaller than those used in other rooms. They were about 13″ high, as opposed to those where more light was required — generally 18″ to 22″. Electrified lamps were often called Electroliers. Complete, undamaged cut glass lamps are rare and expensive.

An early item that we have not found is a chamberstick. This resembled a handled nappy with attached candleholder in the center. It was carried to light the way to the bedroom before electricity came into the home.

From a *Good Housekeeping* article, "My Lady's House: the Dining Room," in April 1893 came this description: "On the low sideboard, a revival of an old style in which a brass rail runs around its width, the glasses of different size and form show with light and shade their artistic curves, whilst the decanter and

Fig. 168. Pair of miniature kerosene night lamps, 7″ h, 12″ with chimney; fair quality; cut in eight-point hobstars, fans, and flutes; signed on wick turner: ABCO NUTMEG. Brass fittings, signed MOFFITBING, are corroded beyond brightening with polish. (Hamstreet)

Fig. 169. Bedroom lamp, 13″. Crystal prism drops hung in every other hole. Should be twice as many. (Hamstreet)

dishes of cut glass add greatly by their polish and brilliancy to this charming scene." Often the most striking exhibit in "this room of rooms" was a punch bowl with cups in the middle of the buffet and candelabra at the ends (fig. C.19).

This 15″ punch bowl on a standard (fig. 170) weighs over twenty-seven pounds. No wonder so much cut glass was broken!

The 14″ punch bowl on a standard (fig. 171), in a split-square design, is cut on a brilliant, colorless blank comparable to the candelabra shown in Chapter 10 (fig. 113).

A punch or eggnog bowl in the 10″ size (fig. 172) was suitable for a less pretentious home if used for punch or lemonade, although for serving eggnog a smaller bowl was used. Notice that the stand is large in proportion to the bowl.

The cordial bottle (fig. 173) held a "strong, sweetened, aromatic alcoholic liquor," often called *liqueur* from the French. The drink was served in tiny, stemmed glasses (fig. 437). We have identified it as "Hob Star," unsigned Gundy-Clapperton of Toronto. (See figs. 416 and 417.) It is, however, signed by the dealer with his personal brand, "G. B. Allen, Vancouver."

This decanter (fig. 174), gracefully formed, is easy to grasp by the neck, whose flutes are decorated where they meet with triple crosshatch, reminiscent of Sinclaire and Dorflinger.

A water set (fig. 175) could be a pitcher or water bottle and tumblers (six or twelve). At first glance, this "Heart" pattern looks like Pitkin & Brooks, registered 22 January 1907. As seen in the catalog circa 1907, however, theirs had the hexad cutting on the heart with

Fig. 170. Punch bowl, 14½″ d × 15″ h, on a standard. Three large twenty-four-point hobstars alternate with X-cut vesicas containing two hobstars and two sections of hobnail. Bold double cuts with beading swing around elements of design, reminiscent of "Parisian," created by O'Connor for Dorflinger. This, too, had curved double miter cuts with beading, made possible by an O'Connor invention. Six areas of large cane with clear buttons are around a smaller hobstar cut on stub that fits into faceted collar. Glass is ⅝″ thick. Punch cups in Cluster do not match bowl, but look well with it. One cup is signed HOARE.

Fig. 171. Punch bowl, 14½″ d × 13½″ h, on a standard cut in chain of hobstars, split squares of silver diamond, kites of cane, and fans. Base has horizontal steps leading up to a "twisted rope" collar around the hole, into which hobstar fits. Although unsigned, we believe it was cut by J. Hoare. The cuts under the scallops and the split silver diamond are typical of his work. Since the tops flair outward, also, the cups with hobstars, fans, and tiny kites of silver diamond go well with the bowl, though they are not identical to it. They are cut on the bottom in a square containing a zigzag star.

Fig. 172. Punch or eggnog bowl, 10″ d × 9½″ h, on a standard. There are short flutes under facetèd collar. Notice that base edge is smooth, whereas the two preceding standards are scalloped.

Fig. 173. Cordial or large cologne, 5″ d × 7″ h; 3½ lbs., in "Hob Star" by Gundy-Clapperton of Toronto, Canada. Signed only with the personal brand of retailer, "G. B. Allen, Vancouver." (Matye)

Fig 174. Decanter, 9″, 12″ with stopper. Two large hobstars with radiant centers are cut on opposite sides. Other two sides have clusters of stars. Between principal designs lie four vertical columns of three hobstars. A twenty-point hobstar covers bottom. Lapidary stopper is made to proper scale. Some call the neck a "double gooseneck."

a miter cut at center top. Neither is it by F. X. Parsche & Sons (Chicago), for their "Heart" had either Russian or hexad, with fine flashing between larger rays and horizontal cuts across the top flashing. This heart has clear hobnail and two miter splits with flashing at top center. Several heart patterns were patented in 1907 and 1908. This was cut by Fry.

The claret jug (fig. 176), as tall pitchers were often called in catalogs, utilizes one of the finer pinwheel patterns These vessels were used for lemonade by those who did not serve wine.

Another claret jug (fig. 177) is shown. Its main motif is the hobstar, while the secondary motif is hobnail. This tall shape and the pattern were typical about 1889.

In an 1889 *Good Housekeeping* magazine, an article described the tall, slender shapes, richly cut with strong handles: "For some distance about the place where the handle is joined to the body . . . the glass is left free from ornamentation, and when the vessel is filled with a colored liquid, lemonade we will say, the handle appears to float on the surface."

The water goblets (fig. 178) are of fine quality with large bowls. Sets of stemware are becoming scarce — especially those in mint condition.

The carafes or water bottles (fig. 179) contrast nicely. The one on the left is of good glass and of a common shape. The other one has an unusual form. With its four large hobstars on the sides and one on the bottom, it would have been more expensive to cut.

A novelty advertised in *Good Housekeeping* in 1889 was an individual water jug that held only two glasses: "a graceful bit to put by one's plate."

The large ice cream tray (fig. 180), 18″ long, is rare in that it has forty-one hobstars! One always dreams of finding the matching saucers. Cut by Straus.

The situation is reversed. Oh, to find the tray to match these saucers (fig. 181)! 6″ in diameter, they are suitable for pudding or ice cream, but too shallow for berries and cream.

In this transitional ice cream tray (fig. 182), a swirl pattern gives a feeling of motion. By Hoare?

Fig. 175. Water pitcher and tumblers in a "Heart" pattern are in #900 by Fry. (Gerritse)

Fig. 178. Water goblets, 6″. Three sixteen-point hobstars and three devices with an X-cut, eight-point hobstar, fans, triangles of silver diamond, a pentagon of crosscut diamond.

Fig. 176. Claret jug, 14″. Three large pinwheels and two large hobstars outlined by double splits with beading. Two triangles of hobnail on sides; a kite of hobnail under fluted lip.

Fig. 177. Claret jug, 14″, has triple notched handle, rayed base. Lip cut in notched vertical prism, splits, and silver diamond; fans on each side. Down front is a chain of five hobstars; on each side are three large, graduated hobstars enclosed by X-splits; remaining triangular areas filled with hobnail. Even rear view is striking. Below handle are two large fields of hobnail and a fan.

The large round tray (fig. 183) in a sort of endless loop design could have been used for sandwiches, cake, or small gelatin desserts to be transferred to individual dessert plates by the hostess. Large trays are scarce and expensive.

Several magazine articles circa 1887 advocated placing a half slice of bread, cut ¾″ thick, in the napkin at the left of each plate. Additional bread was served from the bread tray, whose shape followed that of the silver tray for bread. Later, rolls, such as the Parkerhouse and cloverleaf, became more fashionable. Bread trays are oval and shallow, similar to celery trays.

The first bread tray (fig. 184) in this group is deeply cut in a well-balanced design.

The border of the next bread tray (fig. 185) reminds one of a row of daisies. The radiating vesicas on the flat bottom resemble the petals of a large flower.

This bread tray (fig. 186), to judge by blank, cutting, and the centers on the smaller hobstars, is from the late Brilliant Period.

Fig. 179. *Left to right:* Carafe, 7½″ h × 6½″. Neck fluted and notched; two sets of three horizontal cuts. Six devices, each with eight-point hobstar over diagonal splits and triangles of parallel cuts, alternate with fans. Carafe, 8¼″ h × 5½″. Four large thirty-two-point hobstars separated by fans and silver diamond kites. A sixteen-point hobstar covers bottom. Fluted neck has more complex notching on flute edges. Deeply cut and brilliant.

Fig. 180. Ice cream tray, 18″×10½″, in a Cluster pattern has forty-one hobstars, remaining areas filled with silver diamond and parallel cuts. Average quality. Piece identical to tray signed STRAUS. (Gerritse)

Fig. 181. Ice cream saucers, 6″. Three Gothic arches create hexagonal center with twelve-point hobstar. Tip of arch doubly cut to form a kite containing a zigzag star. Three sixteen-point hobstars lie between arches. (Matye)

Fig. 182. Ice cream tray, 13″×8½″. Six hobstars lie between arms of clear glass (lightly cut with flowers) arranged in swirl pattern. Unusual transitional piece! Tray with arms cut in strawberry diamond signed HOARE. (Gerritse)

Fig. 183. Round serving tray, 12½″×2″, in a strange, but effective, design. Average quality.

Fig. 184. Bread tray, 12″×8″×2″. Four flat pyramidal stars occupy central lozenge. Four prominent hobstars and blazed fans decorate sides. Cane, fine hobnail, and extremely fine silver diamond. Excellent quality.

Fig. 185. Bread tray, 12″×5½″, has a chain of hobstars with crosshatched buttons around sloping sides. Flat bottom cut in graceful design of double-X-cut vesicas with a hobstar in the middle and silver diamond at ends. Remaining areas filled with cane, making a jeweled effect. Average quality. (Matye)

Fig. 186. Bread tray, 13″×5½″. A thirty-two-point hobstar fits hexagonal field in bottom; eighteen-point on ends. Fair quality. (Serres)

Fig. 187. Bread tray, 11½″ × 7½″, unsigned, by Taylor Bros. in "Bellevue." Hobstars encircled by chain of small hobstars (with pentagons of silver diamond between them) at ends of tray defined by deep cuts in concentric circles. Three middle hobstars also surrounded by deep splits. Gently curved edges, cut by a triple miter wheel. Unusual.

Fig. 188. Celery tray, 11½″ × 4½″ × 2″. A figure-eight design.

The superb bread tray (fig. 187), unsigned, has been identified as "Bellevue" by Taylor Brothers & Company, active in Philadelphia 1902-1915. Lafayette Taylor designed this pattern with smooth scalloped edge, called "Colonial Edge" in the catalog. "Bellevue" was a big favorite in jewelry stores.

Shown are two unsigned celery trays. The first (fig. 188) is in a Cluster pattern, cut by many companies. Sometimes the cluster of hobstars encircled another hobstar, in others, they surrounded a hexagonal center like this one. O. F. Egginton's "Arabian" and Enterprise's "Star" are examples of the latter. J. Hoare cut many cluster designs. The cluster was usually combined with other motifs.

For the collector seeking something out of the ordinary, the celery tray (fig. 189) with dentil edge seems to be related to H. C. Fry's "King George," which was cut in squares similar to the outer rows here. Clark did a dentil edge cut in steps on "Prima Donna." The edge on this dish differs from Meriden's "Alhambra" in that each projection has sloping sides. Another mystery to solve! Could it be Canadian?

The celery dish (fig. 190) in "Princeton" is deep enough for serving whole asparagus spears.

The banana made its debut at the 1876 Centennial Exposition. Bananas were wrapped in foil and sold for ten cents apiece, rivaling popcorn and the telephone as a tourist attraction. By the end of the century, Costa Rica was making regular shipments to the United States, and cut glass companies were designing special bowls for the novel fruit

This banana bowl (fig. 191) is a dramatic example of cutting. It was packed away with a cologne bottle (fig. 73) and a powder box (fig. 69) in 1920 at the death of the couple who had received them as wedding gifts in 1909. The three pieces were placed in a shop on consignment by the son and daughter in 1974. There is not a mark of wear or any of the three.

The mayonnaise bowl and underplate (fig. 192) are cut in a pinwheel pattern. Whipped cream was served in similar, but larger, bowls.

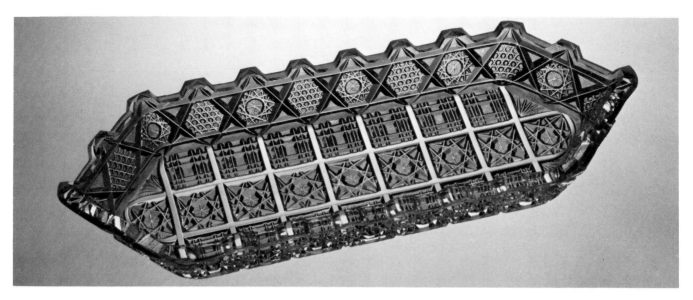

Fig. 189. Celery tray, 12½″ × 4¾″. Bottom cut in squares. Every outer surface cut in fine, sharp silver diamonds. A most unusual treatment.

Fig. 190. Celery dish, 11½″ × 5¾″ × 3″ deep. "Princeton" by Empire. (Matye)

Fig. 192. Mayonnaise bowl, 5″ × 3″, and plate 6″. Similar to a Libbey design of 1900, it features pinwheel and fan around a central hobstar. (Matye)

Fig. 191. Banana bowl, $10'' \times 6\frac{3}{4}'' \times 4\frac{1}{2}''$ deep. Fine, sharp hobnail tusks enlarge the vesicas radiating from center.

Fig. 193. Berry bowl, $8'' \times 3\frac{3}{4}''$, has hexagonal bottom cut in a deep twenty-four-point hobstar. Some authorities consider any combination of silver diamond pentagons and hobstars a variant of "Arcadia." (Matye)

Fig. 194. Fruit bowl, $9'' \times 4\frac{1}{2}''$, circa 1898. Glass is $\frac{5}{8}''$ thick and deeply cut. A Star of David, consisting of a hobstar and six silver diamond points, covers bottom.

The berry bowl (fig. 193) in a variant of "Arcadia" has a primary and a secondary motif, typical of the 1890s.

A fruit bowl (fig. 194), "cut to pieces" as some say, follows. It represents the height of the period from 1895 to 1905.

This fruit bowl (fig. 195) was probably cut circa 1910. The unusual pattern has the same "feeling" as some designs cut by William C. Anderson for his

American Cut Glass Company, especially "Fern," patented 30 May 1911. We call this pattern "Palmette," since it has not yet been identified.

The low bowl (fig. 196), $2''$ deep, is cut in another type of cluster.

Nappies are varied in form and design. A collection of these take little space. They can be used on dining or coffee table to serve candy and nuts. These two (fig. 197) are charming, especially the "Atlantic" by Empire with curled handle.

Fig. 195. Fruit bowl, 9″×4″; 6 lbs. Excellent quality. We call the graceful intaglio pattern "Palmette," for lack of valid identification. Partly polished, partly matte. Tips of petals in center bend clockwise to give an impression of motion.

Fig. 196. Low bowl, 8″×2″, in a Cluster design; brilliant.

Fig. 197. *Left to right:* Bonbon, 5½″, circa 1900, has clear three-petal blossom cut through kite of silver diamond — a "throwback" to an old device in the Middle Period. Bonbon, 6″, with unusual curled handle, in "Atlantic" by Empire Cut Glass Company of Flemington, New Jersey. Crossed bars of cane make a beautiful six-point star with hobstars between the points.

Dessert plates are lovely to collect and use, either in sets or one of a kind. They were sold with a large, matching tray to serve cake at afternoon tea. This one (fig. 198) is finely cut. It would also be suitable for the cracker-cheese-olives course or dessert at dinner.

Extra teaspoons were placed on the table in either a spoon tray (fig. 199) or in an upright spoon holder (fig. 200). The trays, on which spoons lay horizontally, resembled celery trays (9″ to 12″ long), but were shorter (6½″ to 7½″).

The spooner with two handles (fig. 201) is certainly in the hard-to-find category.

The ice tub (fig. 202) was filled with cracked ice and placed on table or sideboard. This one is heavy and well-cut.

The ice bucket with tabs (fig. 203) is less common. The 32-point hobstar bottom makes it superior. Floral cutting on the tabs and below indicate the transitional years circa 1907.

A *Good Housekeeping* article of 1899 stated that bowls for cracked ice, larger than medium-sized finger bowls, were placed at intervals around the table. "A spoonful of the ice is put in each glass and water from the carafe or jug is poured in." It is not generally known that small, individual carafes were sometimes placed at each setting.

Fig. 198. Dessert plate, 7″. Large central hobstar encircled by stars, sections of hexad, and silver diamond (the finest ever seen), making a sort of expanding star.

Fig. 199. Spoon tray, 6¾″×4⅜″×2¼″ deep. Sides turn in slightly. (Matye)

Fig. 202. Ice tub, 5″. Base rayed.

Fig. 200. Spoon holder, 5″, is cut in hobstar, pyramidal star, and silver diamond. Twenty-four-point single star on base.

Fig. 201. Spoon holder, 4½″ h×6″ w including handles. (Miles)

165

Compotes of medium size (fig. 204) were used for jelly or jam on the table and occasionally for bonbons in the parlor. The one on the left is similar to two cuttings signed J. Hoare. Both have interesting stems.

This compote (fig. 205) leans further toward the floral period, yet still has a geometric border.

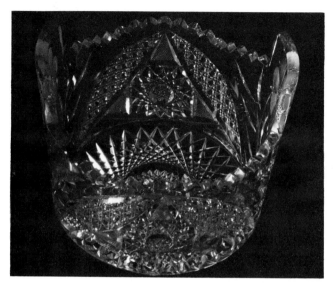

Fig. 203. Ice bucket with tabs, 6½″ d × 5¾″ h, with floral cutting. Thirty-two-point hobstar covers bottom. Vesicas of cane, hobstars, triangles of silver diamond. (Rice)

Fig. 205. Compote, 9″. Note teardrop in six-panel stem. (Matye)

Fig. 204. *Left to right:* Compote, 5½″ h × 6″. Between the arches are complex feathered fans. Jelly compote, 5¼″ h × 6″. Bowl has simple but well-arranged motifs. Base is striking, with its scalloped edge and horizontal steps. (Both from Matye)

This large fruit compote (fig. 206), over 11" high, weighs five pounds. It was used to serve fruit compote (fruit stewed in syrup and served as dessert) or ambrosia (orange sections and coconut). This is one of the finer pieces circa 1906-1909.

For serving mustard, there were small covered mustard jars (fig. 207) with a notched lid to allow a glass or bone paddle to stay in the jar.

Condiment jars also came as part of a caster set (fig. 404).

Horseradish and pickles were popular condiments at a time when salad materials were scarce in winter. These horseradish jars (fig. 208) are interesting cabinet pieces and still useful.

Vinegar and oil for salad were served in special containers, such as these two cruets and the olive oil bottle (fig. 209). A catsup cruet will be shown with Hawkes glass (fig. 301).

Even worcestershire sauce had its own distinctively shaped bottle. These are seldom for sale (fig. 210).

Butter was often placed on the table in a butter tub, similar to the ice bucket shown above. This sometimes had its own underplate. More often, butter rested on a plate covered by a dome.

The cheese dish (fig. 211) looked just like the butter dish, but was larger. The two could be purchased in matching sets. Butter served in a domed dish was in one piece. The plate was passed with a butter knife, so that each person could cut off a piece to place on his own small bread plate. Butter dishes became popular in the United States in the 1870s, although the vogue started in Europe, where restaurants had covered butter dishes on every table. They were pressed glass made in fanciful shapes, such as clocks, helmets, birds on nests, beehives, even a kitchen stove. Cut glass butter dishes depended on beauty of material and design.

Another way to serve butter was to form butter pats in a small wooden mold, place a pat on each small butter chip (figs. 212 and 439), sometimes called a butterette, then put a chip at each place setting just before seating the guests. Extra pats were kept on ice in the butter tub. The wooden butter mold inherited from my mother looks somewhat like a bell. The handle slips through a center hole and is attached to a circle cut on the bottom in a floral pattern. Pulled up into the "ceiling" of the bell, the circle will imprint the pattern on top of the butter packed into the bell. By pushing down on the handle, the formed pat is expelled onto the cut glass chip.

The Domino sugar tray (fig. 212) was a fashionable way of serving sugar cubes. Dainty silver tongs were used to lift the cubes.

Salted almonds were often placed in individual dishes at each place setting (fig. 438).

Fig. 206. Fruit compote, 11" h × 8". Engraved matte flowers have polished highlights, flashed petals, and centers of fine hobnail. Miter leaves polished. Notched stem has a large tear.

In 1905, compotes with tall stems, and even celery dishes on standards, were popular. A writer in *Harper's Bazar* predicted: "If the prevailing fad continues, one may yet see cream-jugs and sugar-basins with standards." This research helps us to date this lovely footed cream and sugar set (fig. 213). These are expertly cut on fine blanks — evidence that one should not generalize and assume that all pinwheel patterns are late and of poor quality.

At breakfast, syrup or sorghum molasses was served in a small jug with a silver-plated lid or no lid at all. Examples (fig. 461) are shown with cabinet pieces in Chapter 19.

Circa 1889, when fashion called for colorful chinaware with a different pattern for each course, it was also stylish to use silk, plush, or embroidered tablecloths. Individual bread plates were adopted to keep the bread off the expensive cloth. Knife rests (fig. 214) were used to prevent grease from soiling the cloth, even if made of washable linen. A large rest was beside the host for the carving knife, and a small individual knife rest was often used at each setting.

Fig. 207. *Left to right:* Mustard jar, 3″, with glass spoon resembling a coal shovel, in J. D. Bergen's "Notched Prism." Lid is notched around edge and cut to admit spoon. A tiny single star is inside the lid under the lapidary knob. Bottom plain. Mustard jar, 4″, has columns of lozenges in silver diamond and pyramidal star between columns of notched vertical prism. Lid is notched around edge and has a single star inside the lid under the knob. Bottom rayed.

Fig. 208. *Left to right:* Horseradish jar, 5″, in notched vertical prism. Unusual stopper matches bottle. Horseradish jar, 3⅝″, has inner stopper, ground to seal jar. Silver lid lined with gold to prevent pitting, and marked "S.W. (the W in a circle with two 'legs') STERLING 937." Centered on the embossed rococo design is engraved *IMM* in ornate script. (Both from Matye)

Fig. 210. Pair of Worcestershire bottles, 8″. Flat-topped stoppers have teardrops. Top quality in every way!

168

Fig. 209. *Left to right:* Oil or vinegar cruet, 5½″ to top of stopper. Stopper not original; could be ground to fit. Fully cut bottom; heavy for its size. Olive oil bottle, 9¼″ in "Harvard." Interesting stopper not original, but could be ground to fit. Oil or vinegar, 7″. Stopper original, numbered to match cruet. "Florence" hobstar, flashed with silver diamond points, principal motif. (All from Matye)

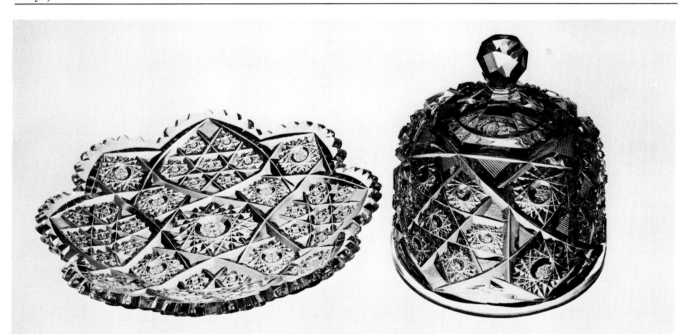

Fig. 211. Cheese dish, 7½″ h; plate 10″, in a Cluster pattern. Design nearly identical with the ice cream tray with forty-one hobstars (fig. 180).

169

Fig. 212. *Top to bottom:* Domino sugar tray, 8½″ l, circa 1917, in cane with crosshatched buttons on sides and floral design on bottom. Note lines cut on tabs to prevent slippage when passing tray. (Matye) Butter chips, ⅝″, have overlapping squares around a central pyramidal button. (Matye)

Fig. 213. Footed cream jug, 4″, and sugar basin, 3½″, circa 1905. Handles double-notched with crosscuts between notches. (Matye)

Fig. 214. Knife rests. *Left row:* 5¾", large facets. 4", ten panels on middle bar, star on ends. 4¼", six panels with notched edges, notched prism ends with star, #57 in M. Bazzett & Co., Chicago, catalog, listed for 75¢ each. Pair of individual rests, 4½", pointed ends. *Right row:* Rare double rest, 5½", ends cut in pattern. 5", signed HAWKES on bar, six panels, faceted ends, heavy. 4¾", similar to above, but shorter shank and lapidary ends slightly larger.

Throughout history, salt has had social, economic, and religious implications. A covenant of salt is mentioned in the Bible. One of the oldest roads in Italy was constructed for shipment of salt. And until today, Persians have had an expression, "untrue to salt," meaning ungrateful or disloyal. We have all heard the saying, "He is not worth his salt."

A great variety of containers, made of many materials, have held this precious substance. They range from the priceless Cellini salt dish to crudely made glass "dips" during the last century. The "standing salt," the oldest and largest, was about 5" high and was placed in front of the person who sat at the head of the table. The "trencher," a deep dish sans cover, was within reach of guests. A small spoon was available for sprinkling salt upon food. "Salt cups," fairly large and mounted on legs, were sometimes used in pairs — one at each end of the table.

Salt dishes, 3" to 3½" in diameter, now known as master salts, were used singly or at each end of the table. By the 1880s, small individual salt cellars or salt dips had replaced them. One could dip celery sticks, scallions, or radishes into the salt (fig. 215).

Salt and pepper shakers (fig. 216) came in matched pairs, either large for placement at each end of the table for sharing, or small, with a pair at each place setting. Some had glass tops; others had sterling silver or pewter tops. Pairs of salt and pepper shakers were not common until after 1875. Brilliant cut glass was made in matching sets, most sets having a salt dish or shaker in the same pattern as the pepper. Even when using matching china dishes, many hostesses preferred cut glass salt and pepper, as well as cream and sugar, containers.

The cracker or cookie jar (fig. 217) looked like a large cigar jar. These are rare and expensive. We have yet to see one of poor quality, so they must have been costly.

Candles were used in chambersticks, in candlesticks, both high and low, and in candelabra (fig. 113). The lowest holder resembled a master salt. A pair of candlesticks 6" tall (fig. 382) will be shown with signed Hoare glassware. The usual height was 9" or 10".

This pair of candlesticks (fig. 218) is clear and brilliant.

The candlesticks (fig. 219) with the swirled "skirt" are unusual because they are hollow from top to bottom.

As for lamps — kerosene or Electroliers — the pair engraved in butterflies and daisies by Pairpoint (fig. 75) and the Harvard-cut lamp shown with Canadian glass (fig. 417) are typical table lamps, above average in quality. Several other types for the table were made. There was one similar to these, but with a so-called "strawberry" dome, shaped like the lid on the banquet mustard pot (fig. 101). The banquet lamp, shaped like our blown-mold lamp (fig. 425), was rather tall and on a pedestal. A lamp with spherical glass lower and upper sections (sometimes with a base and legs) has come to be called a Gone-with-the-Wind Lamp. A few floor lamps were made of cut glass, doubtless for the rich only, or for exhibitions.

Fig. 215. Five individual salts in notched vertical prism. Shamrock master salt, a rare novelty, and spoon, marked STERLING, are from collection of Kay Hamstreet. Master salt in crosscut diamond and fan is from Eleanor McCoy.

Fig. 216. Salt and pepper shakers. *Left to right, top to bottom:* 3½″, pair decanter-shaped, silver tops. Single pepper, 3¼″, sunburst cutting, thin sterling top. Single individual salt, 2″, mother-of-pearl top, pinwheel with blaze near bottom. Three pairs of individual salt and pepper shakers, 2″, in hobstar and fan, tops marked STERLING. (All Matye)

Fig. 217. Cracker or cookie jar, 9¾″ h × 6″, in Harvard and Floral pattern, attributed to Kellner & Munroe. Lid cut to match jar; base has sixteen-point hobstar.

Coal oil was lamp fuel distilled from United States coal, and then from oil shale in Canada. Kerosene was lamp fuel derived from petroleum. The two fuels were identical in use, but the term "coal oil" was used in some areas for both for many years.

Flowers were displayed in baskets, fern bowls, and vases of all shapes and sizes. *Good Housekeeping* in 1893 suggested placing little rose bowls of maidenhair fern and trailing vines on the four corners of a square dining table. "As a general rule, all table decorations are made low." The center decoration "may be of rare cut glass, a fern bowl or basket." A fern growing in the fernery could be "dressed" with fresh flowers, such as sweet peas, by wiring toothpicks to the stems in order to stick the flowers among the ferns. The toothpicks were said to draw moisture from the soil to the flower stems and keep the flowers fresh. It was called a "perpetual table design," to be filled on any occasion.

A "flat" was also used as a centerpiece. This was a shallow wire basket lined with tinfoil and moss.

In addition to cut flowers, indoor plants were abundant in Victorian homes. Plant stands held terrariums, discovered accidently in 1832 by Dr. Nathanial Wood, who placed a butterfly chrysallis in a covered jar with moist dirt. Soon ferns and grass sprang up and flourished, reusing their transpired moisture. The stands also held ferns and fuchsias,

Fig. 218. Pair of candlesticks, 9″, cut in flutes with beaded edges, have teardrops 4¼″ long. Silver-plated liners, where candles rest, were removed for a better picture. (Jo Frazier.)

Fig. 219. Pair of candlesticks, 10″. Skirt has swirl or comet pattern.

Fig. 220. Fern bowl, 7½″ × 4½″, with three feet.

palms, and orange trees that actually bore fruit. Window gardens were popular. This "fernmania," as it was called by Charles Kingsley in 1855, endured into the twentieth century. The author's Georgian colonial house, completed in 1916, has a separate solarium — a room fifteen feet square — with windows covering three walls to admit sunshine to growing plants.

Rose bowls, fern bowls, and baskets are shown elsewhere in this volume. Here are some unidentified ferneries and vases. Most fern bowls had metal liners with small knobs as handles for lifting out the liners.

The footed fernery (fig. 220) of this type was common and not too costly for the average home.

The octagonal fernery (fig. 221) is unusual. It has four feet.

This footed trumpet vase (fig. 222) is 18″ tall — perfect for gladioli or long-stemmed roses. A vase could generally be ordered in sizes from 6″ to 14″ at 2″ intervals. Only a few styles came as large as 16″, 18″, or 20″.

Fig. 221. Octagonal fernery, 7½″ × 4″, has four feet; combined geometric and floral cutting. (Rice)

Fig. 222. Footed vase, 18″, trumpet shape. Four columns of seven silver diamond lozenges separated by wide splits with beading.

The corset vase (fig. 223) is cut in a complex variant of the "Arcadia" pattern, used by several companies as basic motif. The name originated with the Sterling Cut Glass Company, organized circa 1904 in Cincinnati. The shape is exactly like a vase illustrated in *Harper's Bazar* in 1905. The caption read, "Some of the new shapes and patterns in rich cut glass."

The next two vases (figs. 224 and 225) present a contrast in form.

This vase (fig. 226), with a relatively small opening, is thick and heavy. It was probably cut after 1906, when hours could be saved by substituting a single star for a hobstar without detracting too much from the design.

This graceful vase (fig. 227) is also heavy.

The vase with flared top (fig. 228) is cut in a well-integrated pattern on brilliant glass.

The vase with an oblique swirl (fig. 229) resembles a 1903 Hawkes footed vase with hobstars, instead of bull's-eyes, going around the piece. It even more closely resembles a bowl advertised by L. Straus in the *Glass & Crockery Journal* circa 1905. The Straus pattern had bowknots between the bull's-eyes. The superb quality of glass and the cutting are typical of both Hawkes and Straus, the latter of which was a large cutting house that exported much of its glass to Europe. At least the similarity establishes a date of style and manufacture.

Fig. 223. Corset vase, 12″, circa 1905 in "Arcadia" variant, has six panels. On bulbous top are three six-point stars made of splits ending in starbursts. Between these lie feathered gray fans engraved on punties. Bottom cut in a 24-point hobstar.

Fig. 224. Vase, 8″, with bulbous top. Thick notched stem, then vertical prism flairs. Top has butterfly-shaped device created by crossed ellipticals in silver diamond. Shape resembles a vase by J. D. Bergen. (Matye)

Fig. 225. Vase, 9″. Flutes with beading form a corset in the middle. Base has thirty-two rays. Less expensive cutting in terms of labor, but quality is good and shape interesting. (Matye)

Choice of Quality and Price

It is interesting to read advice in an 1899 *Good Housekeeping* magazine: "You may pay any price that you choose, according to the difficulty of the workmanship, but let me assure you that if your means do not warrant a large outlay, the pattern with long wavy lines with beads interspersed are nearly as effective and much less expensive than the more ornate devices, especially if the piece is well covered."

The vase in figure 229 and the Hawkes bull's-eye vase (fig. 319) could be used with even the most modern décor.

It is not possible to establish arbitrary economic classes of glassware customers. It is clear, however, after scanning the information to be found in periodicals published during the Brilliant Period, that there was a rarified level at the top of the social ladder where price was no object, and perhaps three levels of middle-class people who followed the fad to the best of their ability. Below these were the respectable, hardworking poor who bought imitation cut glass, and those so deep into poverty that their only concern was to survive.

Fig. 226. Vase, 10″, is thick, heavy (over 5 lbs.), and clear.

Fig. 227. Vase, 9″. Flutes at top divided by two types of beading. Base is rayed.

176

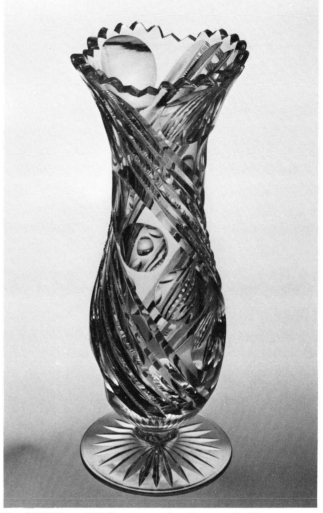

Fig. 228. Vase, 11⅝″. A beautiful pattern on a graceful shape.

Fig. 229. Vase, 12″. Spiral cuts, beading, and bullseye motifs on superb glass create an elegant piece. Note how concave circles vary in size to fit shape of vase.

14

Libbey Cut Glass

In the absence of a signature, it's difficult to identify cutware by companies. Use of blanks from one factory by various cutting shops, the practice of buying blanks from more than one source or of changing their suppliers, workers' movement from company to company in hope of bettering their position, and the copying of designs by rivals all contributed to a melding or overlapping of traits necessary for identification.

This predicament supplies a motive to seek marked pieces. Nevertheless, quality of glass, workmanship, and design should be the deciding factors in purchasing cut glass. Up to a point, one can learn to recognize with some assurance the products of the outstanding makers. In an effort to promote this awareness, we present the rest of our known pieces, with few exceptions, categorically by company.

Libbey's Predecessor

New England Glass Company of East Cambridge, Massachusetts, Libbey's illustrious predecessor, began in 1818 when the four founders — Deming Jarves (a young clerk at Boston Porcelain & Glass Company) and three Boston merchants — took over a failing venture started in 1814. Jarves was appointed "agent" (general manager). He stayed until 1825, when he left to establish a glass factory at Sandwich. Under his leadership, the company prospered. During its first year, forty workers produced glass valued at $40,000. In 1823, 140 workmen made glassware worth $150,000.

During its long tenure (1818-1888), New England Glass Company used nineteen marks on its vast array of products, including flasks, bottles, articles of mercury glass, many types of art glass in color, pressed glass, door and drapery knobs, even railroad lamps. Glass was decorated by cutting, etching, engraving, and gilding.

Early pieces (1825-1850) were similar to those of other companies here and in Europe. They had simple flute or panel cutting and some diamond and prism decoration. We would have judged this celery vase (fig. 230) to have been made by Bakewell, until 1850 a leading manufacturer of lead cut glass. Their metal was

Fig. 230. Celery vase, 8½", cut simply in a chain of English strawberry diamonds and miter cuts, forming bands of plain triangles. Flutes on stem extend upward onto bowl. Thin, wood-polished. Rings when struck.

clear and bright, their designs following Anglo-Irish tradition with emphasis on English strawberry diamond motifs, the glass thinner than that made by the New England Glass Company. The celery vase is identical, however, to goblets "used by Libbey family in 19th and 20th centuries," lent by Miss Sally Libbey, sister of Edward Drummond Libbey, to the 1951 Libbey Exposition at the Toledo Museum of Art. According to Carl Fauster (*Libbey Glass Since 1818*, p. 223), the goblets were made by New England circa 1870. Of course the celery vase is larger than the goblets. Such a round-scalloped edge is seen in a Mount Washington catalog of about 1880 and on a squatty pitcher in "Brazilian" in an old Dorflinger catalog.

Circa 1853, cased and flashed colored blanks cut through to clear in the Bohemian manner by New England could not be distinguished from their European models.

Many men contributed to the success of the company, one of whom was Thomas H. Leighton, a skilled glassblower from Edinburgh. As Italy had done centuries before, England prohibited emigration of glassblowers. By a subterfuge, Leighton came to America. He pretended to go fishing, went to France, then shipped to America, where he eventually contributed six sons and two Scottish cousins to the industry.

The firms' most prestigious engraver was Louis F. Vaupel, already an expert when he arrived from Germany in 1850. He moved to East Cambridge from New York City in 1851 to become head of design and engraving, remaining active until 1885. He made marvelous exhibition pieces for the 1876 Centennial at Philadelphia.

In spite of the capability of making fine products, the parent company was offered for sale in 1877. It had been forced to import costly fuel, was weakened by competition with the cheaper lime glass of the late Middle Period (1864-1876), hurt by the depression of 1873, and beset by labor strife. The general manager, who had been trained at the Mount Washington Glass Company in South Boston before coming to work for New England in 1872, obtained a lease on the company in 1878. To "New England Glass Works" in 1880 he added the words "W. L. Libbey & Son, Proprietors."

William L. Libbey died in 1883. His son, Edward Drummond Libbey (1854-1925), carried on in spite of continuing labor troubles. Edward lost money even after hiring John Locke, a talented English etcher (who invented several types of colored art glass, such as Peachblow and Amberina), so he decided to move to Toledo, Ohio, where natural gas was available for fuel.

In 1888 Edward took 250 workmen and their families, as well as company officials, with him. He also hired a talented young glassblower, Michael J. Owens, who soon was put in charge of production. The new firm was launched by means of a capital stock of $100,000 raised through local businessmen.

The company lost money until 1891 when a strike at the Corning Glass Works in New York caused Edison General Electric to give the contract for hand-blown light bulbs to Libbey. That year the company made a profit of $50,000. Strikers left Corning to work for Libbey, enhancing the Toledo company's capabilities. The name was changed in 1892 from W. L. Libbey and Son Company to Libbey Glass Company.

The World's Columbian Exposition

The World's Columbian Exposition was scheduled to open in 1892 "in commemoration of the four-hundredth anniversary of the landing of Columbus," but was postponed a year due to construction delays. The Fair at Chicago was the perfect medium for publicizing Libbey cut glass. Called a "Dream City" and a "City of Palaces," the ensemble of beautiful white buildings and their settings for exhibits attracted all of the greater and many of the lesser nations of the world.

A favorable, but rather condescending, comment was made concerning this fair's Woman's Building. Designed by Alice Rideout of California in Italian Renaissance style, it measured 888 by 199 feet and cost $138,000. A critic stated that it "lacked boldness and strength of conception, but is charming in its parts and shows close and tasteful attention to its details."

A "monster plaything," the Ferris wheel (fig. 231) with thirty-six cabins like trolley cars (each made to hold ten people) rose 250 feet above the earth. It recouped its cost of $380,000 in a few months. Over two million visitors came to ride in it, and to see such disparate exhibits as a model of Windsor Castle and semi-civilized peoples in transplanted villages. Of such were the handsome Samoan natives and some cannibals from Africa, including forty battle-scarred Amazons from their King's army and sixty savage men.

The Spanish Infanta Princess Eulalia and her Bourbon husband, Prince Antonio, represented her country. They "attracted some surprising demonstrations of toadyism" on the part of some Americans and "a growing love of monarchy among many ambitious people," according to a critic of Mayor Harrison, who kept "prominent citizens at a frigid distance" from his royal guests.

Fig. 231. Ferris wheel at World's Columbian Exposition at Chicago in 1893 rose 250 feet above the earth. (Bancroft's *Book of the Fair*, Vol. II, p.860, copied by Conkling)

In the midst of these wonders, the Libbey Glass Company had erected an exhibition factory, 150 by 200 feet, resembling a palace with a central dome (which served as a smokestack for the furnace) and with two towers flanking the main entrance. Up to five thousand visitors "comfortably entertained at any one time" could watch three hundred Libbey craftsmen "working day and night" blowing blanks and cutting and polishing them from start to finish.

They could also watch the entire process of spinning glass fibers and weaving them into cloth to be used for upholstering furniture, lampshades, and draperies. Glass fabrics did not originate with Libbey. Glass fibers had been spun and woven into cloth as early as 1830 by Signor Olivi of Venice and in the 1860s by Monsieur de Brunfant of Paris. But for fair visitors, glass cloth was a thrilling innovation.

The Crystal Art Room, with mirrored walls and ceiling hung with glass cloth, was the main attraction in the Libbey building. Here were draperies, upholsterings, fire screens, and lampshades ornamented with painted flowers and fruits. Fabrics could be sponged clean without harm.

Among the examples of cut glass displayed about the room against a background of ebony wood and black velvet were ice cream sets encased in brass-bound morocco, a punch bowl priced at $200, and a tall banquet lamp in three sections. A two-piece punch bowl, engraved with hunting scenes and with footed cups to match, was long believed to be one of the exhibits, but there is no confirmation. It was definitely exhibited at the St. Louis Fair of 1904. Recent discovery of a 1910 booklet, "Gifts Universal," illustrated the 12″ Hunting Scene Punch Bowl and Cups, "No. 537," suggesting it was a stock item. Libbey's high quality was justly honored by the award of a gold medal.

The public was duly reminded of this and other honors in subsequent advertisements. In addition to the gold medal at Chicago in 1893, the firm could later boast of gold medals won at the Tennessee Centennial Exposition in 1897, at the South Carolina Exposition at Charleston in 1901, and at the Louisiana Purchase Exposition at St. Louis in 1904.

A spun-glass dress made at $25 a yard for an actress, Georgia Cayvan, was displayed on a mannequin carrying a matching umbrella. The dress had a deeply cut neck, huge puff sleeves with fringes, and a full back (almost a bustle) in a fashion of 1830. Gores were outlined with a braided gimp of glass. At the foot was a puff of glass, and over it a fall of chiffon covered with a gleaming glass fringe. The material, with its brilliant, satin-like surface, resembled grenadine.

The aloof Princess Eulalia was so delighted with all of the Libbey glassware that she ordered a spun-glass dress for herself and appointed the Libbey Glass Company "Glass Cutters to Her Royal Highness Infanta Doña Eulalia of Spain." The dress was finally given by Princess Ludwig Ferdinand of Bavaria to the Deutches Museum in Munich, Germany. An identical dress is now in the Toledo Museum in Ohio. One of Libbey's cut glass designs is named "Eulalia," surely in her honor.

Investment in Libbey's Crystal Palace (against the advice of some of the firm's directors, and financed personally in the main by Mr. Libbey) was certainly justified, both by publicity and by the sale of glassware. Visitors bought many blown or pressed souvenirs to take home. A 12″ plate cut in the "Sultana" pattern, its center engraved with Libbey-over-a-saber and the words "This Trade Mark Cut On Every Piece," was displayed. Thus was the public made aware of the famous mark that would appear in numerous magazine advertisements read by influential citizens at the turn of the century. Cut glass now ranked with sterling silver as a mark of affluence. Libbey was to become one of the foremost names in cut glass and the largest maker to the end of the era. (See fig. 232.)

Fig. 232. American Cut Glass Exhibit at Chicago Fair. (*Bancroft's Book of the Fair*, Vol. I, p.166, copied by Conkling)

Libbey Glassware

Libbey Brilliant glass is heavy and thick, deeply and accurately cut. It shows no loss of sparkle and clarity after years of use. Libbey declared in a 1905 booklet that "the most exquisite effects are obtained from white glassware with a slightly bluish tint . . . found in Libbey Cut Glass."

The company hired the best designers and craftsmen. William C. Anderson designed for Libbey from 1887 until 1906, even while he organized the American Cut Glass Company in 1897 in Chicago, then moved it to Lansing, Michigan, soon after 1900. He created most of American's designs, several of which were patented. At Libbey's, his "Neola" was cut by John Rufus Denman in 1902 on a fabulous mold-blown table, 32″ high and 28″ wide, which was displayed at the St. Louis World's Fair of 1904 where Libbey was awarded the Grand Prize for Cut Glass.

William Marrett worked for Libbey as designer from 1897 to 1903. He originated the "Chrysanthemum" pattern, among others, and created a design based on an idea for a patriotic theme by J. D. Robinson for the famous, 18″ wide, 75-pound McKinley punch bowl (with matching footed cups), which bore shields with stars and stripes on base and bowl. Mr. Marrett and Patrick W. Walker, who came from Corning in 1889, did the cutting. It was to be presented to the president 23 November 1898, but was a week late due to the sudden illness of Mr. J. W. Hahn, who was to make the presentation. Newspapers made fun and said it had been lost. Now the gift *is* lost, but its twin, complete with ladle and twelve cups, has been found by Carl Fauster, Director of Toledo's Antique and Historic Glass Foundation.

When filling orders for presentation pieces or preparing superb exhibition items, it was customary to make two — the second as a back-up piece in case of breakage. To answer the frequently posed question, "How long did cutting take?," we can say with certainty that the McKinley bowl represented four weeks' work by two expert cutters.

Other major pieces were an elaborate floor lamp nearly five feet tall, circa 1904, and the St. Louis punch bowl, 25″ inches high (with two dozen matching cups), cut for the 1904 St. Louis Fair by Rufus Denman. The set was then valued at $2,700. Denman had to hold the bowl on his lap while cutting the pattern. The exertion caused him to lose thirty pounds. Sadly, the first bowl cracked when nearly finished. Another was started at once. It was then "the largest piece of cut glass in the world." It weighs 110 pounds and holds four gallons. The bowl was valued at $25,000 in 1946 when presented to the Toledo Museum of Art by the Owens-Illinois Glass Company. Today it is priceless.

The contributions of Mike Owens should be emphasized. Besides his leadership in the glassblowers' union and his management of the Libbey Pavilion at the 1893 fair, he invented in 1903 an automatic bottle blowing machine which led to lower cost and mass production, revolutionizing the world's glass industry.

In 1896 he left the Libbey Glass Company to make electric light bulbs. Libbey, Owens, and others formed the Toledo Glass Company to make lamp chimneys and tumblers by means of his first invention — a semi-automatic machine to make light bulbs. Toledo Glass, under Libbey's leadership, backed the bottle-making machine, forming the company still known as Owens-Illinois, Inc. It also backed Owen's perfection of the Colburn process for making flat glass automatically, leading to formation of Libbey-Owens-Ford. The Libbey Glass Company of the Brilliant Period is now known as the Libbey Glass Division of Owens-Illinois, Inc. It still makes tableware, but of an entirely different style.

In 1905 Libbey gave an exhibit illustrating the manufacture of glassware to the United States National Museum in Washington (a part of the Smithsonian Institution) — the first such educational exhibit donated to the National Museum by industry. It included a miniature clay furnace; a glass jar containing materials used to make fine glass, such as sand, lead, potash, and saltpeter in proper proportions; and three engraved plaques showing a blower, a cutter, and an engraver.

The first plaque showed the trademark, Libbey-over-a-saber, symbolic of the steel of Toledo, Spain (after which Toledo, Ohio, was named). The *L* and *y* tails nearly meet, but do not quite join. Strangely, in the other two plaques, the tails of *L* and *y* were joined and there was no sword. A beautiful plate showing stages of cutting was also sent, as well as a masterpiece of engraving. It was a 12½″ plaque, known as the Apotheosis of Transportation, modeled from John J. Boyle's sculpture over the entrance to the Transportation Building at the 1893 Columbian Exposition at Chicago. The plaque had been on display at the 1904 St. Louis Fair.

When the taste for Brilliant ware began to decline, Libbey reintroduced stone and copper wheel engraving in an attempt to save the market for fine glass. Realistic designs from nature were executed on heavy glass similar to Hawke's Gravic circa 1910, then on thinner blanks into the 1920s. Both Brilliant or Heavyware (as it was then called in the industry) and Lightware were cut simultaneously. For example, a claret jug, #300, known as "Snowflake" and identified by Mr. Fauster as having been cut circa 1919, had been advertised in a December 1911 *Ladies' Home Journal* This was a "tailored" geometric design, cut well into the Floral Period.

Large shipments of foreign heavyware sold so cheaply that American factories found competition difficult. Of course, World War I cut off raw materials from Germany and other parts of Europe, causing a decline in the quality of blanks — both for Libbey's own use and for other cutting shops who bought from Libbey.

Another important reason for shifting to engraved lightware was that it cost less to produce. It required no roughing or acid dip and little polishing. The waning market for the thinner ware led to a flurry of advertising in consumer magazines in 1919. A 1920 booklet referred to "new shapes of medium weight." These efforts had limited success.

Change to an informal life-style after World War I sparked a return to use of colored glass, another "throwback" to the past. The mother company in New England, in mid-nineteenth century, had produced colored glass, cased or plated-over-clear, with cut or engraved designs through the colored layer exposing the colorless interior glass. This was either left in a matte finish or was polished to match the outer layer.

Several items were exhibited at the New York Crystal Palace Exhibition of 1853.

Research by Carl U. Fauster into the types of ware made by Libbey in the early years in Toledo shows no evidence of color-cased, cut-to-clear commercial ware during the Brilliant Period. None of the six cut glass catalogs from 1883 to 1909 mention colored glass. Mr. Fauster does know of a few signed pieces. He has concluded that the few items in color during the 1890s and early 1900s were either custom-made for individuals or were produced solely for the numerous exhibitions in which Libbey participated.

About the time we entered the war in 1917 and into the 1920s, some color-plated, cut-to-clear was made to sell commercially. It was hoped that a new market would be found for this highest quality of ware that Libbey could produce for the limited luxury clientele. Such items as console sets of bowl-and-candlesticks and vases were made in purple, blue, green, black, and light ruby. Probably amber was made, also.

In 1924 Libbey advertised Safedge Glassware with a beaded rim, which prevented chipping. For the next nine years, Libbey produced mainly commercial ware for hotels and restaurants.

In 1933 A. Douglas Nash designed a new series, cut and engraved with intricate surface detail. Only the most skilled craftsmen could execute his concepts. The series emphasized tall stemware and matching centerpiece arrangements, many with colored parts. The most costly was the Victoria cameo engraved chalice, which required eighty hours of engraving for one piece and retailed at $2,500 a dozen! It was obviously too expensive for the Depression years and was discontinued in 1935. The range of items designed by Nash also included simple crystal pieces for domestic use, as well as complete lines for institutions.

In 1936 the Libbey Glass Company, a division of Owens-Illinois Glass Company, hired Edwin Fuerst to design heavy free-blown and mold-blown pieces, called Modern American, to be introduced in 1939. These had simple cuts; some had engraved animals for surface ornament. They remind one of recent Steuben creations. World War II put an end to this line and to all completely handmade glass. In 1959 an "1818" series, automatically blown, then cut, was made to compete with handcrafted ware, but was not maintained.

After 150 years of glassmaking, Libbey employed in 1968 over two thousand workers and had annual sales of $40 million. Continuing success, one could safely say, depended on integrity, adaptation to public taste, and innovative advertising in the twentieth century. For the reader who wishes to learn the entire history of this famous company, this author recommends Carl Fauster's comprehensive book. (See Bibliography.)

The marks for Libbey are as confusing as were those on New England glass. The first of those that concern us was a paper label (according to Revi) or "enameled, usually in red, and apparently stenciled" (according to John W. Keefe, Assistant Curator of the Toledo Museum of Art). It showed an eagle with spread wings holding three arrows in its claws above TRADE MARK in a circle. A larger concentric circle enclosed a space with the words *LIBBEY CUT GLASS* TO-LEDO, O.

Century magazine of December 1892 carried an advance notice of Libbey's Industrial Palace to be seen at the Chicago Fair. The Eagle trademark was depicted with the admonition, "Ask only for goods with this Trade Mark." The same text and illustration of the Libbey edifice, shown in the 1892 *Century*, appeared in an 1893 *Cosmopolitan* with the same reference to the trademark on the glass, yet Carl Fauster shows an 1892 advertisement in *Cosmopolitan* that makes no reference to finding the Eagle *on* the cut glassware.

Both Mr. Fauster and Mr. Revi describe finding this red Eagle trademark on fair souvenirs (of opal glass supplied to Libbey by Mount Washington), none of which were cut. While Mr. Fauster says that no Eagle trademark has been found on any cut glass, Mr. Revi definitely states that he has encountered Eagle labels on cut glassware.

From 1896 to 1906, LIBBEY was engraved or acid-etched on cutware in a sort of disconnected script over a sword or saber. (See trademarks in Appendix.)

We have found two types of Libbey/saber marks on glass. The earliest coincides with trademark #28180, registered 21 April 1896 "to be cut or etched," and "used since February 17, 1896," according to the patent declaration. In this one, the tail of the *L* swings down below the tail of the *y*, and is clearly separated from it. It was used in advertisements at least through 1899. We could find none for 1900.

From 1901 into 1906, a lower, more streamlined LIBBEY with tails connected, still over the saber, was used in advertising. This was filed 18 May 1905, and was shown in the Patent Gazette 7 August 1906. When etched on glass, a small break in the joined tails appeared under the *e*.

Our evidence so far points to the first saber signature being etched or engraved on the glass from 1896 through 1899. The second was used from 1901 through most of 1906.

Another LIBBEY was registered 19 June 1906 and was used in advertising from 1906 to 1913, according to Keefe. It had no sword, but "The World's Best" was printed on the thickened, joint tail. Even this mark had two printed versions. It was shown in magazines in an ovoid frame in 1911. The slogan on the tail was not etched on the glass.

Whereas in 1896 it was stated that Libbey was *cut* on every piece, by 1899 the words *engraved* or *'graven* were used.

In 1905 and 1906, a blue label with a hole in the center was affixed to the glass over the etched mark to aid the customer in locating the name. Some were square; others were ovoid. Advertisements made much of these "doughnut" labels, a few of which have been found.

A tiny mark, not quite $^3/_{16}''$ wide, with the break in the unified tails, is found on the outside, near the rim, of our three pieces cut in the "Libbey" pattern (fig. 275). This design, similar to Hoare's "Shagbark," is attributed to the year 1910.

Mr. Keefe shows a Libbey-in-a-circle, with thin connected tails, 1919-1930. The letters are thinner and taller and the name more vertical than the earlier marks. The *i* had a hook at the bottom. One of these marks was in an advertisement for Amberina ware in 1917. Engraved crystal in 1922 shows a similar emblem with a straight *i* and joined tails that drop far below the word.

On actual glassware, we have pieces whose styles seem to fit 1906 to 1920, marked with Libbey/circle. Similar to the above, the *i* has no hook, but the tail is thicker than the one described by Keefe, and it has a tiny break below the *e*. Some measure $^1/_4''$; some are a scant $^3/_{16}''$ wide. It would seem that the circle mark we have was used immediately after the sword, circa 1906 onward, concurrently with the streamlined, wider LIBBEY.

Mr. Fauster concludes in his excellent book that a correlation between the year made and the style of the name is debatable.

In 1901, 16 April, a five-point-star-within-a-circle, "used since February 19, 1901," was patented for use on "Certain Named Glass," actually on pressed blanks sold to other companies for cutting. Perhaps in practice it was on a paper label, although registered to be "stamped or etched." We hope so, because the only known Straus etched mark is a tiny five-point-star-in-a-circle.

Dorothy Daniel declared that Libbey never used pressed blanks for its own cutting. We have seen a celery dish signed Libbey/saber that was cut on a mold-blown, figured blank, definitely not blown off-hand, yet not pressed.

"One store in each city sells Libbey cut glass, and no other." So declared an advertisement in a 1909 *Pacific Monthly.* Libbey glass was "big business." Consequently, we have many examples to show.

The plate (fig. 233) in "Princess" was too early for the acid-etched trademark. "Princess" was not assigned to Libbey by William Anderson on his patent drawing #24874, 12 November 1895, for he had just about decided to sell his patterns, or to collect royalties on all cuttings from his designs. Nevertheless, it was sold to Libbey, as was #25512, 19 May 1896, called "Mathilde" by Revi. The only patterns assigned by him to Libbey after these were "Corinthian" (fig. 235), #25570, filed 19 March 1896, granted June 2 of that year; and "Star and Feather" (fig. 267), #38000, filed 26 March and granted 8 May 1906.

The salad bowl with plate (fig. 234) in Libbey's "Harvard" bears no resemblance to the cane or chair bottom of other firms, called Harvard. Its fans fit into the scallops like those in "Princess." Although listed in the 1893 Libbey catalog, it looks like the early 1880 patterns derived from Anglo-Irish designs. An ice cream saucer was shown in the 1895-1896 Higgins and Seiter catalog under the name "Harvard." A tiny

cordial may be seen here under cabinet pieces (fig. 437). Boggess's first book (p. 15) shows a vase in ruby/clear.

The following articles (figs. 235 to 255) are signed Libbey-over-the-saber, except where noted otherwise:

The pitcher or jug (fig. 235) is cut in "Corinthian," created by Anderson. Its signature matches the original saber mark shown in advertisements through 1899. Every glasshouse cut a Corinthian, but they differed greatly. Libbey cut its design on so many items that it is not impossible to collect a fairly complete service.

Fig. 233. Plate, 10″, unsigned Libbey in "Princess," designed by William C. Anderson. Registered design has central fourteen-point hobstar; this one has twenty points.

Fig. 235. Jug, 7¾″, in "Corinthian," #25570 by Anderson, assigned to Libbey, 19 March 1896. Jug, Libbey-saber, is barrel-shaped with thirty-two-point single star on bottom; triple-notched handle; notched flutes around neck.

Fig. 234. Salad bowl, 9″ × 2½″, and underplate, 9¾″, in unsigned Libbey "Harvard." Bold, tailored; heavy glass with "watery," silvery gleam. Wood-polished. Unusual square-over-square in center forms an eight-point star.

Four of Anderson's registered designs were assigned to his own company, American Cut Glass Company of Chicago, 18 May 1897. The next pattern assigned to Libbey that year was by William Marrett, 25 May 1897. Both Marrett and Dennis F. Spillane patented designs for Libbey at the turn of the century. This recital gives insight to the movement of designers from one loyalty to another.

These nappies (fig. 236) are heavy for their size. "New Brilliant" was advertised in a 1905 brochure, "designed to aid in the choosing of acceptable gifts," entitled *The Gentle Art of Giving,* and was still listed in 1908 and 1920 catalogs. Small serving pieces were often called "nappies." Sometimes they were named for their specific use. A 4″ almond dish in this design sold for $2.50 in 1905.

This "New Brilliant' cream and sugar set (fig. 237) would have been within reach of the middle-class family for use at company dinners. It sold for $6 in 1905.

In 1905 a "New Brilliant" jug had two hobstars, one above the other. Tumblers sold for $8 the half dozen; a three-pint jug for $10. In 1908 labor costs were cut by replacing the bottom hobstar with a single fan, as seen in the jug with five tumblers (fig. 238), also shown in the 1920 brochure. Tumblers were listed at $14.20 per dozen and a three-pint jug for $13.50. Each piece is signed Libbey/circle. This is a perfect example of simplification of a pattern to save labor cost

The unusual shape of this nappy in "Colonna" (fig. 239) makes it highly collectible. The design was shown in a 1905 brochure.

This serving dish (fig. 240) has the "watery" look of good, early glass.

The shallow bowl (fig. 241) is typically brilliant-cut on a heavy blank. Design is "Iola."

This rare footed fruit bowl (fig. 242), 13″ long and very heavy, seems to have been made in the 1890s, although it is signed Libbey-in-a-circle. Note the 24-point hobstar on the foot.

Fig. 236. *Left to right:* Nappy, 7″, in "New Brilliant," signed with saber. Nappy, 6″, also saber, has steeper sides.

Fig. 237. Sugar and cream set, 3″ h, in "New Brilliant" is signed Libbey/saber on top of both handles. Handles triple-notched; bases rayed.

Fig. 238. Tankard jug, 8″, and tumblers, signed Libbey-in-a-circle, cut in "New Brilliant" circa 1920. Handle double-notched.

Fig. 239. Nappy, 8″×2⅝″, saber, in "Colonna" comes to a point at top of photo. Point may be used as a handle. (Miles)

Fig. 240. Serving dish, 9″×2″, saber, nearly ½″ thick. Large hobstar covers bottom; alternate points end in eight blazed single stars.

Fig. 241. Shallow bowl, 8″, saber, has a central motif featuring kites of crosscut diamond alternating with fans. Design is "Iola." (Matye)

Carafe and tumbler (fig. 243) in "Cut 208" are signed Libbey/saber and Libbey/circle respectively, probably made in 1906 when the trademark changed. This design was still advertised in a 1920 catalog (p. 300 in Fauster's *Libbey Glass Since 1818*). Notice the unusual broken flute (offset) on the neck.

This heavy compote in "Ozella" (fig. 244) is clear and rings when tapped. Shown in the 1909 catalog, it was surely designed earlier, because this is signed Libbey/saber. Although of the same shape as that shown in another book, this compote is more elaborate. It would be the original version.

The ice bucket (fig. 245) shows a departure from the strictly geometrical cuts of the Brilliant Period.

The banana bowl (fig. 246) exemplifies the use of many of the motifs employed at the height of the period, arranged to fit perfectly the shape of the piece. It is cut all over without appearing "busy."

The set of ice cream saucers (fig. 247) has that "watery" look, and the cuts gleam like silver. The cutting is sharp and deep, the high quality justifying the boastful advertisements.

Seven tumblers in pattern #47 (fig. 248) illustrate geometric cutting of flowers. We missed by one day buying a matching jug. Continuing the search is part of the fascination of collecting. Six are signed Libbey/saber and one is Libbey/circle. The latter is cut on a slightly taller blank and was found separately from the set of six.

Fig. 242. Footed fruit bowl, 13″ l × 7″ w × 7″ h, cut in hobstars, cane, and trellises. Libbey/circle on foot. (Meyer with photograph by Conkling)

Fig. 243. Carafe, 7″, and tumbler, 5½″, in "Cut 208"; the former signed with the saber, the latter in a circle. Broken flutes on neck; single star bottom. (Matye)

Fig. 244. Fruit compote, 8″ d × 5¼″ h, in "Ozella," saber. Note blaze at top of splits. (Hamstreet)

Before moving onward from Libbey-over-the-saber to Libbey-in-a-circle pieces, let us examine some rarities.

The unusual shape of the "Delphos" banana bowl (fig. 249) is enhanced beautifully by the clear, beveled tusks and the fields of sharp, fine hobnail. The smooth, scalloped edge is unusual for a saber piece. This chaste design may be used with the most elegant furnishings, whether modern or traditional.

The tailored appearance of this beautiful ice cream tray (fig. 250) generally appeals to men. The author also finds its disciplined design breathtaking. Its probable date is 1897; its mark is the first Libbey/saber.

Presumably, this coaster, tile, or trivet (fig. 251) — all three names having been used to describe such a piece — was made to support a wine decanter or a teapot.

187

Fig. 245. Ice bucket or tub, 5″×5″, has two X-cut vesicas that meet over a five-point star as its principal device on opposite sides. Remaining areas cut in feathered leaves and star-blossoms. Base has thirty-two rays. (Photograph by Conkling)

Fig. 246. Banana or oval fruit bowl, 11″×6½″, 3″ deep, saber. Unusual four-point star on base fits into an oval frame. Note the many crosscut fans (trellises), flashed single stars, and fans placed to fill irregularly shaped areas.

Fig. 247. Ice cream or berry saucers, 5″, saber. Note the asymmetrical star center. Splits near edge are blazed in a fashion reminiscent of the famous "Neola" pattern.

Fig. 248. Tumblers, 3¾″, in design "#47." Hobstar is a flower supported by a crosshatched stem, with side cuts as leaves. To balance this, a pyramid of cuts is notched horizontally, making small trapezoids.

Fig. 249. Banana or oval bowl, 11½″×8¼″, 4½″ deep in "Delphos," saber. Clear planes make a striking contrast with hobnail, which sparkles.

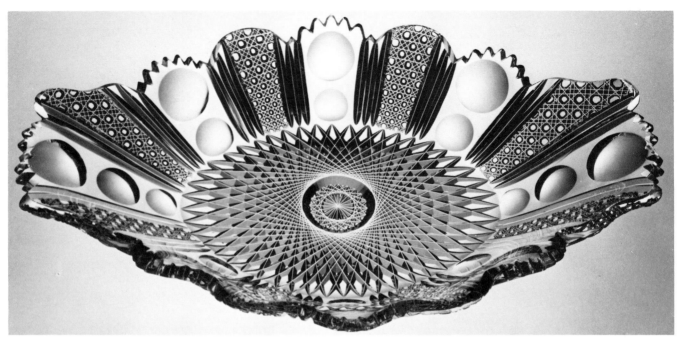

Fig. 250. Fishtail ice cream tray, 15″×9½″, saber circa 1897. Bottom completely covered by forty-eight-point hobstar.

Fig. 251. Coaster, tile, or trivet, 5¼″, saber; excellent quality in glass and cutting. (Bert Hilby)

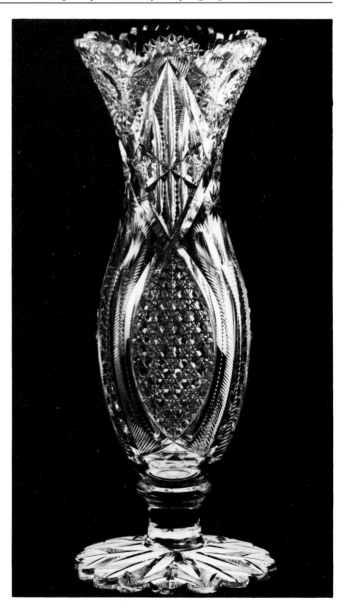

Fig. 252. Footed vase, 18″, in "#163." Libbey/saber below one of the hexad vesicas. Three large vesicas of hexad-of-buttons-and-star motif (a name created by this author) are separated by pairs of deep miter cuts, flashed their full length, that look like stems leading to buds made of flashed thumbprints. Three twenty-four-point hobstars are at top of vase between crossed miter cuts. Small stars and trellises complete top. A clear knop and stem connect vase to its foot, which is scalloped and cut in a flashed, extended single star. (Photograph by Conkling)

Fig. 253. Fruit bowl, 8¼″×3½″, saber, in "Senora." A bold, dramatic design, it has vesicas filled with horizontal cuts forming bars cut alternately in silver diamond and vertical gashes.

Fig. 254. Carafe, 8¼″, in "Senora" and Tumblers, 4″ — all with saber. Bottoms rayed.

Fig. 255. Rose globe, 5½″ h × 7″, in "Senora," saber. Three large twenty-four-point hobstars alternate with vesicas.

Fig. 256. Shallow bowl or nappy, 8″ × 2″, in "Anita." Libbey/circle with separated tails on *L* and *y.* (Matye)

This magnificent vase (fig. 252), in pattern #163 in the 1908 catalog, is fit for the most elegant mansion. The hexad-of-buttons-and-star motif (called a variant of cane or of Russian by others) is found on the finest pieces cut by several companies. (See the "Kensington" Tray by Libbey on p. 232 of Wiener's *Rarities.*) A strong signature appears just below a vesica of hexad.

When we discuss "How to Build a Collection" in a later chapter, think of these matching pieces in the "Senora" pattern, which appeared in a 1904 catalog. All are signed with the saber.

The fruit or berry bowl (fig. 253) shows the unusual design well. We recently saw a one-piece punch bowl in "Senora." It was fabulous! An 8″ bowl sold for $10 in 1905.

The carafe and tumblers (fig. 254) are practical for present use. The carafe is signed on one of the neck flutes. The tumblers are signed inside, center bottom.

The rose bowl (fig. 255) weighs four pounds, which makes it heavy for its size. Note the serrated edge. Rose bowls were used for stemmed roses or to float a single rose in full bloom on the water with the vase half full.

Unless noted, the following pieces are signed Libbey/circle. Several patterns were found in a rare 1919 or 1920 catalog. The only known copy was reprinted by Mr. Fauster in his definitive book on Libbey. We should not automatically assume that all patterns found therein were designed in 1920. Certainly the slightly altered "New Brilliant" goes back at least to 1905 in its more elaborate form.

This nappy (fig. 256), showing the trend toward simpler designs that cost less to cut, was shown in the 1920 brochure with the name "Anita."

"Anita," as rendered on the jug and tumblers (fig. 257), is light, airy, and well-placed. Although miter-geometric, it is a stylized flower design. The quality is superb.

Fig. 257. Jug, 8¼″, and tumblers in "Anita," a tiny Libbey/circle ⅜″ on top of pitcher's handle and ¼″ near bottom on side of each tumbler.

This cream and sugar set (fig. 258) was less expensive and less complex than the old patterns, yet its hobstar has a prominent button showing the depth of cutting.

The spherical pitcher with tumblers (fig. 259) in "Cut #209" was shown in the 1920 booklet and was advertised as "full lead crystal." The glass is brilliant, so we may assume it was made before or after our involvement in World War I.

The champagne cooler (fig. 260) is heavy and well-cut. The shape was sometimes used as a flower pot.

The cake plate (fig. 261) in "Glenda" (also known as "Laurent") on a low foot is cut in an unusual way. The design was advertised in the December 1910 *Cosmopolitan.*

The tray (fig. 262) with central hobstar, whose spokes extend beyond the rim of an apparent wheel, is interesting to study. Shown in the 1920 catalog as "Regis," it was described as "the utmost in design and quality in full heavy weight cut glass . . . the complete surface being cut." It sold for $18.

The central star on this ice cream tray (fig. 263) is cut on the flat bottom. The sides slope upward to form a dish suitable for serving ice cream. The edge indicates late Brilliant Period, but the glass is clear and the cutting is done skillfully.

This extremely simple "Plain Flutes" jug (fig. 264) of circa 1908 is comparable to "Colonial" pattern by Hawkes. An advertisement in *Ladies' Home Journal,* January 1907, remarked that " 'Colonial' appeals to people of refinement and taste who appreciate simple designs and shapes as much as the more elaborate." Customers were urged to have their monograms engraved at a small additional cost. "Let's return to the simple, classic designs of our grandmothers" was the plea by companies who had pushed ornateness to its zenith. Labor cost, as well as change in taste, helped to shape this propaganda. Note that the Libbey pitcher had the same curves and flute cuts on the handle as authenticated pitchers from glasshouses of Ritchie & Sweeney of Wheeling, West Virginia, about 1830-1840 (pl.61, *Cut and Engraved Glass* by Daniel).

Fig. 258. Cream and sugar set, 3″ h, Libbey/circle on top of single-notched handles. Rayed bottom.

Fig. 259. Jug, 7¼″, spherical, with matching tumblers in "Cut #209.", 1919-1920 catalog, all Libbey/circle. Medium-weight jug has sharp diamond in three kite-shaped fields, fern or feather motif at top, cluster of feathered thumbprints at top of cuts, resembling stems, leaves, and buds between the kites. Handle triple-notched.

Fig. 260. Champagne cooler or ice tub, 6″ × 6½″, Libbey/circle. (Gerritse)

Fig. 261. Cake plate, 11″, on low foot, Libbey/circle, in "Glenda" (or "Laurent"). (Gerritse)

Fig. 262. Tray, 12″, Libbey/circle, in "Regis." Intricate maze of deep and shallow cuts. (Gerritse)

Fig. 263. Ice cream tray, 11½″ × 1¾″, Libbey/circle with tails not connected, looks light and airy, yet glass is ½″ thick. Central radiant star is polished. Five curved miter cuts terminate in unpolished kites of silver diamond; feathers are left gray, also.

Fig. 264. Jug, 7½″ h × 6¼″, Libbey-in-a-tiny circle, in "Plain Flutes" has a flute-cut handle. Weighs over 6 lbs.

Fig. 265. Mayonnaise bowl, 5¼″ d × 2¾″ h, and plate, 5¾″ — both Libbey/circle in a later version of "Corinthian." (Rieder)

In a 1920 catalog, another plain "Flute" pattern was illustrated. Pieces in this revival were not carried in regular stock, but were available on special order for those who wanted "plain, heavy Colonial table ware" to blend with period surroundings.

The mayonnaise or whipped cream bowl and plate set (fig. 265) is typical of the Brilliant Period — an altered version of "Corinthian," which dates back to 1896.

Hollow-stemmed champagnes (fig. 266) are hard to find and expensive. These are cut in "Venetta," found in the 1920 brochure, the year the firm was reorganized and renamed the Libbey Glass Manufacturing Company. This may have been an earlier pattern, since the text states: "These patterns are made to order and not carried in regular stock." As in the "Flute" pattern above, "Venetta" could be ordered to "blend with period surroundings."

Early champagne glasses, called *flutes*, were tall, slender vessels that displayed the rising bubbles of carbonic acid to best advantage. McKearin, in *American Glass*, shows two champagne flutes by Bakewell, Page & Bakewell, of about 1825, still copying Anglo-Irish designs in America. Circa 1820, a new process produced a more limpid and lively champagne. Shortly, a new glass with hemispherical bowl on a tall, slender stem was devised to display the new liveliness. Disraeli mentioned in a letter to his sister in 1832 that he had taken champagne from "a saucer of ground glass mounted upon a pedestal of cut glass." The wide saucer does show bubbles well, but such exposure to the air causes the wine to "go flat" too soon, especially in the opinion of Europeans.

The concept of a hollow stem was to allow impurities to sink into the stem, while the drinker imbibed clearer wine at the top. Improved wines made this unnecessary. Besides, the hollow stems are hard to clean.

In the group of pieces (figs. 267 to 272) in "Star and Feather," also known as "Stalks and Stars," we see the beginning of several striking designs in which stylized flowers were made by means of parallel cuts and other devices. Unfortunately, when we first started to collect cut glass, we turned down eight punch cups in this pattern because they were so different from most designs that we never hoped to find a bowl to match. Three years later, I found this punch bowl

Fig. 266. Saucer champagnes, 5″, in "Venetta," Libbey/tiny circle, 1920 or earlier. Fluted, hollow stems with small notches.

Fig. 268. Fruit bowl, 9″×4½″, and celery, 3⅞″, in "Star and Feather," Libbey/saber.

Fig. 267. Punch bowl, 12″×6″, Libbey/circle, in "Star and Feather," was cut on a heavy, clear blank. Design, patented in 1906 and produced for several years, consists of feathered single stars (resembling blossoms or thistles), feathered thumbprints (buds?), and feathered stems. Bud-like flashed ovals did not appear on the original patent drawing, #38000.

Fig. 269. Milk jug, 7⅜″, and tumblers, 3⅞″, in "Star and Feather," saber.

Fig. 270. Water or lemonade tankard jug, 11½″, in "Star and Feather," saber. Use of this design on pitchers is striking. See how it radiates from a point on the front. Handles triple-notched. Both jugs cut on bottom in a thirty-two-point single star.

Fig. 271. Cream and sugar set, 3″ h, in "Star and Feather"; tiny Libbey/circle on top of handles. Bottom cut so that these blooms all seem to originate in the exact center and radiate outward and upward to top of piece. Handles triple-notched.

Fig. 272. Compote, 10″ d × 5½″ h, in "Star and Feather," saber, has scalloped foot. Note thickness of glass. (Rice)

(fig. 267) in mint condition and subsequently twelve other pieces — nearly a complete service. Advice! Never reject a set of good punch cups, tumblers, or stemware. They are becoming scarce.

All pieces in "Star and Feather" shown here — punch bowl (fig. 267), fruit bowl and celery tray (fig. 268), milk jug and tumblers (fig. 269), tankard lemonade (fig. 270), cream and sugar set (fig. 271), and compote (fig. 272) — are signed Libbey/saber except the punch bowl and the cream and sugar, that have Libbey/circle. Note that "Star and Feather" was found in a catalog of 1909, but pattern #38000 was filed by William C. Anderson, assignor to Libbey, 26 March 1906, and it appeared in the Patent Gazette 8 May 1906, proving that designs were often cut long before appearing in the particular catalog stumbled upon by a researcher.

Finding even two pieces in the same lovely pattern could inspire one to start looking for more. The olive or bonbon (fig. 273) matches the bowl (fig. 274). This new departure in cutting came into use circa 1906-1910.

Fig. 273. Olive or bonbon, 7¾″ × 5⅛″, Libbey/circle, has stylized flower with four deeply cut and polished petals, and small flowers and buds, matte finish, less deeply engraved.

Fig. 274. Fruit or berry bowl, 8″ × 4″, Libbey/circle; heavy.

Fig. 275. Ice cream or serving tray, 12″ × 2″, signed on outer edge with tiny Libbey with tails separated, was in a 1910 catalog as "Libbey" design. All cuts polished.

The round ice cream tray or serving tray (fig. 275) and the bowls (fig. 276) in the "Libbey" pattern are all signed with a tiny mark, almost like that seen in an oval cartouche in the magazine advertisements. This design seems to be Libbey's version of J. Hoare's "Shagbark." Close scrutiny reveals that buds in the Hoare pattern have feathery tips bending toward the ends of the buds, while flashing on the Libbey buds is straight. Also, the Libbey flowers are larger. Libbey's blossom centers and the buds are cut in tiny hobnail, curving upward into the glass, giving a sculptured, three-dimensional effect with a silvery appearance. All cuts are polished. A dealer friend, who knew that this had been Mr. Swan's favorite, saved the low bowl for me when her husband's aunt died in 1971 at the age of ninety-seven. This sort of information helps us to visualize the point in time when it was used.

In the October 1910 *Ladies' Home Journal,* there was an advertisement for Puffed Wheat (10¢) and Puffed Rice (15¢), showing Puffed Wheat with peaches and cream served in a cut glass bowl with flowers, buds, and leaves cut in a naturalistic design. Flower centers were composed of tiny hobnails like these. Such a design was "modern" then, and was a welcome departure from traditional geometric cutting. It might be called a "pictorial cutting."

The nuances of shading in this pitcher and tumbler set (fig. 277) compare favorably with Tuthill engraving. Cherries and leaves were cut freehand, for they differ in size and shape on the tumblers. Each cherry has polished highlights on the matte finish. Truly a masterpiece of intaglio engraving! Signed with a tiny Libbey, it was probably engraved circa 1908 to 1912.

Fig. 276. Deep bowl, 8″ × 4″, and low bowl, 8″ × 2″ — both signed near edge on outside. "Libbey" design.

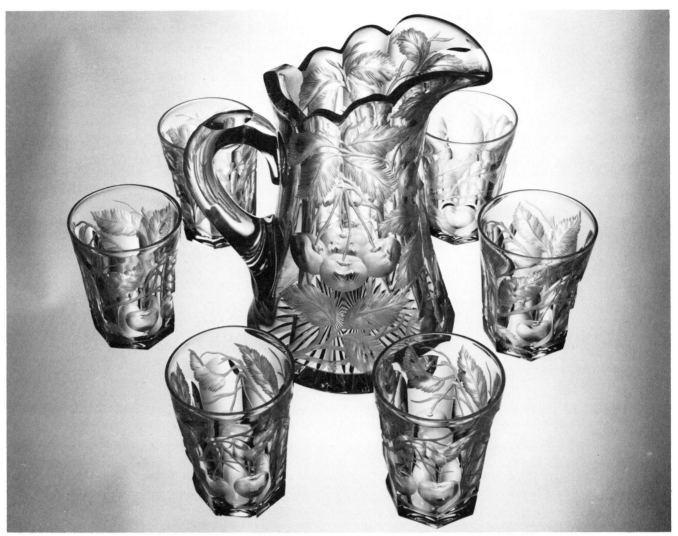

Fig. 277. Pitcher, 9″ × 6″ at base, and tumblers in stone-engraved intaglio cherries, signed with a tiny mark. Eight panels on jug; seven on each tumbler. Jug weighs over 5½ lbs. Deeply cut design wraps around pieces, ignoring line where panels meet, to give a sculptured effect. Handle has intaglio leaves in lieu of customary notching. (Taylor's Treasures)

Fig. 278. *Left to right:* Tumbler, 4″, saber; typical motifs. Whiskey shots, 2¾″, tiny Libbey/circle, with engraved "Rye" motif.

Fig. 279. Compote, 7″, Libbey/circle, circa 1919. Copper wheel engraving of fuschias left in matte for contrast with clear glass. Straight, vertical lines at top of engraved stem, seen from above, add a beautiful touch to center of bowl.

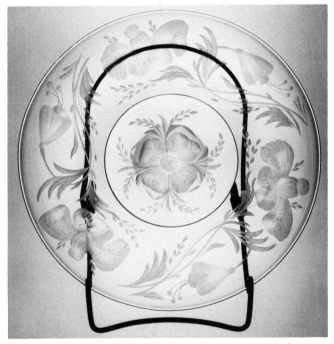

Fig. 280. Plate, 10″, in copper-wheel-engraved flowers, believed to be poppies, also signed in circle. (Gerritse)

One of these whiskey shots (fig. 278) was shown previously (fig. 46) in a close-up of the miniscule copper wheel engraving. These are rare, both in shape and design. A decanter with three indented sides, engraved in rye, barley, and corn, was made to use with these shot glasses. A tumbler, signed Libbey/saber, is shown with the shots to emphasize the small size of the latter.

This dainty compote for jelly or candy (fig. 279) represents artistic design and skilled craftsmanship on lightware glass. The exact shape with twisted stem was shown in the 1919 Libbey booklet entitled "The Gift of Gifts." Only the floral engraving differs from the illustration. It was sold with matching, twisted candlesticks as a console set. The tiny Libbey/circle is stamped in acid on the polished pontil mark of this handblown piece. It rings like a bell.

The plate (fig. 280) is another example of delicate engraving.

The octagonal fruit bowl (fig. 281) in "Wistaria," commonly known as "Lovebirds," is greatly desired by collectors. The genus of this oriental plant, having racemes of white, pink, or purple flowers, is usually spelled *Wisteria* — a publishing error by Nuttall. Only the correct form, "Wistaria," is approved by the International Code of Botanical nomenclature. The plant was named in honor of Caspar Wistar (1761-1818), prominent United States physician/anatomist. The 1920 Libbey catalog showed a full range of items, including a basket, in this unusual design.

Other pieces of Libbey glass are shown elsewhere in this volume for specific reasons: a celery tray (fig. 52), a nappy with handle (fig. 472), an ice cream saucer (fig. 447), a sherbet (fig. 458), a wine (fig. 457), a relish dish with three compartments (fig. 468), and a saucer from a bridge set (fig. 471). All may be compared with items in this chapter for style of design.

Fig. 281. Octagonal fruit bowl, 8″, circle, circa 1920, in "Wistaria" or "Lovebirds." Band of sharp silver diamond frames matte birds and foliage. Alternate sprays polished. Quality in this design varies widely. (Frané)

15

Dorflinger, Hawkes, and Steuben

Both the Dorflinger and the Hawkes glassworks produced large quantities of the finest ware in a great variety of styles. The success of these companies can be traced to the remarkable men who founded them. Both had international reputations.

Christian Dorflinger

Christian Dorflinger (1828-1915) was born in Alsace, France. At the age of ten, he began to learn all phases of glassmaking and decorating under the tutelage of his uncle at the Cristalleries de Saint Louis (in Lorraine), founded in 1767. His father died in 1845.

In 1846 Christian persuaded his mother to move the family to America. He obtained work in Camden, New Jersey, where he earned the respect of colleagues for his knowledge of glassmaking, his energy and perserverance, his business acumen, and especially for his honesty and modesty. By 1853, with the help of friends and with his own savings, he established a glass factory in Brooklyn, New York. There he designed and manufactured lamp chimneys.

The business grew so rapidly that in 1853 he was able to found the Long Island Flint Glass Works, where he broadened his line, adding free-blown tableware. In 1860 he built the Green Point Flint Glass Works on Commercial Street in Brooklyn. Here was cut the famous Lincoln service that launched his reputation. His glass was used in the White House by eight presidents, from Lincoln through Wilson. When he was thirty-three, his gross sales were more than $300,000.

Hard work nearly ruined his health. Advised by doctors to retire, he sold the Long Island Works, left the Green Point factory with trusted associates, and accepted the invitation of a friend, Captain Flower, to rest at his farm in Wayne County, Pennsylvania, near the hamlet of White Mills.

Dorflinger so loved the beauty of the area that he bought Captain Flower's summer home with three hundred acres of timber and farmland and later expanded to fifteen hundred acres. Health restored, he built a small five-pot glass furnace, then brought expert craftsmen from Brooklyn to train local farm boys to make glass of superb quality. He constructed over a hundred houses as dwellings for his workers.

It was through Mr. Dorflinger's generosity that Emil J. Larson, who was a gaffer for sixty years and worked for Victor Durand of Vineland, New Jersey, came to this country. Emil's father, Axel Larson, originally worked for the famous Kosta, maker of fine crystal in Sweden. In 1887 Axel, his family, and two other workers were brought to England to work for Bacchus of Birmingham. The business failed in a few months. Axel, his wife, and ten children were stranded.

Two of the three Swedes went to New York, where they were hired to work for Dorflinger at White Mills. Meanwhile, the Larsons (father and older children) could find only odd jobs in England. They hunted for spilled coal along the railroads for heating and cooking. Two of the older girls worked for Arthur Nash of later Tiffany fame etching and engraving glass.

When Dorflinger learned of their plight, he paid the passage of the whole family to White Mills, where he had a home ready for them. It was indeed the promised land of opportunity. Here an eleventh child was born. They were all welcome to work for Dorflinger, including the girls.

Axel brought with him new shapes and thinner stemware. The new line created a greater demand by cutting shops in a wide area for Dorflinger's glass blanks.

Emil was hired at thirteen. He reached the end of the line, specializing in goblets and small stemware, at seventeen. He started at $20 a week. When he married in 1903 at the age of twenty-five, he was earning $28 per week. He could afford the luxuries of seven suits, a horse, and a surrey with fringe on top.

By 1903, with expanded facilities consisting of twenty-three factory buildings, Dorflinger employed 650 men and boys. A large ship basin was built on the canal that ran through White Mills to Honesdale and on to the Hudson River, from which the huge volume of blown, cut, and engraved ware, as well as blanks for other cutters, could be shipped. Barges returned from New York loaded with sand from France, potash from Germany, and red lead from England. Later, sand from the Berkshire Mountains in Massachusetts was used. The furnace pots were built of fine glazed brick from England. Wood, coal, and water were plentiful around White Mills. The Erie Railroad built a spur station to carry shipments and passengers to and from the glassworks.

In 1868 Dorflinger began construction of a thirty-six-room hotel with a ballroom measuring 31 by 60 feet. It was completed in 1870 and named the St. Charles at a spectacular ball for local dignitaries and for his New York and European friends.

His four daughters were sent to the best finishing schools. They traveled in Europe, but were not allowed to enter their father's factory. It was not acceptable for young ladies of refinement to do this. Their brothers were educated here and abroad

In 1881, when Dorflinger took his three sons into the firm, the name was changed to C. Dorflinger & Sons. William managed the retail and wholesale outlets in New York, Louis stayed at White Mills in the financial management of the business, and Charles helped to operate the plants.

After a fire in 1892, Dorflinger rebuilt the works with even better equipment. The company's greatest prosperity followed during the next twenty years.

The founder, respected and beloved by all who knew him, died in 1915 at the age of eighty-seven. His sons carried on until 1921, when they closed the works forever. The war and Prohibition contributed to the firm's decline, but low-priced ware from Europe was its chief nemesis. By clinging to the old ways and maintaining high standards, Dorflinger found it difficult to compete. Many of the workers went to Corning, New York, where they made Corning and Steuben glass.

Three articles in *Antiques* by Kathryn Hait Dorflinger Manchee (listed in the Bibliography) are recommended for further facts concerning this genius of glassmaking, and for the excellent photographs.

Dorflinger Glassware

The Centennial Set, shown at the 1876 fair, was mentioned earlier, as were the many fine items in the White House. In 1902 Theodore Roosevelt ordered a copy of the Lincoln glassware, replacing the shield with an engraved letter *R*. This is in dispute.

As late as 1963, an engraved goblet, blown and decorated at White Mills in 1917, was given to President Kennedy as a memento of the dedication of the Pinchot Institute in Pike County, Pennsylvania. Dorflinger glass was ordered by the Vanderbilts, Reids, Goulds, and other prominent families. Queen Victoria and King Edward VII had special pieces made for Buckingham Palace. The crystal in a heavy flute pattern was used on the special train carrying the Prince of Wales on an imperial tour of Canada in 1919, and again when he toured the United States and Canada in 1924 (see fig. C.2).

The largest single order came from Mario Menocal, President of Cuba, in 1918. The 2,300-piece set had nineteen different sizes. It cost $60,000. Louis C. Tiffany, who decorated the presidential palace, gave Dorflinger the order. The pattern was relatively simple, with a blaze of flash-miter cutting at the base of each piece and the Cuban coat of arms engraved above this.

A similar flash-miter of varying lengths was used on yachtware for Henry Clay Pierie's yacht, *Yacona*. Crossed yachting flags were engraved above a ribbon bearing the name of the yacht

The factory supplied crystal and cased color blanks to at least twenty-two cutting shops in the area. It made more than five hundred items — apothecary jars, chemical and optical ware among them. These were sent to Dorflinger's showrooms in New York City, "the only store in the world exclusively devoted to CUT GLASS." The cut tableware and the ornamental pieces suitable for decorating the house or for wedding presents are the focus of the collector's interest. Quoting Mrs. Manchee, "Colors included canary yellow, ruby, cased ruby and crystal, shades of green, cased green and crystal, turquoise, the rare poppy color, amethyst, deep 'Stiegel' blue to light blue, amber opalescent combinations, opaque white and rose." A few double-cased items were made.

The beautiful pitcher in green-cut-to-clear on the Dedication Page (fig. C.3) is an authenticated piece that could be mistaken for European. A band of nail-head diamond lies near the base, which is cut in a 64-point single star. Above the band, flowing curves and dainty floral engraving combine with an exquisite handle to form a masterpiece of design.

Some glass items (fig. C.4) were decorated with gold and were marked HONESDALE, where the gold was applied. Some had applied silver in filigree over the glass, or had silver mountings, such as collars, rims, tops, and handles. Some silver fittings were marked with the Dorflinger name; others were not.

In *Harper's Magazine*, January 1897, a goblet was shown representing "our new lines of table service . . . light and graceful; the style refined, and the cutting a new intaglio pattern." Stylized blossoms were cut in the Rock Crystal manner, anticipating the Floral Period by several years.

A less expensive line of etched glassware, as well as lightly cut, thin tableware, was made circa 1910. Three patterns were patented early that year. The legend reads, "For goblets or similar pieces."

Dorflinger glass can usually be positively identified only by comparison with documented pieces, since it was marked with a tiny, round paper label. Within concentric circles on the label are a bottom-heavy wine decanter, with a wine goblet on the left and a cordial glass on the right Above these DORFLINGER is printed. Unless the item was never used, each has lost its signature. Just a few pieces have appeared that are marked on the glass. These were acid-etched by John Dorflinger (1880-1954), a second cousin who kept a small museum-shop in White Mills from 1921 until his death. He had sample pieces of custom orders that were left when the plant was closed. Some commercial pieces have turned up with the name impressed on the base.

According to an 1896 advertisement in *Life*, Dorflinger glass could be ordered with various degrees of cutting. A cigar jar, "all glass-air tight," to hold fifty cigars, was shown. Plain, it sold for $2.25. As illustrated, with thumbprints around stopper and shoulder, and with 2″ flutes around the base, it was $4.50. Richly cut, it cost $10.50. "Also made in sizes for cigarettes, tobacco, and bonbons."

The pitcher and tumbler (fig. 14) seem to be early Dorflinger from one of his Brooklyn firms, as explained in legend and text.

The candlestick (fig. 282), also attributed to Dorflinger, was probably made in the 1870s or 1880s. The band of silver diamond was frequently used by him.

The ice bucket or butter tub (fig. 283) has all of the earmarks of Dorflinger craftsmanship: hand polishing, clarity, freedom from imperfections, and skillful cutting.

Fig. 282. Candlestick 5¼″ h x 5″, circa 1870-1885, has flat ovals on stem; thick base vertical cuts on edge. (Bert Hilby)

Fig. 283. Ice bucket or butter tub, 4″ h x 6″, has clear concave "windows" with crossed triple-miter cut at junctures; twenty-four-point hobstar on bottom.

The "windows" closely resemble those at the top of an authenticated green/clear jug of the Middle Period. Sinclaire cut a similar design that had a chain of hobstars above the punties.

Look back at the 12″ vase (fig. 8), documented as Dorflinger, in sharp relief diamond, cut in the Irish tradition. This is similar to the "Old Irish" pattern of Meriden Cut Glass Company. It has a "tailored" appearance.

Fig. 284. Bowl, 8″, in "Old Colony" in the Irish tradition has original label (in center of radiant star). Rolled edge.

One of the early Brilliant Period patterns, in the style of the 1880s, is exemplified in the signed bowl in "Old Colony" (fig. 284). Its bands of silver and sharp relief diamond were sometimes contiguous and sometimes separated by a clear area, depending on the shape of the article. This pattern was cut on seventeen items. It was exciting to find an original label with not a trace of wear on the glass.

The wine goblets (fig. 285) are attributed to Dorflinger. In McKearin's *American Glass* (pl. 138, p. 341) there is a French pressed goblet, circa 1840, with clear rim, relief diamond, and octagonal foot, which could have been the inspiration for these wines. French craftsmen came to work for Dorflinger, and the master learned his craft in France.

The basket (fig. 286) is apparently a variant of "Marlboro," with the motifs rearranged to fit the shape. Note the silver diamond at the point of attachment of the handle.

The rare orange bowl (fig. 287), authenticated Dorflinger, is large and dramatic. Although many motifs are employed, it is like classical music — altogether lovely.

Fig. 285. Wine goblets, 5⅛″, in sharp relief diamond; faceted knop; octagonal foot. Above knop, eight clear panels end in points extending into the diamonds, making a clear flower form as one looks down into bowl.

Look ahead to the section on cabinet pieces, Chapter 19. The heavy master salts (fig. 442), upper left and right, were cut in a Dorflinger pattern called "Renaissance" circa 1895.

The paperweight-stamp moistener (fig. 288) is a gem, cut in Dorflinger's variation of "Middlesex." The original Middlesex was patented by William C. Anderson for the New England Glass Company, 25 January 1887, #170272 — perhaps his last before moving to Toledo. This was one of the first designs to use the eight-point hobstar as a principal motif. Its upper fan was balanced by an inverted fan. Dorflinger replaced the lower fan by an upside-down silver diamond kite flanked by acute triangles. Shown here, inverted, the piece is a beautiful paperweight. As seen in figure 443, it is a stamp-moistener to hold a damp sponge (the porous, flexible skeleton of a marine animal, not the modern plastic imitation).

The punch bowl (fig. 289) is judged to be Dorflinger, although documentation is lacking. The shapes of the clear triangle and the kites of silver diamond are

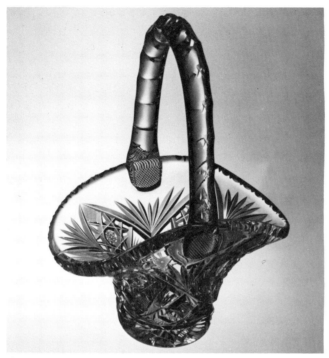

Fig. 286. Basket, 9½″ h; 7″×5″ at edge, in a variant of "Marlboro." Thumbprints on handle with checkered cuts where they intersect. Edge is notched — a long and a short.

Fig. 288. Paperweight-stamp moistener, 3⅜″ d × 1¾″ h, in "Middlesex," weighs 1¼ lbs. Shown here as paperweight. Has a central sixteen-point star with eight silver diamond tips. Eight-point hobstars alternate with fans around sides.

Fig. 287. Rare orange bowl, 15″×9″, 7″ deep, circa 1895-1900, has sections of Canterbury Russian; a large hobstar on each end. (Gerritse)

Fig. 289. Punch bowl, 12″ d × 10″ h, on standard, attributed to Dorflinger. Collar on base resembles a twisted rope. Ladle, 13″, cut in "Middlesex"; silver marked "1223 Gorham Co.," followed by an anchor. Cups in J. D. Bergen's "Electric" cut in a chain of hobstars in lozenges, alternating with fans pointing upward and downward. Bottoms rayed.

Fig. 290. Footed cake tray, 10″ × 5″, in a Daisy design is cut in fine-line, polished cuts. Stem is plain, the apparent cutting near its base being a reflection of the foot. "No. 1175."

Fig. 291. Supreme, 5⅛″ h × 5⅜″; with underplate, 7½. In "Kalana Lily," made to serve grapefruit or a large dessert. Sherbets with underplates, shown in catalogs, were 4″ to 4½″ wide and less deep than supremes.

similar to those in "Middlesex" and "Marlboro," and the relationship of the large bowl to its small stand is similar to that of a punch bowl in the "American" design advertised in *Cosmopolitan,* January 1894. Then, too, the ladle purchased with the bowl is in Dorflinger's "Middlesex," the silver stamped GORHAM.

The punch cups (fig. 289) are cut in Bergen's "Electric." One often has to perform a "marriage" between related designs, since matching sets are rarely found.

As we move into the Late Brilliant or Floral Period, the cake tray on a standard (fig. 290) has been verified as Dorflinger. Both blank and notches on the edge are identical with those in a catalog. Daisies and leaves are like those combined with other motifs, such as the Greek Key in "Athens." Even though the top is flat, it rings when tapped. Footed cake trays are scarce and expensive. Catalog name "No. 1175."

The supreme with underplate (fig. 291), made to serve grapefruit or a large dessert, is delicately acid-etched in "Kalana Lily." Revi shows a goblet, a champagne, and a punch cup. A 6″ master nut dish with four 3″ individual dishes were recently advertised. By these clues, we may assume that there must have been a full table setting in "Kalana Lily." It seems that "Kalana" signified a line of etched lacy and floral designs in the matte finish, for the word was combined with Poppy, Forget-me-not, Crocus, and Queen Anne. Another pattern in the same vein was "Kalana Rose, Band, and Ribbon." It should be noted that "Kalana Lily" was also produced by Irving and by the Tournous Brothers.

Although Dorflinger did some all-over, heavy cutting to answer public demand, much of his glass remained relatively simple in form. The patterns selected for his own family reflect his refined taste for elegant balance of shape, cutting, and engraving, leaving clear areas to reveal the blue-white diamond purity of his crystal.

Thomas G. Hawkes

Thomas Gibbons Hawkes (1846-1913) could trace his ancestry to "Old Singing Waterford," for he was a descendent of the Hawkes and Penrose families who had been glassmakers and cutters in Dudley, England, and Waterford, Ireland, for five generations. He was born at Surmount, his father's estate near Cork, Ireland.

Thomas studied civil engineering for two years, then left for New York City in 1863 at the age of seventeen. In Brooklyn he worked with John Hoare as a draftsman, learned cutting in the shop of Hoare & Dailey, and he did some selling. He moved to Corning in 1870 to become superintendent of the Hoare & Dailey cutting shop, located on the second floor of the Corning Glass Works.

He opened his own cutting shop in 1880, using blanks made by his friend, Amory Houghton, Sr., of Corning Glass Works, which had previously sold its output only to Hoare's shop. He also used Dorflinger blanks, and eventually some imported from European firms (including Stevens & Williams and Thomas Webb in England, Baccarat in France, and Val St. Lambert in Belgium), and a few from Libbey, Fry, Pairpoint, Union, and Heisey.

From the beginning, he was favored by special orders from rich individuals, among them George W. Childs of Philadelphia. In 1885 Hawkes received his first order from the White House: fifty dozen pieces in "Russian" from President Cleveland. In spite of labor disputes with the Knights of Labor union, his business prospered and expanded.

In 1903 he persuaded Frederick Carder to manage a new factory — completely financed by Hawkes — to be called the Steuben Glass Works. Hawkes agreed to take all blanks Carder could make. Orders to Dorflinger dropped sharply. Thomas, his son Samuel, his first cousin Townsend de Moleyns Hawkes, and Frederick Carder opened Steuben Glass Works, 9 March 1903.

Steuben and Frederick Carder

Mr. Carder had been induced to leave Stevens & Williams in Stourbridge, England — partly to answer a challenge in a new land, but also because resentment still rankled against unjust treatment in the old country. In 1891 he had been offered a national scholarship, enabling him to study for three years in Paris, Rome, or London. Stevens & Williams had refused to release him from his contract.

Steuben, under Carder, produced many kinds of art glass, as well as colored and crystal blanks for the Hawkes cutting shop. Any blanks with accidental bubbles or other flaws were returned for replacement. Carder, a genius without question, originated many fine blank forms for Hawkes. Although his long and productive life was mainly devoted to creating new varieties of colored art glass, and although he never would say he liked cut glass, he grudgingly admitted that its brilliancy approached that of a diamond. He had been forced to design cut patterns for Stevens & Williams, but he bowed to popular demand in America as a good businessman.

Soon after Carder began selling his blanks to other outlets besides Hawkes, he established a cutting shop at Steuben. He cut more in the Brilliant style than is generally supposed, using motifs then in vogue. These pieces were sold as Steuben products; Steuben blanks decorated at the Hawkes shop were sold as Hawkes products, with no credit given to the Steuben name. As usual, Carder's products were superb; as usual, he was innovative. His unique style of combining cutting with engraving (most of the latter done at the homes of the engravers) may have accounted for the continuation of his cutting department long after the vogue for cut glass was over.

In 1918, when Steuben ornamental glassware was declared "non-essential" by the wartime government, the company became a subsidiary of Corning Glass Works. Most of the ornamental ware was replaced by bulbs, tubing, and optical glass. Carder's authority was reduced to that of art director. He nearly decided to return to England, but after the war he resumed management of the Steuben plant. Wartime commodities were mainly phased out, and the making of his marvelous colored art glass resumed.

In the post-Brilliant period, unique masterworks were made as presentation pieces. For example, the Queen's Cup given to Queen Elizabeth and Prince Philip by President and Mrs. Eisenhower; the Papal Cup — to Pope Pius on His Holiness's eightieth birthday by Francis Cardinal Spellman, Archbishop of New York; and a Rose Bowl — the wedding gift from President and Mrs. Eisenhower to His Imperial Highness, Crown Prince of Japan.

Mr. Carder retired at ninety-six and died peacefully in his sleep at one hundred years of age.

The lady's cuspidor (fig. 147) in Chapter 11 is attributed to Steuben.

The centerpiece set of vases (fig. 356) in Chapter 17 is believed by two experienced dealers to be a Steuben product. It is shown with Sinclaire glass to illustrate a style made by Sinclaire.

Following the loss of Steuben, Hawkes bought heavy blanks from Libbey, other blanks from the United States Glass Company in Tiffin, Ohio, and some from Val St. Lambert in Belgium. After seeing Tiffin's XX quality metal at the St. Louis World's Fair in 1904, Hawkes had purchased (and continued to buy) XX blanks through the years.

Henry P. Sinclaire, Jr., and Oliver F. Egginton (as foreman) worked for Hawkes. Egginton left in 1896 to establish his own company. Sinclaire had come to work as bookkeeper in 1882, but by 1888 was left in charge when Hawkes was away. By 1890 he was a full partner.

At this time the firm's name was changed from T. G. Hawkes Rich Cut-Glass Works to T. G. Hawkes & Company, and the trademark was devised and used from this year, according to most authorities. How does one explain that a collector/friend of the author owns a 12″ tankard pitcher in "Russian" of finest quality with eight tumblers — all nine pieces acid-stamped with the old signature and dated 1885? Under the quintuple-notched handle, between its top and bottom, is engraved in old English letters, "FWR January 14/85." Perhaps only presentation pieces were marked this early; yet, if so, the trademark must have been designed at that time. It is possible that the set was presented later, but was marked to commemorate an 1885 event.

In any case, the trefoil or shamrock was symbolic of both men's names. The first mark, filed 5 February 1903 as #39884 and copyrighted 3 March 1903 for "Engraved and Cut Glass," was described as follows: "Three segmental lines connected together to form a trefoiled ring inclosing a central ornament and the pictorial representation of two hawkes placed within the lower parts of the trefoiled ring. Used since 1 July 1890." The centered "ornament," a fleur-de-lis, stood for the French name SINCLAIRE; the two birds were a rebus for HAWKES. This same form appeared again as #7942 in the Patent Gazette, 31 October 1905.

In advertisements or on glass, HAWKES was printed within the upper loop of the symbol. (See trademarks in Appendix.) The trefoil enclosed in a circle appeared in magazines during the years 1891, 1892, 1893, 1894, and 1896, with the warning, "Without this trade-mark, no piece is genuine." In 1895 and 1897, the circle was absent and the admonition read, "Without this trade-mark label, no piece is genuine." If "label" meant a paper sticker, we have yet to see one.

No advertisements were found from 1898 to 1901. From 1902 to 1908, a slightly different trademark was shown in magazines. Now HAWKES was printed below the trefoil, the foils were shaped differently, and the birds look less like ducks and more like true hawks with white heads. Now the warning read, "No piece without this trade-mark engraved on it is genuine."

From late in 1908 through 1911, the name was dropped from under the symbol in advertisements, but was retained then and on through the years in the acid-etched mark on glass. This *logotype*, as it is called in the trade, appeared in different sizes, some as small as ³⁄₁₆″ (easily overlooked). On some, HAWKES is directly under the shamrock; in others, it is wider. We have not been able to associate this practice with dates.

Stemware and many small pieces, such as knife rests and the pill bottle in the neck of a water bottle (fig. 20), were signed simply HAWKES in block letters. A 1960 catalog showed the trefoil with the words, "The trademark to look for on large pieces." It is not true that Hawkes signed items with an H, as has been written in a periodical.

The word GRAVIC for "Cut and Engraved Glass" was filed 7 January 1903 and published 3 March 1903, #39883, "Used since 13 December 1902." It reappeared in the Gazette 23 January 1906 as "Ser. No. 7941."

Hawkes thoroughly believed in advertising; Sinclaire did not. In periodicals of that time, advertisements by Hawkes outnumbered all others, even those of his nearest competitor, Libbey. A booklet printed circa 1900 claimed that the Hawkes firm was the "Largest business of its kind."

By 1898 he was filling his third order for the White House. He continued to prosper, in spite of being considered by labor as an "oppressor of humanity" because he hired many apprentices at lower wages. He built a large house in Corning, and bought an estate in Ireland near his father's home, spending every other summer there.

Sinclaire's preference for delicate, engraved designs and Hawkes's for brilliant, geometric cutting resulted in a widely varied display of glassware being sent to the Paris Universal Exposition in 1889. Hawkes glass won the Grand Prix in Group III, thus becoming internationally known. (Two of his winning designs were "Grecian" and "Chrysanthemum.") Subsequently, his products were ordered by the nobility and other fashionable people of Europe.

Hawkes continued to favor brilliant cutting, but broadened his scope when J. Hoare won two awards for engraved and rock crystal glass at Chicago's 1893 Columbian Exposition, and when other companies threatened to outpace him.

In 1902 he introduced his Gravic glass. Gravic depicted natural forms — flowers, birds, fruits — or it combined brilliant cutting with deep intaglio, unpolished engraving of these forms from nature. Pieces were marked with only this word or in combination with the regular trefoil. One should not use the word "Gravic" loosely to describe any such engraved representations of nature, as is the habit of some. Only Hawkes had the right to use this copyrighted term.

Sinclaire broke with Hawkes to form his own company in 1904.

Besides the White House cut glass mentioned previously and glass sold here and abroad from 1880 to 1900, cut glass was furnished during the first half of the new century to many of the richest families in America, such as the Whitneys, Astors, Vanderbilts, Rockefellers, and Armours, and to such internationally renowned people as the Crown Prince of Sweden, Sir Thomas Lipton, Generalissimo Chiang Kai-shek, and President Diaz of Mexico.

The firm originated perhaps a third of the outstanding designs of that period. At one time there were 322 Hawkes patterns on as many as fifty shapes and weights of glass. Classic handcraft equipment was used throughout its history.

In addition to the styles of heavily cut, Gravic, Satin Engraved (begun circa 1903), and Edenhall (a rock crystal type named for the Edenhall Goblet of 1920, which showed scenes from Longfellow's *The Luck of Edenhall*), another cheaper line of cut and engraved ware also appeared in their catalogs and brochures about 1920. (The Edenhall Goblet is considered to be the salient work of its kind. It was engraved by William H. Morse, who was trained in the Hawkes factory.)

Silver mounts made by Gorham and other silversmiths were used until 1912, when Hawkes began to make their own fittings.

Although colored hock glasses in rose, amber, and green were made in stemware sets, few colored pieces appeared in early Hawkes catalogs. A few colored pieces were cut after 1903, but colored ware had not been generally fashionable since the Middle Period. Interest revived in the 1920s.

More could be said concerning the man, Thomas Hawkes: that he was a man of culture, and that he was kind and pleasant to work for (even though he had some enemies in the glassworkers' union). We conclude by saying that his fame was well-deserved. When he died, 7 July 1913, his son, Samuel, inherited the business.

Post-Brilliant Period Hawkes Glassware

The demand for brilliant cut glass having diminished so greatly, the firm turned in the 1920s to making lightweight cut and engraved ware. Engraved monograms on plain pieces were featured, as were delicate, shallow, rock crystal engravings in a continuous, all-over style. A few better engraved pieces were signed by the artist.

Also in the 1920s, Samuel Hawkes introduced a heavy line adapted from the old Anglo-Irish designs of the early nineteenth century. These featured sharp diamond point on a large scale, round and oval bullseyes, and flutes. Patterns were bold, even coarse.

In stark contrast were fine-line cuttings on the *gang wheel*, combined with copper wheel engraved medallions (fig. 311). To all of these were added in the 1920s and 1930s enameled, gilded, and stained wares.

Many of the designs introduced after World War I stayed in the line until the end in 1962. Most were lighter and simpler, but some holdovers from before the war, such as "Queens" (fig. 307), "Kensington" (fig. 323), and certain stone engraved fauna and flora, such as "Satin Iris" (fig. 446), continued to be made.

Samuel had been aided by Penrose Hawkes, who came from Dublin, Ireland, in 1916. (Penrose's father was a brother of Thomas.) When Samuel retired to Florida in the early 1940s, he left the business under the poor management of Bradley Lindsley. In 1949 Penrose Hawkes closed the New York sales office and came home to Corning to salvage the business. The firm lost money after 1956, and Samuel died in 1959.

It was Penrose's sad task to close the factory. He liquidated the business assets in December 1962. He sold the name, trademark, and designs to the Tiffin Art Glass Corporation of Tiffin, Ohio, in January 1964, permitting Tiffin to "use all Hawkes patterns for cut, decorated or plain stem and occasional pieces except, however, silver mounted items." (Tiffin had bought out the bankrupt United States Glass Company in 1963.)

A letter, dated 14 February 1979, from Franciscan Crystal by Tiffin (division of Interpace Corporation) confirmed that "on all of our production we sandblasted the name HAWKES on the base and affixed an.oval blue and white product sticker per attached sample... In 1966, the owners of TAGC sold the company to Continental Can Company and it became known as the Tiffin Glass Company, Inc. Later in 1969, CCC sold the factory to Interpace Corporation and we are now known as the Tiffin Glass facility of Interpace... Our sales of Hawkes crystal continued through 1973 but towards the end we were selling only five of the original Hawkes patterns on an exclusive basis to Tiffany and Company."

Tiffin never published a Hawkes catalog after the firm started making the line in 1964, but sent glossies to customers. In 1969 Tiffin introduced eight patterns — some on old Hawkes shapes, others with the Hawkes-cutting-look on Tiffin shapes.

This somewhat tedious recital is told to clarify confusion regarding very late glassware signed HAWKES.

Penrose Hawkes carried on a retail shop in the old building, selling imported porcelain and glassware. He was a distributor for Waterford glass from Ireland. He also had glass stone-wheel engraved locally by former Hawkes artisans, using both domestic and European blanks (none from Ireland). The former were from West Virginia Glass Specialty Company in Weston; the latter from France. The name HAWKES was marked on the glass with a stylus to prevent confusion with earlier ware. Some pieces were signed HAWKES-CORNING, N.Y. He never signed T. G. HAWKES, as reported in a 1974 periodical. Some of these factual corrections were obtained by correspondence with Mrs. Penrose Hawkes. She quoted Samuel as having said, "There is so much misinformation in all the books on glass."

After Penrose Hawkes died in October 1972, his widow carried on the business until 1975, when the building was purchased from the heirs of Samuel Hawkes by Corning Glass Works.

Every piece described as being signed had the trefoil with HAWKES underneath, with the exception of the tumble-up or boudoir set (fig. 20) and the catsup cruet (fig. 301), which have both trefoil and the name in block letters, and a knife rest (fig. 214) stamped only with HAWKES.

This large, unsigned rose bowl (fig. 292) is fully cut in a design called "Aberdeen" in the patent papers, 14 April 1896. Later it was shown in a Hawkes catalog as "Anson." A 24-point hobstar covers the bottom. "Aberdeen" is scarce; pieces are collector's items. The diamond-shaped areas of crosscut diamond are split from the bottom; between them lie inverted kites of silver diamond.

The famous "Russian" pattern, patented in 1882, was presented previously, and examples (figs. 39, 151, and 156) were shown. Here is a graceful decanter, attributed to Hawkes, (fig. 293) in the most elaborate variation, the Persian, with each button cut in a tiny hobstar. Few Russian pieces were signed.

The dessert plates (fig. 294) in a variant of "Chrysanthemum" are as beautiful as the original design shown at the Paris Exposition of 1889, when Hawkes won a grand prize. These lack only cane on the clear tusks. The design was called "Jubilee" in another book. Since then, a catalog reprint has shown a different design named "Jubilee."

Fig. 292. Rose bowl, 9″ d × 8½″ h, unsigned, in scarce "Aberdeen," later "Anson" in catalog. Heavy and well-cut.

Fig. 293. Decanter, 12″ to top of matching stopper, in Persian variety of Russian, attributed to Hawkes. Rests on a ⅜″ base; cut in an unusual six-point hobstar. Neck has eight flutes.

Fig. 294. Dessert plates, 6¾″, in a "Chrysanthemum" variant. Exactly like patent drawing of 4 November 1890, except that tusks are clear. In registered design, they're cut in cane. (Hamstreet)

Fig. 295. Square bowl, 10″, signed, is an elaborate "relative" of "Chrysanthemum." (Gerritse)

Fig. 296. Rose globe, 7″ h×6″, unsigned, in "Brazilian," typical of "allover" cutting of the period. (Gerritse)

This square bowl (fig. 295) signed Hawkes is obviously related to "Chrysanthemum." Sometimes a cutting shop simplified a pattern after a while to save labor costs. This was certainly not true in this instance.

"Brazilian," #19114, 28 May 1889, was adapted to various articles. Many are unsigned. It consists of fans, eight-point hobstars (sometimes omitted), miter X-cuts, and some silver diamond. The rose bowl (fig. 296) is unsigned.

Fig. 297. *Left to right:* Champagnes, 4¾", in "Brazilian," unsigned. (Author) Tumbler, 3¾", in "Queens," signed, cut with overlapping punties and columns of hobstars. A hobstar covers base. (Matye)

Fig. 298. Fruit or salad bowl, 9″ × 3⅝″, signed, typical of 1895 to 1905.

Fig. 299. *Left to right:* Cologne, 6¾", signed HAWKES in "Cypress." St. Louis or honeycomb neck; half flutes on shoulders; eight-point hobstar and fan. (Matye) Cologne, 6¼", unsigned, tipped to show bottom fully cut in six-point star. Sides have four eighteen-point hobstars alternating with eight-point hobstars. Design also has silver diamond and hobnail, a great variety on a small piece. (Matye)

Look back at the "Brazilian" tumble-up (fig. 20). It is signed on the bottom of the tumbler with a trefoil, ³⁄₁₆″ wide (HAWKES under it, ¼″); on the carafe base with a ⅜″ trefoil (HAWKES is ¹⁄₁₆″ smaller); the pill bottle has HAWKES in tiny block letters on the bottom edge. The pill bottle and carafe are marked *15* with a stylus Part of the eight-point hobstar shows near the base.

Champagnes in "Brazilian" cut for President Diaz of Mexico were slightly more ornate than these (fig. 297). The bowl was deeper and the stem grew wider toward the foot, which had a scalloped edge. These are unsigned and are of finest quality.

The signed fruit or salad bowl (fig. 298) is deeply cut and brilliant. It is a family heirloom from Earle's home in Connecticut.

The signed cologne on the left (fig. 299) is in "Cypress," a version of Anderson's "Middlesex." The cologne on the right is attributed to Hawkes. Both have similar eight-point stars on the sides. The latter piece does not have a matching stopper, and may have been signed only on the missing stopper, or not at all.

Fig. 300. Cream, 4″ d×3⅝″ h; and sugar, 6″ w with handles, signed. Three layers of crosscut diamonds encircle single star on base. Handles double-notched. (Matye)

Fig. 301. Signed catsup cruet, 5¾″, in "Holland," also known as "Centauri." Base rayed; handle triple-notched.

Fig. 302. *Left to right:* Square nappy, 6″, in "Holland," signed in center. Heavy; has "watery" look when viewed from below and feels wood-polished to the touch. Ice cream saucer, 5″, circa 1905-1907, signed OM^{E}G^A, has nothing to do with Hawkes glass. Signature a mystery.

The signed cream and sugar set (fig. 300), circa 1900, is beautifully cut to harmonize with the shape. This same cutting, with the triple row of diamonds double-crossed, is shown in an elegant épergne in Pearson's *Encyclopedia I,* page 90. It is a good example of carrying a design a step further for a larger piece.

"Holland," also known as "Centauri," consists of an eight-point hobstar over a kite of silver diamond. Narrow fans flair upward on each side of the kite. Two hobstars are arranged vertically with larger fans on both sides of the top star. These motifs are repeated around the item. The catsup cruet (fig. 301) and the square nappy (fig. 302) exemplify this popular pattern well. Both are signed. A cruet made to serve catsup had a wider opening than one for vinegar or oil. This cruet's heavy lapidary stopper is marked with the trefoil and is numbered *7* to match a corresponding *7* inside the neck. Hawkes in block letters is stamped beneath the handle.

The ice cream saucer on the right (fig. 302) is an orphan among the Hawkes pieces. It was bought for the mysterious signature, OM^{E}G^A. One can speculate that the large capitals, O, M, and G, were the initials of the maker, or OM^{E}G^A may be the private brand of the distributor. OMEGA was a popular trade name for several products from 1905 to 1907.

"Gladys" (1900-1903) is clearly illustrated in this signed nappy (fig. 303). Purchased at auction, it was described as "American brilliant cut Nappy ca. 1910" in the catalog, with no mention of a signature. A trefoil

Fig. 303. Nappy or dessert plate, 6½", signed, in "Gladys," circa 1900-1903. Wood-polished.

Fig. 304. Powder box, 7" d, in "Odd," signed Hawkes on both pieces. (Meyer, with photograph by Conkling)

Fig. 305. Decanter, 11½"; 14" with matching stopper, signed Hawkes. Unusual shape.

was found near the edge between two scallops when the plate was examined more closely at home. If the auctioneer had known and publicized this, the price would have gone higher.

A 7" puff box (fig. 304) in "Odd" design was shown in a 1911 catalog. Both box and lid are signed in the trefoil. It is heavy and rare.

The signed pyramidal decanter (fig. 305), cut in honeycomb with a chain of hobstars, has a triple-notched handle and a hobstar on the base.

"Brunswick" is one of Hawkes's easy-to-remember designs (ca. 1900-1910), characterized by a chain of hobstars, flutes, and zipper cutting between flutes. It is dramatic in a large item, such as a punch bowl. A tantalus set was advertised in 1903. A similar, but simpler, design with ordinary beading was added to the line in 1904.

A trumpet vase and this "Cream Jug" and "Sugar Basin" set (fig. 306) demonstrate that only the clearest glass could be used for such a pattern. Look ahead to the "Brunswick" cologne (fig. 466) with cabinet pieces for another specimen.

"Queens," cut on the finest Steuben blanks, was widely advertised from 1903 to 1915. It was popular and expensive. In fact, it was a holdover from the Brilliant Period into the 1945-1962 period. Goblets sold for $315 per dozen in 1908. Worth a small fortune now, some pieces, such as tumblers (fig. 297), are hard to find at any price. Advertisements in *Ladies' Home Journal* of 1907 showed a vase-like, footed pitcher

Fig. 306. Cream, 4″ d at base, 3¾″ h; sugar, 5″ d at top, 2½″ h, in "Brunswick." Shapes unusual. Four panel cuts with notched edges on handle of creamer. Bottoms have large hobstars.

Fig. 307. Berry bowl, 8″ × 4″, signed, in "Queens" shows clearly the vertical chains of hobstars that alternate with columns of bullseyes, arranged in one-two sequence. Note flashed bullseye center bottom, resembling a sunburst.

Fig. 308. Champagne pitcher, 13½″, unsigned, in "Queens." This tall, narrow tankard is rare. Graceful triple-notched handle balances shape of pouring lip. Hobstar base can be seen through the side.

with a high handle and a square top, as well as vases in unusual shapes. No pattern name was given then, but in 1903 and 1910, a rose bowl was shown, labeled "Queens." Illustrated here are a berry bowl (fig. 307), a champagne pitcher (fig. 308), a jug (fig. 309), and a 12″ trumpet vase (fig. 310). In Chapter 19, two highball glasses (fig. 456) may be seen. These were found too late to appear in this chapter.

Hawkes also cut a table lamp in "Queens." It is beautiful, but when lighted may be less desirable than a more closely cut design that would diffuse the light and conceal the bulbs.

Fig. 309. Jug, 8¾″, in "Queens," signed below handle, which is cut in a quintuple row of concave diamonds. A twenty-four-point hobstar covers the 5¼″ base. Superb quality!

Fig. 310. Trumpet vase, 12″, in "Queens," signed on top of foot, has faceted knop above foot.

The Gundy-Clapperton Company of Toronto, Canada, cut a similar pattern, usually marked GCCo in a trefoil.

The centerpiece bowl with underplate (fig. 311) in "Gracia" (of the post-Brilliant Period) is similar to "Sheraton" (cut in fine diamonds between the bands) and "Millicent" (with floral engraving between the fine-line bands). These three are considered scarce and desirable to add variety to one's collection. The engraved medallions may have been conceived by Sinclaire before he left in 1904. Volume II of *H. P. Sinclaire Jr. Glassmaker* (p. 32) by Estelle Sinclaire Farrar shows a plate with five similar medallions and rope-like spokes in lieu of fine miter bands. Such bands of fine parallel lines were cut on gang wheels by several firms from 1913 into the 1920s.

"Flutes and Greek Border" was cut by Hawkes circa 1908-1914, when an attempt was made to recapture the interest of customers by going "back to the designs of our grandmothers." These pieces — a berry bowl and a cream and sugar set (figs. 312 and 313) — required much less labor than intricate brilliant

Fig. 311. Centerpiece bowl, 9½″ × 4⅝″, and underplate, 10¾″, both signed in center, in "Gracia" circa 1920. Bands of fine-line cutting and engraved medallions are left gray. Rays in base are polished. Glass is half as thick as earlier pieces.

Fig. 312. Salad or berry bowl, 8″, signed, in "Flutes and Greek Border." Heavy, 4½ lbs.

Fig. 313. Cream, 4¼″ d × 3¼ h, sugar, 3″, signed, in "Flutes and Greek Border." Finest blank.

Fig. 314. Celery tray, 11½″ × 4½″, and bonbon, 6½″, cut in "Gravic Strawberry." Berries and fine leaves in satin; large leaves and stem polished.

Fig. 315. Hexagonal bowl, 10″, 1902-1911, signed HAWKES GRAVIC GLASS on outside near top. A feeling of movement is conveyed by center leaves in a pinwheel conformation. (Gerritse)

Fig. 316. Jelly compote, 6″ h × 7″, signed on polished pontil under paneled stem with teardrop, is engraved in "Floral Spray and Pearls" (our name) in Rock Crystal finish. Knop is cut in flat ovals. Although shallow, it rings like a bell when tapped, and is heavy.

designs, but they exemplify the usual high quality of glass and workmanship. Note that the Greek Key (sometimes called Roman Key in this type of fret) is polished on the cream and sugar set, but left in matte on the bowl.

The celery tray and star bonbon (fig. 314) in "Gravic Strawberry" are excellent examples of Gravic: a combination of intaglio stone engraving and brilliant cutting. The former is signed in the center with the usual trefoil with HAWKES below and GRAVIC GLASS curved above it. The bonbon matches the celery perfectly, yet is center-marked with only the shamrock with HAWKES below — proof that companies were not always consistent in signing their products.

The graceful hexagonal bowl (fig. 315), with stylized blossoms and closed buds, is also signed HAWKES GRAVIC GLASS on the outside near the edge. The pattern is similar in style to "Carnation" in that both have intaglio-cut flowers and leaves, lightly engraved tiny flowers, and a pinwheel-like swirl of leaves in the center. Note the unusual edge with long, smooth scallops — a complete break with the rigid designs of brilliant cutting. This is America's version of French Art Nouveau.

Look ahead in Cabinet Pieces (fig. 446) to see the "Satin Iris" engraved on an ice cream saucer. Hawkes also made a "Gravic Iris," which was slightly more elaborate. A Hawkes relative claims that "Satin Iris" was the last pattern cut by Hawkes (Boggess, p. 60).

This jelly compote (fig. 316) in "Floral Spray and Pearls" (our name for identification) may have been designed by Sinclaire before he left Hawkes in 1904. Sets of glassware have been found signed by both companies, so they must have worked together at times to fill orders after he left. The superb quality and the weight lead us to believe this compote was made before the war. Of course, Dorflinger advertised a light, graceful rock crystal engraving in 1897.

Fig. 317. Sweetpea vase, 8¾″ h × 7½″, in "Regina," signed on top of foot, has flared, undulating edge — a favorite device of Hawkes. Polished pontil mark makes a central bullseye for sunburst. Classic, well-integrated design.

The sweetpea vase in "Regina" (fig. 317) is cut exactly like a tall, slim vase in *Ladies' Home Journal*, 6 June 1907. The advertisement's title was "Wedding Gifts of Hawkes Cut Glass."

Fig. 318. Bowl, 9½″×4″, signed, circa 1906, resembles a "bride's basket" insert.

This signed bowl (fig. 318) is unusual in that it is thick enough for a deep hobstar on the base, yet it gradually thins toward the edge. Pulling out the edge to create the "waves" accomplished this effect. *Ladies' Home Journal* in 1906 showed a basket and a vase by Hawkes with this same daintily notched, crimped edge.

The signed footed rose globe or fish bowl (fig. 319) is cut in a Bullseye pattern, a refreshing change from some of the complexities of the latter days of the Brilliant Period. For those who prefer modern furniture, stressing color and texture on simple forms, this would be appropriate now. The basic shape of this blank was used well into this century.

Several companies — Pairpoint, Bergen, and Straus among them — used the bullseye circa 1898. Hawkes listed "Navarre" in a 1900 catalog, combining this motif with others. The bullseye, called by many names in Europe, is very old.

Fabulous is the word for this tray (fig. 320), the design named "North Star" in a catalog and "Orpheus" by Pearson. Whoever composed the Hawkes advertisement for July 1905 in *Ladies' Home Journal* must have believed his own copy when he described a related design: "Patterns as delicate, intricate and beautiful as lace are seen in pieces of Hawkes Cut Glass...different...unique." If one were asked, "Please pass the cookies," he would indeed be surprised when trying to lift it, because the tray weighs nine and a half pounds empty! Either people were very strong in those days, or many cut glass pieces were impractical. Obviously the plate was free-blown, because one side is noticeably thicker and there are no raised places on the top surface following the indentations, as there would be in a molded blank.

Fig. 319. Footed rose globe or fishbowl, 9½″, signed center underfoot, cut entirely in bullseyes, would make a beautiful fishbowl. Finest blank, later piece, superb glass.

Fig. 320. Rare serving tray, 15″, in "North Star" (or "Orpheus"). Round, signed in center. The hob in the center of each 4½″-star projects 5⁄16″ from the bottom surface by virtue of cuttings around it. The radiant star causes the hob to be thinner in the center.

Fig. 321. *Left to right:* Dessert plate, 7″, signed, in a Wreath and Flower matte engraving with polished cut stars. Dessert plate, 7″, signed, in "North Star," matches 15″ tray (fig. 320). Superb glass required for such cutting.

My husband brought home the 7″ dessert plate (fig. 321, right) as a birthday surprise. He had bought it from a local dealer. I never dreamed that two years after his death I would find the matching 15″ tray in another city and another state, on consignment in a shop.

The dessert plate in a wreath and flower pattern on the left (fig. 321) has the eight-point star so typical of Hawkes, but it also has the light floral engraving, the hanging tassels, and fine-line scalloped edge that show the influence of Sinclaire. Look ahead under Cabinet Pieces (fig. 472) to see a matching handled nappy, and backward (fig. 99) for a silver-mounted cruet in a wreath and flower without the stars. When we asked Mrs. Penrose Hawkes if Sinclaire ever designed for Hawkes after leaving in 1904, the answer was "No."

The anticipated advent of Halley's Comet in 1910 inspired unreasoning fear in the superstitious and creativity in artists. Several cutting shops produced comet designs. This fruit bowl (fig. 322), signed inside center, is one of the most beautiful and rare. The shape is now referred to as a "blow-out" blank.

The design, "Kensington," for the rare footed rose globe (fig. 323), signed HAWKES on top of the foot, was listed circa 1900-1915. "Kensington" was one of the Brilliant Period patterns held over into the 1920s to be made on special order. A plate in this design has no fans.

The signed punch bowl in "Lorraine" and twenty-four matching cups (two were bought after the photograph was taken) in mint condition constitute a rarity (fig. 324). Since the dealer retained eight cups and she mentioned that several were found broken in the house where she bought them from an elderly lady, we may surmise that the original set had thirty-six cups. This pattern was shown in a Hawkes booklet published circa 1900, and was extensively advertised in *Ladies' Home Journal* for several years. In April 1903 a corset

Fig. 322. Fruit bowl, 10¼″ × 4″; 6½ lbs, signed, in a Comet pattern, has fluted vertical walls. Clear planes define the spinning comet. Deeply indented sections alternate two designs. Blank was hand-blown; it varies in thickness, but may have been blown into a mold for shaping.

Fig. 323. Rare footed rose globe, 10½″ h; base and bowl 8″ d, in "Kensington," has chain of hobstars with fans at top, repeated on stem (or knop). Above knop, a faceted section rests on the ball. Scalloped foot is ⅝″ thick and is connected to the bowl by a metal plug. (Miles)

vase, widening gently at top and bottom, was shown. In December 1903 a two-handled low bowl, perhaps for strawberries or cranberry sauce, was illustrated with the words, "Hawkes Cut Glass appears in small as well as large pieces, each one rich, handsome, and rare and all suited for Christmas Presents." In the March 1904 issue, a footed trumpet vase with lapidary knop just above the foot was shown. "Hawkes Cut Glass transmits light colorless as crystal. It does not show a tint yellowish or greenish — and its surfaces do not appear smokey as you hold a piece between the light and your eyes."

The April 1904 *Ladies' Home Journal* pictured an elegant compote in "Lorraine" with a large knop in the stem, cut in hobstars, and an unusual raised platform foot. "Hawkes Cut Glass ranks with Gold and Silver of the highest class for presents and gifts." The December magazine showed an electric table lamp, 23″ high with three bulbs, in this pattern, unnamed in any of the advertisements. The base had horizontal step cutting on a platform and at the "waist" of a corset-type base.

Finally, these car vases (figs. 325A and 325B) with a page from the original English and Mersick Company 1908 catalog listing them at $6 each (whether wholesale or retail is unknown at this time) constitute a rare discovery. Both are signed HAWKES under a trefoil on the flat bottom. In 1984, they might sell at $400 each or more.

How sad that so many masterpieces have been broken and lost to posterity! It is no wonder that prices on the remaining pieces continue to rise.

Fig. 324. Punch bowl, 15″ × 6½″, in "Lorraine," signed, circa 1900, has twenty-four matching cups (twenty-two in photograph). Well-integrated design uses few motifs. Curved splits create arches. Short splits near the three-point hobstar base make notched prism fans. Glass is ⅝″ thick. Handles on cups are triple-notched, a sign of high quality.

No. 10   No. 11

Fig. 325A. Pair of car vases, 8″. One is in brilliant cutting, one in floral engraving with ribbon bows and swags. (Photograph by Conkling)

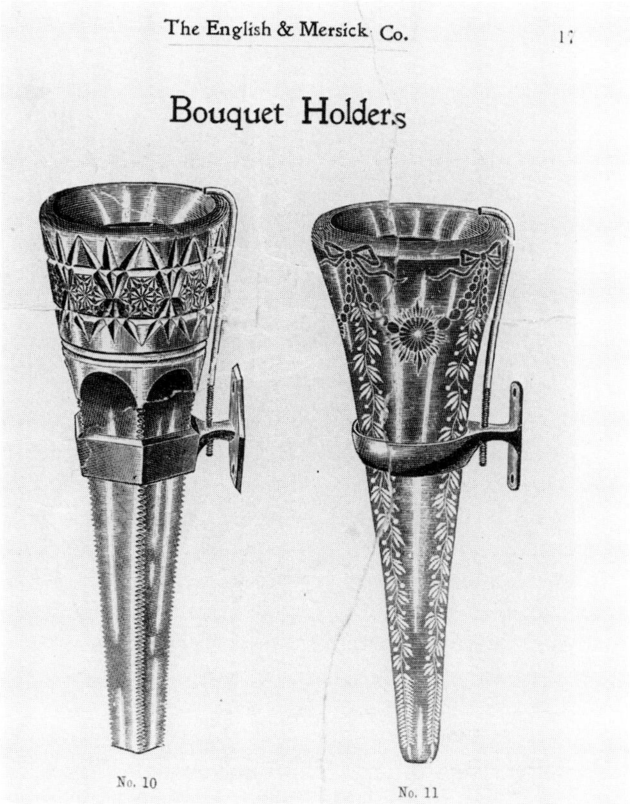

Fig. 325B. Catalog drawings of same car vases with brackets in silver finish. Mountings also came in brass or nickel. Each sold for $6 in 1908. (Photograph by Conkling)

16

Tuthill, Meriden,
Bergen, and Niland

Founded in 1900 as C. G. Tuthill & Company (pronounced Tuttle), the name was changed in 1902 to the Tuthill Cut Glass Company when Charles Guernsey Tuthill, son of Corning's most prestigious architect, was joined by his brother, James F., and his sister-in-law, Susan C. Tuthill. The small firm, employing twelve to fifteen cutters and engravers — about thirty people including clerical help — was located in Middletown, New York.

It is said that Tuthill used Corning Glass Works blanks made according to a special formula supplied by him, exclusively *for* Tuthill. They also used Dorflinger and Pairpoint blanks. The firm produced exquisitely cut and engraved ware until its closure in 1923, when it was sold to Henry Guyard Company of Honesdale, Pennsylvania. Apprentice engravers earned $3 per week. Experts earned $18 to $20 early in the century. The men worked ten hours a day, six days a week.

Charles, who had been trained at Hawkes, created most of the designs. He also did cutting and engraving (with both stone and copper wheels). James Tuthill devised an improved acid polish and also created some designs. Susan managed the factory and guarded the perfection of the products, measuring depth and alignment of every piece with calipers. Tom Mortensen was foreman for over ten years. His death was partly responsible for closing the factory.

Harry Holmbraker, one of the best engravers, used a hundred different copper wheels, the smallest being the size of a pinhead. He engraved a vase with tiny birds (each ¼″ high) with distinctly cut feathers. He is also remembered for a 36″ vase, around which were wrapped engraved, coiled dragons. The vase was a farewell gift for the Chinese ambassador.

Leon Swope stone-engraved beautiful fruit designs at Tuthill from 1911 to 1913. He worked for seven firms across the country during his fourteen-year career.

Although the intaglio flower, fruit, and animal patterns are famous for their realistic artistry and delicate nuances of shading, many designs typical of the Brilliant Period were also cut. Items ranged from small bottles, including inkwells with sterling tops, through tableware, large vases, and punch bowls — even lighting fixtures. One of the biggest orders was a complete dinner service for the Cuban government. Every piece was engraved with the Cuban coat of arms. A year was required to fill the order.

Many articles were stamped with the trademark Tuthill in flowing script. The signature was written in at least two ways. From 1913 to 1918, the single line signature was used. From 1919 to 1923, a double line mark appeared. Unsigned pieces must be identified by comparison with those that are signed or documented.

This footed cream and sugar set (fig. 326) is evidence that geometric patterns were cut by Tuthill. Sets on pedestals are more expensive and were cut on good blanks in all shops.

Look ahead to see an exceptionally fine brilliant cutting on the small bonbon basket (fig. 478, right).

This nappy (fig. 327) has the same hobstars (between bars ending in pentagons of silver diamond) as those on a dish identified as Tuthill in Pearson's *Encyclopedia Vol III*, page 67. Here, kites of cane replace small kites of silver diamond and small hobstars near the center. Nappies with steep sides like this one were often advertised with the comment that they were perfect for serving olives, which would not roll out as they might from a plate.

The dessert plate (fig. 328) in a Butterfly pattern was designed by Thomas Mortensen, who had worked for the Niland Cut Glass Company (Deep River, Connecticut) from 1896 to 1902. While there, he created a butterfly pattern that became popular. At Tuthill's, the same butterfly appeared in this dainty design with flowers similar to those of his Niland cutting. This is an excellent example of an artist's transference of his creations from one company to another. It also exemplifies the difficulty in identifying patterns, even though certain styles typify a firm's mode of expression.

Fig. 326. Footed sugar, 3¾″, and cream, 4″, signed Tuthill with double line on top of handles. Notice scalloped edge used on later pieces.

Fig. 327. Nappy, 7″ × 1½″, sharply cut and heavy, attributed to Tuthill. Notched "spokes" end in pentagons of silver diamond.

Fig. 328. Dessert plate, 7″, unsigned, in "Butterfly." Central star composed of vesicas of extremely fine silver diamond, cut through by lines simulating veins in a leaf. (Ida Frazer)

This compote (fig. 329) for candy or jelly is a late version of "Phlox" on a Libbey blank. It is signed underfoot. The "Phlox" blossoms have five petals. "Primrose" flowers have six.

These European-type champagnes (fig. 330), called parfaits by some dealers, were part of a large set of matching stemware, some of which were signed. The dealer said that her customer took all but these. (Wallace Turner, curator of the Tuthill Museum in Middletown, New York, says that they were not cut by Tuthill.) The shape is like that of the cider, ale, and champagne flutes of the eighteenth and early nineteenth centuries in England and Scotland. "Parfait," which means "perfect" in French, describes the tall glass for ice cream desserts, slightly wider than these and with a round bottom in the bowl to permit a spoon to reach the last bite. These are so narrow and pointed that they appear to be for wine.

This unusual signed vase (fig. 331) has a realistic "Wild Rose" on the bottom. A few rose leaves among the buds and thin stylized leaves decorate the walls. When "Wild Rose" was combined with bands of fine diamond, it was called "Rosemere."

A prime example of Tuthill's "Vintage" is shown in this signed bowl (fig. 332). His intaglio "Grape" won first prize at the St. Louis World's Fair in 1904. In "Vintage," a chain of hobstars is cut to contrast with the stone-engraved grapes. In our opinion, the sculptured roundness of the grapes and the beauty of the leaves is superior to grape designs by other companies, such as Hawkes, Pairpoint, and Sinclaire.

This signed nappy in intaglio Grapes and Pears (fig. 333) is a work of art above and beyond its mundane use in serving food. The delicate shadings produced by gradations in depth of cutting represent the culmination of years of apprenticeship, plus the "eye" of a true artist and lover of beauty.

When appreciation of cut glass began to grow in the 1960s, intaglio pieces were not highly regarded and were often priced much lower than brilliant items. Finding the fruit bowl (fig. 334) was a stroke of luck. The dealer (in antique European furniture and decorative pieces) catered mainly to interior decorators. He handled little American cut glass and obviously did not know what he had, for this bowl was priced lower than his brilliant glassware. We had found a "sleeper."

The jug (fig. 335) and the fruit bowl (fig. 336) are cut in an open petal type of design. The jug is identified by comparison with a signed pitcher of the same size and shape. The bowl, whose design is slightly different, with arrangement of motifs modified to fit the shape, is similar to Tuthill. The blank has the same weight and clarity. It could have been a case of plagiarism by another firm. The rare shape (pinched in at four places to form a sort of square), the clarity, and the weight (five pounds) make it outstanding.

Fig. 329. Compote, 8″×4½″, in a late version of "Phlox," with rolled edge, signed Tuthill underfoot. (Matye)

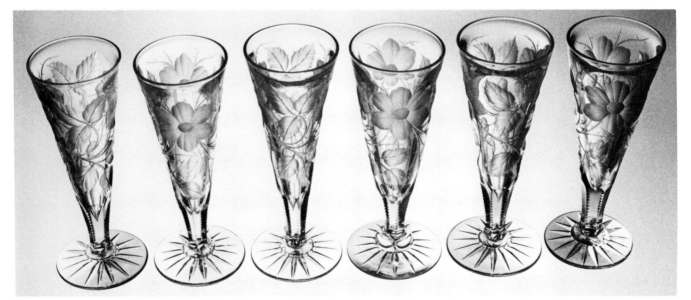

Fig. 330. Champagnes, 6½″, European style, heavy. Meticulously engraved in wild roses with rose leaves and thorns.

Fig. 331. Corset vase, 10″ × 5½″, signed, in "Wild Rose," has full-blown flower engraved on bottom, with finely executed buds and leaves elsewhere. (Gerritse)

Fig. 333. Nappy, 7″, signed, in intaglio "Fruit" — a fine rendering of grapes, pears, and cherries. (Gerritse)

Fig. 332. Bowl, 8″ × 3½″, signed, in "Grapes," often called "Vintage." Combines prize-winning grapes with a chain of hobstars for contrast.

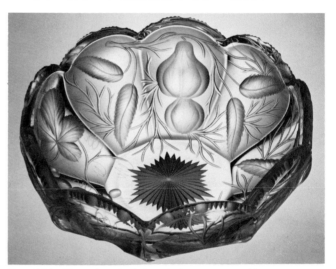

Fig. 334. Fruit bowl, 9½″ × 3½″, unsigned Tuthill, is engraved in the same style as the previously signed dish. Cherries, grapes, and pears carved on nine panels. Fruit, radiant star on bottom, and notches on edge are left gray in matte or satin finish. Highlights polished on grapes add to the illusion of roundness.

Fig. 335. Jug, 8½", in an Open Petal design. Attributed to Tuthill because it matches a signed pitcher. Neck in honeycomb and flute; handle is triple-notched. (Matye)

Fig. 336. Fruit bowl, 8½" × 4", is a close variant of the jug's Open Petal by Tuthill or by another company.

A similar open petal was patented 19 May 1908, #39313, by Louis Hinsberger, in New York City business directories from 1895 to 1910. The Hinsberger patent drawing shows an elyptical miter cut between the petals (a leaf?), and notched prism flairs between leaf and petal, making a feathered effect around the entire flower. Other companies made similar patterns: O. F. Egginton — an open petal with no flashing, called "Sherwood"; Fry — "Ivy" with fans between the petals; and McKee — "Doltec" in imitation cut glass, shown in a 1908 catalog. None of these fits the bowl shown here, but help to establish the date.

Due to the superb quality and smaller quantity of production, in comparison with large companies like Libbey and Hawkes, one can only conclude that Tuthill glass is highly desirable for the serious collector.

Meriden Cut Glass Company (1895-1923)

The Meriden Silver Plate Company, organized in 1869, had produced a line of small articles in cut glass from the beginning. Circa 1895 they added cut tableware of all kinds to the list and adopted the name, Meriden Cut Glass Company, for this branch of the business. Both the silver and glass factories joined a conglomerate, called International Silver Company, in 1898. After International was formed, the cut glass division was separated and combined with a large cut glass department of the Wilcox Silver Plate Company, another predecessor.

Meriden used blanks produced by the Meriden Flint Glass Company until the latter closed in 1896. After that, it cut Mount Washington/Pairpoint blanks as long as possible, then went out of business in 1923 when fine blanks could no longer be found.

The city of Meriden in Connecticut was a nest of fine glass cutting shops and silverware factories. C. F. Munroe, J. J. Niland, and J. D. Bergen are names of other cutting shops in the area that, together with Meriden, supplied cut glass for the silverplated or sterling silver fittings of International Silver Company. The latter was a group of silver firms under one management. This explains why many glass patents were assigned by International.

Unfortunately for collectors, the trademark we seek was on a paper label. This depicted a cut glass plate with THE MERIDEN CUT GLASS CO. curved above the plate, and MERIDEN, CONN., U.S.A. below — the whole enclosed within a circle. Meriden cutware can often be identified by marks on silver mounts, as in the honey pot (fig. 102), humidor (fig. 103), bitters bottle (fig. 104), and butter dish (fig. 105) in Chapter 10. All silver is signed by Wilcox. The candelabra (fig. 113) are not marked, but an identical pair shown in *Hobbies* was signed WILCOX. We have not seen a trademark etched on the glass.

The square nappy in "Cutting No. 225" (fig. 337) was sold by Marshall Field of Chicago in 1911-1912 for $4.50. Alpha Lee Ehrhardt's 1973 price guide considered it to be worth $85 at that time.

The mayonnaise bowl with plate (fig. 338) is cut in "Albany," Meriden's version of the popular bullseye and prism combination begun by several companies from 1898 to 1901. J. D. Bergen in the same city used a flat underplate like this for their ice tub in "Florida." Doubtless both companies had access to the same blanks.

A fine pitcher or jug (fig. 431) in a variant of "Albany" is shown in Chapter 19.

Fig. 337. Square nappy, 7″, by Meriden in "Cutting No. 225." (Matye)

Fig. 339. Fruit bowl, 9″×4½″, in "Alhambra" (or "Greek Key"), patent #41091, filed 14 November 1910 by T. A. Shanley, assignor to International Silver Company. Engraved border in matte.

Fig. 338. Mayonnaise bowl, 4⅝″×2¾″, and plate, 5½″, in "Albany" on heavy, clear blank. Below bullseyes and prisms are three rows of honeycomb. Bottoms are rayed.

Fig. 340. Fern dish, 8½″×3¾″, in "Alhambra" came with a flat edge and silver-plated, metal liner with lip resting on rim.

Thomas A. Shanley, foreman at Meriden from 1904 to 1918, created many beautiful patterns. The author's favorite among all designs is "Alhambra," sometimes called "Greek Key" for the chain-like border engraved near the crenelated edge. This rim reminds one of battlements at the top of a castle wall, and is usually referred to as a *dentil* edge, an architectural term. The contrast offered by bands of sharp, accurate cutting must be seen to be believed. A bowl seems to be partly filled with diamonds of dazzling brilliance. "Alhambra" was filed 14 November 1910 and published 17 January 1911.

The fruit bowl (fig. 339) in "Alhambra" belies the contention that cut glass of the finest quality was gone by 1911.

The fern dish (fig. 340) was photographed upside down to show the perfection of cutting, that caused the radiant miter cuts to meet precisely in the center. Doesn't it resemble a monarch's crown?

The juice glasses (fig. 341) are signed by Roden Brothers, Ltd., of Toronto, Canada, with their ornate *R* flanked by two lions and "R'd 1910." This design appeared in the 1917 catalog under the name "Norman," to be discussed in Chapter 18.

On the celery tray (fig. 341), note how the engraved chain has been slanted gradually to conform to the contours of the heavy Pairpoint blank. A slightly wider dish in an oval shape was used as a bread tray.

The whiskey decanter and shot glasses (fig. 342) exemplify another adaptation of this stunning design. The base of each piece is cut in a hobstar. The decanter's stopper is engraved in the key motif.

Fig. 341. Juice glasses, 3¾″, in "Norman," Roden Brothers' (Toronto, Canada) version of "Alhambra." Bases are rayed. Celery tray, 13″×5″, shows Meriden's "Alhambra" adapted to a long, oval shape.

In this water set (fig. 343), the dentil edge is novel and attractive. A pitcher on a standard was also made with step cutting on the neck and dentil edge at the top and on the foot.

Cracker or cookie jars (fig. 344) are scarce and expensive, but one in "Alhambra" is a prize to be cherished.

The vase (fig. 345) is impressive and is accurately cut on a brilliant blank. This came in several sizes.

A plate was made with rounded scallops — a relief from so many "teeth." It should be recalled that several items in "Alhambra" had silver mountings.

This bread tray (fig. 346) in "Cutting No. 161" was used to serve rolls. The design and cutting rank with "Alhambra" in quality. A large punch bowl on a standard with cups was shown in a catalog. It had to be expensive, even then.

Fig. 342. Whiskey decanter, 11¼″ with stopper, and shot glasses, 2½″. All are cut in a hobstar on base. (Roberts)

Fig. 343. Jug, 10½″; base 6¼″, and tumblers, 3⅝″, in "Alhambra." Each piece has hobstar on bottom. (Roberts)

Fig. 344. Cracker or cookie jar, 9½″, in "Alhambra," has stopper cut to match main pattern. Base has 24-point hobstar. (Meyer)

On a cream and sugar set (fig. 347), "Cutting No. 161" is even finer and more difficult to execute. Such a set cut on footed blanks is rare and expensive.

"Shirley" (also known as "Flora"), another pattern by Shanley assigned to International Silver, is shown here on a dessert plate (fig. 348) and on a large fruit bowl (fig. 349) for use as a centerpiece on the dining table. The patent drawing depicted a bowl divided into three areas like the dessert plate. This fruit bowl, however, is so large that the design has been modified to use four areas of floral cutting. This is an excellent example of the transitional stage between geometric and floral styles. Note that in such a firm as Meriden, the floral sections are far superior to those of many other companies that were cheapening their products by this time. Often blossom centers were merely crosshatched, whereas these have tiny hexagonal hobnails, polished for brilliance.

Fig. 345. Vase, 16″, in "Alhambra." Columns of cane alternate with vertical chain of hobstars and triangles of silver diamond. A twenty-point hobstar covers bottom. Engraved key border in matte appears at base and under dentil edge.

The berry bowl (fig. 350) in "Patrician" by Shanley is indeed a gentle, patrician design and a far cry from the bold, bright cuts of the Brilliant Period. It is called "Othello" by Revi, in whose opinion it is "one of the most beautiful cut glass designs ever made." Remember that this was patented in April 1918, while we were at war.

How sad to learn that this talented designer, Thomas A. Shanley, was working in a laundry in 1919. What a waste!

The candlestick (fig. 351) is attributed to Meriden on the basis of style and the superb quality of the glass. The flashed hobstar with silver diamond points was a favorite device.

The next three items are cut on finest blanks, heavy and clear. This pattern, consisting of hobstars, deep, curved miter cuts, and feathered leaves, has been a mystery for years. After numerous inquiries, we have the opinion of one expert (author/dealer/collector) who believes it to be from Meriden.

The bowl (fig. 352) depicts the pattern most clearly.

The pitcher (fig. 353) is brilliant and heavy, the base covered by a 24-point hobstar. Even the handle is unusual. It is double-notched with double crosscuts down the middle, flutes around the base, and panels on its sides. This was Earle's favorite. The water goblets are also heavy and beautiful (fig. 354).

This large vase (fig. 355), attributed to Meriden, was used in the old Perkins Hotel at Southwest Fifth and Washington streets in Portland, Oregon. Richard S. Perkins (1823-1902), who came from England in 1852 to make his fortune in the cattle business in eastern Oregon, built the hotel in 1891 as an investment and as a place to retire. It became a mecca for cattlemen's conventions, symbolized by a life-sized,

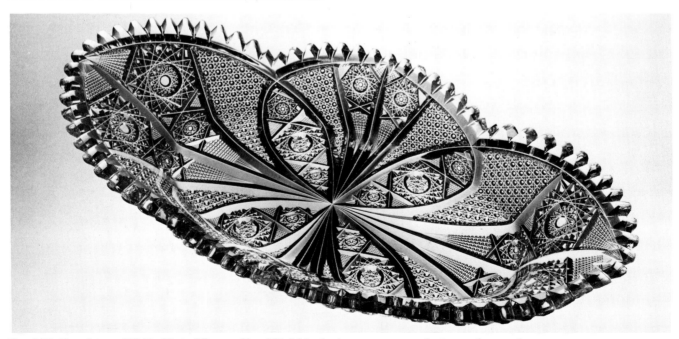

Fig. 346. Bread tray, 13½″ × 7″, in "Cutting No. 161." Much above average in design and execution.

Fig. 347. Footed cream and sugar set, 4½″, in "Cutting No. 161." Triple-notched handle. Fine, accurate work.

Fig. 348. Dessert plate, 7″, in "Shirley" (or "Flora"), patent #44114, filed 7 March 1913, published 27 May 1913.

Fig. 350. Berry bowl, 9″ × 2½″, labeled "Patrician" in catalog (also "Othello"), designed by Thomas A. Shanley, #51938, 2 April 1918. Blank rather thin, yet still of good glass.

Fig. 349. Fruit bowl, 10″ × 4½″, in "Shirley" by T. A. Shanley. Weighs 6¼ lbs. Note four areas of design.

carved, gilded steer in a red-tiled alcove on the roof of the five-story building. Electric lights caused the animal to gleam at night.

In this "second-best" hotel of 125 rooms, each of which rented for from seventy-five cents to two dollars a day, one could buy a meal for twenty-five cents. Heat in hotel rooms was new. Many of the early guests complained that they could not sleep, even with windows open. Few could figure out how to turn off the heat at the radiator.

Because of the financial panic of 1893-1894, Perkins was forced to sell out in 1896. He died in 1902.

Fig. 351. Candlestick, 10″, attributed to Meriden. Large teardrop. (Photograph by Conkling)

Fig. 353. Jug, 10¼″×6¼″ at base, in Feathered Leaf and Hobstar. Weighs 7½ lbs. Front has a sixteen-point hobstar with gray fans above and below. Bottom covered by 24-point hobstar.

Fig. 352. Bowl, 8″×4″, in a Feathered Leaf and Hobstar pattern. Weighs over 4 lbs. Blaze cutting and silver diamond on small vesicas unpolished. Superb glass.

Fig. 354. Water goblets, 6″, in Feathered Leaf and Hobstar. Exceptionally heavy.

234

Fig. 355. Vase, 18″, attributed to Meriden. The ten-point flashed hobstar with silver diamond points is used in many Meriden designs. "Cutting No. 213" also has cane, and "Plymouth" has the crosscut fans, which we call trellises. Base is cut in a thirty-point single star. There are nine flashed hobstars.

In 1906 Lot Q. Swetland bought the hostelry. His uncle, Warren, came from New England to visit. He persuaded Lot to refurbish the hotel in 1908, making it more competitive with the grand Portland Hotel, which had 284 rooms. The Portland charged three dollars for a room and four meals, which were served on elegant dinnerware, including cut glass finger bowls and stemware. Visiting presidents, royalty, and such actresses as Anna Held and Sarah Bernhardt chose the Portland and its elaborate meals and service over the Perkins.

In an effort to attract more affluent guests, the Swetlands changed their décor from a practical Western style to one of refined elegance, using white linen and Spode Blue Tower dishes. They decorated the lobby with large cut glass vases, and took down the golden steer and stored it in the attic. Cattlemen still patronized the hotel, but trade consisted largely of people of moderate means and families looking for a good meal at a fair price.

After Lot's death in 1923, the vase came to his daughter, Mrs. Florence Swetland Roberts, from whom it was purchased in her eighty-fifth year via her niece, Miss Eleanor McCoy. The vase is a part of Portland's historic past. It is also a symbol of the role played by brilliant cut glass in public places, as well as in the home.

Bergen and Niland

Since the Niland and Bergen firms were mentioned in reference to the Meriden group of cut glass companies, a thumbnail sketch of each is appropriate.

In 1880 James D. Bergen and Thomas A. Niland formed a partnership under the name, Bergen & Niland. In 1885 Bergen bought out Niland's interest and formed the J. D. Bergen Company. Thomas continued working for Bergen until 1896, when he established Thomas A. Niland & Company in Deep River, Connecticut, with partners named Jones and Burgess. He sold his interest in the firm to James and Ansel Jones. Thereafter it was known as the Niland Cut Glass Company. While Thomas Niland created most of the designs, a butterfly pattern designed by Thomas Mortensen was one of their most popular patterns. Mortensen went on to act as foreman of Tuthill and cut his butterfly there (fig. 328). Niland returned to Bergen in 1897.

The company had a New York City showroom and did a considerable export business through this branch. The factory closed about 1902. Thomas joined his brother, James, in James's own business in Meriden that year.

James J. Niland had worked in the industry from boyhood, serving a six-year apprenticeship. After learning all phases of cutting in some of the leading factories of England and Scotland, he came to America in 1882 to work for the Bergen & Niland Company. The J. J. Niland Company, started about 1902, produced a line of cut glass "seldom equaled for variety, quality, and moderate prices," according to a 1906 publication. In 1906, fifty skilled workmen were employed, "capable of producing anything in cut glass from a five-cent castor bottle to a thousand-dollar vase." This probably referred to a four-piece vase, 62″ high, made for Tiffany & Company (New York jewelers) in 1906 for $1,000. Among Niland's customers were many leading glass-and-crockery concerns, including Higgins & Seiter in New York City. After 1935 the firm still operated on a small scale. It was closed forever in 1959.

James D. Bergen had learned cutting in shops in New York, in Massachusetts at Mount Washington in New Bedford, and at New England in East Cambridge. He also worked at the Meriden Flint Glass Company as a cutter from 1877 to 1880, when he left to start his own business.

Bergen patented several patterns that followed the trend from brilliant to floral. The 1904-1905 catalog listed all of the usual pieces cut in bold, even spectacular, designs, but is notable for large punch bowls on standards, lamps, and candelabra with silver mounts by Gorham.

The trademark consisted of BERGEN on a band across overlapping world globes, with CUT above and GLASS below. Sometimes, BERGEN in script was acid-etched on the glass.

Mr. Bergen was active until 1917. The shop closed in 1922.

Punch cups in "Electric" (fig. 289) are shown in Chapter 15 with the punch bowl believed to be by Dorflinger. Also, the small violet globe (fig. 483), made from a cut-down cruet, in Chapter 19 is in Bergen's "Golf" pattern.

The next chapter has identified pieces from many different companies, arranged in groups to aid in identifying styles.

17

Other Glassware Companies

Remaining identified pieces are nearly all shown here with brief introductions, except for a longer one in the case of Sinclaire. By expounding at some length on the Sinclaire story, we can perceive more clearly the transition from brilliant to floral design.

H. P. Sinclaire & Company (1904-1929)

When the Brooklyn Flint Glass Works moved to Corning in 1868, Henry Purdon Sinclaire, Sr. and his family moved with the firm, which later became the Corning Glass Works. Amory Houghton, Sinclaire's brother-in-law, was president. Thomas G. Hawkes worked there, and Captain John Hoare had an affiliated glasscutting shop.

H. P. Sinclaire, Jr., (1863-1927) at first declined to follow his father into glassmaking. Spurning the usual college education, he entered Rochester Business University in 1882. A tall, handsome blond with a passion for physical fitness, he was socially popular. He announced that he intended to go into business in New York.

His father's friend, Thomas Hawkes, offered H. P., Jr. a job as bookkeeper in his Hawkes Rich Cut Glass Works. Harry, as H. P., Jr. was called, accepted. A bright young man, he soon learned all phases of the business. He was also a natural salesman.

By 1888 Harry was considered so knowledgeable that Hawkes left him in charge while he went to Ireland every other summer. At twenty-seven, Sinclaire was a partner, secretary, and director. His salary had risen from $600 annually to $1,800.

As a hobby, he had enjoyed sketching birds and flowers observed on hikes through the countryside. He put his talent to work, creating natural designs for engraved glass, using floral and architectural motifs.

Hawkes encouraged Sinclaire in his delicate designs, but did not feel that they would become commercially feasible. In 1889, only three engravers were listed in the Corning directory. Engraving was done to order in the 1890s, but apparently was not shown in catalogs.

Marriage in 1892 and the birth of Robert in 1893 led to thoughts of establishing Harry's own firm. Circa 1897 he opened a china decorating shop (using china from Limoges, Vienna, and Bavaria) with the trademark RAVENWOOD. He continued to differ with Hawkes concerning design. He felt that his engraved ware could compete more successfully with imports from Europe.

His wife died in 1900, leaving four small sons. Then, in 1902, the senior Henry P. Sinclaire died. Harry's brother, Will, succeeded their father as secretary of Corning Glass Works. Samuel and Townsend Hawkes had joined the Hawkes firm. Harry disliked brilliant glass more and more; he also disliked the Art Glass that Hawkes planned for his Steuben Glass Works.

Sinclaire left Hawkes in 1904, establishing his own business, where he could fulfill his dream of making glassware in a style new to the industry. (Marvin Olcott, his partner, took care of the books.) He engraved glass in several depths at several prices. The customer could assemble tableware that harmonized, buying the cheapest items for heavy use, so the price of replacement of broken pieces was minimized.

In 1905, thirty-three engravers and 490 cutters worked in Corning. Sinclaire had fifty employees, eleven of whom were engravers.

He continued to reject advertising as unnecessary for the dissemination of a fine product. Customers included Tiffany in New York, Richard Briggs in Boston, and Banks & Biddle and John Wanamaker in Philadelphia. He did send salesmen "on the road." They carried samples in special trunks, and catalogs with photos and drawings.

The Sinclaire trademark consists of S in a laurel wreath, with a tiny shield in each side of the wreath. One shield bears the fleur-de-lis, symbolizing the French name. The other bears a thistle, representing the family's centuries in Scotland. The whole mark is ⅜″ in diameter. Author Farrar says that there have been forged wreaths on practice pieces and on new glassware. A second authentic trademark: SINCLAIRE in capital letters, is usually found on a rim or foot edge on stemware.

Sinclaire permitted application of the trademark only after the ware passed inspection. The slightest imperfection in blank or cutting condemned the piece to be sold at the factory, unmarked, at twenty-five cents.

C. Dorflinger provided the only glass blanks that satisfied Sinclaire completely. Blanks from secondary suppliers looked pinkish or grayish by comparison. In 1917 Harry complained to his brother, Will, about the quality of Corning blanks. All crystal manufacturers suffered during the war years, being cut off from purchasing war-related substances.

Dorflinger blanks blown for Sinclaire were often designed by Harry. He drew sketches and cut paper patterns. He would fold a piece of manila paper in half, draw a half-form, cut it out, then pin it to the wall. He often made several versions before choosing one. Mrs. Farrar reports that the industry called his patterns "Mr. Sinclaire's paper dolls." His concepts were at times revolutionary. Corning Glass Works supplied his thick mold-blown vases, stands, pitchers, bowls, and soup plates — all his own designs. He also used some Baccarat and Pairpoint blanks.

Before World War I, Sinclaire used a few colored blanks, mainly for hocks, in blue, ruby, green, and amber, some of which came from Steuben. During the war, Dorflinger turned to color and Sinclaire went along.

It is said that the best craftsmen in Corning worked for Sinclaire at one time or another. He had no apprenticeship program. He hired only experts, the most prominent being William Thomas Dow, born in England and nephew of the Egginton brothers. Other experts came from Austria, France, and Germany. In 1904 the ten-hour workday was still in force, although a newspaper had predicted in 1900 that, in the near future, hours would be reduced to nine, possibly even eight, daily.

In attempting to be flexible, and in shifting American taste from brilliant to engraved glassware, Sinclaire produced a panorama of designs difficult to describe.

He used cut motifs with engraved forms in constantly changing relationships, but always with an emphasis on delicacy and harmony, and with areas left clear to display the purity of the glass itself. The few heavily cut designs were the responsibility of someone else, because he did not admire them.

His *silver thread* and silver diamond patterns were geometric in concept, but were brilliant in a subdued sort of way, unlike most "brilliant" ware. Among the rarities in Chapter 11 (fig. 155) is a bowl in which the background is cut in gleaming silver threads.

He also designed sets of plates showing game birds, animals, and fish, as well as landscapes, in fine copper-wheel engraving. His flowers were exquisite, with some portions polished and others in matte finish.

Before the war, some pieces were sandblasted at the Corning Glass Works, then cut through to clear. Others were engraved and lacquered, probably by Ravenwood artists. The author has seen a set of six cigarette holders, each consisting of a round base with rectangular upright center that would hold four cigarettes. The sides of each container were engraved in tiny flowers. The blossoms then were "painted" in pastel colors in lacquer. With this set were six low, rectangular containers with engraved monogram, identified by the auctioneer as fish sauce holders. They were really individual ashtrays. The only decorations aside from the monogram were bands of fineline cutting. These were most likely from the 1920s.

Sinclaire executed jewelers' designs. He made puff boxes and similar pieces whose tops could be ordered in crystal, sterling, or gold. Gorham and Black, Starr & Frost made most of his silver mountings for bowls, pitchers, and vases.

Custom orders for crests and monograms were common. One custom order was unique. Mrs. Farrar relates that the King of Bavaria ordered engraved goblets so thin that they would bend. European firms could not make them. At Sinclaire's, each goblet required three weeks of work. Breakage was great. The wholesale price to Tiffany, who had placed the order, was $1,800 a dozen!

During the depression of 1919-1920 following the war, Sinclaire glassware was in high demand. Finding good blanks was so difficult that Harry decided to make his own at Bath, near Corning. There he made crystal from Dorflinger's formula (hiring Dorflinger craftsmen after Dorflinger shut down forever in 1921) and a new line of colored glass.

Murray Sinclaire joined his father in 1923 and worked hard to maintain the high standards of cleanliness and perfection of product. Nevertheless, competition from Europe, where low wages and living standards prevailed, cut into their success. In an effort to survive, Harry added a line of undecorated glass that was cheaper to make. He also added institutional items, such as communion cups. He made a line of pressed, heat-resistant glass called "Radnt" for pantry use.

An unforeseen heart attack, 21 June 1927, ended the life marked by order and regularity, both qualities so well typified in Harry's designs. Their inspiration gone, H. P.'s sons decided to close down the firm. By 1929 all was finished.

For the center of the dining table, Sinclaire designed a tall oval vase with floral engraving. This was connected by glass chains to four small vases. The chains, as shown in the catalog, hooked over the edges of the vases. These sets were labeled "Centerpiece, 9-pc." Pairpoint made similar sets, with the chains also hooking over the edge.

Fig. 356. Centerpiece set, attributed to Steuben, but typical of Sinclaire and Hawkes. Consists of a vase, 8″, and four smaller satellite vases, 6¼″, connected by glass chains. Textured glass engraved in satin flowers with polished centers. Loops applied to receive chains. (Photograph by Conkling)

Fig. 357. Fruit bowl, 10″ × 3½″, signed Sinclaire, design "No. 1," has six large twenty-point hobstars around base, which is cut in a cluster of seven small sixteen-point hobstars. (Cornwell)

This concept is illustrated by a beautiful centerpiece set (fig. 356), attributed to Steuben. Its chains are hooked through loops. Steuben glass was often adorned with applied loops and other attached forms.

Although this fruit bowl (fig. 357) in design "No. 1" is deeply cut in the brilliant fashion, it has a feeling of open design. It is shaped like a flower. This is item #302 in the 1917 inventory on page 57, plate 12, in *H. P. Sinclaire Jr., Glassmaker*, Vol. I, but was probably designed earlier. It sold for $9.

Fig. 358. Jardiniere, 9¾″ h × 10¾″, signed Sinclaire, in Cane with clear buttons. Pillar-cut "windows" adorn shoulder; a 28-point hobstar covers bottom. Weighs 14 lbs. Glass is ½″ thick. Engraved oval "moons" and small sprays of leaves in matte finish encircle top edge.

The signed jardiniere (fig. 358) is cut on the same kind of blank as the footed "Mazarin" decanter on page 31 in Farrar's second volume. The jardiniere is cut in cane with clear buttons, while the decanter has a different arrangement of lines and starred buttons. Both have clear "windows" (pillar cutting) around the shoulder. The decanter is priced at $150 wholesale circa 1920. The jardiniere was free-blown. When viewed from the side, it is not quite symmetrical. Then, too, there are no "dips" inside the windows to conform to their shape, as there would be in a figured blank.

The plate (fig. 359), whose pattern on a basket was identified in another book as Tuthill, was cut by Sinclaire. This has been proved by correspondence with Wallace Turner, head of the Tuthill Cut Glass Company Museum in Middletown, New York. He has seen the basket in question. It matched a friend's bowl, signed Sinclaire.

The floral engraving on this unsigned bedroom clock (fig. 360) is typical of Sinclaire, although Hawkes and Pairpoint did similar work. Clocks are rare. In 1920 an eight-day movement clock engraved in daisy and leaves (slightly larger than this one) sold for $9.90 at the factory. We missed a similar clock in 1970 for $85, which would probably have sold for $250 or more in 1984.

The signed finger bowl plate (fig. 361), engraved on blank 1070, is clearly hand-blown and thin. The "Rock Crystal Spray" pattern has a fuschia, a carnation, and two other flowers, with a radiant star in the center. This

Fig. 359. Plate, 10″, is unsigned Sinclaire. Fuschias and smaller flowers, exquisitely sculptured, are dramatized by contrasting geometric cutting in the manner of Hawkes Gravic. (Matye)

Fig. 360. Bedroom clock, 6½″, assumed to be by Sinclaire. Face marked "Made in U.S.A."

dainty ware is not yet appreciated by many collectors, most of whom think only in terms of heavy, thick glass with geometric cutting. The plate required hours of skillful engraving and polishing. Eleven plates and eleven saucers (fig. 361), in a different design, were found at the same shop. The author believes that they had been used together as dessert sets.

This vase (fig. 362) is typical of Sinclaire in design, as well as thickness and color of the blank. In a press release describing an exhibition at the Corning Museum of Glass, 15 October 1972, Kenneth M. Wilson, curator, depicted Sinclaire's delicate engraved designs

Fig. 361. *Left to right:* Finger bowl plate, 7″, signed in center, is shown as "Rock Crystal Spray" in a reprint of 1917 inventory, Farrar's book, Vol. I, p. 47. Ice cream or berry saucer, 4½″ × 1⅛″, unsigned, engraved in a simpler Rock Crystal pattern. It is not deep enough to be a finger bowl.

Fig. 362. Vase, 10″, circa 1904-1917, attributed to Sinclaire. Stylized blossoms, chains of "moons," draperies, and bows are typical. Note that the triple leaf motif on foot is similar to that near top of jardiniere (fig. 358). (McCoy)

as being "often based on natural forms, sometimes contrasted with cut elements. Typically, natural motifs appeared as medallions, bands, or panels set off by areas of undecorated glass. Sinclaire, with his architectural approach to design, succeeded in divorcing beauty from price; many inexpensive Sinclaire patterns were as attractive as the most costly ones."

Refer back to figure 47 in Chapter 6 to see another vase in rock crystal engraving, attributed to Sinclaire.

The signed tumbler (fig. 363) is in "Prince Albert." Note the engraved initial. The two wines in "Grapes" are attributed to Sinclaire, partly because the shape conforms to catalog drawings.

Plates (fig. 364), often listed as sandwich or cake plates, came in graduated sizes from 6″ to 10″. This 10″ size in "Strawberry Diamond and Fan" would have made a fine plate for a cold luncheon. It is signed.

The carafe (fig. 365) in "Bengal" is signed on the base. Inventory photographs in 1917 prove that the design was cut on stemware, a handled decanter, several whiskey jugs called demijohns (two with silver mounts), an 8″ dish, a stick bonbon, a pitcher, a 23″ electrolier or banquet lamp, a table lamp, a fernery with screen, a tea caddy (covered jar), and a 9″ bowl with silver rim.

One more piece, a cruet (fig. 464), may be seen with cabinet pieces in Chapter 19.

Fig. 363. *Left to right:* Wines, 4½″, in "Grapes," attributed to Sinclaire. Polished grapes cut in rows; leaves matte. (Author) Tumbler, 3¾″, signed, in "Prince Albert," has a fan above a flute; a hobstar with plain button above a lozenge of silver diamond; rayed base. (Rolland)

Fig. 364. Luncheon plate, 10″, signed, accurately cut in crosscut diamond and fan on superb blank, probably of Dorflinger glass. Unpolished ovals and dots around edge are a sort of trademark for Sinclaire.

Fig. 365. Carafe, 9″, in "Bengal," signed underfoot. On bottom is a twenty-point hobstar. (Photograph by Conkling)

O. F. Egginton Company (1896-1918)

In 1890, T. G. Hawkes gave one share of stock to each of four men who had contributed to his success. One of these was his foreman, Oliver F. Egginton (1822-1900). In 1896, in his seventies, Oliver left to establish his own firm, the O. F. Egginton Company, after declining an offer by Sinclaire to form a partnership. His son, Walter, had been a designer and glasscutter for Hawkes before he joined Oliver in the family business. Walter E. Egginton's name appeared on patented designs. When Oliver died in 1900, Walter took over the cutting firm.

The trademark of the Egginton Rich Cut Glass Company in Corning was registered 23 January 1906. It consists of a new moon with a star within the horns (which nearly meet at the top of the mark). The firm's name, EGGINTON, appears on the moon. Every piece was supposed to be acid-stamped.

The shop seldom used blanks from Corning Glass Works, which had an agreement to supply only John Hoare and Thomas Hawkes. Oliver preferred the glass of Baccarat, Val St. Lambert, Union, Jeannette, and Libbey. He strongly favored heavy brilliant cutting and failed to go along with the new designs when the trend was toward lighter floral cutting around 1910. Just a few designs were stone-engraved. He used acid-dip for polishing. By February 1918, the factory was bankrupt.

Much of Egginton's ware was excellent in quality of workmanship and design.

The "Lotus" pattern (fig. 366) was created by Walter. According to Revi, the "blossom," formed by a silver diamond vesica with three splits, was called a magnolia in the patent specification, so Mr. Revi named the design "Magnolia." Published 24 February 1903, patent #36233 had been filed 19 December 1901. A similar pattern with a large central split and several gradually smaller lateral splits into the silver diamond is sometimes confused with "Lotus." The similar design is "Marquise."

The whiskey decanter in "Lotus" (fig. 367) is unsigned. It went unrecognized until the dish (fig. 366) was purchased, illustrating how adaptation of a pattern to different forms changes the perspective. Both are of highest quality.

The low bowl (fig. 368) in "Cluster" is attributed to Egginton by comparing it with a catalog illustration. It is heavy and sharply cut.

Fabulous is the word for this brilliant bowl in "Roman" (fig. 369), so sharply cut that holding it hurts the fingers. It is signed in the center. The allover cutting, done with utmost accuracy, does justice to the well-integrated design.

Fig. 366. Dish, 7″×2″, signed Egginton, in "Lotus," heavy and sharply cut, rings like a bell. In this form, kites of silver diamond with three splits make a beautiful six-point star.

Fig. 367. Whiskey decanter, 9″, in "Lotus"; uncommon flattened shape. Exquisite stopper is cut in concave hexagonal diamonds; its top is a sixteen-point single star. Bottom is rayed, handle is triple-notched.

Fig. 368. Bowl, 8″×2″, in Egginton's "Cluster."

J. Hoare & Company (1868-1920)

John Hoare (1822-1896) and his father James were born in Cork, Ireland. They both cut glass in Belfast and in England, where John worked for several firms, including Thomas Webb & Sons. John had his own business for five years before emigrating to Philadelphia in 1848.

He started his firm in Brooklyn, New York, in 1853. The date that appears in the trademark — J. HOARE & CO. and 1853 within concentric circles — was adopted early in 1895, but not registered until 12 May 1914. Sometimes NEW YORK is added below the date; more often, CORNING appears in the lower portion. (Our signed pieces are all marked CORNING.) All items were signed after 1895 unless a customer, such as Gorham, asked that the trademark be omitted. From 1900 to 1920, stemware and knife rests were sometimes signed HOARE in capital letters only.

In New York City, Hoare operated under several names, one of which was Hoare, Burns & Dailey. To be brief, he moved to Corning in 1868, being connected with the Amory Houghtons, Sr. and Jr., in their Corning Glass Works, but retaining ownership of the cut glass department under the title, J. Hoare & Company. An understanding existed that Corning Glass Works would not sell blanks to Hoare's competitors, with the exception of Hawkes and Sinclaire.

Corning blanks appear to have been used exclusively from 1868 to 1896. After that period, Hoare used some blanks from Dorflinger, Union, Steuben, and Baccarat. In 1913 a catalog identified items (in handwriting) as cut on mold-blown blanks — one by Fry.

Fig. 369. Fruit bowl, 9″×4″, in "Roman," signed Egginton in center. A radiant star on base consists of six lozenges of silver diamond.

The firm's greatest prosperity was in the 1870s and early 1880s. At that time, it was one of the largest cutting firms in the nation. The shop cut glass for the White House during Grant's administration. Hoare's glassware won awards at various exhibitions and a gold medal at the World's Columbian Exposition in Chicago in 1893. He was the first man to make cut glass for store display windows, and the first to turn glass on a lathe.

John had two sons: John, Jr., a glass cutter, and James, a salesman for the company. In 1887, when John Earle, foreman, resigned, John Hoare, Jr. returned to Corning after three years in the New York sales office to take over as foreman. George M. Abbott, Amory Houghton's son-in-law, became a partner and the name of the firm changed from Hoare & Dailey to J. Hoare & Company.

After the father's death in 1896, the business went onward under his son, James Hoare II, and George Abbott. In 1906 John S. Hoare, son of James II, entered the firm. A branch factory opened in Wellsboro, Pennsylvania, employing two hundred men. Circa 1913, the company started advertising in an attempt to stem the downward trend of business.

In 1916, John closed the Wellsboro factory and moved back to Corning. Bankrupt in 1920, the company closed a short time before James Hoare II died, 4 November 1921.

The earliest piece of Hoare cutware we have may be the "Mikado" tumbler (fig. 455) in Chapter 19. This was designed by George L. Abbott, Hoare's first partner after he came to Corning. The design has been called "Abbott" in his honor, but an 1890 catalog lists it as "Mikado." The patent was filed 15 February 1887. The design features a large pyramidal star, chequered diamond, and fan.

Fig. 370. Footed vase, 14″, signed J. Hoare; ¾″ thick scalloped foot. Three columns of hobstars alternate with three wide columns containing an assortment of motifs, #872 in Hoare ACGA catalog. (Rolland)

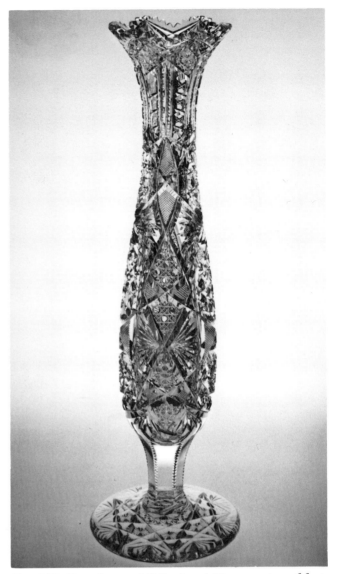

Fig. 371. Footed vase, 17½″, signed Hoare on top of foot. Intricately cut in many motifs, #225 in ACGA catalog.

The signed footed vase (fig. 370), with its complex pattern and fully cut base, is one of Hoare's finest: a sparkling beauty suitable for the richest house, #872.

This footed vase (fig. 371), tall and slender, is fully cut on a brilliant blank. This and all signed pieces shown here have the circular trademark. The exception is the knife rest (fig. 92) in Chapter 10, which has an acid-etched HOARE, barely discernible, on one end of the bar.

The cream and sugar set (fig. 372), signed inside, off-center, shows one of the cluster patterns used often by Hoare, as well as by Fry, Libbey, Straus, and Egginton. Being fully cut on the bottom in squares of silver diamond and fans is a mark of high quality.

Signed punch cups (fig. 170) in a Cluster design are shown in Chapter 13.

The signed fruit bowl (fig. 373) in the shape of Napoleon's hat weighs five and a half pounds; the glass is ½″ thick. Choice of motifs — Cluster and Arcadia — for the shape is superb. No doubt it was cut at the peak of the period in the 1890s.

The signed cluster fruit bowl (fig. 374) with sloping sides has the appearance of an open flower. It is brilliant, though cut on a figured blank. It was shown in a 1910 catalog and again in 1913 as #5134-1894 with the comment, "Figured/Limoge Mould Used." Catalogs seldom admitted using a figured blank. I have named it "Limoge." Revi, page 161, shows a bowl cut by Enterprise Cut Glass Company (Elmira Heights, New York) in a nearly identical pattern that he calls "Star."

Fig. 372. Cream and sugar, 3″, signed Hoare inside bottom of both. Fully cut on bottom in silver diamond squares and fans around a flat star in a square field.

Fig. 373. Banana or oval bowl, 13½″×8½″×4½″, signed Hoare on center bottom. On both sides of Arcadia chain down the middle lies a double row of crosscut squares. (See bowl cut by Andrew Callahan for 1893 Fair, Farrar's book, p. 31.)

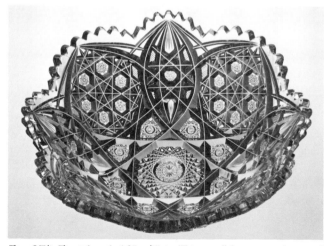

Fig. 374. Fruit bowl, 10″×4″, in "Limoge" (our name) signed inside center. Blank figured, but brilliant.

This rare signed fruit bowl (fig. 375) in a variation of the 1887 Middlesex pattern has a most unusual shape, with straight, sloping sides and a wide, flat bottom. The basal hobstar is rare with its forty-eight points. The bowl weighs nearly six pounds.

The next fruit bowl (fig. 376), also signed, is as dramatic as the one above. Although several motifs are used, the final result is beautiful.

The style of the unsigned ice bucket (fig. 377) is reminiscent of the tailored bowl (fig. 375). Hoare made at least two versions of "Hindoo." This appears to be a variant of the second.

This "Comet" design on a signed ice tub (fig. 378) is strikingly different. The prism flairs are arranged to give an impression of spinning. Doubtless it was one of the designs conceived to celebrate the anticipated, though feared, appearance of Halley's Comet in 1910.

Fig. 375. Fruit bowl, 10″×4″, signed inside center, cut in a variant of "Middlesex." Hoare version separates the fans from the eight-point star by means of single curved splits, as in the Dorflinger design. New England and Hawkes have double splits. Here, every other eight-point hobstar is replaced by a lite of brilliant hobnail. Center of hobstar is cut in a single star like that of the other firms (except, which is clear). Like the Dorflinger, the hobstar is surrounded by fields of silver diamond. A forty-eight-point hobstar covers entire base; 6¼″ in diameter.

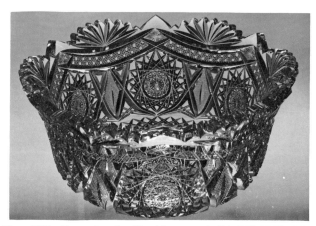

Fig. 376. Fruit bowl, 9″×4″, signed "J. HOARE 1853 CORNING" with the name BARR added to the usual circle. A thirty-six-point hobstar covers bottom (Cornwell)

Fig. 377. Ice bucket, 8″×4½″; unsigned variant of Hoare's "Hindoo." A forty-point hobstar covers base. (Gerritse)

Fig. 378. Ice tub, 8″×5″, in "Comet," signed HOARE, cut in two motifs: hobstar and beaded prism flair. (Miles)

The signed nappy in "Quincy" (fig. 379) was one of many inspired by the return of Halley's Comet.

The signed "Heart" tumblers (fig. 380) are larger and heavier than most. "Heart" was cut by several Chicago firms in 1907: "Heart and Hobstar" (with hexad-of-buttons-and-star on the heart) by Pitkin & Brooks; "Heart" by F. X. Parsche & Son (some with hexad and some with Russian, as seen in a catalog); "Butterfly and Heart" (Russian) by M. E. Scheck. "Thistle," which looked like the others (the heart cut in hexad), appeared in the 1905 catalog of Buffalo Cut Glass Company of Buffalo, New York.

The unsigned server with center handle (fig. 381) in "Nassau" is cut on a thinner, but clear, blank. It is typical of the transitional period from 1908 to 1911; it was shown in the 1911 catalog.

The signed candlesticks (fig. 382) circa 1910, are cut simply, creating a relief from excessive detail, #630 in ACGA catalog. Pairs are scarce.

Other patterns — "Prism," "Monarch," "Mikado," "#225," and "#872" — are shown elsewhere. Consult the Index under "Hoare, J. and Company."

Fig. 379. Nappy, 7″, signed, in "Quincy," a Comet pattern shown in 1910 Hoare catalog. (Matye)

Fig. 381. Cake or doughnut server, 10″, with center handle unsigned, in "Nassau." Dainty engraved fine-line satin leaves and flowers form interesting contrast to geometric cutting.

Fig. 380. Tumblers, 4″, in "Heart," signed inside on center of bottom. Hearts cut in cane with clear buttons; bases rayed.

Fig. 382. Pair of candlesticks, 5¾″, both signed HOARE on a flute near top, above narrow "waist," #630 in catalog.

Reference was made in Chapter 7 to the famous pair of globular bottles, engraved in 1890 on special order, showing horses and stables in exquisite detail. The main commercial thrust, however, at J. Hoare & Company was for the more popular brilliant style of cutting.

J. S. O'Connor — American Rich Cut Glass (1890-1919)

John Sarsfield O'Connor was born in Londonderry, Ireland, in 1831. He was employed by Turner & Lane, cut glass manufacturers in New York City, from 1841 to 1864. Contrary to the belief of some that cut glass was defunct during the Middle Period, this firm made all manner of cut tableware, as well as lampshades and window glass — cut, frosted, and stained. John also worked for Haughwout, served in the Union Army,

then returned to Haughwout as superintendent until it closed circa 1870.

O'Connor then went to work for Dorflinger in White Mills, Pennsylvania, where his many innovations revolutionized glass cutting. He invented a hard-wood polisher and a machine to suck up ground glass, lowering the mortality rate from inhalation of glass by cutters. His special cutting wheel enabled Dorflinger to decorate glass with a curved miter cut. O'Connor created and patented several curvaceous designs for Dorflinger before leaving in 1890 to establish his own shop in Hawley, Pennsylvania.

In 1900, he sold the Hawley factory to Maple City Glass Company and opened a shop in Goshen, New York. He opened a third in Port Jarvis, New York, called American Cut Glass Company in 1902, but closed it in 1903. Its equipment was divided between the Hawley and Goshen shops.

Fig. 383. Tumblers, 4″, in O'Connor's "Princess" (or "Split Square"). Fans, squares of crosscut diamond, and split squares of silver diamond. Wide-mouth jug, 9″; unsigned "Napoleon" (exactly like "Monarch" by Hoare) has three large twenty-four-point hobstars. Base rayed; handle has triple row of crosscut diamonds.

He used a trademark label — O. C. and the words HAWLEY, PENNA. — for many years. Similar labels may have been used in his other shops.

In Hawley, O'Connor used Dorflinger blanks. In Goshen, he used blanks from France. He created many new patterns for his own shops, but patented only "Princess" (under son Arthur E. O'Connor's name), 19 February 1895. This design is illustrated in the three unsigned tumblers (fig. 383) shown with the "Napoleon" jug. We have seen a tankard pitcher in "Princess" with a narrow top, cut on a superb blank. The pattern has also been called "Split Square." At the time the photograph was taken, we had not yet found the iced teas in the next picture.

The wide-mouth jug (fig. 383) and iced tea glasses (fig. 384), both unsigned, are in O'Connor's "Napoleon." Higgins & Seiter's 1899 catalog listed the design as "Napoleon," but had called it "Globe" in 1895-1896. Hoare cut this same design and named it "Monarch." Since O'Connor's trademark was on a paper label, usually removed at once, one may assume that these pieces are "Napoleon," rather than "Monarch."

One may also assume that all iced tea glasses were made after the St. Louis Fair in 1904. A tea merchant at the fair is said to have put ice in his tea, hoping to cool himself during the hot summer, thereby "inventing" iced tea.

T. B. Clark & Company (1884-1930)

Thomas Byron Clark (1864-1944) was born in Meriden, Connecticut, a city noted for silver and glass manufacturers. He was employed by the Meriden Flint Glass Company before going by horse and buggy to Seelyville, Pennsylvania (near Honesdale), in 1884 to establish a cut glass factory, known first as Hatch & Clark, then as Clark & Wood. By 1886, the name was changed to T. B. Clark & Company. Wood continued to work for Clark.

Clark and Wood did not cut glass (although Clark did create some patterns), but they hired fine craftsmen who did superior cutting, mainly on Dorflinger blanks. Only Dorflinger exceeded Clark's output in the Honesdale area. A few years later, Clark built another cutting shop in Hawley, south of Honesdale. A sales office and showroom was maintained in New York City. Clark and Wood established the Wayne Silver Company in Honesdale in 1895 to make silver mountings for their glassware. Also notable is the fact that Clark cut lampshades.

Cut and engraved ware faded about 1920; production of gold-decorated glassware continued until 1930, when the factory closed.

Fig. 384. Iced tea glasses, 6″, in O'Connor's "Napoleon" or Hoare's "Monarch," unsigned. A set of six in mint condition is rarely found.

According to Revi, Clark's daughter denied that her father bought the Honesdale Maple City Glass Company, whose trademarks were a realistic maple leaf and a stylized leaf that was flat on the bottom, Clark used a similar, but less angular, stylized leaf. It was registered 10 June 1910, but had been used since 30 January 1898. Many Clark pieces are signed with a cursive CLARK. A label with CLARK & CO. INC. and a drawing of a cut glass carafe was used until 1898. The first bowl shown here has this rare mark, acid-etched on the glass. A Clark signature is often so faint that it is nearly invisible. Keep looking!

Although some late Clark cutware was mediocre, most was excellent. This low bowl (fig. 385) exemplifies brilliant glass at its best. The mark CLARK & CO. curved above a carafe, both in a circle, dates it as pre-1898. The signature is near the edge over a fan and is hard to see. Design is "Mercedes."

Of the pair of low bowls (fig. 386) in "Huyler," bought together, only one is signed CLARK in cursive. "Huyler" was illustrated in a 1908 catalog. Cluster patterns were made by several companies from 1889 onward for twenty years.

Fig. 385. Low bowl, 10″×2¾″, has a pre-1898, acid-etched Clark signature. Blank is ½″ thick; "Mercedes."

Fig. 386. Pair of low bowls, 9″×2½″, in "Huyler," one signed Clark in script.

Fig. 387. Rectangular tray, 11½″×8″, unsigned Clark in "Jewel" (1896 catalog).

Fig. 388. Fruit bowl, 9½″×3¾″, signed Clark in script, center bottom. Design is called "AU."

The rectangular tray (fig. 387) in "Jewel," shown in an 1896 catalog, was generally used for serving ice cream. It was sold with matching saucers. It is heavy and of good quality.

This signed fruit bowl (fig. 388) is heavy, deeply cut, wood-polished, and was probably made circa 1900.

The cream and sugar set (fig. 389) is unsigned, but is identified as "Galatea" in ACGA catalog. It is heavy, larger than usual, and well-cut.

This plate (fig. 390), in one of many Pinwheel or Buzz Star patterns by Clark, is of fine quality and workmanship. It is signed in script. The owner also has a 7¼″ matching plate, so it must have come in several sizes.

The sugar bowl, pitcher, and tumbler (fig. 391) date from 1909 to 1919, truly into the Floral Period. The pattern closely resembles Irving's "Carnation," but a dealer insisted it was called "Thistle" by Clark. The creamer was shaped like the sugar bowl, but was broken. Quality of glass is good, not excellent. Cutting on the sugar and pitcher is accurate, but is rather poor on the tumbler.

Fig. 389. Cream and sugar set, 3″, unsigned. Hobstar on bottom; handles triple-notched. "Galatea."

Fig. 391. *Left to right:* Sugar bowl, 3½″ h, signed faintly in script, rests on three feet. A thirty-six-point radiant star on bottom. Jug, 9″, nicely cut in same floral design, "Thistle;" petals left gray. Handle is double-notched in concave ovals; base has radiant star. Tumbler, 5″, also has thirty-six-point radiant star on bottom. Only "sugar basin" is signed.

Fig. 390. Plate, 9″, signed in script, circa 1900-1905. (Matye)

H. C. Fry Glass Company (1901-1934)

Henry Clay Fry (1840-1929) was born in Kentucky. At seventeen, he began to work for the glass industry. Traveling for the Phillips Glass Company of Pittsburgh, he met Abraham Lincoln in Illinois (before his election to the presidency) and aroused interest that led to Lincoln's sponsorship of American glass manufacture in 1861.

Fry managed the O'Hara Glass Works, then was president of the Rochester Tumbler Company (founded in 1872), which produced 150,000 pressed and cut tumblers daily.

In 1901 he built his own glasshouse high on a hill in Rochester, where a furious updraft promoted high fusion of his formula. This contained a large proportion of lead and the finest quartz.

Any piece of his superb glass made before he began to make pressed blanks (to be touched up on a cutting wheel to simulate the finer pieces) is now a collector's item. Not only is Fry glass noted for color and brilliance, but also for the unusual shape of his handmade blanks. Some of his designs were floral to please public taste, but many were in the Brilliant tradition.

His most famous creation was a five-part pedestal, holding a large two-part punch bowl and twelve footed cups. The ensemble, cut in vesicas containing various geometric motifs, was four and a half feet high and weighed 150 pounds. It was displayed at the Lewis and Clark Exposition at Portland, Oregon, in 1905, where it won the Grand Medal of Honor.

Fry manufactured many specialities, including heat-proof tumblers for commercial jellies, glass jars for home canning, and bells and ringing tumblers for vaudeville performers.

In 1925 the company went into receivership. In 1934 it closed down completely.

Fig. 392. Serving tray, 11″×1½″, signed Fry in script, in a Flowers and Hobnail design, weighs 4 lbs. Matte flowers and leaves seem to revolve clockwise. Edge cut in long curves and sharp peaks, symptomatic of years 1909 to about 1917.

At an interview with Mrs. Bernice Snead (whose husband was a brother-in-law of Albert Milligan, who had worked for Fry), we learned of an old gentleman named Chalmer Monticue, still living in Freedom, Pennsylvania, a few years ago during her visit there. When Fry's business failed, Mr. Monticue was permitted to keep his equipment in lieu of salary still owed to him. He set up a shop in the rear of the garage of his sister's home and continued to engrave for pleasure until he passed away at ninety-three. He could no longer find good blanks, so he used his daughter's discarded coffee jars. Mrs. Snead had one, simply engraved on sides and bottom in matte flowers and leaves, similar to those on the clock shown here with Sinclaire glassware.

Trademarks include a tiny FRY in script, FRY above a shield, and FRY QUALITY on a shield.

Henry Fry, Jr. was an avid collector of glassware manufactured by other glass companies, making him one of the first cut glass collectors in America.

The signed tray (fig. 392) in a Flowers and Hobnail combination, a transitional design, is dainty in appearance, yet is heavy due to the high lead content.

The geometrically cut nappy (fig. 393, right) is representative of Fry's brilliant cutting circa 1901-1905. The design of the other nappy (fig. 393) still retains a dash of brilliant cutting, yet it caters to public taste of the next ten years. The central flower with fine prism-cut petals and extremely fine hobnail center resembles Fry's "Daisy" pattern, patented by Henry Buckley, 25 November 1913. The method used in engraving pairs of leaves in the patented "Daisy" is the

253

Fig. 393. *Left to right:* Nappy, 6″, swirling effect around polished central blossom. Miter stems and leaves terminate in satin flowers and buds. Nappy, 6″, "America," geometric cutting. (Both from Snead)

same as that followed in engraving the border's blossoms and buds on this handled nappy: a matte finish, highlighted by polished cuts. Neither is signed, but both were brought home by a man who worked in the Fry factory. Nappy on right in "America."

The vase (fig. 394) in "Basket" combines fine-line cutting and engraving. The pattern was registered as #50334, 2 August 1916, by Fred L Anderson of Beaver, Pennsylvania, assignor to H. C. Fry Glass Company of Rochester. It is not signed.

The three pieces of thin glassware (fig. 395) were decorated by diamond-point engraving. Mrs. Snead has sets of this type of ware, given to her and her husband by the brother-in-law who worked in that department at the factory.

L. Straus & Sons (1888-1925?)

Lazarus Straus, his wife, and two sons came to the state of Georgia from Rhenish Bavaria in 1852. In Georgia, he imported and sold fine china and glassware. In 1865 the family moved to New York City, founding the firm of L. Straus & Sons.

They began cutting glass in 1888, employing one hundred expert cutters by 1892. Designers Davies, Siegel, and Richman created forty or more original designs not made by any other companies. Most of them are bold and dramatic; several were patented. Judges at the World's Fair in Chicago in 1893 praised every attribute and gave Straus six awards, more than to any other firm. Straus cut fine glass to order and sold much of it in Europe.

Fig. 394. Vase, 14″, engraved in "Basket" and flora — all in matte finish, with fine-line cutting on the gang (or triple-miter) wheel. Only the basket was registered; other motifs were added to fit the piece.

Fig. 395. *Left to right:* Saucer champagne, 3½", in grape design. Tumbler, 3½", in same grapes. Sherbet, 4", in a formal vine and tassel design. All three pieces are in diamond-point engraving. (Snead.)

A trademark label showing a faceted diamond and the words STRAUS Cut Glass was glued on each piece. It was registered 2 October 1917, but had been used since about 1892. An advertisement in *Century* in 1895 said, "None genuine without the above trade mark." Some Straus ware has an acid-etched star within a circle, from which the date is not yet determined.

A 1900 issue of *China, Glass and Pottery Review* (quoted in *Glass,* February 1979) stated that the company did its own silver mountings, which bore the Straus trademark. Usually silversmiths bought finished pieces of cut glass from cutting shops, then applied their own mounts. Increased rivalry in the market brought prices down so that silversmiths "cut down on the quality of glass purchased in order to make a profit." This inspired some glass companies to make their own mountings.

The heavy orange bowl (fig. 123) in Chapter 11 is deemed by an authority to be a variant of Straus's "Corinthian." The large fan has been added to the basic design.

The dozen tumblers (fig. 396), unsigned, in "Drape" (called "Stars and Banners" by Revi) were purchased in hope of finding a matching pitcher. "Drape," #35323, was designed by Herman Richmond and registered 26 November 1901.

A tumbler (fig. 455) in "Electra" (called "Ulysses" by Revi), designed by Herman Siegel circa 1891, may be seen in Chapter 19.

Heinz Brothers (1901-1927)

After working for Pitkin & Brooks and American Cut Glass Company for many years, the Heinz brothers — Richard, Emil, and Otto — established in Chicago the Monarch Cut Glass Company (1901) with Herman and Frank Kotwitz as partners. In 1902 they bought out their partners' interest and changed the name.

They built a factory in 1905 in St. Charles, Illinois. The brothers became one of the largest makers of cutware in the Midwest, selling all over the United States and Canada, in Germany, and even in St. Petersburg, Russia. They produced over six hundred different articles of fine quality. The factory closed in 1927.

Unfortunately, the Heinz Brothers never used labels or a trademark of any kind, making identification difficult. Some pieces have borne the label of C. E. Wheelock of Peoria, Illinois, which acted as distributor. The label reads RADIANT CRYSTAL, an example of the personal brand of a middleman.

The proportions of the tulip-shaped chalice compote (fig. 397) in "Feathered Star" are lovely. The size of the foot is in perfect harmony with the bowl.

The top of the mismatched boudoir lamp (fig. 482) in Chapter 19 is also in "Feathered Star."

Irving Cut Glass Company (1900-1933)

In 1900, six expert glass cutters formed Irving Cut Glass Company in Honesdale, Pennsylvania. One of these, William H. Hawken, did all of the designing. He had learned blowing, cutting, and designing at Clark's factory in Seelyville.

Fig. 396. Tumblers, 3¾″, unsigned Straus in "Drape." A hobstar is above curved miter cuts, resembling draperies suspended between star tiebacks. Cut on heavy glass of fine quality; much sought after by collectors.

Fig. 397. Chalice compote, 9″×6″, in "Feathered Star" by Heinz Bros. Note formation where stem and foot meet. (Gerritse)

Irving's excellent ware was sold as far away as China, Japan, and South Africa. Much was in the brilliant tradition, yet their most famous pattern was "White Rose" (patented 11 January 1916 by Hawken), which kept the company going for some time during the decline of the Brilliant Period. The matte engraved rose was often combined with brilliant motifs, such as crosscut diamond or cane.

Irving's finer ware was cut on Dorflinger blanks, but late pieces were done on figured blanks from Fry and Libbey. Workers called such pressed blanks "pig iron."

IRVING, in script, was etched lightly on some pieces.

The vase (fig. 398) in a Rose Combination is a good transitional design. It shows the patented flower clearly. Note the scallops, which differ from the early style. The rose was also engraved on light wares — generally pressed blanks.

An ice cream saucer (fig. 446) in the "White Rose" combined with Harvard may be seen in Chapter 19.

The pitcher with six tumblers (fig. 399), signed IRVING on top of the jug's handle, was listed as "Signora" in the auction catalog.

Owanda Glass Company (?-1908)

The only bits of information found on the Owanda Glass Company of Honesdale, Pennsylvania, were that the factory burned down in 1908, and that Fred Leibig cut glass there.

This buttermilk jug (fig. 400) of interesting proportions is attributed to Fred Leibig, cutter at Owanda.

Enterprise Cut Glass Company (1905-1917)

George E. Gaylord founded Enterprise Cut Glass Company circa 1905 in Elmira Heights, New York. He employed about seventy-five men from 1910 to 1917, when he closed down. The war ended his main supply of blanks from Belgium and those from Union Glass Works of Somerville, Massachusetts. Gaylord had worked for both T. B. Clark of Honesdale and Quaker City Cut Glass Company in Philadelphia. He died in 1924.

No marks were used on Enterprise glass, so identification is difficult. Some of their patterns were similar to current designs. "Rose" resembles "White Rose" by Irving, but has fewer petals. "Star" is similar to one of Hoare's Cluster patterns. "Buzz" employs the pinwheel, common to many cutters at that time.

Fig. 398. Vase, 12″, in Irving's "Rose Combination" — the matte rose with polished jewel center combined with cane (clear buttons), ellipses containing zigzag stars, and silver diamond. Good quality glass. (Matye)

Fig. 399. Pitcher, ¾″, signed Irving on top of handle, and tumblers, 4″, not signed, in "Signora." Handle triple-notched; base rayed. (Photograph by Conkling)

Fig. 400. Buttermilk jug, 6″ h × 5½″, attributed to Fred Leibig of Owanda Glass Company. Under pouring lip are two small hobstars and six small triangles of silver diamond. Base has thirty-two rays. (Photograph by Conkling)

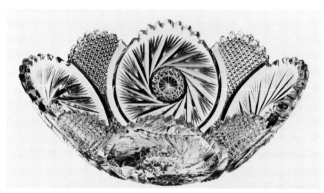

Fig. 401. Banana or oval bowl, 10″ × 6½″ × 4″ h, by Enterprise. Pinwheels outlined by deep miter cuts; base cut in a hobstar. (Photograph by Conkling)

"Sunburst" used a device used by others. Gaylord did, however, cut intricate, superior designs, two of which are "Majestic" and "Imperial" — second to none.

This oval or banana bowl (fig. 401), cut in pinwheel and hobnail, is striking and brilliant.

A. H. Heisey & Company (1895-1958)

A German from Hanover, Augustus H. Heisey founded this company in 1895 in Newark, Ohio. An experienced glass man, he chose Newark for the availability of natural gas for fuel.

Although the name is known for simple, harmonious designs on pressed glass, sturdy enough for use in hotels, bars, and restaurants, the factory "made all types of glass from heavy pressed pieces to the most delicate blown crystal," as well as frosted figurines.

Quoting further from a letter from Louise Ream, president of Heisey Collectors of America, 19 April 1977: "They used over 200 etchings and possibly more cuttings than that. Also, most or all of the most famous cutting companies at one time or another used Heisey blanks...Hawkes, Clark, Pairpoint and many, many more...Hunt and Newton are two more."

Evidently some cutting shops that used Heisey ware ground off the embossed H-in-a-diamond to conceal the origin of their blanks. This is based on a statement by a cutter who reported that his first assignment as an apprentice in a well-known establishment was to grind off the Heisey mark.

The Heisey cutting department, formed about 1915, did the lighter type cutting prevalent at that time, resembling Sinclaire and Pairpoint to some extent. Some special orders were filled, however, that differed from the regular line.

One of the engravers was Emil Kroll, considered to be one of the finest in the world, from the Court of Franz Josef of Austria. His brother, a cousin, and two sons also worked for Heisey.

Prior to 1900, Heisey had no trademark. Use of the embossed H-in-a-diamond began 1 November 1900. The mark was registered in 1901. PLUNGER CUT, registered in 1905, was placed on pressed and polished ware. A trademark for pressed or blown ware was granted in 1906. About 80 percent of all pieces were marked with the embossed *H*; others had paper labels that were white on a blue ground. In 1909, another trademark was registered: the diamond without the *H*.

In 1920 colored ware was added to the line, as well as enameled, milk, custard, iridescent, and silver-trimmed glass. The company was sold to Imperial Glass Company of Bellaire, Ohio, in 1958.

The hair receiver (fig. 163) in Chapter 13 was mold-blown, with the mark impressed inside the bottom while the glass was still malleable. In Louise Ream's opinion, it was engraved by Sinclaire "since an authority on cut glass identified a pitcher" she has in that pattern as Sinclaire. We have seen two other pieces in this same design: a puff box and a small jelly compote. Now that we know of Emil Kroll and his relatives, it seems just as likely that the engraving was done in the Heisey shop.

Corning Pyrex Ware

There is one more category of "cut" glass to see. It is so unusual that a photograph is warranted. With our entry into World War I in 1917, customs, fashions, and attitudes changed radically. Luxury items were out; practical products were in. PYREX ovenware (borosylicate glass) was made by the Corning Glass Works. Who would expect this mundane product to be decorated by cutting?

Fig. 402. Teapot, 9″ from tip of spout to back of handle; 5½″ h, signed PYREX, acid-etched on bottom. Embossed on lid: CORNING PYREX MADE IN USA PAT MAY 27-19. (Bert Hilby)

This teapot (fig. 402), signed PYREX, has lightly cut vine leaves. The patent date, 27 May 1919, is embossed on the pressed lid. A metal ball serves as handle. From this hangs a chain attached to a tea ball. The pot was blown and its trademark is etched on the bottom.

On 8 July 1924, the Giometti Brothers in Corning (1902-1933) registered a design consisting of fine-line bands and circles containing flowers for cutting on Pyrex brand glassware. Perhaps they cut the teapot pictured.

Having seen so much American cut and engraved glass of the Brilliant Period, we now move on to comparisons with European and Canadian pieces.

18

European Versus American

Some collectors are like the visitor to an art gallery who declares, "I don't know much about art, but I know what I like." He buys indiscriminately, accumulating a hodge-podge of styles and values. If he can afford not to worry about the future value of the pieces, all is well. If, however, the time comes when ill health overtakes him, or he needs money, or he must move to a smaller home, it will behoove him to know what he has and to own probably American rather than European cutware.

European or American

We are not saying, "Don't collect *old* European cut and engraved glass." Some of it is lovely and may complement the style of your décor perfectly. Just remember that, to judge by prices, Americans do not value it as highly as old American, nor do Europeans prefer ours to their own at this time.

Two years ago, I met a dealer who had made a trip to Ireland. There she purchased an American Brilliant covered butter dish, signed HAWKES, for $35, brought it home, and sold it for $300. By the same token, we bought the graceful Dutch decanters (fig. 7) in Chapter 2 for a third to a half of the price of American decanters of comparable quality. They had been in the shop for at least a year.

Let us now review the kinds of European glass one may actually have an opportunity to purchase. Few specimens of early glass are available to the ordinary collector. Most are in museums, or are priced far beyond the means of all but the very rich, yet some fine articles do appear at moderate prices.

English, Scottish, Danish, and Irish Glassware

As reported in Chapter 2, reactions to John Ruskin's derogatory remarks concerning cut glass, as well as the usual periodic change of taste, brought a "quieter," less dramatic form of cutting to England during the second half of the nineteenth century.

The claret jugs (fig. 403) with figural spouts were made circa 1880-1900. Patricia Wardle (*Victorian Silver and Silverplate*) says that characteristic of the period

1880-1901, were "glass claret jugs of various shapes, often decorated with elaborate engraving or cutting and with silver mounts. The latter range from the plain and functional with straight handles and little decoration to elaborate mask spouts and acanthus-leaf handles derived from Renaissance originals." However elaborate the silver, note that the glass of these jugs is thin and the cutting shallow, as compared with American brilliant cutting of the same era. The English jugs are lovely, but they do not sparkle like American glass.

Some English glassmakers used more soda, producing glass with a yellowish tinge. English glass weighed less than the American. The Irish and Bohemian combined potash and lime, giving a slightly gray color. The Americans' use of potash and oxide of lead made glass heavier and more light refractive.

There is never a sudden shift in styles. An English court decanter shown at our Centennial Exposition at Philadelphia in 1876 had practically the same shape as my "Russian" decanter by Hawkes (fig. 293) in Chapter 15, but it had a faceted stopper. The neck was cut in honeycomb (St. Louis diamond) and the body in flat-topped relief diamonds with a band of strawberry diamonds around the shoulder. This brilliant style was going out as ours was coming in.

The six-bottle caster set (fig. 404), cut in notched vertical prism, is a good example of British glass with a slightly off-color hue. One rarely finds a set with all original pieces and stoppers, however, so this set is desirable. It is useful for holding condiments at the table, even today.

At a recent auction, Danish cut glass items of this period were so "brownish" that we would not have taken a piece as a gift. This is not to say that all Danish glass is off-color. A friend has a large vase of a better color, but it is not colorless and brilliant like the American.

The acid-polished English knife rests (fig. 405) have good clarity, but the cutting is not as sharp as American glass. They were purchased to illustrate the satin-lined cases of the times, used both in England and America, for sets of tumblers, stemware, and other pieces for presentation as gifts.

Fig. 403. *Left to right:* Claret jug, 11″, has a figural spout, a Viking with full beard, and engraved silver band with beading around edge. Lid is marked: Mappin & Webb, Prince's Plate, Rd. 71552, Sheffield & London. Narrow flutes around base, which has a single twenty-four-point star. (Willits) Claret jug, 10″, also has a Viking spout and plated, engraved top. Lid has no trademark, but is surely from the same company. "I 185" is scratched in the lid, perhaps to identify model. (McCoy)

Although the tray (fig. 406) has scallops similar to some cut here circa 1917, the rather prim "tailored" design seems to be English, rather than American. Proof is lacking, yet we can use this to convey the style of English cut glass early in this century.

Stevens & Williams of Brierly Hill, Staffordshire, established in 1776, was mentioned previously in connection with the cameo glass reproduction of the Portland vase by John Northwood, and concerning Frederick Carder's tenure there. In addition to colored Art Glass, such as Satinglass, Alexandrite, Peach Bloom, Cameo, Silver Deposit, and many other dramatic forms late in the nineteenth century, Stevens & Williams cut and engraved a high grade of crystal. Some pieces were sturdy. Others were delicate and lovely, such as this water lily vase (fig. 407) in the

Fig. 404. English caster set in silver-plated frame on four ball feet. All original. Mustard jar with spoon (marked W&H, 1852) and two bottles have silver tops. Three bottles have glass stoppers. Marks on silver are English, but unclear.

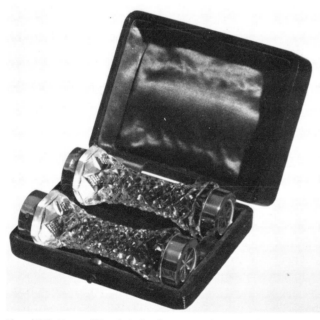

Fig. 405. Pair of English knife rests in box lined with Kelly-green silk satin. Box snaps shut and is leather-covered. Ends of rests cut in a star and banded in silver stamped "L&S, anchor, Y, and a lion" (Lister & Sons, Newcastle 1888). Bars cut in crosscut diamond and small fields of silver diamond (the *real* English strawberry diamond).

Fig. 406. Round tray, 11″, is ½″ thick. Believed to be English, although the motif found in central kites may be seen in Averbeck's "Saratoga" and in Fry's "Frederick."

Fig. 407. Vase, 9½″, signed "S, a fleur-de-lis, and W over ENGLAND." Engraving and cutting consist of water lilies, fluted arches with rounded tops, and swirls that represent water. It could have been designed by Frederick Carder in the 1890s before he came to America (Matye).

French Art Nouveau style, the New Art that took hold in Europe and America in the 1890s. It was a decorative style in architecture, stained glass windows, furniture, and objects such as jewelry, vases, and grooming accessories. It borrowed twisting plant forms from nature. We see it in the ladies with flowing hair, amid leafy vegetation, on silver-backed hair brushes and hand mirrors, and on posters of the period.

Thomas Webb & Sons, established at Stourbridge in a coal, iron, and clay district, was inspired by the Great Exhibition of 1851 at the Crystal Palace, located in London in a huge structure sheathed in glass. The finest designs and methods of manufacturing world-wide were shown, and so led to the introduction of many new kinds of Art Glass in England. Webb made all the types mentioned concerning Stevens & Williams and more, as well as excellent table glassware.

Thomas Webb perfected the *lehr*, a moving oven for annealing glass. When he died in 1869, sons Thomas Wilkes, Charles, and Walter formed a partnership. They produced crystal in many forms, in addition to the cameo work of George and Thomas Woodall.

The company showed tableware at the Crystal Palace in 1851 and won prizes, but at the Paris Exposition in 1878, the only award won by T. W. Webb was for chandeliers. Work in clear glass continued, but their main emphasis was on fancy colored, iridescent, and cameo. About 1906, Bohemian factories did heavy enameling to simulate cameo. Webb dropped the cameo and resumed cutting flint glass.

Truly handmade, Webb cut glass is famed for its crystal purity and fine polish. The designs have tended to accentuate the beauty of the glass itself and the form of the piece, rather than to multiply the points of illumination by means of deep complex cuttings. The English have not cared for the "cut-to-pieces" style of the Americans.

This heavy fruit bowl (fig. 408) was made in our post-Brilliant Period. The author sent photographs of this bowl and of the next item to England. In a letter from Dema Glass Limited Glassware Manufacturers, incorporating Edinburgh Crystal Glass Company/Thomas Webb & Sons (the title on their letterhead), Director, S. R. Eveson remembers that this bowl was made as late as the 1930s. Footed, it was labeled "New York" shape. Without a foot, as is the one illustrated here, it was called the "Worcester" shape. Although heavy and clear, the glass does not have the lively sparkle of American products.

In the same letter, Mr. Eveson replied concerning the decanter (figs. 409A and 409B):

> We have one here at the works which appears to be almost identical in shape but which has a different kind of stopper. The one we have was made at our associated Scottish factory (which was at that time The Edinburgh & Leith Flint Glass Works), probably 30 or 40 years ago. It bears the "Edinburgh, Made in Scotland" back stamp etched on the base. Have you looked for a similar stamp on your decanter?

Fig. 408. Fruit bowl, 10″ × 5″, signed "Webb, MADE IN ENGLAND." Shape is "Worcester." Cutting design 3961 ½. Weighs 8 lbs.

Of course, we did look and found none. Based on the numerous marks of wear and the target stopper (which was used concurrently with the mushroom stopper during the early nineteenth century), it is apparently much older than "30 or 40 years ago."

While seeking a possible American origin, we learned that Charles Bonnert of Baltimore patented a bottle (#36262, 31 March 1903) with a hole in the center that resembles this one, but it had the same thickness all around the hole, while ours is larger at the bottom.

Pairpoint made an engraved bottle in green, that was somewhat thicker at the bottom. However, the glass was thin and had a protruding lip and a spherical blown stopper. Steuben carried Blank 1071, similar to Pairpoint's decanter.

Recently, a decanter by Hawkes, cut geometrically, was advertised in a national magazine. This is evidence that Hawkes made a decanter with center hole.

The engraving on our decanter, however, does not resemble American work by any company. It is partially polished to a silvery sheen, unlike any seen on American glassware.

One reads that liquor containers of a cheap material, perhaps pottery, were made many years ago in this shape, so that the bartender could put several over his forearm to carry them from the storeroom. One reads, also, that farm laborers in America had water bottles with a larger hole to slip over the shoulder.

We may suppose that the shape originated in the practical, cheaper bottles, then was copied in fine cut-and-engraved glass. Final proof of age of this piece is still a mystery, but it was surely made in Scotland and cut in England.

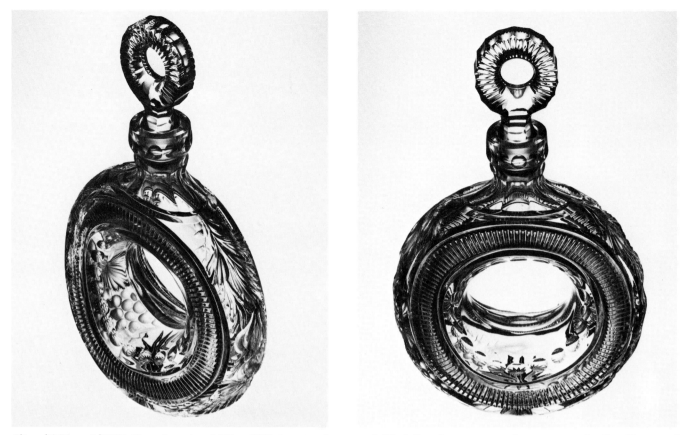

Figs. 409A and 409B. Rare decanter, 11″ h × 6¼″, is cut and engraved. Neck fluted; concave circles cut around collar. Front and back have two deep miter cuts with miter radiants between cuts. Just inside hole is a chain of punties. Down sides, which broaden at base, cascade engraved leaves and fruits, polished to a silvery sheen. Below these are clusters of grapes, polished to rock crystal (as are sixteen rays on base). Stopper is a pinch-pressed "wheel" or "target," completed by cutting.

Modern Irish Waterford cut glass can be seen in every city, so there is no need to show it here. The original Waterford Glass House 1783-1851, called also Waterford Flint Glass Manufactory (or Works) was revived on a small scale in 1947 as a "pilot factory." Little progress was made. It was then taken over by the Irish Glass Bottle Company.

The Irish Republic was seeking new ways to improve the economy and to prevent emigration of its young people to foreign countries. The existing plant was closed in 1951, and a new, modern factory was constructed just one hundred years after the original firm went out of existence. Master artisans from Germany, Italy, and Czechoslovakia were brought in to train young Irishmen. The number of employees rose from fifty in 1950 to more than 2,500 in 1979. A vigorous advertising campaign was launched. World-wide acceptance created a need for a second factory in 1967 and a third soon after.

The glassware is handblown and handcut, yet the cuts are few, compared with our American heirlooms of the Brilliant Period. Many modern Waterford pieces are copies of the old pre-1851, "tailored" designs, but many are simple and modern. All kinds of pieces are produced — even fine presentation and commemorative items for dignitaries. Waterford is one of the better imports.

German and French Cut and Engraved Glassware

A lack of sharpness led the author to discover that a shoe perfume (fig. 166) in Chapter 13 and the toothpick holder (fig. 440) in Chapter 19 were imported. Some American factories and wholesale houses, such as Pitkin & Brooks, carried European imports made to their specifications, along with American glass, including small items such as toothpick holders and knife rests. Higgins & Seiter illustrated this very toothpick holder in 1899 under "Bohemian Glass Novelties." It sold for thirty cents.

Fig. 410. Candy dish, 9″ from tips of handles, has a silver frame, sculptured in flag lilies. It is marked: S. 12776 (a new moon and a crown) 800 WTR JOH. CHR. WICH. NURNBERG. (Matye)

Another example of Art Nouveau, so popular from 1890 to 1910, is this graceful candy dish (fig. 410) made in Nürnberg, Germany. It rests in a silver frame sculptured in flag lilies with flowing lines. The glass insert, thinner than American, is engraved on the sides in a natural plant design, that is left gray. It has simple, polished bulb leaves on the bottom. Contrast this with American engraving shown previously.

Also made in Germany is the decanter (fig. 411). Standing 15″ high, including the fully cut stopper, the piece is cut in motifs so like American ware of the period that, without the mark on the silver neck band, identification would be doubtful. The "new moon and crown" was the sign adopted by federal law, 16 July 1884, and applied to silver, 1 January 1888, to identify *fabrication moderne*.

French glass makers were noted from earliest times for stained glass windows. England required their assistance in glazing churches as early as the eighth century. The French made tableware always, but did not develop a distinctive style until late in the eighteenth century. In 1764 a glassworks was founded by the Bishop of Metz under a permit from Louis XV in the small town of Baccarat, located 250 miles east of Paris in the foothills of the Vosges Mountains. (Remember that English lead crystal began in 1780.)

Baccarat has been noted from the beginning for superbly pure crystal. Since 1817, the firm's glass has contained about 30 percent lead oxide with a firing temperature of 2,600 degrees F. It is interesting to note that, since earliest times, Baccarat imported its potash from America. Much of their glass has used only a limited prismatic effect, employing mainly cut panels and flutes to enhance its innate beauty. But circa 1910, some geometric cutting and some engraving, similar to Sinclaire designs, was done.

This unsigned tray (fig. 412) is probably late nineteenth- or early twentieth-century Baccarat. A local jeweler who handles the finest imports judged it to be Baccarat, as did a well-known dealer/author/collector. A photograph was also sent to the New York office of La Compagnie des Cristalleries de Baccarat. It was then forwarded to Paris. The Paris office did not recognize it as a contemporary piece.

The Baccarat trademark (a large circle enclosing a decanter in the center, a tumbler on the right, and a stemmed goblet on the left, with BACCARAT inside the top of the circle and FRANCE inside the bottom) was devised in 1830. Only since 1937 has this trademark been applied to the glass with fluoric acids.

Fig. 412. Tray, 12″, attributed to Baccarat, circa 1912, is made of beautiful, clear glass. (Matye)

Fig. 411. Decanter, 15″, has fully cut stopper with teardrop, resembling a four-petal flower when seen from above. Upper neck and lip are of silver, marked "new moon and crown 900 T over M 19." The 900 is the same as American coin silver. Body has three pinwheels alternating with hobstars and fans. (Matye)

Canadian Cut and Engraved Glassware

Glass staple products made in Canada's own factories in the 1840s and 1850s were window glass and bottles. These expanded to include lampwares in the 1860s, and finally in the 1880s to pressed tablewares. Some of the many patterns may have been made on molds bought from United States companies. As in the States, Canadian pressed glass around the turn of the century tried to imitate the more expensive cutware.

The *Year Book* of 1876 supplies figures to prove that in that year, Canadian glassblowers supplied the home market with nearly a million items of glass. High customs duties on imports (30 percent in 1891) protected domestic manufacture.

The word "flint" was a trade name in Canada for colorless glass. Very little lead glass was produced there. The general output was of the cheaper lime glass, introduced in the 1860s. Much of it resembled United States ware, since workmen often went to Canada from the States. Early efforts in cutting, practiced from the mid-nineteenth century, consisted of decorations on special items or orders. Canadian cut glass was not then the true cut glass described in this book.

Aside from common bottles, pressed and blown tableware (colored and clear), craftsmen made many *whimseys*, including: canes, hats, paperweights, and *drapes*. Drapes were composed of a series of glass ornaments held together by glass chains. They were a manifestation of the Victorian love of florid and senti-mental decoration. Cuspidors were also blown of clear or green bottle glass and coated with opal (milk glass). Designs were cut through the outer covering to clear. Engraving and frosting (sandblasting) cut-to-clear were also used.

The St. Lawrence Glass Company of Montreal (1867-1875) claimed to produce "the finest kinds of pressed and cut Flint Glassware," yet their advertising material mentions only cut lampshades, and "flint" meant "colorless." They used the pure white sand from the Berkshire Mountains in Massachusetts, so presumably the color was good.

The Nova Scotia Glass Company of Trenton (1881-1892) was reported in the *Halifax Morning Chronicle* of 31 January 1885 to be decorating its pressed or mold-blown pieces with both engraving and cutting. The cutters were mostly Bohemians.

The Lamont (Diamond) Glass Company, also of Trenton, Nova Scotia (1890-1902), advertised "a general line of Blown and Cut Glassware, Cut Door Lights a Specialty."

Robert McCausland of Toronto (1856-?), a firm of artists in stained glass, furnished church windows as far North as Aklavik on the fringe of the Arctic Circle, and as far South as San José, Costa Rica, as well as to cities in the United States. They also cut glass, but did not manufacture it from raw materials.

Other Canadian cutting houses, about which information is scant, are George Phillips & Company of Montreal, Quebec (1907-?), and the following in Ontario: Belleville (1912-?), Lakefield (1915-1920), which sometimes marked glass with a small Union Jack, and Ottawa (1913-?).

It is not difficult to recognize glassware from Canada cut on Canadian or on most European blanks, since their lime formulas lacked our brilliance. It can be more difficult to discern the difference when United States blanks were used, especially when the patterns are nearly identical to ours. Much of the latter was cut by artisans who had first worked here. Then, too, some Canadian agents sold United States glass, stamped with their private brands.

The following examples are cut on blanks from the States or on the best from Europe. Since only the most brilliant glass is suitable for our collection, we had no desire to own ordinary specimens.

The compote (fig. 413) is signed ELITE-on-a-maple-leaf, the trademark of Gowans, Kent & Company. Mr. G. H. (Harry) Clapperton had moved from Stourbridge, England, to Toledo, Ohio, in 1885 when he was twelve. At seventeen, he began a ten-year apprenticeship with the Libbey company there. By 1900 he was a qualified cutter. That year he moved to Canada, where he found work at Gowans-Kent. In 1897 the firm was listed in the Toronto Directory as a wholesale dealer in crockery and glassware, with no mention of manufacturing. It is said that he originated glass cutting in Canada at this firm, which then cut both geometric and natural designs. It is also said that he was reputed to be the foremost cut glass designer in Canada, second to none on the continent.

In 1905, Mr. Clapperton formed his own business, making and cutting all designs himself. He was joined by Mr. N. F. Gundy a year later under the name, Gundy-Clapperton Company. Within ten or more years, the original management took control, and the name was changed to Clapperton's, then to Clapperton & Sons, at which time the trademark was changed from GCCo-in-a-shamrock to C-in-a-shamrock. From some period in the early 1920s, the mark began to be omitted from smaller items.

Gundy-Clapperton did not *make* glass. Early in this century, blanks were obtained from Baccarat of France, Val St. Lambert of Belgium, Libbey of Toledo, Ohio, H.

Fig. 413. Compote, 8″, signed "ELITE" on a maple leaf in a circle (Gowan, Kent & Co., Ltd., Toronto, Canada), has a 2″ gallery. Flutes on stem widen at top to make six-point flower form, as one looks down into center.

C. Fry of Rochester, Pennsylvania, and Union Glass of Summerville, Massachusetts.

In 1913 the firm was cutting the "Colonial" pattern, "now so much in vogue among the fastidious few 'who know'. Ornate richness gives place to the quiet dignity of gracefully flowing line." This opinion is quoted from an article written in 1913 (publication unknown) by a visitor who spent a few hours in this "largest plant of the kind in Canada." The unknown writer declared that "Cut Glass is now a fine art — a sister art to painting and sculpture." He especially praised Gundy-Clapperton's intaglio work — the only such work being engraved in Canada at that time. He praised a design showing a bird and vines, and remarked on the combination of "mitre and intaglio work," which must have resembled Hawkes's Gravic.

Cut glass from Clapperton & Sons, still being produced in 1967 at publication of an article by Elizabeth Shepherd (archaeologist and lecturer on cut glass), made use of Val St. Lambert blanks. Gundy-Clapperton, prior to World War I, cut all of the items popular in the States and utilized all of the cut motifs and floral engravings now familiar to our readers. It is said that the firm made "nothing but cut glass, and nothing but the best." These examples bear out that statement. They are all marked with the early signature, 1905 to 1915 or so.

Fig. 414. Cologne, 6¾″, signed "GCCo" in a shamrock. Bottom rayed. (Matye)

Fig. 415. Vase, 12″, signed "Gundy-Clapperton and Birks" (distributor), has unusual shape. Blank of finest crystal. (Gerritse)

The cologne bottle (fig. 414), signed with the GCCo-in-a-shamrock trademark, is indistinguishable from one of ours. Incidently, cologne was often called "toilet water" then.

The fine vase (fig. 415) is signed BIRKS with the Gundy-Clapperton trefoil — an example of the common practice of adding the distributor's name to that of the cutter. The author has also seen G. B. ALLEN and DINGWALL above or below the cloverleaf.

On this round tray (fig. 416) in "Hob Star," the shamrock is in a circle. Both glass and workmanship are excellent.

The tray enabled us to recognize the unsigned 21″ table lamp (figs. 417A and 417B) in "Hob Star." The patterns and quality are identical. This is Harvard at its finest. The light is distributed by the elaborate pattern, so that the whole dome becomes filled and radiant. Even the base seems to be illuminated. Pearson shows an 18″ lamp (Encyc. I, p. 104), signed CGCo with the same top, but with a different base.

Fig. 416. Round tray, 12½″, signed "Gundy-Clapperton," superbly cut in "Hob Star"; thirty-two points. (Rolland)

Fig. 417A. Table lamp, 21″ h × 12″, unsigned Gundy-Clapperton in "Hob Star." Two sockets for long bulbs are marked "250 W, HUBBEL (in an oval) 250 v." Central hobstar has forty-eight points; otherwise, it matches the tray (fig. 416) perfectly.

Fig. 417B. Table lamp dome, seen more clearly. Accurate cutting.

The cordial bottle, in Chapter 13 (fig. 173), another example of "Hob Star," is signed G. B. ALLEN VANCOUVER.

The domino or loaf sugar tray (fig. 92) in Chapter 10 is cut in a transitional combination. A chain of flat stars, like that around the gallery of the Elite compote (fig. 413), is cut on the bottom, while matte tulips decorate the sides. This was "Tulip," their "Industrial design #3888." Only the tulip was registered by Gundy-Clapperton.

Finally, we have a signed specimen of Gundy-Clapperton engraving: a cream and sugar set (fig. 418) with strawberries and leaves in matte finish. The scalloped edge resembles United States glass from 1910 to 1917.

In 1921 G. H. Clapperton opened Quinte-Clapperton Amalgamated in Deseronto, Ontario. It burned in 1931. The firm returned to Toronto.

Roden Brothers of Toronto, manufacturers of silver-plated ware at least as early as 1891, cut both geometric and floral designs in lead glass. This berry bowl (fig. 419) in "Edna," signed with an ornate *R* flanked by lions, compares favorably in brilliance and sharpness of cutting with our extraordinary Egginton bowl (fig. 369) in Chapter 17. The scalloped edge is different from any United States glass we have seen. Elizabeth Shepherd states that Roden Brothers signed some of their glass PORTE/&/MARKLE in a circle.

Turn back to Chapter 16 to see the three juice glasses (fig. 341), signed on the bottom with Roden's trademark and "R'd 1910." Herein lies a mystery that took a great deal of correspondence to solve. When slightly altered, this fabulous "Alhambra" design, originated by Meriden Cut Glass Company in Connecticut, became "Norman" at Roden Brothers in Canada. "Norman" was filed 9 November 1910 by Thomas and Frank Roden, and was registered the next day. Quoting from a letter from Janet Holmes, Curatorial Assistant at the Royal Ontario Museum, "The registration was for the castellated edge and border pattern." (Remember that the filing date for "Alhambra" in the United States Patent Office was 14 November 1910.)

Two deviations from the Meriden pattern occur on "Norman." First, the bottom hobstar (in the vertical columns lying between strips of cane) on jugs and vases is replaced by a single star fitted into a diamond-shaped (lozenge) field. Second, the juice glasses signed RODEN have a single star on the bottom, whereas water tumblers and whiskey shots in "Alhambra" have a fully cut hobstar. "Alhambra" cracker jar, decanter, water jug, and vase all have a beautiful hobstar base. It is impossible to tell from the catalog whether other "Norman" pieces have this base.

Fig. 418. Cream and sugar set, 3″, is signed "GCCo" in a trefoil beside creamer's handle. Engraved "Strawberry" design in matte finish; handles triple-notched; base rayed.

Fig. 419. Berry bowl, 8″ × 3¾″, signed by Roden Bros. of Toronto. Edge is cut in small flutes separated by triple-miter cuts. Design is "Edna."

"Norman" is the only pattern marked "Registered Design" among dozens in the 1917 catalog, but from the Commissioner of Patents in Ottawa, through Mrs. C. White, came the information that design #3114, called "Old Irish," was registered 12 November 1910. A bowl is shown with the same scalloped edge and fields of sharp relief diamond as in Meriden's "Old Irish." Only a band of sharp diamond between scallops and fields is different. This may be due to the depth of the bowl illustrated on the patent paper. (See Pearson *Encyc. III*, p. 180, for Meriden's "Old Irish.") Numerous designs for Roden were registered, but nearly all concerned cutlery or medallions.

A Canadian firm making plated ware in Hamilton, Ontario, in 1879 was called Meriden Britannica Company. It was founded that year to produce 1847 Rogers Brothers silverplate and sterling ware. About 1912, it merged with International Silver Company of Canada, which was incorporated in 1924 to include Standard Silver and William Rogers & Son. George Wilcox was the first president. Later, more companies joined.

There is no example in this collection of glass marked with the letters NACGMCo, with the *o* inside the *C*. The letters are arranged inside a circle between points of a six-pointed star within the circle. Sometimes a number appears in the center; sometimes NATIONAL is above the number and ASSOCN below it. (See trademarks in the Apendix.)

With the help of Virginia Wright, Assistant Librarian of the Corning Museum of Glass, a mystery has been solved. A few writers and dealers have suggested that the mark is Canadian. I wondered about the coincidence between the letters in this sign and the initials of the National Association of Cut Glass Manufacturers, organized in Buffalo, New York, 17 August 1911. The association was incorporated in Pennsylvania, 9 March 1921, and remained active until 1942.

Miss Wright learned that the trademark symbol was adopted in 1922 to indicate that "glass so marked was made to the top standards of cut glass manufacture." The association included both United States and Canadian members. The number 3 in the center of a label was assigned to the George Phillips Company in Montreal. One may assume that each member had an assigned number. One may also assume that the symbol may be seen on either Canadian or United States cut glassware.

The present House of Birks in Montreal, well known for silverware and jewelry, has a long and complicated history. Its founder, Henry Birks, was born in 1840 of English parents. He entered business at seventeen and founded Henry Birks & Company, a retail store, with a staff of three in 1879. His business policies were unusual, dealing only with cash and one price for all.

He opened his first factory in 1887, making jewelry. In 1893 he admitted his three sons as equal partners and changed the name to Henry Birks & Sons. He operated a glass factory from 1894 to 1907, when he sold it to George Phillips & Company and bought the Gorham (silver) Company of Canada. He expanded greatly by absorbing other companies, having branches in the major cities of Canada and in London, England.

In 1893, Henry Birks & Sons of Montreal was an agent for Libbey cut glassware. Revi lists six other Canadian firms as agents for Libbey. One was Gowans, Kent & Company of Hamilton and Toronto, who also cut their own glass. Mr. Hazen Wright, Head Office Buyer for the modern Henry Birks & Sons of Montreal in 1976, remarked that Wood Gundy, a very old Canadian cutting firm in Deseronto, like Roden, imported blanks for cutting from such fine companies as Val St. Lambert and Baccarat. Both Wood Gundy and Roden Brothers did special work for Henry Birks & Sons, who etched the name BIRKS on many pieces. Mr. Wright believes that heavy lead crystal was never manufactured in Canada. All pieces were imported as blanks, were cut, then given an acid dip to achieve a brilliant finish. Was the Gundy of Wood Gundy the same as the gentleman associated with Clapperton?

New or Old?

When buying crystal goblets, wines, dessert dishes and the like to use when entertaining, one can find good quality new Baccarat, Val St. Lambert, and Waterford at a jewelry or large department store. There is also 20 percent lead crystal by Fostoria, made in America. It is available in pressed reproductions of old pieces found in the Henry Ford Museum, for example, at a lower price. Possible breakage and replacement may make this the sensible thing to buy. Obtaining a complete matching set is no problem in this situation for as long as the pattern is current.

Nevertheless, the lady of the house probably washes her delicate crystal herself. If so, why not enjoy antique cut glass? It will continue to increase in value, whereas new pieces, even the finest, will not be worth more until many years hence. A new piece, no matter how expensive, depreciates in value like an automobile as soon as the customer walks out of the door. Just try to get what you paid for it!

Lowell Innes, New Englander and recognized authority on old glassware, recently appeared on the television program, *Antiques*, with its host, George Michael. His advice is to study good books on the kind of antique you wish to collect, to visit museums where you can find authenticated pieces, and to look at collections belonging to individuals. You should also ask the collector if you may touch the items in question in order to experience the "feel" of the sharpness and the weight. Also, you may ask the owner to tap the edge of bowls and compotes to hear them ring.

By the time you have studied the photographs in this volume, you should be well acquainted with American use of motifs in designs. It is not always possible to find collectors to visit. You may hear someone's name mentioned, but would not dare to call as a stranger to request an appointment. In fact, some individuals are reluctant to admit visitors, or even to reveal that they own a valuable collection.

Instead, go to reputable dealers and ask for information. Most are happy to inform a prospective customer. Go to large antiques shows, where many dealers come to display their wares. Most shows are under supervision of association officers who do their best to insure that items for sale are really old, or if new are so labeled.

New European glass may appear among old American at auctions, where the catalogs may not discriminate or may be in error. This new glass may be thick and truly cut and engraved, but the cutting is usually large and sparse. Engraved flowers are usually flatter. They do not have the fine nuances and many levels of cutting that we find in old glass from either Europe or America.

Other imports are not truly cut. They are blown or pressed into a figured mold to form the miter cuts and hobstars, with a few gray cuts around a molded pinwheel.

Baskets with wide handles that come up out of the body (fig. 420) are nearly always modern European. This one was purchased in 1968 from a dealer who called it "antique" and charged accordingly. Impressed by the signature, FRY, scratched on the side of a miter cut on the rayed base, the buyer gladly paid the inflated price for a new imported basket. (A genuine Fry signature would have been acid-etched.) The owner still likes her basket, but is chagrined to learn that its origin was misrepresented.

Most American baskets of the Brilliant Period had handles made separately and fastened to the body, but a Mount Washington catalog of the early 1880s does show a "Russian" basket with an undulating edge. The handle is wide and comes out of the body. During the Brilliant Period, most pieces were cut entirely, or mainly, in one motif or design (such as hobnail or sharp relief diamond.) Doubtless there are few of those early baskets extant.

Fig. 420. Modern imported basket, 8″ h × 9¾″ × 6″, has "Fry" scratched on side of miter cut on rayed base. Hobstar, hobnail, and sharp diamond — all polished. Zigzag stars, crosscut squares, silver diamond, and single stars on buttons in center of hobstars are left gray. Buttons and nailheads are not symmetrical. (Gilbert)

Fig. 421. Decanter, 12″, and wine goblet, 4½″, are modern imports, attractive until examined closely. Star in center of pinwheel and flashing — left gray — are typical of new European ware. (Kriska)

In March 1981, such a basket, cut in mixed brilliant motifs, was displayed at a show. It engendered much controversy among dealers as to whether it was new European or old American. This author agreed with an experienced dealer that it was indeed of the American Brilliant Period — an exception to the rule. One must rely on the brilliance of the glass and the cutting to determine age and provenance. Visit stores that import modern glassware for comparison.

A new bell has a clapper (or tongue) whose chain is attached to the bell by means of a plastic button glued to the glass. An old bell has a chain whose top link was imbedded in the hot glass.

The only modern cut glass we have seen that compares in brilliance and workmanship to that of the American Brilliant Period belongs to a lady whose son was stationed in Germany in the American Air Force in 1974. He had three pieces made to order for his mother. He was told that this excellent cut glass is never made for export. Its patterns were similar, but not identical to our old glass.

Imports graduate from good to unbelieveably poor, obviously pressed or mold-blown and inaccurately cut, if cut at all. This modern decanter and its wine goblet (fig. 421) are good compared with some imports. Large cuts were really cut, but do not meet accurately around the body of the decanter. Acid polishing has removed sharp edges. Finally, crosscuts (also hastily done, with cuts incomplete or going past the goal), small fans between vanes of the buzz, and zigzag stars in the

center are left gray. The owner, a dear friend, gave permission to make pejorative remarks concerning her glass. She now regrets her purchase, since the price of the new glass was substantial.

Browse through stores, look at labels, and compare the new glass with these photographs and with authentic examples wherever you can find them. Some labels read "Cut Lead Crystal," when the only "cut" consists of a rough, unpolished zigzag star.

In this dessert or luncheon plate (fig. 422), cut in 1972, one sees design and skillful cutting by Louis Iorio, an expert of the old school. It is a fine piece within the limitations imposed by the present-day dearth of good lead blanks. Louis Iorio was one of the first employees of the Empire Cut Glass Company, which located in New York City in 1895, then moved to Flemington, New Jersey, under the aegis of Henry C. Fry.

Empire at its peak used the finest of Fry blanks. For comparison with the modern plate (8″, 11 ounces), see the nappy (6″, 16 ounces) in Empire's "Atlantic" pattern (fig. 197) in Chapter 13, made circa 1903. The nappy with curled handle sparkles and was wood-polished. It may have been designed and cut by Louis Iorio, since he was responsible for many Empire patterns. When Empire closed in 1925, Louis took his last pay in cutting equipment. In his own shop, Mr. Iorio and his son William continued to cut glass in the old manner.

Fig. 422. Plate, 8″, engraved "L. Iorio #146″ in one of the miter cuts. Also signed top center with acid-etched trademark, IORIO in a circle. Outline miters of vesicas and fans are polished; silver diamond, cane, and zigzag stars are left gray. Blank is thin and lightweight.

In 1972, Louis designed and cut a series of three hundred plates, offered as "Artist Originals." Each was different, numbered, and signed. This one is #146. Disappointed to find that cuts were unpolished, and that the piece was "grainy" and weighed only eleven ounces, I complained. William courteously explained that only occasionally does a fine old blank come to light. He added, "Generally speaking, present-day costs involved in producing this type of cut glass puts it far beyond the reach of most collectors and it is therefore not practical to produce such ware today." Feeling ashamed, yet grateful that the great man was still so skillful at the age of ninety, I refused the offer of a refund and placed the plate in my collection.

In 1977 "Mr. Cut Glass," as Louis is known, was still active at ninety-five. Son William was cutting and engraving glass and grandson Ric Iorio at twenty-eight was creating colored glass in the Art Nouveau tradition. The family has a collection dating from 1500 B.C. to the present.

Cut or Pressed?

Remember that cut glass is a handmade product. As in oriental rugs, variations in the design appear. If irregularities are too noticeable, skillful cutting is lacking. The piece may have been done by an apprentice, or late in the period by an indifferent workman. Some of the poorest pieces I've seen were wedding gifts in 1919. The cutting was badly done on inferior blanks. The finest examples of cut ware approach perfection and uniformity, as in Hawkes and Dorflinger pieces circa 1890 and in the "Alhambra" items by Meriden, made about 1911. Even here, slight differences in execution of an element are seen.

The original carving of the mold for either a mold-blown or pressed item was accurately done, therefore all copies are the same. For example, the concave diamonds in the pressed "Vernon" celery vase (fig. 13) in Chapter 3 are more apt to be uniform than the St. Louis neck on the wine bottle (fig. 9), also in Chapter 3. Use calipers to measure motifs, if in doubt.

Color is another difference. The punch bowl and cups (fig. 423), pressed early in this century, exemplify this criterium. The color is dark — a sort of gray. The edges are rounded, mold marks show clearly, and the bowl emits a short-lived ring when struck by fingernail or pencil. (Some sound more like a dull thud. Cut glass bowls ring like a bell unless cracked, heaven forbid!) This punch bowl was made by McKee Glass Company of Jeannette, Pennsylvania. The embossed trademark, PRESCUT, was registered in 1904, and the pattern, "Nortec," was patented in 1908. Nortec was first produced in 1907, the third in a series of patterns ending in "tec": Aztec, Toltec, Nortec, Fentec, and so on until 1915.

Originally located in Pittsburgh in 1850, McKee Glass Works made commercial ware, such as bar tumblers and lamp chimneys, but only a few pressed tableware patterns. After many changes, the firm emerged in Jeannette as a part of the National Glass Company under Andrew Smith (1908). The "tec" patterns were all geometric, but an imitation of engraved floral ware (1904) was named "Rock Crystal." (Do not confuse this with polished engraving on handblown lead glass.) In 1919 McKee started a new line that was pressed and lightly engraved. The company used the hand method of pressing until 1927. A great deal of McKee glass is still available.

Most pressed glass made to imitate cut glass, especially when made of the cheaper soda-lime developed during the Civil War while lead was scarce, has such rounded edges that no one could mistake it for cut. Cheap to make, requiring bicarbonate of soda and a changed formula of lime and other ingredients, it was clear, but does not ring when tapped. It is also lighter in weight. It was often called "the poor man's cut glass." We exclude the compote (fig. 13) in Chapter 3 and the lamp (fig. 425), to be discussed shortly, both made in the last quarter of the nineteenth century. They are much better than the inferior mass-produced ware made after 1900.

Reprints of glassware illustrated in the Butler Brothers' general merchandise catalogs of 1905 and 1910 show that this "make-believe" cut glass was sold in vast quantities. Butler Brothers was the largest wholesale firm in America, with "more than 32 acres of floor space in just two of the many buildings."

Fig. 423. Punch bowl, 14½″×8″, and cups in "Nortec," pressed pattern registered in 1908 — a good example of pressed lime glass in imitation of cut glass.

The trademark PRESCUT is mentioned in one section of the 1905 Butler catalog. Among the assortments (the assortment plan having begun in 1887) is one consisting of a covered butter dish, a spoon holder, a cream pitcher, and a sugar bowl. The set sold wholesale for the incredible price of 33 cents! It was described as a new design, an "exact reproduction of genuine cut glass, extra heavy, and brilliantly fire-polished." Suggested selling price was 50 cents.

An 11½″ punch bowl, separate stand, and twelve handled cups, identical to my mother's two-piece compote (fig. 424), sold wholesale for 75 cents for the set. In 1910, iridescent 9″ berry bowls with a wavy edge and embossed designs in gold, green, and violet sold for 89 cents a dozen. Isn't it shocking that people will now pay so much for cheap, pressed glass with a mechanically achieved iridescence? Cut glass is worth every cent because it represents years of labor and dedication.

Mother used the fruit compote (fig. 424) as a centerpiece on her dining table. Together with a pair of pressed candlesticks (fig. 426, right), the compote made a fine console set. When lifted off, the top can be used as a large bowl, while the base (whose edge can be seen as a shadow) can serve as a vase.

At a recent show, there was a table lamp with hobstars and other motifs common to cut glass. From a distance, when lighted, it looked like cut glass. It was priced at $350, but would sell for at least $2,200 if it were what it pretended to be. As I stood looking at it and touching it, a customer asked me if I knew whether it was cut. I simply replied, "Close your eyes and touch it." He was learning to discriminate.

Fig. 424. Fruit compote on separate standard, 9″ h × 10″, imitates cut glass motifs. Mold marks (four-part mold) visible on foot and on bowl as ridges through the kites of rounded diamonds.

While examining the photographs of pressed glass, look at the pretty, mold-blown desk or dining table lamp (fig. 425) in "Pineapple and Fan" (or "Shepherd's Plaid"), made by the Model Flint Glass Company in Albany, Indiana, between 1892 and 1901. Later it was made by the Indiana Glass Company in Dunkirk. The plain diamond and fan surface is blunt, and mold marks show, but the color is very good.

Fig. 425. Kerosene lamp, 16½″, 20″ including chimney, in "Pineapple and Fan" or "Shepherd's Plaid". Mold-blown; four seams on base, top, and middle. Silver-plated and brass metal fittings are above oil font.

Fig. 426. *Left to right:* Cut candlestick, 8″, one of a pair (Matye) Pressed candlestick, 8″, one of a pair in same colonial style. Note blunt edges and mold marks. (Author)

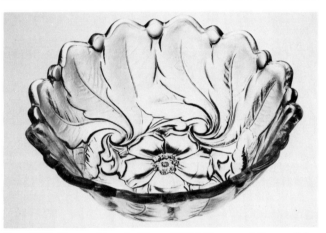

Fig. 427. Pressed bowl, 9″, in "Wild Rose and Leaves" by Indiana Glass Company, circa 1920-1940. (Bert Hilby)

For direct contrast between cut and pressed, examine these candlesticks (fig. 426), which are so similar in design. On the left, the piece has cut notches on the stem and a sharply cut twenty-point hobstar on the foot. The candlestick on the right is attractive, but the glass has a gray cast. Unfortunately, lighting makes the cut stick on the left appear to be darker than the pressed. This is an illusion. The pressed piece has round edges and several bubbles. Mold marks show in the picture.

This inexpensive pressed berry bowl (fig. 427) is shown merely to educate the novice collector. It was made as early as 1920 and sporadically into the 1940s by the Indiana Glass Company, and was sold in department stores for a few cents. The "Wild Rose and Leaves" pattern can now be considered a collector's item, in the same category as Depression Glass. A 1975 price guide listed its value as $5. The absolute beginner might have heard of natural flower forms in glass decoration and might mistake this for engraved ware. Of course, a dealer would know and would price it accordingly, but an individual owner at a house sale might be as ignorant as the buyer. Many people believe they inherited cut glass, when in fact they have ordinary pressed soda-lime glassware.

There is nothing wrong with collecting pressed ware, the glass of the people. Pattern glass made before the Civil War is pressed and valuable. But when paying for cut glass, be sure that you get it. Our best advice to the new collector is to buy only from established dealers who know their merchandise, and who will stand behind their sales. They have a reputation to uphold and will be frank and helpful. Only after having bought from reliable proprietors for some time, and after having observed collections and studied books on the subject can one safely buy at house sales or auctions.

Auctions are especially risky sources from which to purchase cut glass. Catalog descriptions are frequently faulty. Besides, most auction houses now print disclaimers of responsibility in the catalog, such as this actual statement:

> All items are sold "as is" and neither (the name of the house) nor the consigner makes any warranties or representations of any kind with respect to the property, and in no event shall they be responsible for the correctness, genuineness, attribution, condition, or provenance of the property and no statement in the Catalog or made at the Sale or in the Bill of Sale or advertisement shall be deemed such a warranty or representation or an assumption of liability.

I do recommend that you go to auctions while learning. You can see much European glass to compare with American Brilliant ware. Sometimes a collection of the latter is offered from a known estate. Many times, new pieces from Europe are mixed in with the old American. By recording prices, you can verify that a piece you felt was antique was indeed so. New pieces that go for from $45 to $65 would sell for $175 to $225 if from the Brilliant Period.

A modern European cut-and-engraved large, oval fruit bowl sold recently for $65. If it had been from the Brilliant Period, it might have sold for $165 to $185 at the auction and perhaps $235 in a shop. Yet eager buyers bidding against each other may run the price even higher than a shop dealer would charge. It is easy to get carried away and pay more than an item is worth.

Never go in while the sale is in progress and buy without having examined the piece closely, catalog in hand. From a distance, every article looks beautiful under the lights. Jot down in advance the highest figure you will be willing to pay. If you take time during the bidding to think about it, you may lose the piece. A tentative decision on price in advance can prevent panic and a rise in blood pressure.

At an auction, there is always a risk that a piece may be cracked *after* you have examined it. It is nerve-wracking to stand by during the pre-sale period and watch person after person pick up the bowl you desire and set it down carelessly, "dinging" it against a neighboring teapot. Take one last careful look just before you're asked to take a seat.

The other source for collectors is the private home. Many estate or house sales are now managed by professionals; some have an officer stationed outside the door, giving out numbers, admitting only a few customers at a time. Usually the finest cut glass has been kept by the family or sold before the general public is admitted at prices as high as those in a store. Mediocre pieces are often overpriced. If, however, the family holds the sale, the seller may have already approached a dealer, only to find that his offer is low, and so has decided to keep the cut glass in the house sale. In this case, the collector may make a "good buy," provided he can get to the coveted piece in time.

If the glass is priced high by a professional manager, leave a reasonable bid. You may be surprised by a call saying you can have it at your price.

Best of all is the rare instance when the collector hears of an elderly person who is disposing of treasures, or of another collector who has decided to sell duplicates or to upgrade his collection. The buyer is under no pressure to make a quick decision. He gladly pays more than a dealer can afford to pay, and less than a dealer must charge.

19

Why and How to Build a Collection

The ideal time to choose a category of antiques to collect is before society at large has discovered its desirability. In the 1930s, one could buy oak furniture in secondhand stores for "a song." A dresser may have cost $12; a rolltop desk, $25. Now the same dresser may be priced at $200 and the desk at $500 or more.

Only recently have collectors become interested in Art Nouveau items. Even more recently, Art Deco has become popular. We bought a Handel pictorial lamp, made circa 1912, for $110 in 1966. In 1984 it was worth at least $500.

Vogue magazine in March 1979, page 124, made an interesting observation concerning cut glass: "Fifteen years ago, serious auction houses wouldn't even sell cut glass. Now the demand is enormous, and prices only go up ... To determine current market value, multiply the original price thirty times."

In 1948, Samuel Hawkes estimated that a 9″ berry bowl, comparable to those of the Brilliant Period, would cost $100 to produce. In 1958, a signed Libbey bowl could be bought for $12. In 1968, when the theoretical cost of production had risen to $200, such a bowl could still be bought for $48. The same bowl in 1978 may have been priced at $175 to $250, depending upon where it was found. In 1985 it may have been marked $285 to $350.

A friend's cookie jar, bought from a dealer (who charged reasonable prices) for $190 in 1971, was sold to a collector for $460 in 1975. In 1985 it would probably bring $750 to $850.

In 1973, I saw at an antique show a beautiful, tall table lamp with silver base, with the dome cut in a circle of hobstars and Harvard. The price, $1,995, seemed shocking then. When I expressed surprise, the dealer explained that she had sold this and two others at $500 each to a doctor and his wife in 1970. The wife died. Three years later, this dealer had to pay $1,475 apiece at auction to get them back — nearly triple her selling price.

In 1979, a lamp of comparable value went for $3,000 from one collector to another. A dealer would have asked $3,500.

Prices continue to rise on the finest glass simply because people crave beautiful objects that can never be reproduced.

The United States Customs Service now considers an object to be antique if it was made one hundred years before purchase. The standard used to be 1830 or older, because the invention of machines generally displaced hand labor from that date. Although only some of our glassware is one hundred years old, the handcrafting of the rest does place it in the antique category, according to some authorities. Any art object that can never be reproduced may be called antique. Such items as Depression Glass, even though made shortly after cut and engraved glass of the Brilliant Period, is considered collectible because it was machine-made and was cheap at its inception.

It is wise to compare prices, for dealers from certain sections of the country can charge and get more than others. Some dealers add a set mark-up to the purchase price, regardless of market value. Most will offer to buy at from 35 to 65 percent of the retail value, hoping to double their investment on the average. Some may take a piece on consignment, making 20 to 50 percent profit, since their money is not tied up while the glass remains in the shop as when an outright purchase is made.

In the case of one dealer noted for high prices, a piece priced at $550 by another merchant was bought for $500 with the courtesy discount. He immediately repriced it at $1,200! Whether it sold at this price is unknown. Even if he lowered it to $1,000, he would have made a large profit.

Most dealers are not greedy. They love the merchandise they handle and probably started as collectors. They are happy to make a fair profit in order to repeat the cycle of finding more merchandise to sell. In addition to the usual expenses of rent, utilities, freight costs, storage, and taxes, money is spent for travel — locally or even across the country — in search of worthy items for stock.

Attend shows and auctions, visit shops, and learn the current prices. Take notes for reference. Memory cannot be relied upon here.

Published price guides are useful, but due to lack of space for detailed descriptions and photographs, most guides present brief descriptions that are difficult to visualize. The quality is impossible to verify. Guides tied directly to illustrations in a book are much more helpful. If accumulated over a long period of time, the prices may be obsolete by the date of publication. Use price guides as one criterion only — not as a final judgment.

In any case, buy the best and most unusual pieces you can afford, because these are the ones you can always sell if you need to do so. At first, Earle and I bought largely from a dealer in this area whose prices seemed high at the time. We complained to each other, but kept going back because she had the finest glass. She was about two years ahead of others as far as prices were concerned, or so it seemed. Looking back, her prices were modest by comparison with those of today. More important, we obtained the fine pieces when they were available.

Advanced collectors are never interested in ordinary items; the uninitiated think the lowest price is high. Two or three years after purchase of a good item, you can probably get your money back from a dealer, and you can make a profit when selling to another collector by asking less than a dealer has to charge. If the collector wants your piece badly, he may pay you full retail price, happy to find this unique or scarce item. You must make at least some profit to reimburse insurance costs and money lost by being idle for months or years. Collectors often upgrade their collections or sell a piece similar to another one in order to buy something different.

Friends have asked, "What if we have a depression?" Granted, buyers would be harder to find, but some people are so well off that they would hardly feel the economic pressures. One might have to hold the glass longer, but the value would still be there. The desire for precious art objects no longer being made increases with the years.

The Ones that Got Away

Sometimes he who hesitates is indeed lost. We were so used to deciding jointly on any large purchase that we literally lost a chance in a lifetime. While I was in France in 1968, Earle was offered a pair of Russian candelabra for $325. He waited for my return, not realizing how scarce they are. They were sold immediately, of course. Who knows what they would sell for now? Perhaps $2,500?

In Chapter 14 on Libbey glass, an incident was related in which we foolishly passed by eight cups in "Star and Feather" because the pattern was different from the more common miter-cut ware. Another error of omission in the early days of collecting (1967) was to hesitate to buy a rectangular ice cream tray and eight matching individual dishes for $200. A dealer bought the set, took it to a show, and sold it for $400 while we were making up our minds.

We also turned down an enormous floor vase in cobalt blue made by Hawkes about 1921 for a hotel in California. We first saw it in that state for $625, then later in Washington for $725. Samuel Hawkes had engraved his signature on the bottom. I wanted to buy it for its historical value, but Earle was not satisfied with the simple cutting around the top. Live and learn!

The largest "boat" we missed was the Hawkes punch bowl with wide sterling silver rim by Gorham and twenty cups, made in 1912 as a special order for John Jacob Astor IV. In December 1969, the set was advertised by a Texas dealer. We sent for a polaroid picture and saw that this 24″ bowl was truly fabulous. It had been purchased from the Gorham Silver Company by an unnamed gentleman when Mrs. Astor failed to pick it up after her husband drowned. Owned by this family until 1969, the daughter, then in her eighties, sold it to the Texas dealer. Best of all, it had never appeared in any book. The price was $4,700. This would have been the central attraction of our proposed museum. We considered the purchase for three days, then regretfully declined.

Types of Collections

There are many ways of pursuing glass collecting. Since it is rather expensive, it would be wise to consider several before going very far. One may collect one category of item, made of different materials. Imagine a lone cut or engraved glass specimen among a group of different types of art glass in any kind of item: barber bottles or cruets, for example. Hair receivers have been made of pottery, porcelain, pressed glass, cut blown glass, silver, and other materials. Whatever you decide, you may usually place one of cut glass among the others.

Ways to Build a Collection

Unless money and space are limitless, it is wise to consider in advance several avenues to a purposeful collection.

All Glassware of One Pattern

By collecting only one pattern, such as "Star and Feather" by Libbey or "Brunswick" by Hawkes, one could conceivably assemble a complete service. You can rarely discover all components of an original set of cutware at once. As an example of the many items sold as a set, a No. 40 Cocktail Set in "Savoy" was listed in a 1904-1905 catalog of J. D. Bergen.

Fig. 428. *Left to right:* Jug, 6¾″, for cereal cream or invalid's tray. Holds a pint. Base rayed; handle double-notched. Carafe, 7¼″ h × 6¼″, cut like jug.

Fig. 429. Bowl, 9″ × 4″, has unusual gallery. Engraved matte lines define links of a chain of alternating hobstars and triangles of hobnail (Gerritse)

Fig. 430. Nappy, 11½″ including handles, matches bowl (fig. 429). Note crosshatching on thumb rests. (Gerritse)

1 No. 585	1 quart Decanter	$13.75
1 No. 583	1 pint Decanter	9.40
1 No. 631	½ pint Bitters Bottle,	
	Sil. Pl. Spout	8.15
1 No. 858	1 pint Mixing Tumbler	5.00
6 No. 939	Cocktail Glasses	15.00
1 No. 2004	16-inch Mirror Tray	10.00
		$73.80

All of these accoutrements for drinking were placed on the mirrored tray. One can see how unlikely it would be to find the entire set intact. (Decanters and jugs were usually described by their capacity, rather than by height as we do now.)

It was a pleasant surprise to find a small jug to match the carafe (fig. 428) four years apart. The small size of the pitcher is uncommon. For this reason, it was priced higher than the novice collector would expect.

The bowl and large nappy (figs. 429 and 430) make dramatic use of a band of crosscut diamonds in contrast with an unusual border.

Fig. 431. Jug, 8¼″, in Meriden's "Albany," unsigned as usual. Entire bottom covered by a thirty-two-point hobstar; lip fluted; handle triple-notched. Beading has a row of fine cuts, then two prisms cut in a short and a long. Tumblers, 4″, flair and become thin at top — a perfect complement to the jug, which widens at the base. Tumblers' beading is a row of short notches, then a row of three shorts and a long. Bottoms rayed.

Fig. 432. Sugar and cream set, 3″, cut in flute and notched prism or beading. Bottoms rayed; handles single-notched.

Closely Related Patterns

It is also pleasant to assemble closely related designs. Some patterns were cut by many, and some in several variations: Harvard, Strawberry Diamond and Fan, and Russian, for example. The following four photographs show pieces in Prism, or in Bullseye and Prism, which are attractive.

The jug (fig. 431) is like the catalog illustration of Meriden's "Albany." The quality and color are certainly up to Meriden's standard. The tumblers have a different beading but complement the shape of the jug. They are of superbly clear glass with paperweight bottoms. We first bought a Fry pitcher in notched prism to go with the tumblers, but it looked too heavy.

J. D. Bergen used the notched prism in many patterns. It was combined with Bullseye in "Florida" (1904-1905 catalog). Pairpoint patented Punty and Prism patterns in 1898 and 1901, and L. Straus & Sons in 1898. These dates are mentioned to dispel the illusion that these less-expensive-to-cut designs were introduced late in the period.

The mayonnaise bowl with plate cut on heavy blanks (fig. 338) in Chapter 16 also shows Meriden's version of Bullseye and Prism.

The cream and sugar set (fig. 432), inherited from Mother Swan, had constant use. It was cut on heavy blanks. The lip on the cream jug was nicked. We had it smoothed by a professional.

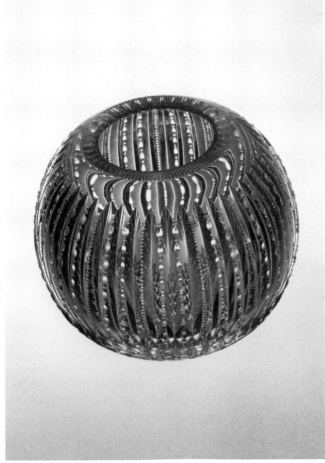

Fig. 433. Rose globe, 5¾″ h × 7″, cut in notched vertical prism: two prisms in a long, then a short notch; one in fine beading. Top edge has parallel cuts; base covered by a twenty-four-point hobstar.

Fig. 434. Wine decanter, 15″, circa 1904-1912. Fine lapidary stopper, eight-point hobstars on opposite sides, two radiant stars on alternate sides, thickened base. Bottle is less closely cut than some, but shows wine's color to advantage. Wine goblets, 4″.

The rose globe (fig. 433) with a hobstar on the base has beading to match the pitcher (fig. 431), but no bullseyes. The "bent" prisms at the top are an optical illusion.

All of the above items look well together. Slight differences simply break the monotony of identical designs.

Combining Compatible Patterns

The next choice is to combine compatible patterns. The cone-shaped wine decanter and wine goblets (fig. 434) do not match, yet are attractive together.

Among the six punch bowls in the collection, only two have matching cups. With three, we have placed cups with compatible designs. It is thrilling to find matching cups with a bowl, but it seldom happens. Incidently, punch cups were often called "lemonades." Some were without handles and had underplates; some, with or without handles, were footed.

Cabinet Pieces

If you have limited display space, cabinet pieces are an excellent choice.

Collecting Small Objects

With limited display space and/or money to spend, one can collect one each of many small objects, representing many patterns and makers. Here are five items (fig. 435) suitable for display in a small area. The butter pat is well cut. The miniature cruet may have been one of a set of individual oil cruets or a salesman's sample, but was more likely blown as a *whimsey* (or *friggar*) from the remains of a batch of glass. Perhaps the blower made this tiny cruet, then passed it to a friend in the cutting department to finish as a gift for the gaffer's wife or sweetheart. The hatpin holder cut in a prism pattern has a solid bottom and a central hole on top encircled by five holes for hatpins. Some American

Fig. 435. *Left to right:* Butter pat or butterette, 2⅛″, nicely cut on a clear blank. To the touch, it feels oily or slick — a sign of acid polishing. Miniature cruet or whimsey, 5″. Stopper has a tiny teardrop and some sharp diamond cutting to match bottle. Below are engraved leaves and flowers. Hatpin holder, 5″; columns of notched prisms varied by crosscutting long notches every other row. Cordial, 3¾″. Although bowl is simply cut, lapidary knop has a teardrop. Individual toothpick holder, 2″, decorated only with vertical and horizontal prisms.

Fig. 436. *Left to right:* Smelling salts, 2¾″, with inner glass stopper, ground to fit opening, and lift-off silverplated top, is cut in bullseyes and miter, similar to a Bergen salt shaker. Wine, 5″, with oval thumbprints on a textured blank. Stem in six panels has teardrop. Sample compote, 4⅛″, is a rarity. Call bell, 4″. Clapper is a brass ring on a chain. (All from Matye)

holders looked like a slender bud vase or toothbrush holder with a wider foot, except for the closed top with holes. The dainty cordial suggests that a collection of different cordials would be pleasing. The toothpick holder came with three others, proving that it was meant for the individual place setting. In the days before dental floss, toothpicks were thought to be a necessity.

This group (fig. 436) includes a smelling salts container, a wine glass, a miniature compote (a rare salesman's sample), and a tea or call bell.

These pieces (fig. 437) are a tiny cordial in Libbey's "Harvard," a napkin ring, match and toothpick holders on heavy bases, (resembling those in a Pitkin & Brooks catalog of 1904), and a shot glass. The latter is a sharply cut example of early (circa 1880) Strawberry

Fig. 437. *Left to right* Cordial, 3¼″, in Libbey's "Harvard." Teardrop goes through knop and stem to rayed foot. Napkin ring, 2¼″, by Empire. Match holder, 3″, probably an import with paperweight base. Toothpick holder, 2¼″, matches match holder. Whiskey double shot, 2¾″, in "Strawberry Diamond and Fan," has rayed base. Fine quality.

Fig. 438. Set of nut dishes, 2½″ × ⅞″, in crosscut diamond on bottom, sharp relief diamond on sides, and fans on corners. Miniature bowl or salesman's sample, 4″. Very thin, but well cut, with flashed hobstar in center.

Diamond and Fan made by many houses, such as New England and Mount Washington. It was also cut in red, green, and yellow cut-to-clear.

The nut dishes (fig. 438) are in a design typical of the 1880s. Menus often called for almonds. The miniature bowl must be a salesman's sample. It is too thin to be a toy, or even a pin dish.

The individual nut dish (fig. 439), upper left; the master salt below; and the two butter chips on the right are all of fine quality.

Objects in Different Patterns

For collectors with limited space, toothpick holders (fig. 440) are practical and available. Some were imported, but many were produced here. The middle holder is an import. It feels less sharp to the touch.

Knife rests (fig. 441) came in many shapes, sizes, and cuttings. Prices are rising rapidly.

Master salts (fig. 442) were passed with a tiny spoon for sprinkling food. Or, a master salt was used to put salt into the small individual salt dishes, or "dips," at each place setting. The spoons are also collectible.

Three sets of salt dips in contrasting shapes are shown with a paperweight-stamp moistener (fig. 443). The former are useful today for celery and carrot strips.

The first patent for a salt shaker (fig. 444) was issued 15 September 1863. Shakers were made of many materials, including silverplate and sterling, pewter, glass with silver deposit, ceramic, colored art glass, and pressed and cut colorless glass. There is great variety among shakers in cut glass. Bargains can still be found in the plainer ones, so feel free to use them. Elaborate shakers in good condition are scarce.

Cream and sugar sets are found in many shapes and sizes. Several have been shown here, but none are more charming than this small individual cream and sugar (fig. 445) cut by Egginton.

Fig. 439. *Left to right:* Individual almond dish, 4″. (Nash) Master salt, 3″, wood-polished. Two butterettes, 3″, cut in crossed ovals, eight-point hobstars, and clear pentagons.

Fig. 440. Toothpick holders. *Left to right:* American, 2⅝″, with flared top and wide rayed base is cut in punties, fans, and stars. Imported, 2″, shown in 1899 Higgins & Seiter catalog, p. 53, at 30¢ each. American, 2¼″, cut in honeycomb panels and beading.

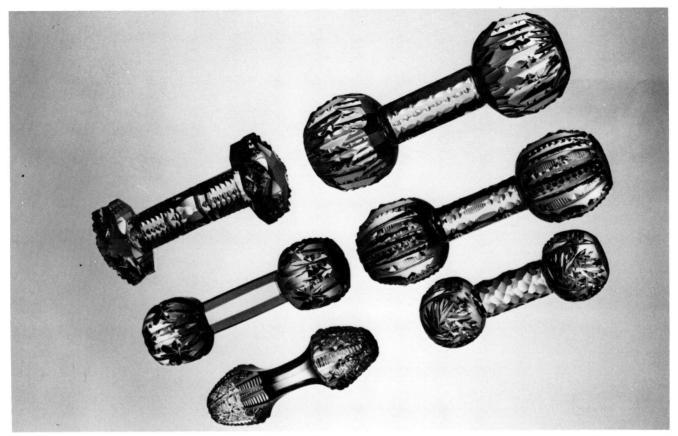

Fig. 441. Knife rests, 4″ to 5¼″, were cut in many designs. The small rest with scooped shank has complex ends. The other small rest with honeycomb shank has two pinwheels on each end. (All from Matye)

Fig. 442. *Top Row, left and right:* Heavy master salts, 1¾″h x 2¾″, in Dorflinger's "Renaissance," advertised in 1893. *Top row, center:* Lighter master salt with beaded prisms. *Lower row, left and right:* Identical oval tubs with tabs and underplates, cut in cane with clear buttons. *Center:* European, set in a Russian enamel metal frame decorated in red, white, turquoise, dark blue, and green enamels. (All from Matye)

Fig. 443. *Top to bottom, left to right:* Round salt dips, 1½″, the smallest we have seen. Paperweight-stamp moistener in Dorflinger's "Middlesex" can serve as a master salt. Cavity smaller than those in fig. 442; seems to have been made to hold a sponge for wetting stamps. Inverted: a beautiful paperweight (fig. 288). These dips have notched and plain prisms on sides, and sharp relief diamond on bottom. Oval salt dips have lapidary sides and single stars on bottom. This shape was also made in pressed.

Fig. 444. Five salt and pepper sets. *Left to right:* Pair, ¾″, in honeycomb and beading with sterling tops marked "RW, a moose head with antlers, & STERLING 761," signifying R. Wallace & Sons Mfg. Co., Wallingford, Connecticut. Pair, 3″, with bowknots and flutes, pewter tops with mother-of-pearl insertions. Pair, 5¼″, cut in zigzag prisms; glass tops; imported? Pair, 2¼″, cut in vertical prism; nickel tops. Pair, 2½″, has flute divided midway by X-cut, making bowknot effect; glass tops.

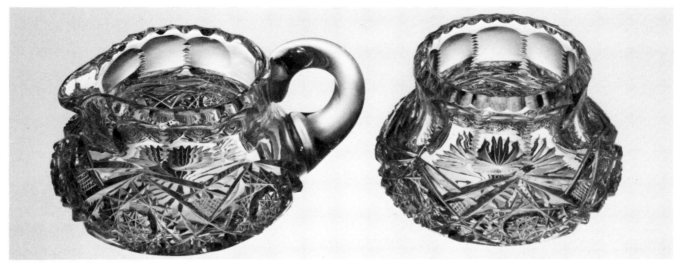

Fig. 445. Individual cream and sugar, 2½″, has chain of hobstars around each bowl. Cut by Egginton. (Rice)

Fig. 446. Ice cream saucers, 5″. *Left to right:* Irving's "Rose Combination." Blank is second rate, "grainy" and "wavy." In 1916 and later, good blanks were hard to find. (Author) Intaglio "Iris" signed with Hawkes trefoil. Open blossom partially hidden; buds clearly shown. (Matye)

Every collector desires an ice cream tray and matching saucers. These are scarce and expensive. Sets also require more space for display. It is not difficult, however, to find an occasional saucer, so why not collect one of a kind and enjoy a variety of patterns?

These ice cream saucers (fig. 446) exemplify the transition from geometric to floral cutting in well-known designs by Irving and Hawkes. They are "Rose Combination" ("White Rose" combined with cane) and "Iris," respectively. Hawkes did engrave a more finely delineated Iris with long engraved leaves and small flowers, artistically filling the large areas between the irises. This was signed HAWKES GRAVIC. Hawkes claimed that every piece was signed.

The next saucers (fig. 447) for berries or ice cream contrast nicely. On the left is a Cluster pattern called "Athole" by Pitkin & Brooks. On the right is a Star signed Libbey/saber.

A Hawkes ice cream saucer and a rectangular bonbon (fig. 448) offer contrast in design and quality. The saucer, whose "color is the perfect pellucid white so highly prized," as stated in an advertisement extolling Hawkes's products, is of the highest quality. The superficially attractive bonbon is a late piece, quickly made to save expense. It has been cut on a figured blank. The inner surface dips in slightly at each button of the Harvard cutting, showing that the pattern was "roughed in" on the mold. When held up to the light, the clear partitions on the sides with Buzz and Cane look wavy and muddled. In addition, the cane is not sharp and the Harvard buttons are not symmetrical.

This serving dish or nappy (fig. 449) is deeply cut in an interesting pattern. Examine it carefully.

Many cabinets have a groove at the back of each shelf. A row of dessert plates could thus be used with smaller cabinet pieces. Several have been shown elsewhere in this volume.

Fig. 447. Berry or ice cream saucers. *Left to right:* Larger than usual, 6″; unusual cluster in P&B's "Athole" (catalog). Fine, brilliant pattern. Signed Libbey/saber, 5″, has five-point star with wide and narrow mitered petals and small hobstars between points. (Both from Matye)

Fig. 448. *Left to right:* Ice cream saucer, 5″, signed Hawkes; excellent. Rectangular bonbon, 4″ × 7″, 2½″ deep. Unusual shape and design on a poor blank. (Both from Frazer)

Fig. 449, Nappy, 7″. Large central hobstar is unusual in that its twenty points are cut in silver diamond. Chains of silver diamond lozenges have split ends, almost to the middle.

Fig. 450. Punch cups, all handles plain. *Center:* Cluster and vesica, signed J. Hoare. *Top, then clockwise:* Pinwheel with zigzag star center. Bottom fully cut; three hobstars above a fan alternate with acute angle cuts and tiny fans above small zigzag star. In J. D. Bergen's "Electric," a chain of double fans alternates with star of four overlapping triangles. "Korea," signed P&B, has border chain of hobstars and a stylized matte engraved blossom (patented) on bottom. Bottom fully cut in hobstar in a square; each of four vesicas outlined by two miter cuts; only one prism thus formed is beaded.

Frequently, one to three tumblers or cups are for sale. Usually they are priced lower than if in a set. Buy one and add it to your group. Setting the table with a different tumbler at each place, or serving punch in assorted cups, can certainly stimulate conversation.

All but one of these punch cups or lemonades (fig. 450) has been taken from one of our sets.

The following tumblers may have been shown in sets; some have not.

Three tumblers (fig. 451), signed Libbey, are cut in contrasting styles.

Of these tumblers (fig. 452), one is Libbey, and two are unidentified.

Four tumblers (fig. 453), include a less expensive one with a simple design, two signed Libbey, and one called a "champagne tumbler" in one catalog.

Of these four (fig. 454), the first is O'Connor's "Princess," patented 19 February 1895 by Arthur E. O'Connor for the John S. O'Connor shop at Hawley, Pennsylvania. Revi says that it was a production item in their Goshen, New York, shop, also. Pearson calls the pattern "Split Square." the next is signed Libbey/saber. The third is Straus's "Drape". And the fourth is from the Middle Period, believed to be early Dorflinger.

Fig. 451. Tumblers. *Left to right:* Signed Libbey/circle; panels of notched prism, hobstars, and fans. Libbey/saber, "Star and Feather." Libbey/circle, "Cut #209"; kite of sharp relief diamond, feathered thumbprints like flowers, and cuts resembling stems and leaves.

Fig. 452. Tumblers. *Left to right:* Libbey/circle, "Anita"; hobstar and beading, resembling blossoms and long leaves. Notched prism design, paperweight bottom, clearest glass. Blazed single star with hobstars and sections of both silver and crosscut diamond.

Fig. 453. Tumblers. *Left to right:* Simple cutting, zigzag stars and fans. Libbey/saber, "#47." Libbey/saber; "Senora" has two deeply cut hobstars and notched horizontal prisms. Unusual flared edge; cut in three large hobstars separated by two vertical beaded prisms. This shape labeled Champagne Tumbler in one catalog.

Fig. 454. Tumblers. *Left to right:* O'Connor's "Princess" (1895), hand-polished on wooden wheel; crosscut diamond, fans, and split squares of silver diamond. Libbey/saber, heavy; X-cut notched prisms resemble one motif in "Spillane," #38002, 8 May 1906. Unsigned Straus "Drape." Polished pontil on bottom, punties around base, simple engraving, probably early Dorflinger.

Fig. 455. Tumblers. *Left to right:* J. Hoare's "Mikado," or "Abbott" after its designer, 4″; large pyramidal star and checkered diamond; bottom cut in an eight-point flashed star with pyramidal center. Highball, 5″, cut in pinwheel, fan, and kite of silver diamond; rayed base — a less complex cutting on a fine, heavy blank. (Rolland) Clark's "Prima Donna", or "Triple Square" (named for motif between hobstars, also fitted into squares); 4″, a twenty-four-point hobstar covers base. (Rolland) "Electra" (called "Ulysses" by Revi) by Herman Siegel for Straus in 1890. Base rayed; vertical cuts under hobstar.

Fig. 456. Highball tumblers, 5″ h, 2⅝″ at top, in "Queens," signed HAWKES below trefoil; an inch taller, and slimmer than water tumblers, which are often 3″ wide at top.

The first of four tumblers (fig. 455) is the "Mikado" by Hoare, patented 15 February 1887. The designer, George L. Abbott, was Hoare's first partner after he came to Corning. This tumbler and the fourth, in Straus's "Electra" (1893 catalog, called "Ulysses" by Revi), came from the home of a prominent politician who was once mayor of Minneapolis. His granddaughter recalls his sumptuous mansion. The second is a

highball tumbler, which is taller and narrower than a water tumbler. The third, heavy and ornate, is cut in Clark's "Prima Donna."

The two highball tumblers (fig. 456) in "Queens," signed HAWKES, were found too late to place in the chapter on Hawkes glassware. They are an inch taller than water tumblers and an inch shorter than iced tea glasses.

Fig. 457. *Left to right:* Saucer champagne, 4″ × 4″, has family name engraved on one vesica. Note unusual stem in broken flute (offset). Water goblet, 6½″ × 3½″, has all-over hobstars, with lapidary knop low in the stem; unusual hobstar underfoot; came from Iorio collection. Excellent quality. Wine goblet, 5″, Libbey/circle; teardrop at base of stem. (All from Gerritse)

The tumbler was originally a drinking vessel with straight sides and rounded bottom, without footing or stem. It did not stand upright, but was served full of liquor to be drunk at one draught. The tumbler was then put down on the table, bottom side up. Today any vessel without foot or stem is called a tumbler.

One might collect different types of stemware, such as champagnes (which are scarce), water goblets, or wines, or many patterns in one category. Whole suites of wine glasses were sold to those who served a different wine with each course, but these are rarely found intact. They included saucer champagnes, clarets for red wine, wines for white wine, cocktails, crème de menthe, sherries, and cordials. It would be interesting to find one of each in the same pattern, or even of different designs to illustrate size and shape.

These three — a saucer champagne, a water goblet, and a wine — show widely diversified cutting (fig. 457). The wine is signed Libbey.

Sherbets are hard to find. They were perfect for serving homemade sherbet, pudding, gelatin dessert, or ice cream. On the left (fig. 458) is a variation of Libbey's "Sultana." On the right is a pinwheel pattern by Hoare. Both are heavy and cut nicely. Very large sherbets were called supremes.

Small covered boxes are attractive. These two (figs. 459 and 460) exemplify well-known patterns: "Comet" and "Florence Star." Many came with a powder puff. In cut glass, they were fitted with matching cut glass or sterling silver lids. Cheaper pressed boxes usually had plated lids. Powder boxes were also made of pottery,

Fig. 458. Sherbets: *Left to right:* Unsigned Libbey, 3½″, in a variation of "Sultana," patented 15 January 1901 by William Marrett. Only the contents of the "fill-in" sections differ from registered drawing. This one substitutes hobnail for silver diamond; fans are not flashed, but were in the drawing. Unsigned Hoare. Pinwheels alternate with stars boxed by cuts and small triangles of fine silver diamond.

porcelain, art glass (such as pink satin), and metals, including silverplate, but the majority were in pressed or cut crystal. Matching puff boxes and hair receivers are worth seeking.

Broaden your collection to include ointment, rouge, patch, and sachet jars, as well as hair receivers. (A patch or beauty mark was a small piece of black silk or court plaster stuck on the face or neck to hide a defect or to heighten beauty.) Use these jars in bedroom or bath to hold cotton balls, bobby pins, spools of thread, aspirin tablets — sundries of many kinds.

Fig. 459. Puff box, 4¼″ d × 3″ h, circa 1910, in a Comet pattern that uses fine silver diamond in the flashing lights that swirl around a central hobstar, left gray for contrast. (Matye)

Fig. 460. Puff box, 4¼″ d × 3″ h, cut on top in a "Florence" variation; central button in high relief. The original "Florence" flashed hobstar with silver diamond points, #190053, was patented 23 April 1889 by Wm. C. Anderson, assignor to Edward D. Libbey; it was named for Libbey's wife. (Matye)

One could conceivably collect syrup jugs (fig. 461), although they are not plentiful. The one on the left has no lid. The jug on the right has a silverplated top and handle, similar to the Hawkes jug shown earlier (fig. 97).

Cruets are more plentiful. They came in a variety of shapes and were used for vinegar and oil, served separately at the table. Their stoppers had a longer neck than did the cologne bottles.

The first cruet (fig. 462) is simply cut, but of good glass.

The next (fig. 463), with step cutting on the neck, an engraved flower, and pointed stopper, is more ornate.

These three cruets (fig. 464) are all cone-shaped with wide bottoms and lapidary stoppers. The first two are signed by Pitkin & Brooks; the third by Sinclaire.

The next three (fig. 465) have triple pouring lips and lapidary stoppers.

Perfume and cologne bottles (fig. 466) are attractive and are still not exorbitant in price. These two are in Hawkes's "Brunswick" (signed) and Hoare's "Pluto" (unsigned). Several other examples were shown previously in this volume.

"Toilet water" (from *eau de toilette* in French) was an important amenity in the day when clothing was incredibly complex and difficult to clean. A great many such bottles were sold.

Fig. 461. Syrup jugs. *Left to right:* Jug, 6″, has a heavy bottom, so is not easily tipped over. Jug is cut in alternate columns of two rows of beading, followed by lozenges of silver diamond (English strawberry diamond) and zigzag stars. Base rayed. Jug, 4¼″, with silver-plated top and handle is cut in American strawberry diamond and fan (crosscut diamond). Resembles an egg-shaped sugar shaker, circa 1885, by Mt. Washington.

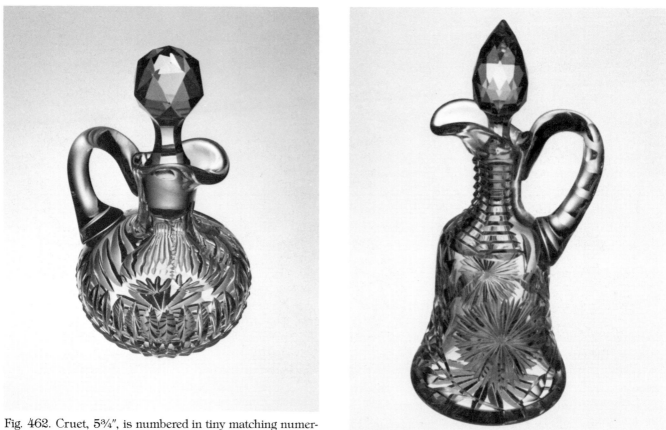

Fig. 462. Cruet, 5¾″, is numbered in tiny matching numerals scratched on stopper and neck, proving that stopper is original.

Fig. 463. Cruet, 8″. Handle is double-notched; base rayed.

Fig. 464. Cone-shaped cruets. *Left to right:* Signed P&B, 7¾"; single-notched handle; stopper not original, but could be ground to fit. Signed P&B, 6"; hobstar, bullseye, and miter cuts; a honeycomb neck and double-notched handle. Signed Sinclaire, 7½"; cut in notched vertical prism and English strawberry diamond; handle single-notched (All from Matye)

Fig. 465. Cruets with triple pouring spouts. *Left to right:* Flashed single stars and fans, 5½". Four eight-point hobstars with starred buttons; double-notched handle, 5½". Decorated by vertical beading only; good blank; triple-notched handle, 6". (All from Matye)

Fig. 466. Cologne bottles. *Left to right:* Stopper and bottle, 6″, in "Brunswick" signed Hawkes. Base rayed. In this variation of Hoare's "Pluto", 6¼″, a chain of stars encircles base; prisms go around middle. Lapidary stopper numbered to match bottle.

Fig. 467. Center vase, 5½″ h × 6¼″, small in scale, cut in honeycomb neck and top. Base rayed. Five hobstars around sides alternate with crossed ellipses.

Fig. 468. *Left to right:* Relish dish, 7″ × 2″, trefoil shape; three compartments; signed Libbey/saber. Triangular bonbon, 6½″. (Both from Matye)

A collection of finger bowls or small vases would also be feasible for the cabinet. This center vase (fig. 467) is small enough to place in a cabinet, or to use on a small apartment dining table. Vases in this shape were made in various sizes. Some were massive. (See fig. 22, Chap. 6.)

Nappies with Unusual Shapes, Compartments, or Handles

Dishes of unusual form are sought by collectors to add interest to their display.

The relish dish (fig. 468) with three compartments is signed Libbey/saber; the triangular bonbon is also extraordinary. Both are of high quality.

Try to find one leaf-shaped nappy (fig. 469). We have not seen two alike.

This square bonbon (fig. 470) in "Broadway," found in the G. W. Huntly 1913 catalog, adds interest to a collection.

The club and heart saucers (fig. 471) are doubtless remnants of two sets that were sold in silk-lined boxes as prizes for bridge clubs. A card table set for serving ice cream consisted of four nappies: heart, club, spade, and diamond. The set was often purchased with matching oblong tray for serving ice cream, and a 9″ or 10″ plate for serving cake or cookies. Dorothy Daniel reported that a card table set in the "Corinthian"

Fig. 469. Bonbon, nut, or olive nappy, 7″×5¼″, shaped like a leaf, clear fluted "stem" making a handle; overlapping miter-cut ovals. (Matye)

Fig. 470. Square bonbon, 7″, in "Broadway," listed in G. W. Huntley's 1913 catalog. (P&B had a similar pattern with added hobstars; J. D. Bergen's "Golf" is nearly identical.) (Hilby's Antiques)

Fig. 471. *Left to right:* Club saucer or bonbon, 5″×3¾″, cut in "Corinthian" adjusted to clover or club shape, faintly signed Libbey/saber. Heart saucer or bonbon, 5½″.

Fig. 472. Handled nappies, 5″, without handles. *Left to right:* Libbey/circle circa 1907 in "Iola." Hawkes wreath and tassel engraving in "Empire," signed. Matches 7″ dessert plate (fig. 321).

Fig. 473. Relish dish, 9″ without double-notched handles. Cut in flowers with centers of tiny hobnail; blossoms around edge made of fine diamond and splits; miter leaves and stems. A hobstar is on bottom center.

Fig. 474. Footed nappy, 6″ d, 9½″ with handles, 3⅝″ h. Pattern similar to J. D. Bergen's "Golf." (Serres)

pattern by Libbey, cut on fine blanks, was in fact the first of its kind to be sold as a unit. Heart-shaped nappies, however, were also sold separately as gifts on Valentine's Day and for birthdays and wedding anniversaries. This club nappy in "Corinthian" is signed Libbey/saber.

These signed nappies with handles (fig. 472) are of finest quality. On the left by Libbey is "Iola"; on the right by Hawkes is "Empire."

The large relish dish or nappy (fig. 473) with four compartments and two handles is cut on a good, heavy blank. It is a transitional piece of high quality circa 1907-1912. A sectional nappy with two handles was called a "cabaret."

Footed Nappies and Compotes

About 1905, footed pieces, even celeries and banana bowls, were a fad. The next two items (figs. 474 and 475) are good examples of this trend. The first footed nappy with two handles is clear and heavy — one of the better pinwheel cuttings after 1900. The second is also cut on a fine, heavy blank.

This miniature compote (fig. 476) is perfect for serving honey. It is heavy for its size and does not rise with the spoon during service. It rings like a bell when tapped. It can also be used for bonbons, paté, or cheese spread. A fine cabinet piece, it was probably cut by Tuthill.

A compote (fig. 477) for serving jelly, jam, or candy makes a good beginning if one wishes to specialize in compotes. They range from cabinet pieces to large. dramatic specimens.

Fig. 475. Footed nappy, 5″ w with handles, 3½″ h, cut in a chain of hobstars. Foot has a hobstar — a sign of quality. (Rice)

Fig. 476. Miniature compote, 5″ × 2″, has engraving (satin flowers, polished leaves) on bowl and underfoot. Petals textured; centers cut in finest silver diamond ever seen. Tuthill?

Larger Pieces, Sets, and Baskets

Sets of water jugs and tumblers, decanters and wines, ice cream trays and saucers, and especially punch bowls and cups require more display space. Even some fruit compotes are too large for a cabinet. Fruit, berry, and banana bowls (usually called "oval bowls" in catalogs) came in every design, usually 8″ to 10″ in diameter. They quickly fill a shelf.

A collection of wine decanters and/or whiskey bottles would make a varied display. Many shapes have been shown here.

The word "decanter" was derived from the Latin, *de* (from) plus *canthus* (spout or rim of a vessel). It first had an alchemical sense: to pour off from a precipitate so as not to disturb the sediment. It now refers to an ornamental glass bottle for holding and serving wine, brandy, or the like.

Another costly, but worthwhile, collection could consist of jars, such as cracker jars, tobacco humidors, and jars for cherries, caviar, pickles, or horseradish.

Vases came in all sizes and can be placed in every room. We have shown many, from tiny violet globes and bud vases to some 18″ high.

Baskets are scarce, probably because handles have been broken. Small baskets were used for bonbons. Large ones held fruit or flowers, often as a table centerpiece, and were classified as "vases."

Here are two lovely bonbon baskets (fig. 478), small enough for the cabinet. The one with the twisted handle resembles a signed Clark bowl and the Straus version of "Corinthian." The other has been positively identified as Tuthill by comparison with a signed plate.

This medium-sized fruit or flower basket (fig. 479) has many elements of design, yet it is graceful and well-integrated.

Fig. 477. Jelly compote, 8″, is well-cut, of superior quality.

The designer of a superb flower basket (fig. 480), over 13″ high, has created a dramatic effect by means of miter cuts, flutes, and cane, with not a hobstar in sight! It has the purity of an early Dorflinger design.

Fig. 478. Bonbon baskets. *Left to right:* 4½″ h, 4″ w, 6″ l. Closely resembles "Corinthian" by Straus. An eighteen-point hobstar with six points of fine diamond forms a Star of David in bottom. Note twisted handle. 4½″ h, 4½″ w, 6″ l. It matches a signed 5″ Tuthill plate exactly. Four kites of hobnail radiate from center. Plain handle is double-notched by small cuts.

Fig. 479. Fruit or flower basket, 8½″ h, 6″ w, 10″ l. At each end is a flashed star with fine cuts across flashing, outlining the star. A sixteen-point hobstar covers base.

This large flower basket (fig. 481) strongly resembles the basket on page 433 in Revi. The latter is by the Paul Richter Company (1914-1940) of Maywood, Illinois, in his "Floral" pattern. His blanks were purchased from Libbey-Owens Glass in Toledo, and were polished by means of his secret acid-bath formula. Although this basket fits the criteria, many companies cut similar floral patterns after the Brilliant Period faded away. This basket was doubtless one of the best. Proof of origin of the Richter basket is evidence of the age of this example.

Fig. 480. Flower basket, 13″ h, 5¾″ w, 9¾″ l, may be early Dorflinger. Polished pontil mark on bottom, horizontal steps on base. Above this, a band of diagonal prisms, then a section of flutes and beading. A border of cane, edged above and below by two deep cuts with serrated prism between cuts, leaves only thumbprint scallops on the edge. Handle has a double row of concave ovals and miter cuts at point of attachment. A brilliant "tailored" effect!

Fig. 481. Flower basket, 16″ h, 8¾″ to top of bowl, 5½″ w, 11¼″ l, circa 1914-1930. Flower petals are fine, matte parallel lines; centers are polished hobnail; leaves, miter-cut and polished. (Matye)

Expensive and Rare Items

Umbrella Stands

A collection of umbrella stands would be the ultimate in rarity, requiring a large investment It would also be the ideal way to display a collection of antique canes and/or umbrellas and parasols.

Lamps, Candlesticks, Candelabra

Lamps in mint condition and with matching parts are equally rare and expensive. Few were made; many were broken. In spite of scarcity, invest only in those of fine quality. We have seen a few late floral cuttings on inferior glass. In each case, they were on smaller lamps.

Candlesticks — singles or in pairs — and candelabra are difficult to find, but are well worth the effort Prices are rising rapidly.

Architectural Cut Glass

One could conceivably collect only architectural cut glass, such as window panes, chandeliers, hanging bowls or globes, or even doorknobs. These are all the rarest of the rare.

Silver-Mounted Cut Glass

In Chapter 10, a wide variety of silver-mounted pieces was shown. Some collectors have a strong aversion to this combination of materials; others find it exciting. Most pieces are expensive and many were engraved as presentation pieces. Finding either plain or inscribed silver-mounted items is a challenge. Some glass without silver was also inscribed with names and/ or dates. Some had events, messages, or mottos.

Colored Cut and/or Engraved Glassware

Since relatively little was produced during the Brilliant Period, either solid or colored-cut-to-clear pieces are scarce and expensive.

The pair of candlesticks (fig. C.1) in solid apple green was made during the Middle Period, circa 1860 or earlier.

The decanter and wines in green- and red-cut-to-clear (fig. C.2) by Dorflinger we call "Prince of Wales." They were ordered for his special train in 1919 and 1924 on state visits to Canada.

The stunning pitcher on the Dedication Page (fig. C.3), with band of nailhead diamond near the base, is engraved in flowing curves and dainty floral designs above the band. It is attributed to Dorflinger, who often used green-cut-through-to clear.

Mismatched, Improvised, and Converted Pieces

The purist does not want mismatched pieces. Some collectors are not that particular and will accept "married" sections of different designs. If you wish to buy an article with mismatched parts at a lower price, that is your prerogative. Just remember that most dedicated collectors try to find pieces in their original form and as nearly perfect as possible. By all means, learn to be observant and to be sure that parts match, if you care and if you expect to get your money back some day. Check secondary motifs as well as primary. Small pieces, such as punch cups, may omit some motifs found on the bowl, but those present must be the same.

Butter domes and plates, any pieces with underplates (such as bowls for salad, whipped cream, or mayonnaise), and punch bowls with separate standards should be examined carefully. Even mismatched cream jugs and sugar basins have been sold to unwary buyers.

The boudoir lamp (fig. 482) is a good example of pieces that match in size, but not in design.

Lamps have been constructed by using a vase for the lower part and an inverted bowl as a shade. This is not unacceptable if both are cut in the same pattern, yet the purist would reject even this.

Fig. 483. Violet globe, 2½″ h × 3¾″, in "Golf" by Bergen, was converted from a broken cruet. Pinwheels alternate with a fan above two zippered triangles and a single star. (Matye)

Fig. 482. Boudoir lamp, 13″ h, 6″ d at top, has a dome in Heinz Bros.' "Feathered Star" (fig. 397). Base, with its different type of star, and panels cut in stylized flowers, obviously does not match top. (Gerritse)

Fig. 484. Centerpiece vase, 5¾″ h × 8½″, is actually an inverted punch bowl base. Transitional pattern, circa 1908, has hobstars and triangles of silver diamond under a Gothic arch. Flowers have matte silver diamond centers; the rest is polished. Bottom shows wear, proving it has been used as a vase for a long time.

We have seen attractive lamps with a silk shade over a vase with a hole bored in the bottom, through which to thread a hollow tube holding a wire. A better way is to place the vase on a platform, bending the rod around behind it to avoid destroying its original condition. Lamps have been made of statuettes in this fashion.

Broken pieces are sometimes altered by a glass cutter who specializes in repairs. It does seem a shame to throw away a broken piece if it can be used in any way.

This violet globe (fig. 483) in "Golf" by Bergen has been converted from a cruet with a broken top by grinding and beveling the edge. If parallel miter cuts had been made on the edge, the change might have been undetectable. This is of fine quality and well worth saving.

We were astonished at the ingenuity of a dealer several years ago. She freely admitted she had bought at auction a broken cut glass floor lamp. The stem was a hollow metal tube, containing the electric wire, enclosed in a glass tube cut in a circle of hobstars every few inches. She bought it for "a song," then commissioned a cutter to sever the tube between designs, shape the sections, and notch the ends, thus creating a dozen "napkin rings." We did not have the courage to ask if she apprised her customers of the conversion.

This centerpiece vase (fig. 484) is really an inverted punch bowl base. Some bowls were made to fit over a base with a solid top. Ordinarily the bowl has a stub that fits into a hole in the base, in which case it could never double as a vase. This stand is cut beautifully, so it should be used. Chances of finding a matching bowl are extremely remote.

Some conversions were made at the time of manufacture. Goblets were made into bells when the foot was accidently broken. Tumblers blown into a mold were converted to hats by shaping the edge into a hat brim. Such novelties as hats and shoes were popular in the Victorian era. Most were pressed.

It is unlikely that the reader will ever encounter a converted piece. If so, the price should be greatly reduced. How can one tell if it has been altered? By being well acquainted with the great variety of items that were made and with their original shapes.

20
Choosing Glassware

To sum up the criteria discussed previously for choosing cut and engraved glassware of high quality, let us review the marks of excellence.

A good blank is the first essential element. It is heavy for its size and thickness, due to high content of lead. If shaped like a bowl, it rings when tapped gently with fingernail or pencil. If it does not ring, look for a crack, which may be at the bottom of a miter cut.

In daylight, when outside foliage is viewed through an uncut section of a good piece, leaves are not distorted by swirls and shadows. The glass should be perfectly clear and free from bubbles or seeds (unmelted sand or bits of clay.)

The blank should have been freely hand-blown and generally symmetrical, although a large hollow piece (such as the Sinclaire jardiniere shown in fig. 358) may be slightly lopsided. A tray (such as the Hawkes plate in fig. 320) may be thicker on one side. There are exceptions to this rule. Some of the finest pieces have been blown into a paste mold, as when shaping a box or when a bowl had indentations to produce a more dramatic form (fig. 322 — the Hawkes bowl in a Comet pattern). The mold was plain and nothing but air has touched the refractory or inner surface. Some call these "blow-out" blanks.

The inside surface should *not* follow the contours of outer cutting, because this is the sign of a figured blank, in which the design was partially programmed by forming the main "cuts" in the mold.

A fire-finished pressed piece (with a few light cuttings added) is liable to deceive the novice, since mold marks were erased by the heat. Fire-finishing helped, but could not restore the luster destroyed by the plunger that ruined the refractory inner surface as it made contact wih the hot glass. The "cuts" of the large motifs are too perfectly proportioned and the edges are not sharp.

Acid-polished cut glass, if left in the bath too long, can also lose its sharpness. Hand polishing on a wooden wheel is generally preferred over acid polishing, although some of the latter was skillfully done.

Avoid a pebbly or grainy finish made by acid. Learn to use the sense of touch to detect the difference. Wood polishing leaves a smooth finish that is highly superior.

Cutting must be done accurately, evenly, and symmetrically. Cuts do not run past the point of intersection. Buttons (hobs) are uniform in size and shape. On rayed bases, the rays are of equal length.

Look at miter cuts through a magnifying glass. Wheel marks that are slightly visible are proof of cutting. Marks that are clearly visible indicate haste and careless smoothing and polishing.

Handles must be applied vertically. A lopsided handle is a detriment. If a piece has two or three handles, make sure they match in size and placement.

Engraving should be sculptured realistically, with veins in leaves following nature's curves — not hastily cut in straight lines. Carved at various depths to resemble flower, fruit, or butterfly, the representation should not be merely a flat, gray form. Patterns should be harmoniously arranged to complement the shape of the piece, whether they are free forms copying nature, or precise geometric motifs, such as the key border on the "Alhambra" celery dish (fig. 341). The engraving may be left gray in a satin or matte finish, may be polished back to clarity (rock crystal), or may be a combination of the two, depending on the desired effect.

Judging by the reaction of visitors, only a few people welcome the quiet dignity of the thin, delicate rock crystal cuttings of Pairpoint and Sinclaire. In shops, customers usually pass over them for the heavier, more flamboyant brilliant cutware. If you find one, perhaps it will turn out to be a "sleeper," whose value will appreciate greatly as interest in all types continues to grow. In fact, prices have risen rather suddenly on such items as Pairpoint candlesticks.

A signature is desirable, but not essential. Some poor pieces have been signed. A magnifying glass should be carried when glass hunting. Even with poor vision, one may read a faint or very small mark with such an aid.

Damage

If a piece was used — not packed away all these years — there are bound to be some marks of wear. Before defining limits, we must agree on terminology.

A *chip* is a piece of glass that has separated from the body of the item, leaving irregular, sharp edges.

A *flake* is a thin layer of glass that has split from the item, leaving a smoother surface than the chip.

A *crack* is an actual separation that will potentially continue to lengthen and will ruin the value of the piece.

A *fracture*, caused by striking the piece, consists of tiny cracks radiating from the point of impact.

Bruises (wear marks) are tiny scratches, usually on the bottom of pieces where they have rubbed against the surface of table or shelf. Many Victorian tables and buffets had marble tops that were harder than glass. Scratches may also appear inside a bowl used with a metal *frog* (flower holder) for displaying flowers.

A *heat check* is a tiny white line that appears at the point of attachment of a handle. It was caused (when the gaffer was applying the handle) by a difference in temperature between piece and handle. These should have been of the same degree of heat.

Sick glass is a chemical disintegration of the glass due to a faulty formula, generally characterized by too much alkali in the mixture. The glass may appear to be damp and give off an odor of ammonia; it may finally flake off. *Crizzling* was the name used in England during the 1670s when Ravenscroft was developing a lead glass formula. Before using oxide of lead in his new "flint" glass, he found that within a few months it gradually devitrified, losing its transparency. Any crizzling seen today was caused by excess borax in the formula.

Another type of flawed glass exists. It is sometimes called *scissile*. Imperfect fusion has caused a network of minute fissures, visible only when held up to the light. We had some tumblers with this condition, noticed only by chance. The condition never worsened.

When we started to collect, every piece had to be "mint," or nearly so. Pragmatism has now taken over to some extent. If damage can be corrected without showing, the item is purchased. Twice, early in our experience, the agreement was for the dealer to have the repairs done. If it turned out well, we took the piece and paid for the repairs. The risk was his. Now, I feel capable of judging whether it will be successful, so I take the gamble on my own.

Dealers often have to take a whole collection in order to obtain a few choice pieces. Since they must also sell the damaged and/or inferior pieces, they must ask high prices for the finer items to compensate for low prices. The wise collector is selective and will pay the price for good examples in excellent condition.

A few people are not so particular. A friend has offered to buy any damaged pieces I have. She does not want to invest heavily, yet likes to display pieces in a case. A bowl from the Swan estate was cracked in transit from the East. We were reimbursed by insurance. My friend admired it, but would not take it as a gift. We had to accept five dollars, while feeling embarrassed to take anything.

A damaged piece is acceptable on two conditions: that it is rare or unique, and that an unbroken one will probably never be found. This can be compared with the situation where shards of broken glass are dug up at the sites of old factories and placed in museums as evidence of early work.

Repairs

Chips and flakes. If a bowl's entire scallop is broken off, nothing short of recutting the entire edge can be done to replace it. (Enough clear headroom must be present to avoid cutting into the pattern.) Rough scallops can be polished, however. Cuts between scallops can be altered and the opposite side can be made to match.

If chips on the edge of a tumbler, cup, or finger bowl are so deep that the grinder must go into the pattern (or even too close to it) when cutting down the edge, forget it. On the contrary, shallow flakes can be eliminated without harm. If a clear rim permits cutting down a tumbler or cup, others in the set may be made to match it when the difference in height is apparent. In our opinion, nevertheless, it would be preferable to leave them in their original condition, even if one is cut down. (A cut-down item is always offered at a lower price or given at no cost with a set.)

Fairly large chips on sharp edges of corner fans on a rectangular tray were successfully corrected, but chips ground on the foot of a compote resulted in a change in form from round to oval. This we declined to buy, even though the top was perfect.

Cracks and fractures. Cut glass is vulnerable to sudden changes in temperature. High-temperature glass used in cooking utensils expands in 1,000 degree F heat by a coefficient of 32. Art or lead glass expands from 115 to 140. At the bottom of a deep miter cut, the glass is much thinner than at the top. A sudden change causes the thin part to expand or contract more rapidly than the main body of glass, and a crack will follow the cut.

A dealer in finest antiquities of many types related an unfortunate incident in her shop. Her associates had just returned from a buying trip in winter. As they unpacked a geometrically cut glass lamp, a young man who was learning the business was eager to light the lamp. He put in bulbs and plugged in the cord. A loud "ping" was heard. All were horrified to see the dome fall apart in two perfect halves.

Leave your glassware packed for several hours when coming in from the cold. In the "good old days," people knew that a kerosene lamp chimney would crack if a cold draft struck it.

If a piece has been hit, look at the point of impact to see if cracks have developed. Check to see if glass has been cracked while removing a rim for resilvering.

Silver rims have sometimes been added to conceal chips on the edge of bowls and boxes. Examine carefully to see whether the mount is old. If it is plain with no hallmarks, it is probably not original.

The mouths of decanters are often nicked by being hit with the stopper. Both the edge of the opening and the bottom of the target stopper of the ring decanter (fig. 409) were chipped. I could not refuse this lovely piece, so I had it smoothed, admonishing the glass cutter to be sure that the stopper's shoulder was level with the opening when he finished.

A set of finger bowls was bought because it matched jug and tumblers. Every bowl had one or more flakes. With plenty of clear headroom above the notched prism pattern, they were all ground to the same height. The edges were rounded and the repair was barely detectable, even though it was not the same as if fire-finished.

Heat checks. The heat check on a cream jug handle may or may not develop into a crack (which can usually be detected by one's fingernail). In any case, the price should be lower, and one should not pick up the piece by the handle.

Bruises. Scratches from wear, if not too noticeable, are regarded favorably as signs of age. If so visible that they detract from beauty, those on a plain surface can be polished out. It is said that a few unscrupulous dealers have made them deliberately on new pieces. If so, these could probably be detected by observing that they are parallel to each other. Valid marks go in random directions.

Sick glass. If glass is really breaking down, nothing can be done. A decanter, vinegar cruet, perfume bottle, salt container, or vase can become cloudy due to a chemical reaction with the contents if not washed frequently. If the inner surface actually breaks down, there is no remedy. An attempt may be made to conceal the condition by covering the bottom with oil. I smelled an oily substance resembling Vicks nose drops in a decanter for sale.

On the contrary, residue from contents, which appears as a whitish coating, can sometimes be removed. Three examples of success should suffice:

A butterfly and floral bowl (fig. 71) was for sale in a home shop. It had white rings halfway up the sides. The lady said they would not wash off after she had used the bowl for some time to hold flowers. I asked if the water was "hard" in her town. It was. I suggested that she soak the bowl in a vinegar solution for half an hour, assuming that the rings were calcium deposits. If the rings disappeared, we would buy the bowl. They did and we did!

The ring decanter (fig. 409) was gray in the bottom. I tried vinegar and water and shook rice around after soaking the piece in soap solution. Neither worked. A lecturer on antiquities suggested dishwasher detergent. Fearfully, I tried it by dissolving the granules in hot water (shaken in a jar), then letting the solution cool before pouring into the decanter. After soaking overnight, the glass became clear. Normally I would not use a detergent of any kind.

A tall trumpet vase (fig. 222) was cloudy at the base. Neither vinegar nor detergent helped much. I bought jeweler's rouge (a fine abrasive) at a hobby shop that sells leather and tools for creating designs thereon. The clerk said they spread oil on a piece of leather, rub on the rouge, and strop their carving tools on the leather strip.

A stick was sharpened to fit down into the narrow point at the bottom of the vase. Over this, I put a piece of cloth, into which was rubbed salad oil. The rouge was rubbed on the oiled cloth and the stick pushed up and down inside the vase. The glass is nearly clear.

Damaged silver mounts. Silver mounts are sometimes dented. Inquire of a silversmith whether removal and straightening are possible, or even worth the risk and cost.

If a piece is broken, its resale value is gone or greatly diminished. Not wishing to throw it away, one can attempt to mend it. Mends will show clearly, unless they're along lines of miters.

In the November 1968 *Connoisseur*, John F. Mills gave advice on mending. Pieces must be clean and dry. He recommended Duroflex as the most convenient adhesive. One should apply a minimum amount, hold firmly until set, then remove excess glue quickly by means of a cotton swab dipped into acetone or methylated spirit.

Other adhesives include Araldite 101 and 103, which should be used only by a professional. They are difficult to remove.

"A self-made adhesive can be prepared by dissolving pieces of Perspex in glacial acetic acid 5 millilitres with ethylene dichloride 195 millilitres," according to Mr. Mills. I have had no experience in this area and quote an expert's advice for your information.

Washing Cut Glass

As stated in a June 1893 *Ladies' Home Journal* article on the care of cutlery and glass:

> To some women their cut glass is as precious as their diamonds; indeed some of it is almost as costly. As in the case of gems, the value is increased with the depth and amount of cutting... Only the wealthy can set their tables with the finest cut glass, but all can have dainty shapes in clear glass.

The best advice on washing glass comes directly from advertisements of the period. Competitors of Ivory Soap, whose advertisements gave advice for washing everything from linoleum to the baby, derogated the use of soap. Pearline was one of these:

> Nothing mars the Beauty of Choice Glassware as the Filmy Cloud that remains after Washing with Soap in the Old-Style-Way. The Remedy is Simple: Stop using Soap — and Wash All Glass with PEARLINE ... in warm suds. Rinse in Clear Water of the same Temperature. Dry in Sawdust — if you have it handy. Polish with Linen Cloth. (Quoted from a 1907 *Ladies' Home Journal*)

In a 1912 *Ladies' Home Journal*, Ivory gave this advice:

> Cut glass is easily chipped. It is best, therefore, to wash it, one piece at a time, in a wooden tub or a padded dishpan. Never put cut glass in very cold or scalding hot water. To wash: Make a suds of Ivory Soap and lukewarm water. Let the glass remain in the suds a few minutes. Then go over it with a medium stiff nail-brush. Rinse twice in water of same temperature as the water used for washing. The first rinsing water should be clear. To the second, add a little bluing; bluing gives a brilliancy to cut glass that cannot be produced in any other way. Dry with a soft flannel or a piece of cheesecloth which has been washed. Polish with soft tissue paper.

> If you have a great deal of cut glass and use it frequently, it is a good idea to provide yourself with a supply of jewelers' sawdust, which can be dried and used over and over again. After washing the cut glass, place it in a box and pour sawdust over it. Rub the glass with handfuls of sawdust, and it will soon be dry. Any sawdust that may have attached itself to the glass can be removed with a brush.

I have followed this method, except for the sawdust, using either Ivory or a special liquid called Crystal Wash. The sawdust would save a great deal of time if one used the glass often. In lieu of that, I use pieces of old linen tablecloth or cloth diapers and rub each large miter cut. Fortunately, one can still buy liquid bluing, which really improves the color of the glass.

Both acids and alkalis can eat into the surface of glass. Most detergents and many soaps contain alkali. Never put ammonia, lye, or a product containing borax in the water.

An apparent contradiction appeared in the June 1893 *Ladies' Home Journal* in advice on cleaning bottles. Directions were to put one tablespoon of muriatic acid to a pint of water into the bottle, cork it, and let it stand twelve hours. (Perhaps this solution would be as safe as vinegar, which is acetic acid.) Shake well, then wash with soap and water, using cloth and wire to rub the interior, or put in shot and shake the bottle. One would have to use the wire carefully to avoid scratches. This I would never do.

A dealer/friend has had success in clarifying the bottom of decanters by filling them with glycerin, letting them soak for several weeks, then washing as usual.

English author Moore recommends using strong soap diluted with water, then shaking with a handful of shot in the bottom of a closed object. He tells of breaking a few raw eggshells into the article with a little cold water (warm if the piece is greasy), shaking it well, and rinsing with fresh water. His glassware shines after this treatment. The eggshells seem harmless.

Another English author suggests that, after rinsing and drying the glass, one should wipe it and the glass shelves with a chamois that has been rung out in methylated spirits and water. We have not tested these ideas or that of leaving potato peelings in water overnight in a decanter, as described in an old Higgins & Seiter catalog.

A Hawkes advertisement in 1909 suggested, "Oil Your Cut Glass with a rag moistened with '3-in-One Oil,' polish briskly with dry, soft cloth to bring back the original sparkling brilliancy."

The modern Steuben company advises frequent washing in warm — never hot — soapy water. Remove stains by rubbing with half a lemon or by washing with vinegar. "Rinse each piece thoroughly and dry it with a lint-free towel." Soft water gives the best results.

Never use abrasives, such as scouring powder or steel wool. And never put your collectibles in a dishwasher.

Sweet liquids occasionally cause decanter stoppers to stick. Do not use force or hot water. Apply warm water to the neck of the piece and rub soft soap around the opening. Soak, if necessary.

You may have seen cut glass for sale with stale food dried in the miter cuts. An old toothbrush is perfect for cleaning the cuts.

Visitors ask how often I wash my glass. Those pieces in enclosed cases can last up to a year, if not used for serving food. Large pieces displayed in the open, even when covered with cloth or paper, must be washed every two or three months. They accumulate skum from the city's air pollution, even when windows are closed.

The two worst enemies of cut glass are the faucet on the sink and a sudden temperature change. Move slowly and do not hit faucet or sink. Place a rubber mat over the divider of a double sink, and pad the drainboard with towels, especially if you have ceramic tile. Put one piece at a time into a rubber or plastic dishpan.

When washing a large punch bowl, get someone to hold it while you wash and rinse. Holding a heavy, slippery piece with one hand is risky.

Remove rings and bracelets when handling glassware. We have seen several deep scratches inside vases and bowls made by a diamond on the hand while drying the glass.

Do not replace stoppers in jars or decanters until every drop of water has evaporated. Better still, leave lids off.

Further Care

Heat from a candle flame or hot molten wax will crack fine glass. Always put out the flame before it has burned to within 3" of the crystal.

In wrapping glass, do not put newspaper or brown wrapping paper next to the glass. Use tissue paper first. The residual sulphur in all three may have an adverse effect over a long period of time, especially in the presence of moisture. Ink in the newspaper would be the most harmful. When storing for weeks or months, first wrap in clean white cotton or linen cloth. Tissue will encourage retention of dampness. Better still, store in open air in a cabinet, if possible.

Flowers allowed to stand in water can etch glass and make it cloudy. If you wish to use your vases while entertaining, do so, then empty and wash when guests have departed. (The same advice applies to wine decanter and spirits bottles.) It would be tempting fate to let the flowers remain for days while they wilt and disintegrate. Use artificial flowers, or leave vases empty on a daily basis.

Never stack cut glass pieces, with the possible exception of ice cream saucers and small plates. If you do, place a piece of cloth or paper towel between them to prevent glass from grating against glass.

Allow enough space between pieces on your shelves to avoid one striking another; move slowly when putting glass into the case or removing it.

Bare wood or marble can scratch fine glass. It is advisable to cover shelves with cloth, felt, or paper. On the contrary, cut glass can mar surfaces of fine wood. Some dealers and collectors stick small pads on the bottom of each piece to prevent scratching furniture. This detracts from the appearance of the glassware, as does placing stickers on the glass for identification or pricing. Stickers left on for a long time are difficult to remove. I have had to resort to typewriter fluid, but hastened to wash it off quickly.

Either place a piece gently on the furniture, or put it on a plateau or doily. Pads for hot dishes covered by silvery aluminum, found at variety stores, are not elegant, but they do reflect light up through the glass.

Displaying Glassware

China closets with glass windows on sides and front are satisfactory for all but tall vases and punch sets. Plate grooves on shelves or separate metal plate easels show plates to advantage and save space. Plastic holders are transparent and do not detract from the design, but they may melt on a hot day.

Rarely, pieces have broken spontaneously for no apparent reason, just while sitting on a shelf. The cause is believed to be improper tempering at the time of manufacture.

Regardless of how it looks outside the house, I have put aluminum foil on the inside of windows in two rooms set aside for the collection. The foil is effective in reflecting heat and in keeping room temperature down.

Old sectional bookcases, with glass doors that can be raised and pushed back into the case, are excellent for any pieces small enough to fit. In 1968, four-section bookcases could be bought for about $50 each. In 1980 they sold at $50 or more for each section at auctions. One might find them for less at house sales.

Our experience in finding an eight-foot showcase may be helpful. In 1968, Earle and I went to several firms that handled secondhand cases. They were priced from $250 to $300; most were in poor condition.

I had seen cases in thrift stores (such as Salvation Army) where reconditioned merchandise was displayed. Theorizing that these cases were donated by stores, I called every thrift store in the yellow pages. I finally found a case for sale for $40, went to see it, and paid $60 (plus $20 to have it delivered), feeling guilty even after donating an extra $20 over the price. It is in mint condition and presently holds fifty-five pieces.

The case has four mirror-lined sliding doors in the back and a 10″ shelf that is perfect for small items. The shelf and floor are covered with off-white formica, which did nothing for showing the designs of the glassware. Besides, the surface of the formica is smooth. Even a slight earthquake tremor might cause the upper pieces to slide off the shelf and to crash down upon those below.

Although black velvet (as used by Libbey in the 1893 Columbian exhibit) or blue (as Earle desired) are recommended as a background for cut glass, moss green velvet was chosen because the room, a former solarium, was already painted celery green. To hold the velvet in place, and to provide a cushioned base to prevent sliding, I bought rubberized non-skid yardage (used under scatter rugs to prevent slippage), cut it to fit both shelf and bottom of the case, then covered it with the velvet. The velvet was cut with a 2″ allowance on all four sides, turned under, and sewn underneath to the rubber material.

One china closet from England in Art Nouveau style was already lined with gray velvet. I lined another English case in red embossed wallpaper to accent a color in the rug.

If we had much colored glass, I would group these together. In my opinion, they would detract from the crystal.

Decorating with Cut Glass

Cut glass can be used as part of the home décor. Nineteenth-century houses often had eighteenth-century furniture or pieces made in the Victorian period, which were derived from many styles. Even the most modern homes, whose décor depends on plain lines, geometric form, color, and richness of materials for effect, could be compatible with such patterns as the Hawkes bullseye vase (fig. 319) and the notched prism basket (fig. 480).

With a large collection, feature a few pieces in each room. Keep the rest in cabinets or in a special room. The home should not resemble a shop. Hopefully, the color pictures here (figs. C.9-20) may suggest ways of using the glass in our time. Vases, baskets, candlesticks, and decanters may be placed to enhance the appearance of a mantel, a bookcase, or the piano. The buffet is a perfect setting for punch bowl, cups, decanters, and candelabra. A fruit compote, épergne, or flower center on the dining table is beautiful, especially if reflected in a mirrored plateau.

Living in a small apartment need not deprive the cut glass aficionado of enjoying a small collection. So-called "cabinet pieces" are precious and lovely to look at.

Lamps may obviously be used for the purpose for which they were intended. Their great monetary value, however, precludes use in a location where someone may trip over the cord, or where a child throwing a ball indoors may lead to disaster.

Nearly every visitor inquires, "Do you use your cut tableware?" My answer: "Rarely, and only with certain guests — those who appreciate its value, but are not too nervous at the prospect to enjoy it." Considering that each piece of stemware is worth from $60 to $300, I would be nervous if children were present, or if a large group were chatting and milling about.

Insuring the Collection

Some companies offer an "inland marine" policy separately for objects in the fine arts category. Generally, a better price can be found if the endorsement is attached to the homeowner's policy, dealing with the same firm for both.

A flat rate is usually charged to cover breakage, fire, theft, and transportation to a show. (My broker asks me to notify him if the glass is being transported for display purposes.) An additional endorsement at a different price can be added to cover breakage caused by an earthquake (called "catastrophic insurance"). Location in respect to the crime rate and construction of the building may enter into the company's choice of premium.

Certain firms have a limit on how much they will insure. My broker had to change companies after the first refused to go above a certain figure.

Appraisal of Value

Most companies will accept a recent bill of sale to establish a value of a piece. If one has had the glass for some time, replacement value would be much higher than the purchase price. In this case, the broker accepts my evaluation. I cannot afford to over-insure my glass. He feels that I know as much or more than most appraisers in the area, since most of them cover so many fields.

If you need a professional appraisal, save time and money by having a descriptive list with your estimate of replacement value ready for the appraiser to verify or change. After the initial establishment of value, the insurance company will probably accept your own annual upgrading of value.

Take photographs of all of your pieces for reference in case of theft or breakage. Number them to agree with your catalog.

Cataloging the Collection

A card file divided into categories is most helpful. I first record a new piece on a wide sheet, lined for bookkeeping, under these headings: date purchased, name of item, catalog number, source of purchase, pattern name and maker, and present value (in pencil to prepare for the next report to the insurer), and insured value. You may discover that pieces similar to yours have risen and you may wish to make a pencil notation, including date and price. Keep checking to see if a genuine trend has developed.

After recording a new piece on the sheet, I fill out a card for the file. On the card is recorded the same information, plus a brief description (size, motifs) and other pertinent information (age and style, for example).

Categories and numbers set up to organize the record are: Baskets 1-25; Bottles, Colognes, Perfumes 26-50; Bowls 51-150; Boxes and Jars 151-175; Butter and Cheese Dishes 176-190, et cetera. The number ranges were chosen arbitrarily to provide room for additions within a category. This system may not work for you, but may serve as a model. It is important to devise some form of record. For those who buy a piece or two at first and then embrace collecting cut glass as a hobby, acquisition can become an addiction. Unless one has money to burn, planning is essential.

American and Canadian Trademarks or Signatures

TRADEMARKS

M. J. Averbeck

T. G. Hawkes & Co.

1892-1896

J. D. Bergen Co.

A. H. Heisey & Co.

1895-ca. 1913

T. B. Clark & Co.

J. Hoare & Co.

1896-1900

1901-1906

C. Dorflinger & Sons

Hunt Glass Co.

1901-shaped blanks
(Libbey)

O. F. Egginton Co.

Irving Cut Glass Co.

1906-1919

Empire Cut Glass Co.

Laurel Cut Glass Co.

1919-1930
W. L. Libbey & Son

H. C. Fry Glass Co.

Meriden Cut Glass Co.

311

Mt. Washington/Pairpoint

Taylor Brothers Co.

F. L. Morecroft (Ideal Cut Glass Co.)

C. G. Tuthill & Co.

Pitkin & Brooks

Quaker City Glass Co.

National Association of Cut Glass Mfgrs.
(members in U.S. and Canada)
1911-1942

H. P. Sinclaire & Co.

L. Straus & Sons

CANADIAN TRADEMARKS

Roden Brothers
Toronto, Ont. 1910

Gundy-Clapperton
Montreal, Que. 1905

Gowans, Kent & Co.
Toronto, Ont. 1905

Annotated
Bibliography

Books

An American Lady. *The Ladies' Vase or Polite Manual for Young Ladies.* 8th ed. Hartford: Wm. James Hamersley, 1852 (1st ed. 1847).

Ash, Douglas. *How to Identify English Drinking Glasses and Decanters 1630-1830.* London: G. Bell & Sons, Ltd., 1962. Precise, chronological descriptions, illustrated by line drawings and photographs. This survey ends in 1830 because "Thereafter, cut glass, which was the most popular, became like the architecture, furniture, and silver of the period, subject to the excessive elaboration to which our Victorian ancestors were so devoted, and glass objects often appeared more like coarse jewelry than functional vessels... The period is usually of little interest to the collector of the glass of earlier times."

Avila, George C. *The Pairpoint Story.* New Bedford, Mass.: Reynolds-DeWalt Printing, Inc. and the author, 1968. Excellent account of the company's evolvement from the Mt. Washington Glass Co. Photographs not found elsewhere; some difficult to decipher.

Boggess, Bill and Louise. *American Brilliant Cut Glass.* New York: Crown Publishers, Inc., 1977. Over 600 pieces illustrated. Thumbnail sketches of important firms; sixty previously unidentified patterns; pragmatic advice for the collector.

Bessy, Maurice. *Magic and the Supernatural.* London: Spring Books, 1964. A pictorial history to which we referred only once concerning natural glass: obsidian.

Brooks, John A. *Glass, 100 Masterpieces of Crystal and Color.* New York: Golden Press, 1973. Brief historical review of glassmaking and decoration from ancient Egypt to America in the present. A brief survey with relatively few, but large, pictures; 80 pages. Very little on American glass.

Brown, Dee. *The Year of the Century: 1876.* New York: Charles Scribner's Sons, 1966. A fascinating account of the state of our nation at the time of the centennial celebration at Philadelphia. The author relied heavily on newspapers, letters, diaries, and biographies of principal personages, as well as governmental reports and historical studies.

Burton, John. *Glass.* Philadelphia: Chilton Book Co., 1967. After some history of glassmaking, his philosophy, and accounts of visits to glass centers in Europe, Mr. Burton gives directions for making glass objects in your own home. Many good illustrations.

Butler, Joseph T. *American Antiques 1800-1900, A Collector's History and Guide.* New York: The Odyssey Press, 1965. A fresh appraisal of nineteenth century styles in home furnishings with a guide for the collector who wishes to integrate antiques in modern settings. Historical survey; well-illustrated. One chapter on glass in general; very little on cut glass.

Cantor, Jay. "Mansions for Millionaires," *Discovering Antiques; the Story of World Antiques,* Vol. 2. New York: Greystone Press, 1973. This is one article among many found in this twenty-volume, superb full-color work, obtained from its original publisher, British Publishing Corp. Explores the arts, crafts, styles, and fashions from the Renaissance to the twentieth century — from America, England, Ireland, Scotland, the Continent, even Persia and Turkey. Most illustrations are in full color. Articles on European glass, and those on early American, give insight on the origins of our Brilliant Period glass.

Cohen, Hal. L. *Official Guide to Silver and Silverplate.* New York: House of Collectibles, 1974. Retail prices of silver and silverplate of the post-Civil War era, 1865-1920, current at date of publication. A cross-section of American silversmiths' hallmarks of the nineteenth century are given, but the book's value to us lies in the many illustrations of cut and engraved glass with silver mounts.

Cole, Ann Kilborn. *The Golden Guide to American Antiques.* New York: Golden Press, 1967. A small paperback, 4" × 6", containing excellent advice for the novice collector.

———. *Antiques: How to Identify, Buy, Sell, Refinish, and Care for Them.* New York: David McKay Co., Inc., 1957. Contains nothing on cut glass, but does offer valuable advice to the beginning collector — advice that applies to our specialty.

Conkey, W. B. *The City of Palaces.* Chicago: W. B. Conkey Co., 1895. Authoritative book on the Columbian Exposition of 1893.

———. *Wonders of the World's Fair,* Part 1. Chicago: W. B. Conkey Co., 1894. Excellent illustrations and text.

Contini, Mila. *Fashions from Ancient Egypt to the Present Day.* New York: Crescent Books, 1965. Nearly 550 illustrations, all but a few in color. Excellent text. Complexity of Victorian fashions indicative of preoccupation with ritual in social life.

Corning Glass Works. *This Is Glass.* Corning, N.Y.: 1957. A 64-page booklet defining types and properties of glass; glassmaking by hand and by machine; how it is used.

Cudd, Viola N. *Heisey Glassware.* Brenham, Tex.: Herrmann Print Shop, 1969. Good introduction to Heisey glassware.

Bancroft, Hubert How. *The Book of the Fair.* Vols. 1 and 2. Chicago: The Bancroft Co., 1893. Two large volumes, well-illustrated. Material on cut glass (pp. 147, 166, 841, 882) and on Pairpoint silver (p. 152).

Bettmann, Otto L. *The Good Old Days — They Were Terrible.* New York: Random House, 1974. The author is founder of the famed Bettmann Archive in New York, a picture library of three million prints and photographs. This book is fascinating.

Daniel, Dorothy. *Cut and Engraved Glass 1771-1905: The Collector's Guide to American Wares.* New York: M. Barrows & Co., Inc., 1966. The first serious effort to examine the genesis and qualities of American ware. The author presents in detail fifty representative patterns of the Brilliant Period. A standard work.

Davidson, Marshall B. *American Heritage History of Antiques from the Civil War to World War I*. New York: American Heritage Publishing Co., Inc., 1969. History of home furnishings and decorative arts, covering exact period of our concern. Well-illustrated.

———. *History of Notable American Houses*. New York: Heritage Publishing Co., Inc., 1971.

Davis, Derek C. *English and Irish Antique Glass*. New York, Washington: Frederick A. Praeger, 1965. Well-written and informative.

Davis, Frank. *Antique Glass and Glass Collecting*. London, New York, Sydney, Toronto: Hamlyn, 1973. "His survey of glass is like a voyage of discovery."

Ditzel, Paul C. *Fire Engines, Firefighters*. New York: Crown Publishers, 1976. Vivid descriptions of equipment for fighting fires, a scourge of the nineteenth century in America.

Eastwood, Maud. *The Antique Doorknob*. Forest Grove, Ore.: Times Litho, 1976. Compilation of information, long neglected, concerning a fascinating collectible. It is evident that Maudie has researched her subject thoroughly and joyfully.

Ellis, Rev. John, editor in chief. *Chicago and the World's Columbian Exposition*. Chicago: Trans-Continental Art Publishing Co., 1895. Fairs of former times compared with that of 1893.

Elville, E. M. *English and Irish Cut Glass, 1750-1950*. London W.C.2: Country Life, Ltd., 1955. One of the few books that bring us up to mid-twentieth century.

Farrar, Estelle Sinclaire. *H. P. Sinclaire, Jr., Glassmaker*, Vols. 1 and 2. Garden City, N.Y.: Farrar Books, 1974 and 1975. Mrs. Farrar, with access to family members and many Corningites associated with the glass industry, presents an account of her grandfather and his unique products. The 1917 inventory photographs are useful for identification of our glassware.

Farrar, Estelle Sinclaire, and Spillman, Jane Shadel. *The Complete Cut and Engraved Glass of Corning*. New York: Crown Publishers, Inc., 1979. Well-documented volume with more than 750 illustrations.

Fauster, Carl U. *Libbey Glass Since 1818*. Toledo, Ohio: Len Beach Press, 1979. In the glass industry since 1930, the author is highly qualified to write this history. Part Three contains four reprinted catalogs, never before reproduced.

Freeman, Dr. Larry. *Grand Old American Bottles*. Watkins Glen, N.Y.: Century House, 1964. Bottles of all types, as well as "a social history of liquid refreshment habits from Colonial America down to the present." The reader can appreciate the scarcity of cut glass bottles.

Furnas, J. C. *The Americans: a Social History of the United States 1587-1914*. New York: G. P. Putnam's Sons, 1969. Detailed, well-researched; a pleasure to read. 400 pages.

Gardner, Paul V. *The Glass of Frederick Carder*. New York: Crown Publishers, Inc., 1971. An excellent work by the curator, Division of Ceramics and Glass, National Museum of History and Technology, Smithsonian Institution. Black-and-white photographs, color plates, and catalog line drawings.

Encyclopaedia Britannica, Inc. "Glass" in Vol. 10. Chicago: William Benton, publisher, 1967. Articles on John Ruskin, Egypt, and other subjects also consulted.

Hartshorne, Albert. *Antique Drinking Glasses*. New York: Brussel & Brussel, 1968. A pictorial history of drinking vessels in England from Roman times to 1800; scholarly, authoritative.

Harris, Nathaniel. *Victorian Antiques*. New York: Golden Press, 1973. A review of the various styles from Greek and Roman revival to Art Nouveau in the decorative arts. Only 80 pages; few, but excellent, photographs.

Haynes, E. Barrington. *Glass Throughout the Ages*. Baltimore: Penguin Books, 1964. Revised; originally published in England in 1848. Part II is a detailed survey of table glass in eighteenth-century England. Part I traced the development of glass from ancient Syria and Egypt through Europe, Scandinavia, and Russia to modern times.

Hughes, G. Bernard. *English Glass for the Collector 1660-1860*. New York: MacMillan Co., 1958. Detailed descriptions and excellent photographic examples of decorative styles in English glass.

———. *English, Scottish, and Irish Table Glass from the Sixteenth Century to 1820*. New York: Bramhall House, 1961. Development of flint glass, decoration; illustrations and descriptions of glassware by categories.

Ives, Prof. Halsy C. (introduction by). *The Dream City*. St. Louis: N. D. Thompson Publishing Co., 1893. "A Portfolio of Photographic Views of the World's Columbian Exposition."

Jefferson, Josephine. *Wheeling Glass*. Columbus, Ohio: The Guide Publishing Co., 1947. This small volume of 86 pages clears up mysteries concerning the rise and fall of early glassmakers from 1819 on through the Middle Period. It contains notes on such names as Sweeney, Ritchie, and Hobbs-Brockunier.

Kovel, Ralph and Terry. *Know Your Antiques*. New York: Crown Publishers, 1967. The section on cut glass is necessarily limited, but would be useful as an introduction to the novice.

Kraus, Michael and Vera. *Family Album*. New York: Grosset & Dunlap, 1961. A well-illustrated social history of our nation, as late as 1914.

Lagerberg, Ted and Vi. *Collectible Glass Book 3: Durand Glass*. New Port Richey, Fla.: Modern Photographers, 1967. Some Durand, colored cut-to-clear; a few pieces of Dorflinger and Pairpoint crystal shown, but mainly Durand Art Glass in color. Many gems of information concerning glassmen not found elsewhere.

Lichten, Frances. *Decorative Art of Victoria's Era*. New York: Bonanza Books, 1950. Ninety-six pages of illustrations and fourteen two-color pages.

Longstreet, Stephen. *We all Went to Paris, Americans in the City of Light 1776-1971*. New York: MacMillan Co., 1972. Specific information on the critic, John Ruskin (pp. 124 and 125); nuggets of materials concerning artists, writers, and socially prominent individuals of the Golden Age.

Lungberg, Ferdinand. *The Rockefeller Syndrome*. Secaucus, N.J.: Lyle Stuart, Inc., 1975. Well-documented; revelatory information on the rich and super-rich.

McKearin, George and Helen. *American Glass*. New York: Crown Publishers, 1941. Detailed exposition of seventeenth, eighteenth, and nineteenth-century glassware houses and their products. Book has two thousand photographs and one thousand drawings. (Little on cut glass.)

———. *Two Hundred Years of American Blown Glass*. New York: Crown Publishers, Inc., 1950. An excellent history of American blown glass; 114 illustrations.

Massengill, Samuel Evans, M.D. *A Sketch of Medicine and Pharmacy*. Bristol, Tenn: The S. E. Massengill Co., 1943. Fascinating review of medicine and pharmacy from the Stone Age to modern times. Pertinent to our study are sections on nineteenth-century medicine and on female physicians.

Moore, N. Hudson. *Old Glass, European and American*. New York: Tudor Publishing Co., 1924. Excellent profiles of each country's glass. American section includes Mexican. Has 223 photographs.

Munsey, Cecil. *Collecting Bottles*. New York: Hawthorne Books, Inc., 1970. Well-researched, well-written work on history, manufacture, collection, and decoration of bottles (including cutting and engraving).

Norbury, James. *The World of Victoriana*. London: Hamlyn Publishing Group, 1972. Illustrates progress of furniture and the decorative arts in Britain and America from 1837 to 1901. Over 150 photographs and engravings.

Otto, Celia Jackson. *American Furniture of the Nineteenth Century*. New York: Castle Books, 1965. Helps the reader to more readily visualize the setting for cut and engraved glass of the period.

Padgett, Leonard E. *Pairpoint Glass*. Des Moines, Iowa: Wallace-Homestead, 1979. Traces history of Mt. Washington glass from 1837 to the present. Many types of glass, including cut and engraved. Over seven hundred photographs, some in color.

Papert, Emma. *The Illustrated Guide to American Glass*. New York: Hawthorne Books, Inc., 1972. Traces development of glassware in America. One chapter on cut and engraved. Adequately, but not lavishly, illustrated.

Pearson, J. Michael, and Dorothy T.
The Pearsons were first collectors, then dealers in cut glass. The five Pearson books are listed here in chronological order, rather than alphabetically by title.

_____. *American Cut Glass for the Discriminating Collector*. New York: Vantage Press, 1965. Some brief histories of prominent companies are given, but the main attraction to readers was the hope of identifying patterns of their own glassware, and the pleasure of seeing fine pieces arranged by categories.

Pearson, J. Michael. *A Study of American Glass Collections*. Miami: The Franklin Press, Inc., 1969. Additional patterns illustrated and companies discussed; photographs of rarities found in collections.

_____. *Encyclopedia of American Cut and Engraved Glass 1880-1917, Vol. I: Geometric Conceptions*. Miami Beach: J. Michael Pearson, 1975. Geometric patterns categorized to facilitate identification of pieces.

_____. *Encyclopedia, etc., Vol. II: Realistic Patterns*. Miami Beach: J. Michael Pearson, 1977. Engraved designs from nature, often in combination with cutting.

_____. *Encyclopedia, etc., Vol. III: Geometric Motifs*. Miami Beach: J. Michael Pearson, 1978. Continuation of Vol. I, with a pattern index of all three volumes.

Pešatová, Zuzana. *Bohemian Engraved Glass*. Feltham, Middlesex, England: Hamlyn Publishing Group, Ltd., 1968. The story of Bohemian cut and engraved glass since the time of Caspar Lehmann at the end of the sixteenth century. Techniques of cutting and engraving; more than 130 plates.

Peterson, Arthur G., Ph.D. *Trademarks on Glass*. DeBary, Fla.: available from author, Box 252, Zip 32713, 1968.

Rainwater, Dorothy T. *American Silver Manufacturers*. Hanover, Pa.: Everybody's Press, 1966. Excellent reference on maker and trademarks. Essential for identification of marks on silver-mounted glassware.

Revi, Albert Christian. *American Cut and Engraved Glass*. New York: Thomas Nelson and Sons, 1965. After a brief résumé of the development of the industry in America, Revi presents facts and figures concerning manufacturers, state by state, Over five hundred illustrations including photographs, patent drawings, and some catalog reprints.

_____. *Nineteenth Century Glass*. New York: Thomas Nelson & Sons, 1959. Good background reading on the genesis of glass around the Mediterranean in ancient times. Author then skips to the nineteenth century. Each chapter is concerned with a type of art glass made here and in Europe.

_____. Editor. *The Spinning Wheel's Complete Book of Antiques*. New York: Grosset & Dunlap, 1972. Selected articles (1945-1972) from the periodical cover many types of antiques. Among thirty-four articles on glassware, seven are on cut glass: Dorflinger, Gillinder, Irving, Lackawanna, Laurel, Halter, and Sinclair.

Roberts, Patricia Easterbrook. *Table Settings, Entertaining, and Etiquette*. New York: Bonanza Books, no date, but Library of Congress Cat. Card #67-25918. A mélange of historical information on table settings and up-to-date references and advice on beautiful settings. Lavishly illustrated in both color and black and white.

Rockwell, Robert F. *Frederick Carder and His Steuben Glass 1903-1933*. West Hyack, N.Y.: Dexter Press, Inc., 1966. Booklet containing a vignette on the creative genius of decorative art glass, with twenty-six pages of superb color photographs. Only three cologne bottles are of cut crystal.

Salter, Stefan. *Joys of Hunting Antiques*. New York: Hart Publishing Co., Inc., 1971. With little pertaining to our subject, this anecdotal record of hunting antiquities in Europe and America serves as an inspiration for the cut glass collector.

Savage, George. *Glass*. New York: G. P. Putnam's Sons, 1965. Succinct overview of glassmaking from ancient times. Includes oriental, European, English, Irish, and American glass. Illustrations mainly from museums.

Schwartz, Marvin D. *Collector's Guide to Antique American Glass*. Garden City, N.Y.: Doubleday & Co., Inc., 1969. History, style and identification of various types of American glass; one excellent chapter on cut and engraved.

Seale, William. *The Tasteful Interlude: American Interiors Through the Camera's Eye, 1860-1917*. New York: Praeger Publishers, 1975. Old photographs of Victorian interiors from Boston to Santa Fe, with descriptive text written by an historian who had restored five American houses when this was written. Recommended for the cut glass collector.

Sears, Stephen W., and the editors of *American Heritage: Hometown, U.S.A.* New York: Simon & Schuster, 1975. Visual history of life in "smalltown" America at the turn of the century. Excellent text and captions.

Shull, Thelma. *Victorian Antiques*. Rutland, Vermont: Charles E. Tuttle Co., 1963. Covers fifty-seven categories of Victorian antiques.

Simpson, Jeffrey. *The Way Life Was: a Photographic Treasury from the American Past*. New York: Praeger Publishers; printed in Milan, Italy: Amilcare Pizzi, 1974. Many aspects of our people from 1880 to 1915 — the "400" of New York's high society and its teeming slums, the Indians, sod houses of pioneers of the plains, and prostitutes of New Orleans.

Skelly, Leloise Davis. *Modern Fine Glass*. New York: Richard R. Smith, 1937. After a brief historical introduction, modern twentieth-century glass from Europe, U.S.A., and Mexico described. Photographs are good.

Spillman, Jane Shadel, and Farrar, Estelle Sinclaire. *The Cut and Engraved Glass of Corning 1868-1940*. Corning, N.Y.: Corning Museum of Glass, 1977. Over one hundred photographs of pieces at the museum and information on Corning, the "cut glass city of New York state."

Stevens, Gerald. *Early Canadian Glass*. Toronto: McGraw-Hill Ryerson, Ltd., 1960. The author is a leading expert in the field of Canadiana. This book is the first general summary of what is known of early Canadian glass. Information on cut glass is limited to Gundy-Clapperton of Toronto.

Tardy. *Les Poinçons de Garantie Internationaux pour L'Argent*, 10th Edition, Paris SE: Tardy, 21, Rue des Boulangers (no date). Silver trademarks of Europe. Book is written in French.

Time-Life Books Editors. *This Fabulous Century 1900-1919*, Vol. I. New York: Time, Inc., 1969. Excellent portrayal of all segments of society from the small prairie town to the immigrants' ordeal in the city slums to the luxuries of the very rich. Rare photographs.

315

Unitt, Doris and Peter. *Book of Marks: Antiques and Collectibles.* Peterborough, Ontario, Canada: Clock House, 1973. Emphasis on Canadiana; includes U.S. and European marks on silver, ceramics, and glass.

Van Tassel, Valentine. *American Glass.* New York: Gramercy Park Publishing Co., 1950. A small volume with seventy-five photographs; one chapter on cut and engraved glass (twelve pages) — appropriate reading for the beginning collector.

Wardle, Patricia. *Victorian Silver and Silver-Plate.* New York: Universe Books, 1963. Useful as a means of visualizing development of style in a complex period. Some examples of glass used in conjunction with silver are shown.

Warman, Edwin G. *American Cut Glass, a Pattern Book of the Brilliant Period 1895-1915.* Uniontown, Pa.: E. G. Warman Publishing, 1970. Small volume with notes on the development of cut glass, useful to the novice collector. Drawings of various pieces have pattern names, but are not identified by companies.

Watkins, Lura Woodside. *Cambridge Glass 1818 to 1888.* New York: Bramhall House, 1930. Story of New England Glass Co. of Cambridge, Mass., at one time the largest glasshouse in the world; based on research done by "visiting thirty families whose families had been connected with the works," and by studying documents. Other Cambridge factories are reviewed in the final chapter. Excellent!

Wiener, Herbert, and Lipkowitz, Frieda. *Rarities in American Cut Glass.* Houston, Tex.: The Collectors House of Books, 1975. Primarily a feast for the eyes: photographs of some of the finest existing pieces owned by the authors (both of whom are collectors and dealers). Forty-six pictures of scarce colored glass are also shown.

Wills, Geoffrey. *Glass.* London: Orbis Publishing, 1975. Part of a series. Succinct data; diagrams and color pictures of European glass of many types.

Wilson, Kenneth M. *New England Glass & Glassmaking.* New York: Thomas Y. Crowell Co., 1972. Comprehensive history of New England glass by its leading authority, now curator of the Corning Museum of Glass. Nearly four hundred illustrations.

Serial Publications

Babson, Roger W. "Great Fortunes of History." *The Mentor,* November 1921, pp.3-12.

Baker, Lillian. "Hatpin Holders: Look-alikes and Reproductions." *Antique Trader,* 17 December 1974.

Beach, Stanley Yale. "Automobiling: The Closed Car." *American Homes and Gardens,* April 1910, pp.138,139.

Boggess, Louise. "Little Known Signatures." *The Collector,* April 1975, pp.3,5-7.

———. "Cut Glass: The Brilliant Period." *American Collector,* October 1976, pp.14,15,28.

———. "Reflections on Glass: Tuthill Cut Glass Known for Fine Glass." *The Collector,* November 1978, p.12.

Bologna, Sando. "Barber Bottles." *Antiques Journal,* November 1977, pp.16-18.

Bull, Jerome Case. "The Modern Swordswoman." *Munsey's Magazine,* July 1897, pp.491-496.

Call, Thomas S. "The Automobile and Its Relation to Suburban Life." *Suburban Life,* July 1905, p.15.

Carter, Herman C. "Milady's Dresser Accessories." *Antique Trader,* 29 January 1974, pp.36,37.

Cowie, Donald. "Prime Irish Antiques." *Antiques Journal,* March 1974, pp.10-12.

———. "Collecting as an Investment." *Antiques Journal,* March 1975, pp.14-16.

Crane, George. "Within the House: The Decoration Value of Glass." *American Homes and Gardens,* September 1913, pp.332,333.

Daniel, Dorothy. "Brilliant Cut Glass: How to Identify It." *Antiques Journal,* July 1968, pp.14,15,34.

De Vilbiss, Philip. "Trash or Treasure?" (Puff boxes). *Antique Trader,* 4 July 1972.

———. "Pass the Cuspadora." *Antiques Journal,* May 1975, p.49.

Dow, Joy Wheeler. "Principals of Home Decoration." *American Homes and Gardens,* July 1905, p.35.

Elder, Robert A., Jr. "Damage in Ceramics and Glass." *Antiques Journal,* May 1975, pp.10-13.

Evans, Elliot. "Shreve & Company of San Francisco Flatware, Part 1," *Spinning Wheel,* September 1978, pp.30-32.

Farrar, Estelle Sinclaire. "Cut and Engraved Glass of Corning, N.Y. 1869-1940." *American Antiques,* May 1977, pp.25-29.

Fauster, Carl U. "Libbey Colored-cased Glass Circa 1920." *Glass,* January-February 1973, pp.30-34,38,39.

———. "The McKinley Bowl" (and the story of its twin). *American Antiques,* September 1976, pp.35-38.

Fitzpatrick, Paul J. "The Saga of an American Glasshouse" (Bakewell). *Glass,* January-February 1973, pp.13-22.

———. "White House Drinking Glasses." *Antiques Journal,* April 1975, pp.22-26,46.

———. "American Cut Glass at the 1876 Centennial." *Antiques Journal,* December 1975.

———. "Baccarat: Crystal of Kings." *Antiques Journal,* August 1976, pp.12-14,46.

———. "Baccarat: Lasting Excellence." *Antiques Journal,* September 1976, pp.23,24,55.

———. "Waterford Glass," Parts 1 and 2. *Antiques Journal,* May 1977, pp.16-19,48, and June 1977, pp.30-32,53.

———. "White House Dining Customs." *Antiques Journal,* March 1978, pp.44-46,55,56.

Fleisher, Mark. "Glass Manufacture in Corning, N.Y." *Antique Trader,* 15 August 1972, p.46.

Fleming, Joan. "Brides of Yesteryear." *Antique Trader,* 17 December 1974, pp.54,55.

Foglesong, Katie. "Iowa Antiques Class Studies Castor Sets." *The Collector,* July 1976, p.9.

Fornwalt, Russell J. "Collectors Beat the Inflation Heat by Investing in Art and Antiques." *Antique Trader,* 9 July 1974, p.48.

Freeman, Dudley. "Those Were the Yuletide Parties." *National Star,* 28 December 1974.

Gaines, Edith. "Woman's Day Dictionary of American Glass." *Woman's Day,* August 1961, pp.19-34.

———. "Woman's Day Dictionary of Sandwich Glass." *Woman's Day,* August 1963, pp.21-32.

Gores, Stan. "Glass Souvenirs of the 1876 Centennial." *Glass,* November-December 1972, pp.23-28.

———. "A Chip or Flake?" *Antiques Journal,* April 1974, pp.37,55.

———. "1879 Price List Sheds Light on Gillinder & Sons and Their Glass." *Antiques Journal,* May 1978, pp.32,33,54.

Herrick, Christine Terhune. "New China and Glass Ware." *Harper's Bazaar,* Part 1, Vol. 39, 1905, pp. 476-479.

Holzer, Harold. "Personal Relics from the Past: Ladies' Victoriana." *Antique Trader,* 11 March 1975.

Horton, Christine. "Patterns, Patents and Trademarks of Cut and Engraved Glass," Parts 1 and 2. *American Antiques,* May 1977- pp.19-24, and August 1977, pp.21-26.

———. "Cut Glass — 1880-1915." *American Antiques,* May 1976, pp.34-40.

_____. "Giants in Glass Houses — American Cut Glass 1880-1915: The Brilliant Period." *American Antiques*, September 1976, pp.27-33.

Hubbard, Clarence T. "Mastery in Glass" (Libbey). *Antiques Journal*, May 1971, pp.22,23,42.

_____. "Where's the Twin?" (McKinley punch bowl). *Antique Trader*, 1 August 1972, p.51.

Jenkins, Dorothy. "Salt Dishes." *Woman's Day*, March 1966, pp.15,101,102.

_____. "Cut-Glass Patterns." *Woman's Day*, April 1969, pp.35, 82,84.

Koehler, Margaret H. "Pairpoint Glass." *Antiques Journal*, January 1975, pp.18-21,50.

Laing, Trusy. "Cigar Smoking Popularized by English King." *Antique Trader*, 20 March 1973, p.62.

McCulloch, Lou W. "The Art of Mourning." *Antiques Journal*, October 1977, pp.19-21,51.

Macswiggan, Amelia E. "Baccarat: The Crystal of Kings." *Antiques Journal*, September 1973, pp.16-18,52.

Manchee, Kathryn Dorflinger. "Dorflinger Glass," Parts 1,2, and 3. *Antiques*, April 1972, pp.710-715; June 1972, pp.1006-1011; July 1972, pp.96-100. Authentic; glass photography at its best.

Manley, C. C. "Acid etched Glass: an Underrated Art." *Antiques Journal*, September 1977, pp.21,22,53.

Mathews, James. "The Powder Jar Collections of Roe Lair." *Antique Trader*, 8 October 1974, p.61.

Mebane, John. "What's New That's Old." *Antique Trader*, January 30, 1973, p.48.

_____. "Heart-shaped Antiques." *Antiques Journal*, February 1974, pp.13-15.

"Sugar Shakers." *Antiques Journal*, May 1975, pp.56,57. E. K. Metcalf, "Hints for Convalescent Children." *Ladies' Home Journal*, February 1910, p.60.

Michael, George. "A Visit with Lowell Innes." *American Antiques*, December 1976, pp.43-45. (Mr. Innes is an expert on *Pittsburgh Glass 1797-1891*, the title of his excellent book.)

Miller, Yvonne. "Vinaigrettes Make 'Scents' for Collectors." *Antique Trader*, 22 May 1973, p.47.

Mills, John Fitzmaurice. "Problems and Solutions II." *Connoisseur*, November 1968, p.165. (Cleaning cut glass.)

Moffett, Cleveland. "The Edge of the Future: Sudden Rise of the Horseless Carriage." *Suburban Life*, July-December 1905, pp.153-160.

Neale, Harriet M. "Home Furnishing and Decoration — V: Table Glass Ware." *Good Housekeeping*, Vol. IX, 1888, pp.111-112.

Poese, Bill. "Hand Me Down the Walking Cane." *Antique Trader*, 17 December 1974, pp.52,53.

_____. "Victorian Stickpin Holders." *Antique Trader*, 21 January 1975, p.49.

_____. "Vaseline Glass." *Antiques Journal*, April 1976, pp.50-52.

Poole, Hester. "Elegance, Taste and Art in the Home. The Celebrated Dining Set of Mrs. George W. Childs of Philadelphia," (three articles). *Good Housekeeping*, 15 May 1886, pp.1-5; 1 March 1890, pp.193-195; April 1894, pp.151-156.

Power, Esther H. M. "Reflections on Dorflinger Glass." *Antique Trader*, 2 April 1974, pp.41,42.

Ray, Marcia. "Inventive Ladies of '76." *Spinning Wheel*, July-August 1976, p.24.

Revi, Albert Christian. "A Cut Glass Door Panel." *Spinning Wheel*, November 1968, p.58.

Rivera, Betty. "Collectible Parasols." *Antiques Journal*, November 1977, pp.44,45.

Rodger, William. "English Table Glass of the 'Golden Age'." *Glass*, January-February 1973, pp.4-10.

Rogers, Jo Ann. "Superstitions." *Antique Trader Annual of Articles* Vol.V, p.101.

_____. "Ric Iorio and His Art Glass." *Antiques Journal*, April 1977, pp.22-24.

Russell, J. Almus. "Taught to the Tune ... District Schools of Yesterday." *Antiques Journal*, February 1976, pp.20-23.

Sandlin, Lesley McGee. "A Passion for Pattern Glass." *American Collector*, August 1977, pp.10,11,18. (Concerns collections of both pattern and cut glass by Bob Batty and where they may be seen.)

Schuessler, Raymond. "When They Wired Up America." *NRTA Journal*, September-October 1976. (NRTA means National Retired Teachers Association.)

_____. "Homes — the Splendid Age." *NRTA Journal*, May-June 1977.

Singleton, Esther. "Perfume Worship in All Ages." *Cosmopolitan*, Vol.16, November to April 1893-1894, p.476.

Stam, Michele L. "The Victorian Use of Indoor Plants." *Spinning Wheel*, May 1978, pp.18-22.

Stout, Sandra McPhee. "McKee Glass." *Antiques Journal*, October 1973, pp.36,37,59.

Thomas, Diane. "Victorian Chatelaines." *Antiques Journal*, October 1973, pp.10-12.

_____. "Milady's Hatpins through the Years." *Collector's Weekly*, 3 December 1974, pp.1,3.

_____. "Variety Marks Hatpin Holders." *Collector's Weekly*, 3 December 1974, pp.1,2,6.

Upton, Charles A. "Cambridge Glass." *Antique Trader*, 30 January 1973, p.39.

Waterfield, Marge. "Yes, There Really Was a Lydia Pinkham." *Antique Trader*, 24 April 1973, p.52.

Wright, Lacy (reporter's interview with Mr. Wright). "Working in the Cotton Mill." *Poverty Law Review*, November-December 1977, pp.4,5.

Four more anonymous articles should be listed:

"The Century of Meriden" Sec.3, pp.132,133. Meriden, Conn., 1906.

"Clippings of Cuttings" (information on L. Straus & Sons). *Glass*, February 1979, p.17.

"Hatpin Holders." *Antiques Journal*, December 1977, p.37.

"Hatpins." *Woman's Home Companion*, January-June 1911.

Finally, we have three booklets:

The Eventful Twelve Hours, or the Destitution and Wretchedness of a Drunkard. An original booklet published by the American Tract Society in New York (no date).

The Sandwich Glass Museum Collection (forty pages). Boston: Nimrod Press, 1969. (Photographs and notes on history of the company and on the exhibit, with one page of blown, cut, and engraved glassware.)

Tools of the Glassmaker. New York: Corning Museum of Glass, 1980.

Catalogs

M. J. Averbeck (manufacturing jewelers in New York), No. 104, 1900-1910, reprinted by Cerrito Printing, El Cerrito, Calif., 1973.

J. D. Bergen Company 1904-1905, reprinted by Cembura & Avery Publishers, Berkeley, Calif., 1973.

Butler Brothers, reprints of glassware sections in 1905 and 1910 catalogs, Chattanooga, Tenn.: Antiques Research Publications. Valuable for comparing this cheap, imitation ware with real cut lead glass.

W. G. Crook Illustrated Catalog of 1888 (reprinted selections from this "Busiest House in America," located in Nelsonville, Ohio), Kermit, Tex.: Collector's Weekly, 1972. Cut glass salts, peppers, and casters illustrated.

Dorflinger & Sons reprint. Hanover, Penn.: Everybody's Press, 1970. Factual introduction concerning history of company.

Alpha Ehrhardt. *Cut Glass Price Guide.* Kansas City, Mo.: Heart of America Press, 1973. Reprints of pages from catalogs from 1898 to 1923, showing original prices for comparison with 1973 values. Dates help reader to trace evolution of design. Trademarks.

Empire Cut Glass Company 1905-1910 reprint. Flemington, N.J.: edited by William L. Iorio, 1980.

Harper's Bazaar: 1867-1898, Victorian Fashions and Costumes. New York: Dover Publications (edited and introduced by Stella Blum), 1974. Selected reprints from "A repository of Fashion, Pleasure, and Instruction." Detailed engravings.

Jo Evers. *Standard Cut Glass Value Guide.* Paducah, Kentucky: Collector Books, 1975. Reprint of pieces arranged categorically, showing company, pattern sizes, and current values.

T. G. Hawkes & Company reprint. Corning, New York, 1960.

Hawkes Cut Glass (reprint of an 1897 or 1898 booklet of thirty pages, telling the Hawkes story. Good illustrations of thirteen patterns.) Kermit, Tex.: Collector, 1976. Reprinted for the California Regional Group of the National Early American Glass Club.

Higgins & Seiter catalog (original), circa 1901 or 1902.

Higgins & Seiter catalog (reprint) of 1899, American Historical Catalog Collection, Princeton: Pyne Press, 1971. Has historical introduction.

John F. Hotchkiss. *Cut Glass Handbook and Price Guide*, 2nd. ed., Des Moines, Iowa: Wallace-Homestead Co., 1970. Concise information on collecting; a section of photographs of pieces with prices; a cross reference price guide for four books on sale in 1970 (prices now obsolete, but useful in comparison with the present); condensed version of 1960 Hawkes catalog.

Thos. J. Juzek & Co., Catalog 1910-1911 (original) of Elgin, Illinois, wholesale jewelers. Out of 728 pages, sixteen are devoted to "fine, rich, deep-cut glassware." Not one example of floral cutting or engraving is shown. Companies of origin not given.

Lamps & Other Lighting Devices, 1850-1906. American Historical Collection, Pennington, N.J.: Pyne Press, 1972. An historical introduction, followed by sketches of seven glass companies specializing in lamps, adds to our background knowledge, but has few references to cut glass lamps or candlesticks.

Marshall Field & Co. 1895-1896 Illustrated Catalog of Jewelry and European Fashions (reprint), Northfield, Ill.: Gun Digest Publishing Co., 1970. Most of the illustrations are woodcuts, an art form that has nearly passed away. The company's motto has always been, "Give the lady what she wants!"

Libbey Glass Company Cut Glass, June 1st 1896 (reprint), Toledo, Ohio: 1968.

C. F. Monroe catalog (Meriden, Conn.), reprinted by the American Cut Glass Association, 1981(?).

Mt. Washington Glass Co. (reprint) of the 1880s with Price List and Pattern Key, Clinton, Md.: Leonard E. Padgett, 1976.

F. X. Parsche & Son Co. (Chicago), reprinted by Donald C. Parsche, 1981.

Pennsylvania Glassware 1870-1904. Reprints from catalogs of Cascade Glass Works, 1870; Phoenix Glass Co., 1893; Agnew Co., 1894; T. B. Clark & Co., 1896; United States Glass Co., 1904 — with an historical introduction. Princeton: Pyne Press, 1972.

Pitkin & Brooks, circa 1907 (reprint), Berkeley, Calif.: Cembura & Avery Publishers, 1973.

Quaker City Cut Glass Co., reprinted by the American Cut Glass Association, 1980.(?)

Roden Brothers catalog and price guide. Peterborough, Ontario, Canada: Clock House, 1974. Reprint of 80 percent of 1917 catalog from Roden Brothers of Toronto.

Sears, Roebuck & Company. Fall 1900 catalog (miniature reprint), Northfield Ill.: DBI Books, Inc., 1970.

Sears, Roebuck & Co., #117, 1908: "The Great Price Maker" (reprint). Chicago: Follett Publishing Co., 1969.

Silver Plate and Sterling Silver, reprinted selections from the W. G. Crook, Nelsonville, Ohio, illustrated catalog of 1888. Kermit, Tex.: Collector's Weekly, 1972.

St. Aubin, Jr. *Pairpoint Lamps, A Collector's Guide* (selected reprints). New Bedford, Mass.: Pine Trees Press, 1974. Only two brilliant cut and one engraved floral are shown among 112 lamps, yet the book is worthwhile for its insight into décor of the period.

Steuben Glass catalog, "The Ornaments of Spring," Seattle, Wash.: Frederick & Nelson, Division of Marshall Field & Co., 1967.

Steuben Glass booklets: "Enjoying Steuben Glass," by Louis Redmond, and "Your Steuben Glass and How to Care for It" (anonymous and not dated). Both from Corning Glass Center, Corning, N.Y.

Taylor Brothers & Co., Inc. (Philadelphia) reprinted by the American Cut Glass Association, 1981(?). Copyright by Florence Taylor Vay.

Victorian Silverplated Holloware. Rogers Brothers Manufacturing Co., 1857; Meriden Britannia Co., 1867; Derby Silver Co., 1883 — reprinted by American Historical Catalog Collection, Princeton: Pyne Press, 1972

Wallenstein Mayer & Company catalog of 1913, partially reprinted. Cincinnati, Ohio: D. James, 1967. The great majority of patterns are deeply cut and brilliant; only a few are floral. The firm called itself the "Jewelry Headquarters of the Middle West."

Index of Illustrated Designs or Patterns

Documented pattern names are italicized. The others are generic, descriptive names in common usage. Company attributions without proof are in parentheses.

Pattern Names	Company	Figure Number
Aberdeen, later *Anson*	Hawkes	292
Abbott. See *Mikado*		
Albany	(Meriden)	86,338,431
Alhambra	Meriden	339,340,341,342, 343,344,345
America	Fry	393
Anita	Libbey	256,257,452
Anson, formerly *Aberdeen*	Hawkes	292
Arbutus	Pairpoint	71,72,73
Arcadia variation	unknown	114,193,223
Argus	(New England)	12
Ashburton	(New England)	12
Athole	Pitkin & Brooks	447
Atlantic	Empire	197
AU	Clark	385
Basket	Fry	394
Bellevue	Taylor Brothers	187
Bengal	Sinclaire	365
Bird, engraved	unknown	5
Block	(several firms)	134
Block Diamond	Smith Brothers, Dorflinger, or Mt. Washington	62
Border	Pitkin & Brooks	30
Bow and Festoon, our name	Hawkes	115
	(Sinclaire)	117,362
Bowa	Pitkin & Brooks	53
Brazilian	Hawkes	20A&B,296,297
Broadway	G. W. Huntley catalog	470
Brunswick	Hawkes	306,466
Bullseye	Hawkes	319
Butterfly	Tuthill	328
Butterfly and Daisy (Late Daisy)	Pairpoint	68,69,70,75A&B
Butterfly and Thistle	Pairpoint	74
Byzantine variation	Meriden	130
Cane, clear button	Sinclaire	358
	unknown	139,160
Cane-on-Cane	unknown	142A&B,143
Cane and Pillar	unknown	133
Caprice	Bergen	53

Pattern Names	Company	Figure Number
Caroline	Hawkes	395
Centauri. See *Holland*		
Chair Bottom. See *Harvard*		
Chelsea	Pairpoint	77,78
Cherries, engraved	Libbey	277
Chrysanthemum variation	Hawkes	294,295
Cluster	Egginton	368
Cluster patterns	Hoare	170,372
	Straus	180
	unknown	196,211
Colonna	Libbey	239
Comet	Hoare	378
Comet and Swirl patterns	Hawkes	322
	Hoare	379
Corinthian	Libbey	136,235,265,471
Corinthian variation	(Meriden)	105
	(Straus)	478
"*D*"	Fry	40
Daisy. See *Butterfly and Daisy*		
Daisy	Pairpoint	67
Daisy	unknown	146
Delphos	Libbey	249
Diamond Poinsettia (Star Flower)	Morecroft, Ideal	54
Drape, (*Stars and Banners*)	Straus	396,454
Eden	Quaker City	150A&B
Edna	Roden Brothers	419
Electra (*Ulysses*)	Straus	455
Electric	Bergen	289,450
Elfin	Hoare	145
Emblem	Bergen	23
Empress	Quaker City	88
Feathered Leaf and Hobstar	(Meriden)	352,353,354
Feathered Star	Heinz Brothers	397,482
Flag Lilies, engraved	unknown	410
Flora. See *Shirley*		
Floral patterns, examples	Libbey	279,280
	Sinclaire	359
	(Steuben)	356
	Dorflinger	Dedication page
	unknown	473,481
Floral Spray and Pearls, our name	Hawkes	316
Florence variation	Libbey	209,460
Flowers and Hobnail	Fry	392

Pattern Names	Company	Figure Number
Flute	Dorflinger	C.2
Flutes and Greek Border	Hawkes	312,313
Flute and Notched Prism	unknown	432
Galatea	Clark	389
Genoa	Averbeck	58
Georgia	Higgins & Seiter catalog	60
Gladys	Hawkes	303
Glenda (Laurent)	Libbey	261
Golf	Bergen	483
Gracia	Hawkes	311
Grain, engraved rye	Libbey	46,278
Grapes, engraved	(Fry)	395
	(Thomas Webb)	409A&B
	(Sinclaire)	363
	(New England)	16
	Pairpoint	76
Grapes, Cherries, Pears	Hawkes	333,334
	Heisey	163
Grapes, Pears	(Pitkin & Brooks)	161A&B
Grapes, Pears, Plums	(Fry)	45
Grapes (Vintage)	Tuthill	332
Greek Key. See Alhambra		
Harvard or Chair Bottom	(Kellnor & Munroe)	217
Harvard	unknown	134,164,167,209
Harvard	Libbey	234,437
Harvard and Floral	(Kellnor & Munroe)	217
	(Washington Cut Glass)	37
Harvard and Hobstar	unknown	36
Heart	(Fry)	175
Heart	Hoare	380
Heart shapes	unknown	468,471
Hindoo variation	(Hoare)	377
Hob Star	Gundy-Clapperton	173,416, 417A&B
Hobstar and Cane	unknown	132
Hobstar and Feathered Leaf	(Meriden)	352,353,354
Holland (Centauri)	Hawkes	301,302
Horse, engraved	(Pitkin & Brooks)	144
Huyler	Clark	386
Iceland	Hawkes	141
Iola	Libbey	241,472
Iris, engraved	Hawkes	446
Irish Waterford style	Dorflinger	8,285
Jewel	Clark	387
Kalana Lily, etched	Dorflinger	291
Kensington	Hawkes	323
Korea	Pitkin & Brooks	59,450
Late Daisy. See Butterfly and Daisy		
Laurent. See Glenda		
Libbey	Libbey	275,276
Limoge, our name	Hoare	374
Lorraine	Hawkes	324
Lotus (Magnolia)	Egginton	366,367
Lovebirds. See Wistaria		
Magnolia. See Lotus		
Majestic	Quaker City	90
Marlboro	(Dorflinger)	286

Pattern Names	Company	Figure Number
Mercedes	Clark	385
Middlesex	Dorflinger	288,289,443
Middlesex variation	Hawkes	299
	Hoare	375
Mikado (Abbott)	Hoare	455
Monarch or *Napoleon*	(Hoare or O'Connor) 104,383,384	
Nassau	Hoare	381
Nevada	Mt. Washington/Pairpoint 64,65,66	
New Brilliant	Libbey	236,237,238
Norman	Roden Brothers	341
Nortec, pressed	McKee	423
North Star (Orpheus)	Hawkes	320,321
Notched Prism	Bergen	207
Notched Prism	unknown	19,435,452,465
Notched Prism and Flute	unknown	432
Odd	Hawkes	304
Old Colony	Dorflinger	284
Open Petal and variation	Tuthill	335,336
Orpheus. See North Star		
Othello. See Patrician		
Ozella	Libbey	244
Patrician (Othello)	Meriden	350
Palmette, our name	unknown	195
Phlox	Tuthill	329
Pineapple	Laurel	80
Pineapple and Fan (Shepherd's Plaid)	unknown	425
Pinwheel patterns	Enterprise	401
	Owanda	400
	unknown	50,124,153,177, 411,450,455,458,470
Plain Flutes	Libbey	264
Plaza	Pitkin & Brooks	129
Pluto variation	Hoare	466
Prima Donna (Triple Square)	Clark	455
Prince Albert	Sinclaire	363
Prince of Wales	Dorflinger	C.2
Princess (Split Square)	O'Connor	383,454
Princess	Libbey	233
Princeton	Empire	190
Prism, formerly *White House*	Libbey	28
Prism and Bullseye	Straus	29
Queens	Hawkes	297,307,308 309,310,456
Quincy	Hoare	379
Regina	Hawkes	317
Regis	Libbey	262
Rock Crystal Spray	Sinclaire	361
Roman	Egginton	369
Roman Rosette, pressed	Sandwich	11
Rose Combination	Irving	398,446
Royal	Hunt	38
Russian, Canterbury	unknown	39
Russian, Cleveland	unknown	151,166
Russian, Persian	(Mt. Washington)	156
Russian, Persian	(Hawkes)	293

Pattern Names	Company	Figure Number
Rye. See Grain		
St. Regis	Hawkes	97A&B
Senora	Libbey	253,254,255,453
Shepherd's Plaid. See *Pineapple and Fan*		
Shirley (Flora)	Meriden	348,349
Signora	Irving	399
Silver Thread and Floral	unknown	155
Split Square. See *Princess, O'Connor*		
Stalks and Stars. See *Star and Feather*		
Stars and Banners. See *Drape*		
Star and Feather (Stalks and Stars)	Libbey	267,268,269 270,271,272,451
Star Flower. See *Diamond Poinsettia*		
Strawberry, engraved	Gundy-Clapperton	418
Strawberry, Gravic	Hawkes	314
Strawberry Diamond and Fan	(Hawkes)	18
	(Mt. Washington)	63
	Sinclaire	364
	unknown	127,364,437,438,461
Sultana variation	Libbey	458
Sunburst	(Pitkin & Brooks or Enterprise)	31
Thistle	Clark	391
Tiffany	unknown	108
Triple Square. See *Prima Donna*		
Tulip, engraved and cut	Gundy-Clapperton	92
Ulysses. See *Electra*		
Venetta	Libbey	266
Vernon Honeycomb, pressed	New England	13
Victoria	Pairpoint	79

Pattern Names	Company	Figure Number
Vine and Tassel, our name	Fry	395
Vintage (Grapes)	Tuthill	332
Water Lilies	Stevens & Williams	407
Whist	unknown	149
White House, later *Prism*	Libbey	28
Wild Rose	Tuthill	331
Wild Rose and Leaves, pressed	Indiana Glass	427
Wistaria (Lovebirds)	Libbey	281
Worcester	Thomas Webb	408
Wreath and Flower	Hawkes	99,321,325A&B
Wreath and Tassel	Hawkes	321,472
Zipper	Meriden	103
Numbered Patterns		
#1	Sinclaire	357
#47	Libbey	248,453
#RC 155	Sinclaire	47
#161	Meriden	346,347
#163	Libbey	252
#208	Libbey	243
#209	Libbey	259,451
#225	Hoare	371
#225	Meriden	337
#630	Hoare	382
#872	Hoare	370
#900	Fry	175
#1490	Hawkes	20A&B

Index

About the Author

Martha Louise Swan graduated first in her class from Connecticut College (New London) in 1937 with a double major: Romance languages and music. With her election to Phi Beta Kappa in her junior year, she became a Winthrop Scholar. She was offered a year's graduate scholarship to the Sorbonne in Paris, but declined because of Hitler's threat to peace.

After raising four children with her husband, an accountant/musician, she earned a Master of Education degree at Lewis and Clark College (Portland, Oregon) in 1964. Through the years, she has taught public school music, French, and Spanish, as well as private lessons in voice and piano.

The origin of her interest in cut glass is described in the introduction to this volume. The author carries the reader back to the Gilded Age between the 1876 Centennial Exposition and World War I, vividly portraying the role of cut glassware in the upper layers of society. Such exquisite glassware has never been reproduced and probably never will be.

Value Guide to
American Cut and Engraved Glass

The Brilliant Period
in Historical Perspective

Martha Louise Swan

The first value guide (1986) was prepared in consultation with Carol Weir, an active dealer in cut glass and a prominent member of the American Cut Glass Association. In the second edition, I had additional advice from Robert Hall, a dealer who often sells rarities. He is also a member of ACGA.

For this edition, the basis for price revision is careful observation of retail prices charged by dealers across the country for pieces comparable to those in my book. Each value stated is based on glassware in excellent condition. If damaged, a discount should lower the price.

Appreciation of the unique qualities of cut and engraved glass of the American Brilliant Period, 1876–1916, has resulted in steadily rising prices in the last thirty years. As examples continue to disappear into private collections and museums—or through breakage—values rise.

Prices are influenced by several factors. They vary geographically, depending on supply and demand. Certain well-known dealers attract customers who have fine glassware to sell; they are able to charge more, if they so desire. Also, profit margins differ widely from dealer to dealer.

"Sleepers" may sometimes be found at house sales or in shops whose owners know little about cut glass. Occasional bargains are found at auctions, if the collector is knowledgeable and careful.

Values listed here, in American dollars, from low to high, may serve as a guide to the present worth of the exact pieces shown in the book. The item numbers correspond to the photographs (figures) in the volume. Matching sets sell for more than single items from a set.

Neither author nor publisher can be blamed for loss resulting from use of this price guide. It is a value guide—not a price catalog.

Fig.	Item	Value Low–High		Fig.	Item	Value Low–High	
3	Bowl	$ 250–	300	31	Jug	$ 450–	500
4	Plate	300–	350		Tumblers,		
5	Cream and				each	45–	65
	sugar	350–	375	32	Sauce or		
6	Shade	25–	35		Cologne	150–	200
7	Decanters,			33	Spoon Tray	125–	175
	pair	750–	850	34	Jug	325–	375
8	Vase	450–	550	35	Bonbon	140–	165
9	Bottle	200–	250	36	Bowl	365–	450
10	Decanters,			37	Footed Rose		
	each	325–	450		Globe	190–	260
11 Upper R	Plate	70–	85	38	Spoon Tray	260–	330
Lower L	Plate	70–	80		Bonbon	75–	100
Upper L	Cup Plate	55–	65	39	Jug	275–	350
Lower R	Salt	115–	135	40	Jug	240–	275
12	Decanter	165–	210	41	Fern Dish	50–	60
	Goblets, each	45–	55	42	Vase	85–	135
13 L	Compote	110–	140	43	Bowl	175–	225
	Celery Vase	165–	210	44	Bowl	280–	340
R	Compote	70–	80	45	Bowl	300–	375
14	Pitcher	200–	250	46	Shot Glass	85–	130
	Tumbler	30–	40	47	Vase	140–	170
15	Decanter	260–	310	48	Vase	500–	600
16	Decanter	550–	600	49	Vase	300–	400
18	Cream and			50	Vase	160–	210
	Sugar	150–	175	51	Vase	80–	110
19 L–R	Violet Globe	75–	85	52	Celery	195–	230
	Bud Vase	30–	40	53	Celeries, each	195–	230
	Bud Vase	25–	35	54	Bowl	175–	200
	Footed Violet			56	Bowl	150–	200
	Globe	180–	250	58	Bowl	550–	650
20A&B	Boudoir Set	650–	750	59	Punch Bowl	650–	700
21	Jug	325–	425		Punch Cups,		
22	Flower Center	650–	750		each	40–	60
23	Saucers, each	95–	105	60	Whiskey Bot-		
24	Pair of Bon-				tles, pair	2,500–	3,000
	bons, each	65–	85	62	Tumblers,		
	Larger Bonbon	85–	110		each	45–	60
25 L–R	Sauce Bowl	90–	110	63	Tray	900–	1,000
	Finger Bowl	60–	80	64	Cheese	650–	700
26 L–R	Bonbon	120–	140	65 L–R	Cheese	650–	700
	Olive	100–	130		Butter	550–	650
27	Bowl	190–	220	66	Butter	385–	450
28	Lemon or			67	Glove Box	1,150–	1,300
	Pins	55–	75	68	Cream and		
29	Cream and				Sugar	340–	400
	Sugar	195–	250	69	Puff Box	225–	250
30	Bowl	230–	260				

Fig.	Item	Value Low–High		Fig.	Item	Value Low–High	
70	Cheese and Crackers	$ 350–	400	108	Bowl	$ 850–	950
71	Bowl	295–	350	109	Bowl	450–	525
72	Jewel Box	550–	650	110	Martini Pitcher and Spoon	1,400–	1,650
73	Cologne	200–	250	111	Carafe	450–	550
74A&B	Flower Center	650–	825	112A&B	Ash Tray	400–	500
75A&B	Table Lamp	3,500–	3,800	113	Candelabra, pair	2,800–	3,500
76	Jam Jars, each	75–	110	114	Candelabra, pair	1,050–	1,150
77	Centerpiece	750–	800	115	Vase	2,500–	3,000
78	Footed Vase	350–	450	116	Picture Frame	375–	450
79	Footed Vase	350–	450	117	Umbrella Stand	4,000–	4,500
80	Glass Panel,	unique		118	Umbrella Stand	4,000–	4,500
81A&B	Doorknob	180–	225	119	Whiskey Jug	4,000–	4,200
82	Doorknob	175–	195	120	Jug	550–	650
83	Bowl Shade, rarity	2,500–	3,500	121	Punch Bowl	2,200–	2,500
86	Decanter	550–	600		Punch Cups, each	55–	80
87	Vase	1,100–	1,200	122	Bowl	500–	600
88	Vase	3,000–	4,500	123	Orange Bowl	650–	750
89	Champagnes, each	160–	200	124	Compote	1,000–	1,200
90	Punch Bowl	3,500–	4,000	125	Compote	1,150–	1,250
91A&B	Silver Figural Candelabra	1,400–	1,550	126	Compote	850–	950
92	Knife Rest	95–	115	127	Butter	500–	600
	Sugar Tray	135–	155	128	Sauce Boat	300–	375
93	Bride's Basket	265–	350	129	Canoe	375–	415
94	Coasters, each	20–	25	130	Bonbon	500–	600
95 L–R	Puff Box	125–	140	131	Bonbon	300–	375
	Pomade Box	30–	45		Stick Bonbon	250–	275
96	Trinket Box	230–	275	132	Triple Heart	900–	1,000
97A&B	Syrup Jug	325–	375	133	Footed Decanter	950–	1,050
98	Sugar Sifter	200–	250	134	Slipper	350–	425
99	Oil Crust	185–	220		Paperweight	295–	335
100	Decanter	650–	750	135	Napkin Rings, each	75–	115
101	Banquet Mustard	400–	450	136	Bell	250–	300
102 L–R	Lady's Flask	165–	210	137	Bowl	350–	400
	Honey Pot	275–	350		Saucers, each	120–	130
	Tooth Powder	275–	350	138	Footed Decanter	800–	900
103	Cigar Jar	900–	1,000		Wines, each	85–	125
104 L–R	Bitters Bottle	350–	400	139	Tray	800–	850
	Barber Bottle	250–	325				
105	Butter	600–	675				
106	Decanters, pair	1,600–	2,000				
107	Bowl	500–	600				

Fig.	Item	Value Low–High		Fig.	Item	Value Low–High	
140	Wine Caddy	$ 130–	150	171	Punch Bowl	$ 3,000–	3,500
141	Wine Washer	400–	460		Punch Cups,		
142A&B	Water Goblet				each	50–	75
	and Wine,			172	Eggnog Bowl	1,000–	1,100
	each	225–	260	173	Cordial or		
143	Finger Bowl	200–	250		Cologne	275–	325
144	Cigar Ash Tray	250–	325	174	Decanter	650–	750
145	Demitasse			175	Pitcher	385–	450
	and Saucer	250–	315		Tumblers,		
146	Cuspidor	275–	300		each	55–	70
147	Cuspidor	650–	750	176	Claret Jug	450–	550
148	Footed Tray	700–	800	177	Claret Jug	850–	975
149	Bridge Set,			178	Goblets, each	100–	125
	complete	500–	600	179 L–R	Carafe	225–	250
150A&B	Flower Mug				Carafe	350–	450
	or Spooner	325–	350	180	Ice Cream Tray	1,050–	1,100
151	Decanter	650–	750	181	Ice Cream		
	Goblet	140–	170		Saucers,		
	Champagne	130–	160		each	130–	150
	Wine	125–	150	182	Ice Cream Tray	900–	950
152A&B	Compote-Vase	1,000–	1,200	183	Round Tray	650–	750
153	Epergne	750–	850	184	Bread Tray	800–	850
154A&B	Table Lamp	5,000–	6,000	185	Bread Tray	360–	410
155	Bowl	450–	550	186	Bread Tray	360–	410
156	Footed Bowl	800–	950	187	Bread Tray	650–	700
	Plateau	300–	350	188	Celery Tray	395–	425
159 L–R	Tobacco Jar	450–	500	189	Celery Tray	450–	550
	Cigar Jar	480–	520	190	Celery Tray	240–	280
160	Inkwell	450–	550	191	Bowl	700–	800
161A&B	Collar Box	750–	850	192	Mayonnaise		
162	Dresser Tray	800–	900		and Plate	210–	260
163 L–R	Puff Box	190–	240	193	Bowl	250–	325
	Hair Receiver	175–	225	194	Bowl	500–	600
164	Puff Box	285–	340	195	Bowl	375–	425
165	Atomizer	150–	175	196	Low Bowl	265–	300
	Perfume	70–	80	197 L–R	Bonbon	85–	110
166	Shoe Perfume	150–	190		Bonbon	250–	300
167	Trinket Box	110–	160	198	Dessert Plate	200–	250
168	Pair of Minia-			199	Spoon Tray	175–	200
	ture Lamps,			200	Spoon Holder	295–	325
	each	80–	110	201	Spoon Holder	300–	350
169	Bedroom			202	Ice Tub	250–	300
	Lamp	900–	1,000	203	Ice Bucket	300–	375
170	Punch Bowl	3,000–	3,500	204 L–R	Compote	180–	225
	Punch Cups,				Compote	180–	225
	each	45–	65	205	Compote	175–	225
				206	Compote	650–	750

333

Fig.	Item	Value Low–High		Fig.	Item	Value Low–High
207 L–R	Mustard	$ 45– 60		219	Candlesticks, pair	$ 850– 925
	Mustard	65– 85			(single for less than half)	
208 L–R	Horseradish	145– 200		220	Fern Bowl	200– 260
	Horseradish	145– 200		221	Octagonal Fern Bowl	210– 275
209 L–R	Oil Cruet, as is with original stopper	90– 115 / 125– 150		222	Vase	550– 650
				223	Vase	550– 650
	Olive Oil, as is with original stopper	120– 150 / 125– 155		224	Vase	195– 260
				225	Vase	295– 350
	Oil Cruet	130– 160		226	Vase	295– 360
210	Pair of Worcestershire Bottles, each	285– 340		227	Vase	260– 360
				228	Vase	550– 650
211	Cheese	650– 700		229	Vase	450– 550
212	Domino Sugar	150– 200		230	Celery Vase	150– 210
	Butter Chips, each	35– 45		233	Plate	450– 500
213	Cream and Sugar	450– 550		234	Bowl and Plate	850– 950
214 L row	Knife Rests, each	45– 55		235	Jug	425– 500
				236 L–R	Nappy	125– 150
	Knife Rests, pair	45– 55			Nappy	110– 125
R row	Double Knife Rest	110– 120		237	Cream and Sugar	260– 310
				238	Tankard Jug	375– 400
	Knife Rests, each	60– 70			Tumblers, each	45– 65
215	Individual Salts, each	22– 32		239	Nappy	200– 260
				240	Dish	200– 275
	Shamrock Salt	55– 60		241	Shallow Bowl	325– 360
	Spoon	30– 40		242	Footed Fruit Bowl	1,700– 2,000
	Master Salt (diamond/fan)	40– 50		243	Carafe	275– 300
					Tumbler	45– 65
216 Upper R	Salt and Pepper set	60– 75		244	Compote	550– 650
	Single Pepper	22– 25		245	Ice Tub	285– 350
	Single Individual Salt	20– 22		246	Oval Bowl	450– 550
				247	Saucers, each	120– 150
Lower R	Salt and Pepper Sets, each	25– 45		248	Tumblers, each	55– 70
217	Cracker Jar	950– 1,050		249	Oval Bowl	900– 1,100
218	Candlesticks, pair	750– 850		250	Ice Cream Tray	2,000– 2,200
	(single for less than half)			251	Trivet	120– 135
				252	Vase	2,200– 2,500
				253	Bowl	400– 500
				254	Carafe	325– 395
					Tumblers, each	90– 100

Fig.	Item	Value Low–High		Fig.	Item	Value Low–High	
255	Rose Globe	$ 750–	850	282	Candlestick, higher if a pair	$ 150–	175
256	Shallow Bowl	200–	250	283	Ice Bucket	375–	400
257	Jug	325–	375	284	Bowl	235–	265
	Tumblers, each	50–	65	285	Wines, each	130–	150
258	Cream and sugar	200–	230	286	Basket	525–	625
259	Jug	440–	500	287	Bowl	1,200–	1,450
	Tumblers, each	50–	65	288	Paperweight-Stamp Moistener	150–	195
260	Champagne Cooler	450–	500	289	Punch Bowl	1,900–	2,100
261	Cake Plate	750–	850		Ladle	475–	575
262	Tray	750–	850		Punch Cups, each	45–	55
263	Ice Cream Tray	650–	750	290	Footed Cake Tray	650–	750
264	Jug	275–	325	291	Supreme and Plate	165–	210
265	Mayonnaise and Plate	250–	300	292	Rose Bowl	1,200–	1,400
266	Champagnes, each	165–	200	293	Decanter	750–	850
267	Punch Bowl	1,000–	1,100	294	Dessert Plates, each	300–	350
268	Bowl	350–	400	295	Square Bowl	450–	550
	Celery	175–	225	296	Rose Globe	600–	700
269	Jug	440–	475	297	Champagnes, each	140–	185
	Tumblers, each	55–	75		Tumbler	225–	275
270	Tankard	500–	600	298	Bowl	350–	400
271	Cream and Sugar	300–	360	299	Colognes, each	135–	165
272	Compote	550–	650	300	Cream and Sugar	225–	260
273	Bonbon	150–	170	301	Catsup Cruet	350–	395
274	Bowl	250–	300	302	Square Nappy	185–	225
275	Tray	800–	900		Saucer	65–	80
276	Deep Bowl	340–	385	303	Dessert Plate	185–	225
	Low Bowl	325–	370	304	Powder Box	650–	750
277	Pitcher	1,300–	1,500	305	Decanter	650–	750
	Tumblers, each	200–	250	306	Cream and Sugar	380–	410
278	Tumbler	45–	65	307	Bowl	800–	900
	Shot Glasses, each	90–	125	308	Tankard	1,300–	1,500
279	Compote	190–	250	309	Jug	1,050–	1,300
280	Plate	600–	650	310	Vase	900–	1,100
281	Octagonal Bowl, fine (quality varies widely)	1,300–	1,500	311	Centerpiece	460–	550
				312	Bowl	325–	375
				313	Cream and Sugar	225–	275

Fig.	Item	Value Low–High		Fig.	Item	Value Low–High
314	Celery	$ 350– 375		346	Bread Tray	$1,100– 1,250
	Bonbon	200– 260		347	Cream and	
315	Bowl	600– 700			Sugar	1,050– 1,150
316	Compote	190– 240		348	Dessert Plate	140– 190
317	Vase	350– 400		349	Bowl	450– 525
318	Bowl	300– 350		350	Bowl	350– 450
319	Footed Rose			351	Candlestick,	
	Globe	400– 450			single	300– 325
320	Tray	1,500– 1,700			pair	650– 750
321 L–R	Plate	225– 250		352	Bowl	385– 485
	Plate	550– 600		353	Jug	750– 850
322	Bowl	1,200– 1,400		354	Goblets, each	200– 250
323	Footed Rose			355	Vase	1,800– 2,000
	Globe			356	Centerpiece	
	(extreme				Set	750– 850
	rarity)	8,500– 9,500		357	Bowl	500– 600
324	Punch Bowl	2,300– 2,600		358	Jardiniere	3,500– 4,500
	Punch Cups,			359	Plate	425– 500
	each	65– 85		360	Clock	350– 450
325A&B	Car Vases,			361	Plate	45– 65
	pair	750– 850			Saucer	12– 15
326	Cream and			362	Vase	275– 375
	Sugar	350– 395		363	Wines, each	65– 70
327	Nappy	265– 315			Tumbler	50– 65
328	Dessert Plate	250– 300		364	Plate	600– 700
329	Compote	275– 300		365	Carafe	450– 500
330	Champagnes,			366	Dish	250– 275
	each	125– 150		367	Decanter	1,000– 1,100
331	Vase	485– 600		368	Bowl	625– 650
332	Bowl	850– 900		369	Bowl	650– 675
333	Nappy	450– 525		370	Vase	900– 1,000
334	Bowl	850– 900		371	Vase	1,050– 1,150
335	Jug	525– 650		372	Cream and	
336	Bowl	375– 485			Sugar	285– 325
337	Square Nappy	195– 250		373	Bowl	1,200– 1,500
338	Mayonnaise			374	Bowl	325– 375
	and Plate	250– 350		375	Bowl	650– 750
339	Bowl	900– 1,000		376	Bowl	500– 600
340	Fern Dish	950– 1,100		377	Ice Bucket	550– 650
341	Juice, each	150– 200		378	Ice Tub	975– 1,075
	Celery	1,450– 1,500		379	Nappy	230– 260
342	Decanter	1,950– 2,200		380	Tumblers,	
	Shot Glasses,				each	65– 95
	each	200– 225		381	Cake Server	475– 550
343	Jug	1,900– 2,100		382	Candlestick,	
	Tumblers,				pair	400– 460
	each	250– 275		383	Jug	450– 550
344	Cracker Jar	2,000– 2,200			Tumblers,	
345	Vase	3,500– 4,000			each	50– 75

Fig.	Item	Value Low–High		Fig.	Item	Value Low–High	
384	Iced Tea, each	$ 200–	250	418	Cream and Sugar	$ 195–	250
385	Low Bowl	475–	600	419	Bowl	265–	325
386	Pair of Low Bowls, each	385–	425	420	Basket	65–	90
387	Tray	650–	750	421	Decanter	60–	75
388	Bowl	340–	400		Wine	30–	35
389	Cream and Sugar	250–	310	422	Plate	110–	150
390	Plate	250–	300	423	Punch Bowl, pressed	50–	75
391	Sugar	100–	125		Punch Cups, each	6–	10
	Jug	250–	300	424	Compote	50–	70
	Tumbler	35–	45	425	Kerosene Lamp	500–	600
392	Tray	600–	700	426 L–R	Candlestick, cut	100–	120
393 L–R	Nappy	125–	155		Candlestick, pressed	30–	50
	Nappy	150–	250	427	Bowl	20–	35
394	Vase	250–	300	428	Jug	260–	280
395	Champagne	22–	30		Carafe	250–	275
	Tumbler	20–	25	429	Bowl	300–	350
	Sherbert	22–	30	430	Nappy	350–	400
396	Tumblers, each	75–	100	431	Jug	350–	425
397	Compote	325–	365		Tumblers, each	50–	65
398	Vase	195–	250	432	Cream and Sugar	185–	225
399	Pitcher	295–	385	433	Rose Globe	400–	500
	Tumblers, each	45–	60	434	Decanter	275–	300
400	Jug	350–	375		Wines, each	75–	95
401	Bowl	300–	375	435	Butter Pat	32–	40
402	Teapot	200–	250		Miniature Cruet	95–	120
403	Claret Jugs, each	450–	500		Hatpin Holder	110–	140
404	Caster Set	250–	300		Cordial	45–	60
405	Knife Rests, pair	135–	150		Toothpick Holder	18–	26
406	Tray	185–	240	436	Smelling Salts	50–	75
407	Vase	180–	210		Wine	60–	85
408	Bowl	200–	250		Sample Compote	140–	165
409A&B	Decanter	2,000–	2,200		Bell	60–	85
410	Candy Dish	150–	200	437	Cordial	70–	85
411	Decanter	230–	300		Napkin Ring	85–	100
412	Tray	250–	350				
413	Compote	250–	350				
414	Cologne	210–	250				
415	Vase	450–	600				
416	Tray	950–	1,000				
417A&B	Table Lamp	4,700–	5,500				

Fig.	Item	Value Low–High		Fig.	Item	Value Low–High	
437, *contd.*	Match Holder	$ 55–	65		Salt and Pepper Set	$ 15–	25
	Toothpick Holder	55–	65	445	Cream and Sugar	190–	230
	Double Shot Glass	50–	65	446 L–R	Ice Cream Saucer	40–	50
438	Nut Dishes, each	40–	50		Ice Cream Saucer	120–	140
	Miniature Bowl	50–	60	447 L–R	Ice Cream Saucer	130–	160
439 Upper L	Almond Dish	35–	45		Ice Cream Saucer	120–	140
Lower L	Master Salt	35–	45	448	Saucer	120–	140
Right	Butter Pats, each	30–	40		Bonbon	45–	60
440 L–R	Toothpick Holder	65–	75	449	Nappy	135–	165
	Toothpick Holder	40–	45	450 Center	Punch Cup	45–	65
	Toothpick Holder	40–	50	Top (clockwise)	Punch Cup	30–	45
441 L row	Knife Rests, each	60–	75		Punch Cup	45–	75
					Punch Cup	40–	55
R row	Larger Knife Rests, each	80–	90		Punch Cup	40–	60
	Smaller Knife Rest	120–	130		Punch Cup	55–	80
442 Upper, L&R	Master Salts, each	55–	75	451 L–R	Tumbler	50–	65
					Tumbler	55–	75
Center	Master Salt	50–	65		Tumbler	55–	65
Lower, L&R	Master Salts, each	35–	45	452 L–R	Tumbler	45–	65
					Tumbler	50–	60
Center	Master Salt	35–	45		Tumbler	45–	65
443 Upper L	Salt Dips, each	12–	16	453 L–R	Tumbler	30–	40
					Tumbler	55–	70
Upper R	Paperweight-Stamp Moistener	150–	185		Tumbler	90–	100
					Tumbler	60–	80
Lower L	Salt Dips, each	22–	25	454 L–R	Tumbler	55–	70
					Tumbler	50–	70
Lower R	Salt Dips, each	12–	16		Tumbler	75–	100
					Tumbler	30–	40
444 L–R	Salt and Pepper Set	20–	30	455 L–R	Tumbler	55–	75
	Salt and Pepper Set	20–	30		Tumbler	50–	70
	Salt and Pepper Set	40–	50		Tumbler	100–	125
	Salt and Pepper Set	15–	20		Tumbler	65–	80
				456	Highball Tumblers, each	265–	300
				457	Champagne	95–	120
					Goblet	100–	125
					Wine	95–	120
				458	Sherberts, each	50–	75

Fig.	Item	Value Low–High		Fig.	Item	Value Low–High
459	Puff Box	$ 185– 220		C.1	Candlesticks, pair	$ 350– 450
460	Puff Box	190– 230		C.2	Decanter	750– 850
461 L–R	Syrup	225– 265			Red Wines, each	150– 200
	Syrup	190– 235			Green Wines, each	125– 150
462	Cruet	90– 105		C.3 on Dedication Page	Pitcher, engraved	1,600– 1,900
463	Cruet	115– 130				
464	Cruets, each	125– 160				
465	Cruets, each	125– 165		C.4	Honesdale Cameo Vase	600– 750
466	Colognes, each	230– 250		C.5	Red Overlay Pane	unique
467	Center Vase	375– 425		C.6	Perfume	140– 165
468	Relish	230– 265				
	Triangular Bonbon	175– 225				
469	Bonbon	195– 240				
470–	Bonbon	150– 175				
471	Club Bonbon	110– 145				
	Heart Bonbon	95– 125				
472	Handled Nappies, each	140– 185				
473	Relish, four compartments	300– 400				
474	Footed Nappy, two handles	175– 225				
475	Footed Nappy, two handles	180– 235				
476	Miniature Compote	110– 125				
477	Compote	475– 550				
478	Baskets, each	450– 500				
479	Basket	2,000– 2,200				
480	Basket	1,300– 1,500				
481	Basket	1,100 1,200				
482	Boudoir Lamp	300– 350				
483	Violet Globe	40– 50				
484	Center Vase	80– 125